AF685586

MICROPROCESSORS: HARDWARE, SOFTWARE, AND DESIGN APPLICATIONS

MICROPROCESSORS: HARDWARE, SOFTWARE, AND DESIGN APPLICATIONS

WUNNAVA V. SUBBARAO, Ph.D., P.E.
Associate Professor, Department of Electrical Engineering
Florida International University
Miami, Florida

Reston Publishing Company
A Prentice-Hall Company
Reston, Virginia

Library of Congress Cataloging in Publication Data

Subbarao, Wunnava.
Microprocessors : hardware, software, and design applications.

1. Microprocessors. 2. Microcomputers. I. Title.
TK7895.M5S83 1984 621.3819'58 83–21297
ISBN 0–8359–4394–1

AIM® is a registered trademark of Data Processing Consulting, Inc.
Apple® is a registered trademark of Apple Computer, Inc.
ATARI® is a registered trademark of Atari, Inc.
Commodore™ is a trademark of Commodore Business Machines.
Intel® is a registered trademark of Intel Corporation.
Rockwell 6502® is a registered trademark of Rockwell International Corporation.
TRS-80® is a registered trademark of Radio Shack, a division of Tandy Corporation.
VIC-20® is a registered trademark of Commodore Business Machines.
Z80® is a registered trademark of Zilog, Inc., with whom Reston Publishing Company is not associated.

© 1984 by Reston Publishing Company, Inc.
Reston, Virginia 22090
A Prentice-Hall Company

All rights reserved. No part of this book may be reproduced in any way, or by any means, without permission in writing from the publisher.

10 9 8 7 6 5 4 3 2 1

Printed in the United States of America

This book is dedicated to my beloved parents

Mr. Wunnava S. Venkateswarao
and
Mrs. Wunnava S. Ranganayakamma

without whose help and sacrifice my education and this book would not have been possible.

CONTENTS

Preface

This book is intended to be used as a text for courses in microprocessors and microcomputer-based system designs at junior and senior levels. Also, it is intended to be a self-teaching book for a practicing engineer specializing in digital, control, and instrumentation systems and in acquiring knowledge of microprocessors and design skills using microcomputers.

In the last few years, microprocessors and microcomputers have virtually revolutionalized the fields of digital electronics, control systems, and instrumentation. With microprocessor-compatible analog to digital (A/D) and digital to analog (D/A) integrated circuits freely available, microprocessors/computers are finding new applications in the analog field. Currently there is no field in engineering where micros are not used.

The advances in microprocessors themselves are astounding. The development of architectures from 4-bit to 8-bit to 16-bit microprocessors and the introduction of single-chip microcomputers and support devices have made the usage of micros very efficient, economical, flexible, convenient, and expandable in respective applications.

There is an abundance of material available regarding each of the microprocessor devices and systems, but it is scattered and noncorrelative. A person wishing to learn about micros is often confronted with a lack of good instructional material and resulting confusion.

In this book, a genuine effort has been made to introduce the study of microprocessors and microcomputer systems systematically, with practical and operating software and hardware examples. Front-running microprocessors (8-bit) such as Intel 8085, Motorola 6800, Rockwell/MOS Technology 6502, Zilog

Z-80 and RCA 1802 have been chosen for discussions in this book. A systematic study of these micros will help the reader comprehend 16-bit micros and bit-slice micros very easily. Throughout the book, numerous working examples have been given to provide more understanding of the concepts and systems. Wherever appropriate, single-chip microcomputers such as the 8048/8748, 6805/68705, and 6500/1 have been introduced in sufficient detail, with practical operating design examples.

In addition, other microcomputer-related bussing and interface concepts such as S-100, multibus, exerciser, and RS-232 have been introduced with practical hardware and software examples.

Chapter One covers the basic concepts of microprocessors such as architecture, registers, data transfers, instruction formats, and so on. In addition, software concepts of stacks, subroutines, interrupts, and I/O interface are introduced. A study of this chapter will provide the basic knowledge of microprocessors.

Chapter Two deals with the specifics of the 8085 microprocessor, its instruction formats, and a typical 8085 microprocessor-based system such as the SDK-85, and bus structures such as S-100 and multibus.

Chapter Three deals with the applications of the 8085-based system with software and hardware details. Some of the typical applications are data handling and data coding systems, data serialization with RS-232 interface, and single-chip micro 8748 application.

Chapter Four concerns the architectural features of the 6800 microprocessor and typical 6800-based microcomputer systems such as MEK 6800, Exerciser bus structures, and interface.

Chapter Five is devoted to practical applications such as waveform and timing generation, data acquisition, and A/D and D/A operating interface using the 6800-based microcomputer. A data acquisition example is presented to introduce the single-chip micro 6805/68705.

Chapter Six describes the architectural features of the 6502 microprocessor and a typical 6502-based microcomputer system, such as the AIM-65.

Chapter Seven is devoted to 6502-based microcomputer applications such as moving display, stepper motor control, position controllers, and XY graphics interface. An operating traffic light controller example is presented with the single-chip micro 6501.

Chapters Eight and Nine include the architectural features of Z-80 microprocessors and the design of a typical Z-80-based microcomputer system. Several practical examples, such as component testers, industrial control, and monitor routines, are presented.

In Chapters Ten and Eleven, architectural features of the low-power CMOS 1802 microprocessor and 1802-based microcomputer configuration are presented along with practical applications such as industrial timer, data entry, and validation.

All the microcomputers chosen are inexpensive single-board stand-alone systems highly suited for learning and microcomputer-based system applications. The discussions presented are all practical examples, most of them worked out by the research students in the Electrical Engineering Department of Florida International University. These applications can be implemented with any other microcomputer systems with appropriate modifications. The problems at the end of each chapter are especially designed to represent various applications of microcomputers, and readers are encouraged to solve them and implement them on any microcomputer system of their choice. This will greatly improve the knowledge and scope of their understanding. Nothing replaces hands-on experience, and students are requested to read the material and implement it on their microcomputers.

Any five chapters can be covered in a one-semester course, which will provide a solid base in at least two microcomputer systems. The entire book fits nicely in a two-semester sequence at the junior/senior undergraduate level in engineering, computer science, and other related disciplines. This book is a result of the courses taught by the author in microprocessors over the past several years at Florida International University and his association with Burroughs Corporation in microprocessor-based designs.

Many people have helped in the preparation of this book, and the students in the Electrical Engineering and Technology and Computer Science departments at F.I.U. are particularly helpful. Special mention should be made of Al Rojas, Arturo Suarez, Jerry Chang, Richard So, Rene Zuleta, Alan Geoffory, Phil Vallejo and Hugo Amezequetta, who have conducted extensive experimentations on various systems to support the discussions in the book.

I would like to acknowledge the encouragement and guidance rendered by my Chairperson, Dr. James Story, and the professional courtesy extended by senior colleagues, Professor Manuel Cereijo and Mike Urucinitz at F.I.U. I would like to show my gratitude especially to my wife, Sunanda, and my children Madhavi and Manoj, who showed great understanding throughout the preparation of this book, and to Ronnie Marino, who has done an outstanding job of typing and retyping the manuscript.

Wunnava V. Subbarao

MICROPROCESSORS: HARDWARE, SOFTWARE, AND DESIGN APPLICATIONS

CHAPTER ONE

General Concepts of Microprocessors

1.1. INTRODUCTION

In this chapter, we will be introduced to general concepts associated with microprocessors and microcomputer systems. Most contemporary leading 8-bit microprocessors such as the Intel® 8085, Motorola 6800™, Rockwell 6502®, Zilog Z-80™, and RCA 1802 are made with NMOS/CMOS technology and are contained in standard 40-pin DIP integrated circuit packages. The technology is progressing so fast that the semiconductor manufacturers could put a whole microcomputer system consisting of input/output circuitry in addition to the microprocessor on a single silicon chip.

A programmable digital system, the microprocessor can accomplish any task that a conventional digital system can do within the allowed time constraints.

1.2. ARCHITECTURE OF A TYPICAL MICROPROCESSOR

A microprocessor consists of several registers, an arithmetic logic unit (ALU), a control unit, and address, data, and control buses as shown in Figure 1.1. A register consists of several bits of information, each bit corresponding to the Q output of a flip flop as shown in Figure 1.2. An 8-bit register consists of eight such flip flops, interconnected. All the registers are capable of storing digital information (in the form of 1s and 0s), and can be used as counters or shift registers, depending on the instruction. All these are interconnected.

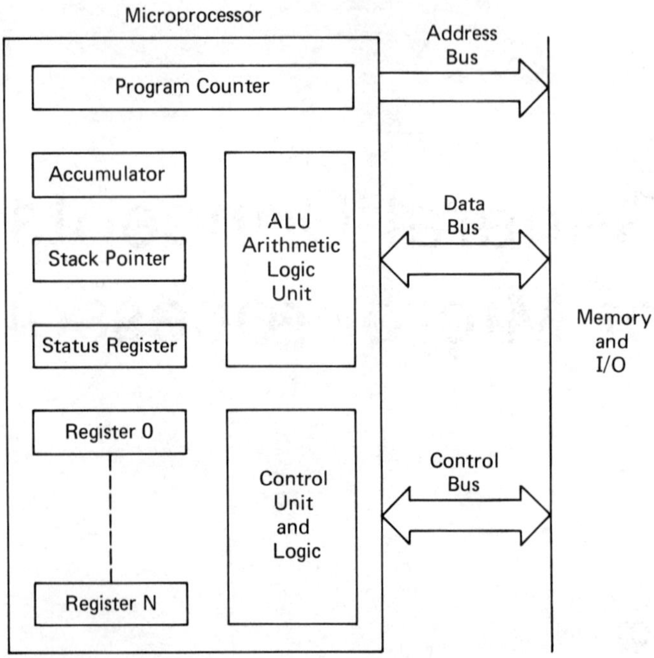

Fig 1.1. Typical microprocessor architecture.

Registers and Flags

Some of the registers of a microprocessor are special-purpose and have identified tasks. The other registers are general-purpose and are used for storing information while it is being processed. Referring to Figure 1.1, we can identify the special-purpose register functions readily.

Program Counter (PC)

This register acts as a counter and contains address information about the memory location from which the microprocessor obtains instructions or

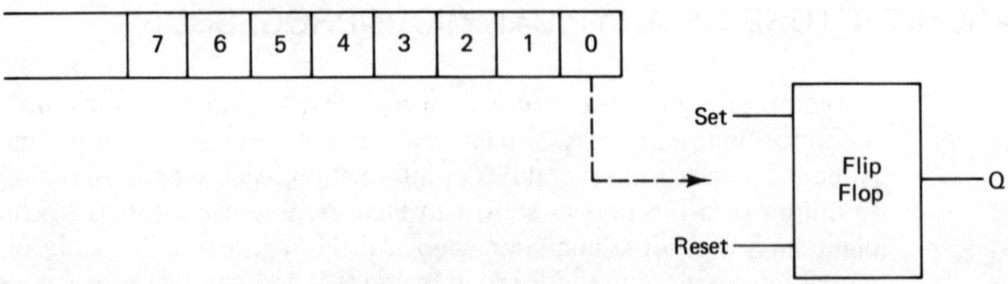

Fig 1.2. Typical register structure. Each bit corresponds to flip-flop.

data information. Each time the microprocessor accesses memory, the program counter is incremented to point to the next location from which the next instruction or data is to be fetched.

Accumulator (ACC)

This register contains data on which the microprocessor usually does logical manipulations. Also, in most of the microprocessors, the accumulator is the entry and exit register for the data transfer between the microprocessor and external memory and input/output (I/O) devices. For an 8-bit microprocessor, the accumulator is eight bits wide.

Stack Pointer (SP)

At times the microprocessor may have to suspend its present operation and take up a different operation in response to interrupts or subroutines. In such a case, it will store the digital information pertaining to the present operation in a certain part of the memory called stack, so that it can fetch it back, after the interrupt or subroutine is completed, to continue the present operation. The stack pointer register contains the address information of the location of the stack.

Status Register

At times it becomes necessary to know about the status of an operation, such as whether there was a carry in a just concluded addition operation. The status register contains such information. Examination of the status register helps the microprocessor to make proper decisions. The status register is also known as the flag register.

Arithmetic Logic Unit (ALU)

All arithmetic operations on data are carried out in this register. The final digital data is then transferred to the accumulator.

Control Logic Unit (CLU)

This is the heart of the microprocessor. This unit consists of several registers such as instruction registers and data routing circuits such as multiplexers and decoders. The instruction register decodes the instruction being processed and properly establishes data paths among various elements of the microprocessor through its multiplexer and decoder network.

Other Registers

The other registers are general-purpose and are used by the microprocessor to store the data temporarily while it is being processed. These registers have a similar structure to that shown in Figure 1.2.

Address, Data, and Control Buses

Any microprocessor communicates with outside memory or input/output devices such as displays, printers, keyboards, or other data entry mechanisms through its three buses, as shown in Figure 1.1. A bus is a group of electronic connections through which electronic signals are transmitted.

Address Bus

This is a unidirectional bus that contains the address information being put out by the microprocessor. Most contemporary 8-bit microprocessors have an effective 16-bit address bus and are capable of addressing any one out of 65,536 possible locations (recall $2^{16} = 65{,}536$ in the binary world).

Data Bus

This is a bidirectional bus through which data information flows from the micro to outside the digital system during the "write" operation and into the micro during the "read" operation. The size of this bus determines the size of the microprocessor. An 8-bit data bus signifies an 8-bit processor (8085, 6800, 6502, Z-80™, 1802, e.g.), and a 16-bit data bus refers to a 16-bit processor (8086, 68000, Z-8000, e.g.).

Control Bus

This bus contains control information flowing between the micro and the outside world for proper data transfer and timing. "Read/$\overline{\text{write}}$," "bus enable" and "clock timing" signals are usually the control signals originated by the microprocessor. "Interrupts," "reset," and "hold" control signals are usually initiated outside the digital system to reach the microprocessor.

We will demonstrate these concepts with some example problems.

Example 1.1

In a specific 8-bit microprocessor, the stack pointer is 8 bits wide and the program counter is 16 bits wide, as shown in Figure 1.3.

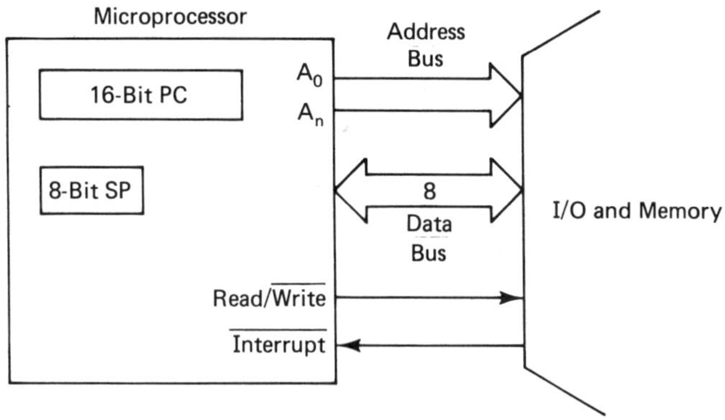

Fig 1.3. Microprocessor driving memory and I/O for Examples 1.1, 1.2, and 1.3.

(a) How wide is the effective address bus? Why?
(b) How many total memory locations can be addressed in real time?
(c) How many memory locations are there in the stack part of memory?

Solution

(a) *Address Bus Width.* The address bus is 16 bits wide, since the program counter that contains the address information to be put on the address bus is 16 bits wide.

(b) *Addressable Memory Locations.* 65, 536 (2^{16}) locations of memory can be accessed, one location at a time, as a function of the contents of the 16-bit address bus.

(c) *Stack Memory.* Stack pointer, which addresses the stack part of the memory, is 8 bits wide. Consequently, the stack memory contains 256 (2^8) locations.

Example 1.2

In the microprocessor circuit of Figure 1.3, following normal logic conventions,

(a) When are read and write operations performed by the microprocessor? How does data flow?
(b) When is the interrupt recognized?

Solution

(a) *Read and Write.* When the Read/$\overline{\text{Write}}$ control signal is at a high level (logic 1), the microprocessor performs the "read" operation. It reads information from the location addressed by the address bus. Similarly, when the Read/$\overline{\text{Write}}$ control signal is at a low level the "write" operation is performed.

(b) *Interrupt.* This is a low active logic signal, and the microprocessor recognizes it when it goes to a low logic level.

Instructional and Data Formats

For typical 8-bit microprocessors, the instructions and data are expressed as 8-bit words or bytes. In the microprocessor industry, hexadecimal notation, as shown in Table 1.1, is used extensively.

Instructions may be one, two, or three bytes long, as shown in Figure 1.4. The first byte of the instruction is always the operational code or "op code," which corresponds to the actual binary or hex code. This code specifies what kind of operation should be performed. Depending on the addressing modes, the second and third bytes may be the data or address of the data. We will discuss these addressing modes with specific microprocessors in later chapters.

Example 1.3

In the microprocessor circuit of Figure 1.3, the address bus $A_{15}...A_0$ contains 1010 0011 1100 0001.

(a) What is the location accessed by the microprocessor?

(b) If the accessed location contains an op code corresponding to the instruction "clear accumulator," what is the sequence of events?

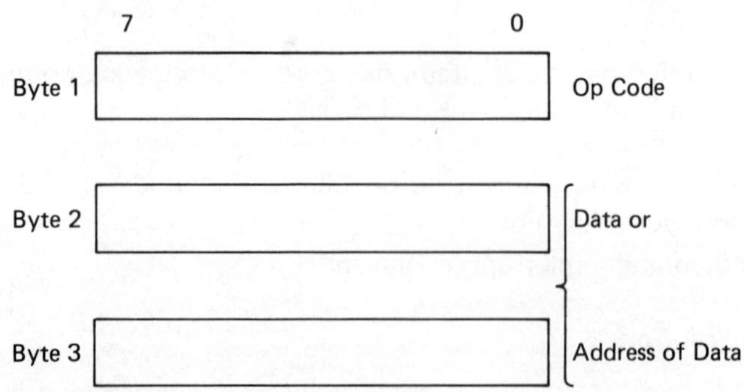

Fig 1.4. Typical instruction and data format.

Table 1.1. Binary, Decimal, and Hexadecimal Representation of Numbers.

Binary	*Decimal*	*Hexadecimal*
0000	0	0
0001	1	1
0010	2	2
0011	3	3
0100	4	4
0101	5	5
0110	6	6
0111	7	7
1000	8	8
1001	9	9
1010	10	A
1011	11	B
1100	12	C
1101	13	D
1110	14	E
1111	15	F
10000	16	10

Solution

(a) *Location.* The contents of the address bus correspond to the location being addressed. Referring to Table 1.1, the location is $(A3C1)_{Hex}$.

(b) The microprocessor clears its accumulator. The program counter is incremented to refer to the next location, A3C2, from which the microprocessor will fetch its next instruction to continue the operation.

1.3. CONCEPTUAL OPERATION

The microprocessor is a programmable logic element that obtains information or data from memory or I/O (input/output), manipulates the data sequentially, and puts it back in the memory or I/O. Figure 1.5 shows a typical microprocessor-based computer system.

Microcomputer System

As shown in Figure 1.5, a microcomputer system consists of I/O interface devices, ROM (read only memory) and RAM (random access memory) devices connected to the microprocessor through its address, data, and control buses.

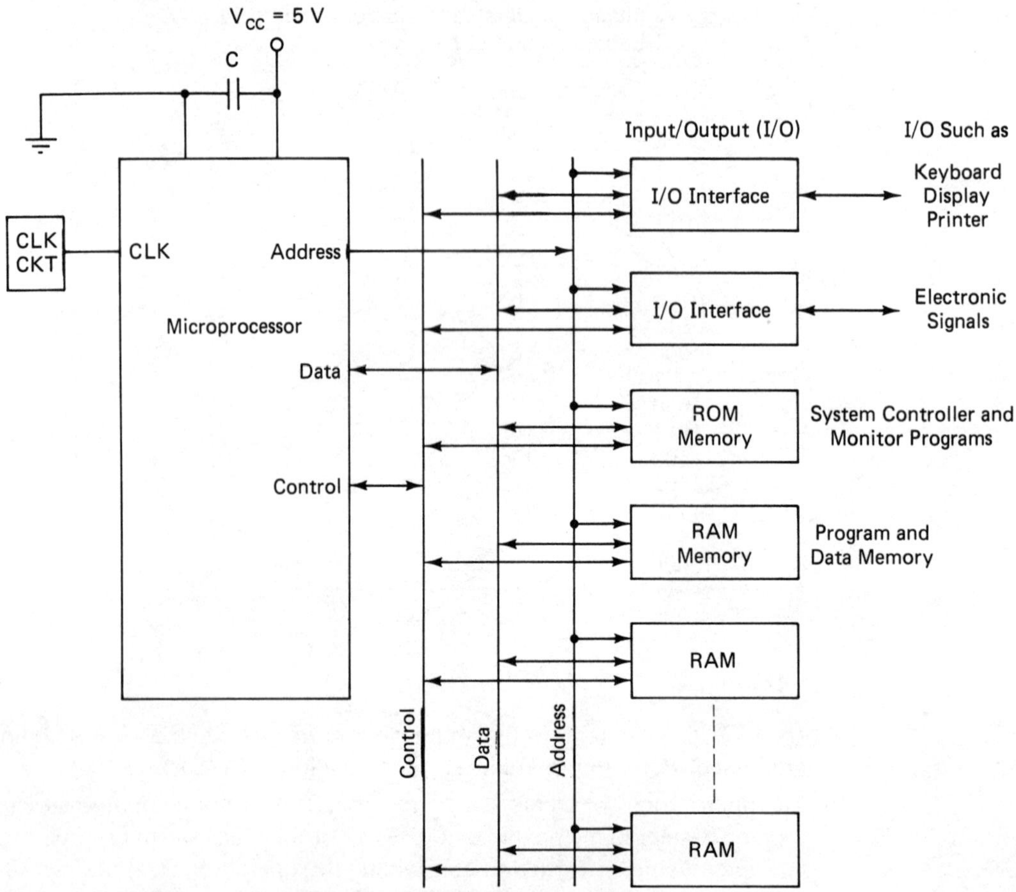

Fig 1.5. Typical microprocessor-based microcomputer system.

All these devices are tristate, and proper decoding of the address bus allows any of these devices to be selected. The data then flows between the microprocessor and the selected device(s).

The I/O interface devices establish a logical and electronic match between the microprocessor and the actual input/output systems, so that data can flow smoothly.

The ROM devices can only be "read" by the micro and contain preset programs that run the microcomputer system in a predetermined way. The contents of the ROM are nonvolatile and remain unchanged even if the power to the system is turned off. Fixed programs are stored in ROM.

RAM is the actual read/write portion of the memory, and the microprocessor can read or write the data. Alterable programs and data are contained in the RAM.

Sequence of Operations

To execute a program, the microprocessor reads the program memory and interprets the first byte of the instruction as the operational code (op code), which tells the microprocessor what to do with the information contained in the following byte or bytes. This part of the operational sequence is called the "fetch cycle." After the data corresponding to the first instruction is properly operated on, the microprocessor advances to obtain the next instruction, and the process is repetitive. The sequential advancement of the microprocessor is actually accomplished with the help of the program counter discussed earlier.

While the microprocessor is executing the main program, it may be necessary to respond to a more urgent event occurring in the system, which requires the attention of the microprocessor immediately. The servicing of such an event is accomplished with the help of interrupts and stacks.

Interrupts and Stacks

The interrupt is a hardware control signal from the I/O to the microprocessor requesting attention. It is a useful feature, especially when the microprocessor is interfacing with a slow I/O system. When the I/O system is ready to give out or accept data, it will inform the microprocessor by activating the interrupt input. The microprocessor, which may have been executing another program while the I/O was not ready, responds to the interrupt by suspending the main program and taking up the "interrupt service routine," which is another program intended to service the interrupt and the I/O. Figure 1.6 shows the typical interrupt structure.

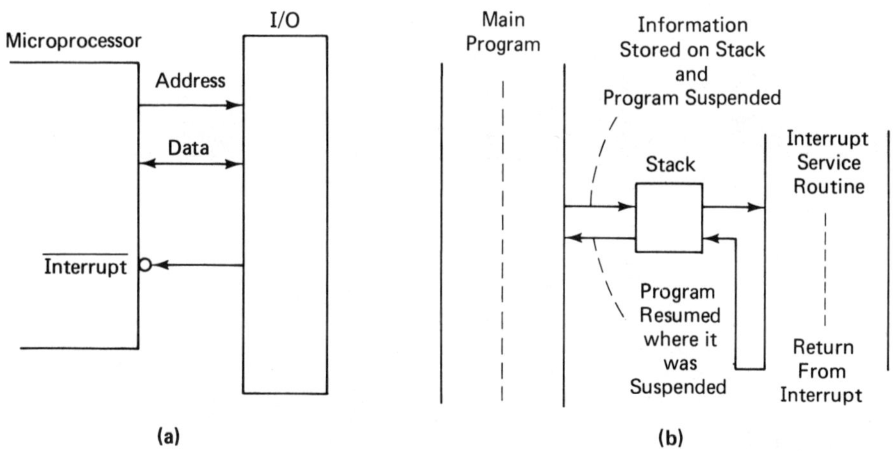

Fig 1.6. Interrupts: (a) Occurrence of interrupt from I/O; (b) sequence of events in interrupts.

Before actually executing the interrupt service routine, the microprocessor may store the information pertaining to the main program in the predetermined part of the memory called stack. This will enable the microprocessor to continue the main program without loss of data when it finishes the interrupt service routine and returns to the main program via a "return from interrupt" instruction.

Subroutines

It is quite possible that a microprocessor may execute a similar type of program many times in the course of a main program. The repeated occurrence of a program can be put together and called a subroutine. Whenever required, the microprocessor may perform the subroutine program via a "jump to subroutine" instruction. It will return to the main program with a "return from subroutine" instruction, which is usually the last instruction in subroutine programs.

As shown in Figure 1.7, the subroutines can be nested. A microprocessor executing subroutine 1 may go to subroutine 2. After completing subroutine 2, it will resume subroutine 1. After its completion it will resume the main program. The subroutines can be nested to any degree.

Again, to maintain the continuity of execution of programs, before executing the new subroutine, the information pertaining to the present program or routine being executed is stored on the stack. Thus, the amount of stack memory available effectively determines the degree of nesting.

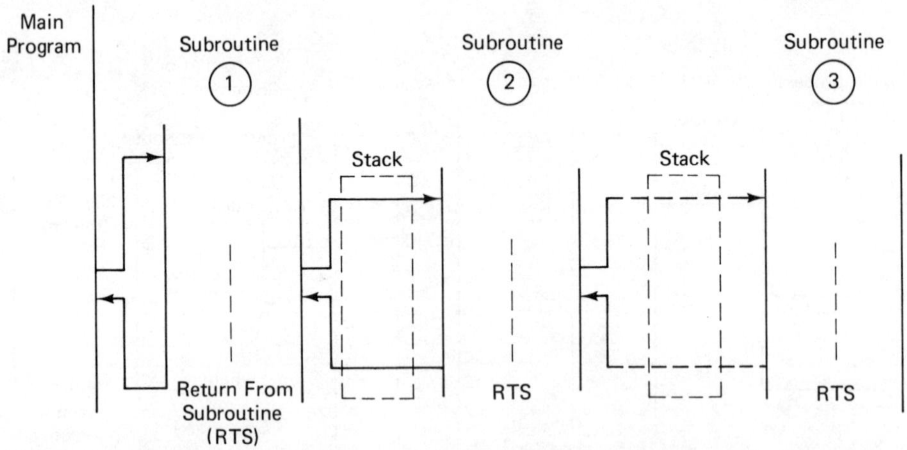

Fig 1.7. Subroutines and nesting.

Example 1.4

As shown in Figure 1.6, a microprocessor such as the M-6800 is controlling a printer. Each time data is given, the printer takes 2.5 milliseconds (ms) to print it and then sends a low active interrupt to the microprocessor requesting new information to be printed, whenever it is ready.

(a) If the micro takes an average of 5 microseconds (μs) to execute a typical instruction, and if the interrupt service routine for the printer takes 25 such instructions, compute the actual percentage of time the microprocessor is devoting to the control of printer.

(b) How many such printers N can be handled by a single microprocessor if the interrupts are structured.

Solution

(a) The interrupt occurs once every 2.5 ms when the printer requests new information from microprocessor by activating the interrupt input line going low.

The interrupt service routine (ISR) to put new information into the printer takes

$$T_{ISR} = \underset{\text{(no. of instructions)}}{25} * \underset{\text{(time for instruction)}}{5} = 125\ \mu s$$

Thus, the microprocessor attends to the printer for 125 μs for each 2.5 ms as shown.

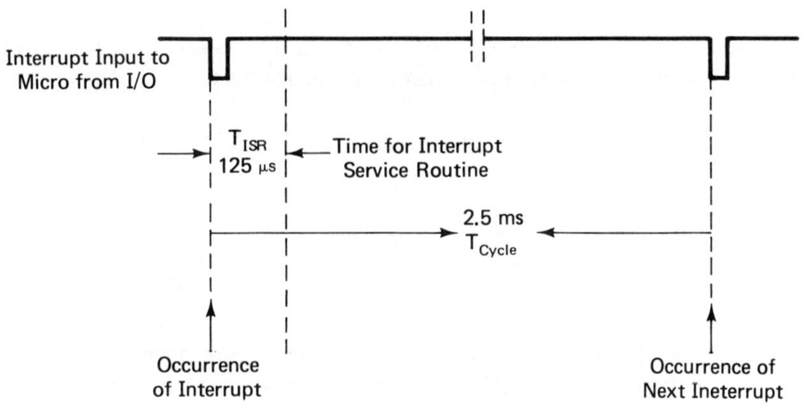

Percent of micro time for printer:

$$\frac{T_{ISR}}{T_{Cycle}} = \frac{125\ \mu s}{2.5\ ms}\ \%$$

$$= \boxed{5\%}$$

Thus only 5 percent of micro time is required for servicing a single printer.

(b) If the interrupts are linearly structured (one following the other), up to 20 printers, each requiring 5% of micro time, can be handled:

$$\boxed{N = 20}$$

Example 1.5

In a 6502-based microcomputer system, the stack memory is 256 bytes. The 6502 microprocessor consists of a 16-bit program counter, an 8-bit accumulator, two 8-bit index registers, an 8-bit status register, and a 9-bit stack pointer.

(a) Find how many bytes of stack memory S_m are required to store all the information contained in the microprocessor.

(b) How many nested subroutines, N_s, are possible?

(c) If each stacking or unstacking of memory takes 20 μs, what is the time involved in nested subroutines of the sixth degree in conducting stack-related operations,

Solution

(a) *Number of Bytes of Stack Memory.* For each stack operation required, memory can be easily computed as follows:

Micro Registers	*Required Storage*
16-bit program counter	2
8-bit accumulator	1
two 8-bit index registers	2
8-bit status register	1
Total bytes	6

The stack pointer, which keeps track of the position of the stack, is not stored on the stack. Thus, the amount of stack memory S_m required to store the information contained in the microprocessor is 6 bytes.

$$\boxed{S_m = 6 \text{ bytes}}$$

(b) *Nested Subroutines.* With each stack operation requiring 6 bytes, and with available stack memory space of 256 bytes, we can have $^{256}\!/_6 = 42\frac{2}{3}$ stackings; or, the number of subroutines N_s each requiring a stack operation, is 42.

$$\boxed{N_s = 42}$$

(c) *Timing.* For six nested subroutines, the time required is

$$T_{\text{Stack (6)}} = 6\,(\underset{\text{For Stacking}}{20\ \mu s} + \underset{\text{For Unstacking}}{20\ \mu s}) = 240\ \mu s$$

$$\boxed{T_{\text{Stack (6)}} = 240\ \mu s}$$

1.4. INPUT/OUTPUT (I/O) STRUCTURE

I/O Data Flow: Bus Structure

For conducting any control system applications, a microcomputer system should have access to the input/output (I/O) devices and systems. Usually these I/O devices or systems communicate with the microcomputer via some standard "bus" structures such as S-100, SS-50, IEEE-488, etc. The bus, as we discussed earlier, is a collection of electronic signals with specified voltage levels and electronic and timing properties and a well-defined electronic layout structure. We will elaborate on this when we deal with specific microprocessors.

Memory Mapped I/O

Some microprocessors such as the Motorola 6800 consider a typical I/O to be no more than a memory location. Thus all the data transfer features between microprocessor and memory apply for a typical I/O interface. All the instructions of the microprocessor can be used to manipulate the I/O data. This type of I/O is known as memory mapped I/O.

I/O Mapped I/O

Some microprocessors such as the Intel 8085 consider the I/O to be distinct from the normal memory and carry special I/O instructions. Because of the streamlined I/O instructions, at times the I/O bound data transfer may be faster and more efficient. This is known as I/O mapped I/O.

Both memory mapped and I/O mapped I/O are used extensively in industry, and we will present them in more detail with each specific microprocessor.

1.5. SUMMARY

In this chapter we introduced the basic concepts relating to microprocessors such as registers, flags, instruction formats, and a conceptual computer operation. The registers act as data storage elements, which have the capability to act as counters or shift registers. The flags are flip flops that are set or reset to indicate the status of a previous operation. The ALU in any microprocessor coordinates all arithmetic and logical operations on the data. The instructions always contain an op code as the first byte to specify the type of operation to be done. The following bytes of an instruction may contain data or the address of data.

Interrupts are hardware signals to the microprocessor from the I/O devices requesting its attention. The microprocessor stores its registers in a separate part of the memory called stack when it responds to interrupts or subroutines. Inevitably the microprocessor operation centers on reading data from memory or I/O, manipulating it and writing it back in memory or I/O to accomplish any given task.

Some micros consider I/O as similar to memory (memory mapped I/O), and some micros distinguish I/O from memory (I/O mapped I/O).

Even though most micros differ from each other in the details of their architecture and instructions, the basic concepts discussed in this chapter are applicable to all.

Problems

1.1. A microprocessor is nothing more than programmed logic, as shown in Figure 1.8. Using logic elements such as AND, OR, NOT gates and

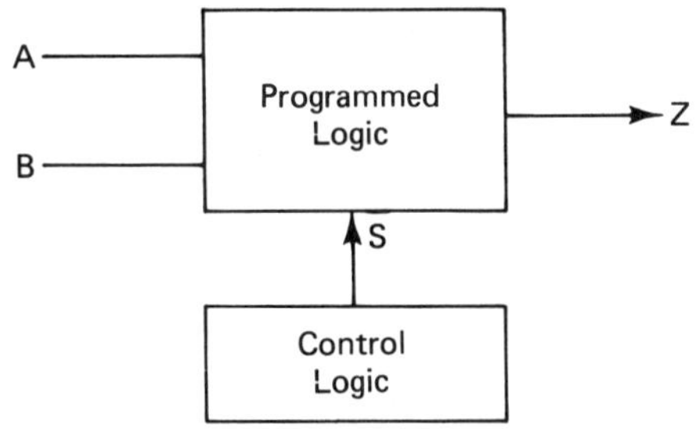

Fig 1.8. Programmed logic (Problems 1.1 and 1.2).

multiplexers, synthesize the network to accomplish the following:

If S = 0, transfer contents of A to Z
If S = 1, transfer contents of B to Z

1.2. Repeat Problem 1.1 using multiplexers for programmed logic and decoders for control logic.

1.3. In addition to being programmed logic, the microprocessor contains several registers to store data. Registers are arrays of flip flops. Figure 1.9 shows a simple internal structure of a microprocessor, where all the elements are connected to the common signal path called a bus.

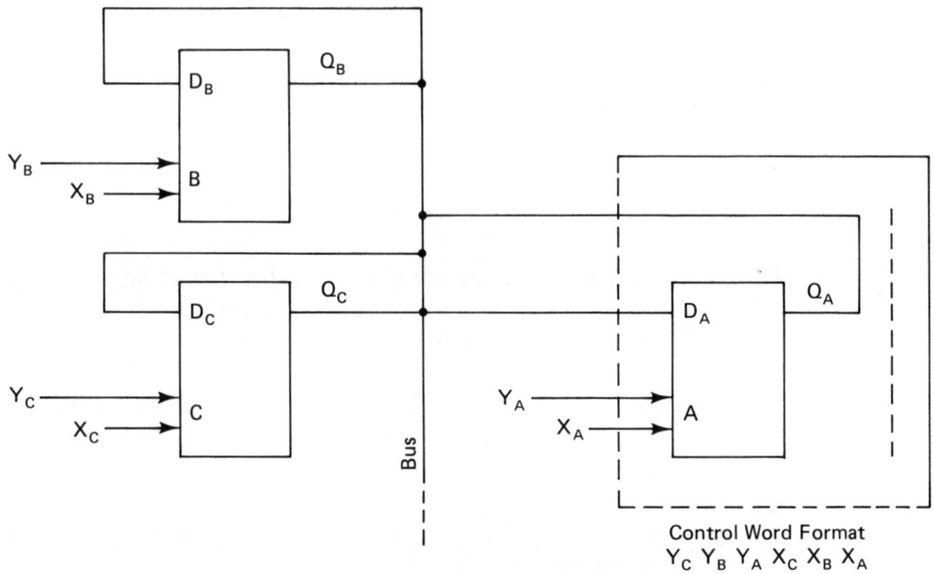

Fig 1.9. Microprocessor bussing concepts for Problems 1.3, 1.4, 1.5, 1.6, and 1.7.

(a) What type of output configuration should the elements have in order to be connected to bus? (Totem pole, tristate, open collector, etc.)

(b) Can all the elements be active on the bus all the time? Why?

(c) Are the concepts of wired OR, wired AND applicable for the busing under consideration?

1.4. Consider each element in Figure 1.9 as a conventional D type flip flop. X and Y are control signals that control the operation of each element as shown.

X	Y	Operation
0	0	Element disconnected from bus. Control given to ALU.
0	1	Element puts output on bus.
1	0	Element accepts input from bus.
1	1	Element in refresh mode.

(a) What is accomplished if the control word is

$$Y_C Y_B Y_A X_C X_B X_A = 001010 = (0A)_{Hex}$$

(b) What is accomplished if the control word is $(00)_{Hex}$?

1.5. In Figure 1.9, it is necessary to transfer the contents of B to C. What is the control word?

1.6. Write a sequence of control words to accomplish the following in sequence:

Transfer B to A

Transfer C to B

Transfer A to C

No transfer for awhile

Repeat the above four-step process.

1.7. In the microprocessor industry, some of the control signals are referred to as write when the element is putting output on bus, and read when the element is accepting input from bus (X is similar to read and Y is similar to write). Using real flip flop devices such as 7474 D flip flops, implement the structure of Figure 1.9, with all the necessary logic and interface devices (be sure to use tristate or open collector devices to be connected to the bus).

1.8. An 8-bit microprocessor operates on 8-bit registers (8 flip flops interconnected). Using octal D type latches such as SN 74373 for each element, repeat Problem 1.7. Clearly show all your interfacing drivers. (Note: for 8-bit data, 8-bit buffers such as SN 74365 are required.)

1.9. In addition to data transfers, arithmetic and logical operations are done inside a microprocessor using its ALU as shown in Figure 1.10. Consider that ALU control signals $Z_2Z_1Z_0$ become active when X and Y are inactive.

(a) Explain the necessity of the temporary register T.

(b) How does the data transfer take place between accumulator, ALU, and accumulator?

1.10. Consider that the control of ALU operation is as shown:

Z_1	Z_0	Operation
0	0	No operation. Control given to X and Y for data transfer
0	1	Add T to A
1	0	Subtract T from A
1	1	Invert contents of A

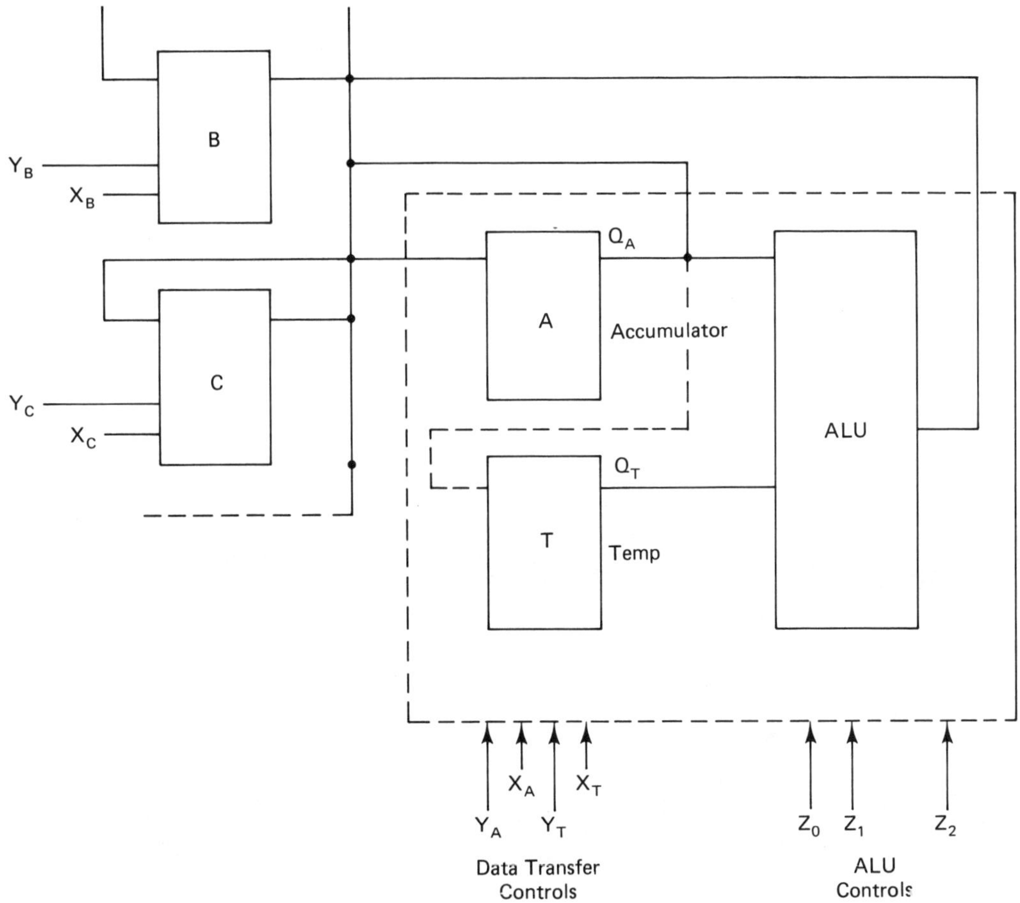

Fig 1.10. Conceptual microprocessor (Problems 1.10, 1.11, and 1.12).

Taking the data transfer codes from Problem 1.4, write a sequence of control words in the format

$$Z_1\ Z_0\ Y_C\ Y_B\ Y_A\ X_C\ X_B\ X_A$$

(MSB) (LSB)

to accomplish

(a) B + A (add B and A and store in A)

(b) C = $\overline{B}$ (invert B and store in C)

1.11. Using the format of Problem 1.10, write a conceptual program (series of control statements) to clear the accumulator to an all-zero condition, and transfer those contents to other registers B and C.

1.12. Explain briefly the difference between subroutines and interrupts in a typical microprocessor system.

1.13. In a particular microprocessor-based system, a page of memory is dedicated for a stack. It is required to store a program counter and two general purpose registers on stack for each subroutine or interrupt. How many subroutines or interrupts can be nested?

CHAPTER TWO

8085 Microprocessor and Microcomputer Systems

The 8085 microprocessor developed and marketed by the Intel Corporation is perhaps one of the most widely used 8-bit microprocessors in contemporary applications. It is a 40-pin integrated circuit, fabricated with NMOS semiconductor technology. It is software compatible with the earlier 8080 microprocessor and has some added features and a convenient interrupt structure. In this chapter we will discuss the 8085 microprocessor and associated devices. This will enable us to understand any 8085-based microcomputer, such as the SDK-85, and to develop operating system designs using such a microcomputer.

2.1. GENERAL ARCHITECTURE OF THE 8085

The basis for any microprocessor operation is its register architecture and flag structure. These help the internal data transfers and indicate the status of the processor to the user for decision making.

Registers, Flags, and Bus Structure

As shown in Figure 2.1, the 8085 consists of

16-bit program counter	PC
16-bit stack pointer	SP
8-bit accumulator	A

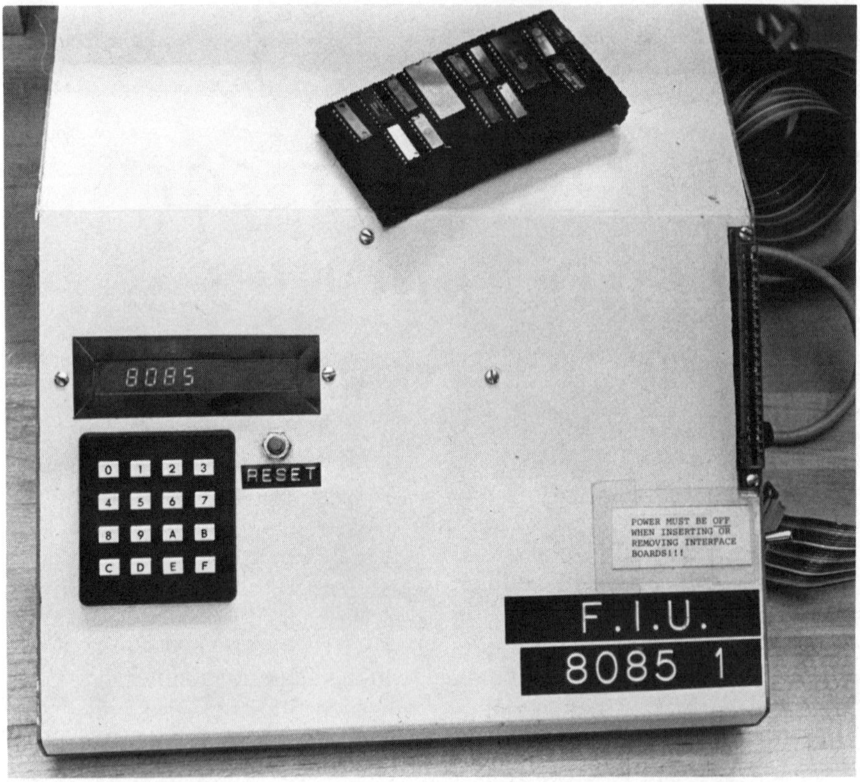

8085-Based System Developed at Florida International University.

Six 8-bit registers paired as	BC
	DE
	HL
and	
8-bit arithmetic logic unit	ALU
8-bit flag register	FLAG

The 16-bit program counter can address up to 65,536 (64K) memory locations. The 16-bit stack pointer helps to set up the stack part of the memory anywhere within the 64K memory space. Because of the 8-bit accumulator and ALU, the data manipulations are byte oriented.

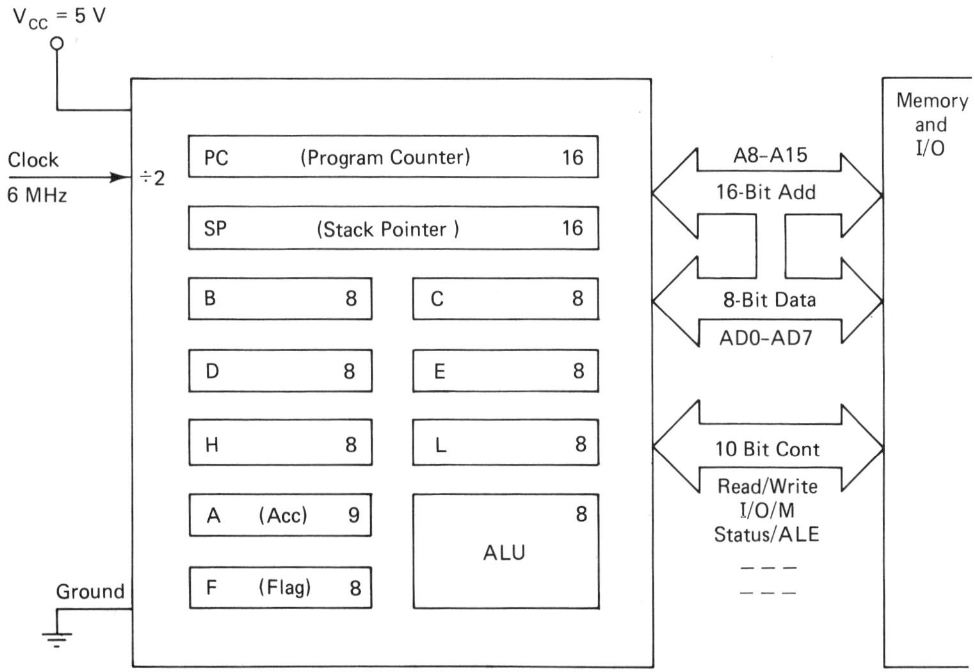

Fig 2.1. The 8085 programming structure with registers and buses.

The six general purpose registers B, C, D, E, H, and L can be used for data storage within the processor. They can also be operated in pairs, to obtain a 16-bit data format for indirect addressing.

The flag register has five effective flag bits: carry (C); auxiliary carry (AC); parity (P); sign (S); and zero (Z), as shown in Figure 2.2. These bits are set as a result of certain operations, as defined in the Figure 2.2. The flag bits help the decision making and branching to a different program location, under software control (making use of the conditional jump instructions of the 8085 instruction set).

The 8085 bus structure consists of an effective 16-bit multiplexed address bus, an 8-bit data bus (which is multiplexed with the lower order 8 bits of the address bus), and a 10-bit control bus, which consists of control signals such as read, write, and so on, as shown in Figure 2.1. When the address bus is active (when addressing a location), AD0...AD7 and A8...A15 lines contain the actual address information from the program counter. Then the address bus is deactivated, and the data transfer takes place between the 8085 microprocessor and addressed location on lines AD0...AD7. All the memory and I/O devices connected to the 8085 bus are structured to respond to this multiplexed feature, and the data and address are never scrambled.

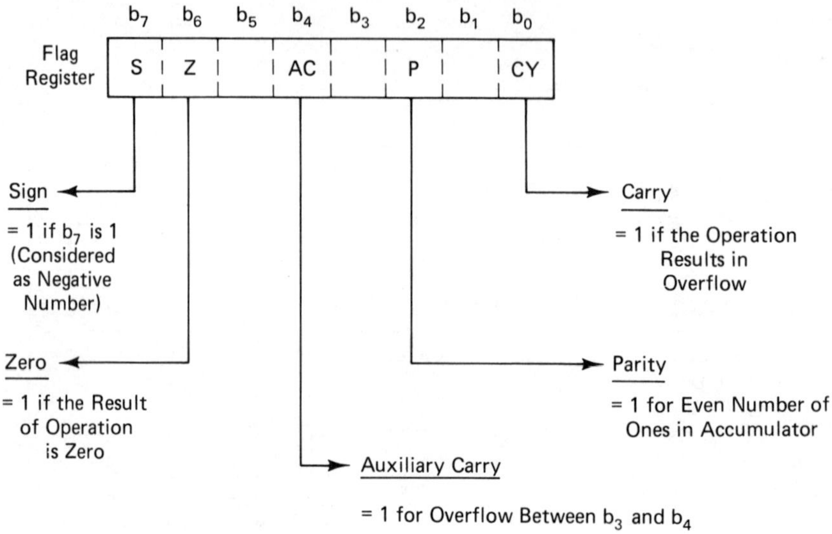

Fig 2.2. The 8085 flag register format.

8085 has a ÷ 2 and clock-shaping circuit internally and thus operates on half the external clock frequency.

Reset and Interrupt Vectors

The sophisticated but flexible interrupt structure of the 8085 makes it much more powerful than its predecessor 8080. Figure 2.3 shows the reset and interrupt signals associated with the 8085. A vector is a specified address to which the microprocessor goes, in response to the corresponding reset or interrupt signal.

$\overline{\text{Reset In}}$ is a low active system level interrupt of highest priority, which vectors 8085 to start executing the program at 0000 location. Also, the 8085 puts out a "Reset Out" signal in response to $\overline{\text{Reset In}}$, which in turn resets other devices in synchronization. Table 2.1 shows the features of other interrupts.

Trap is a nonmaskable interrupt of next priority that forces 8085 to vector to the 0024 address and start executing the program contained in there. The restart interrupts 7.5, 6.5, and 5.5 are maskable under software control and vector the 8085 to the locations as shown in Table 2.1, to execute the respective programs.

INTR, which is the lowest priority interrupt, can also be masked under software control. 8085 responds with interrupt acknowledge $\overline{\text{INTA}}$ to the I/O

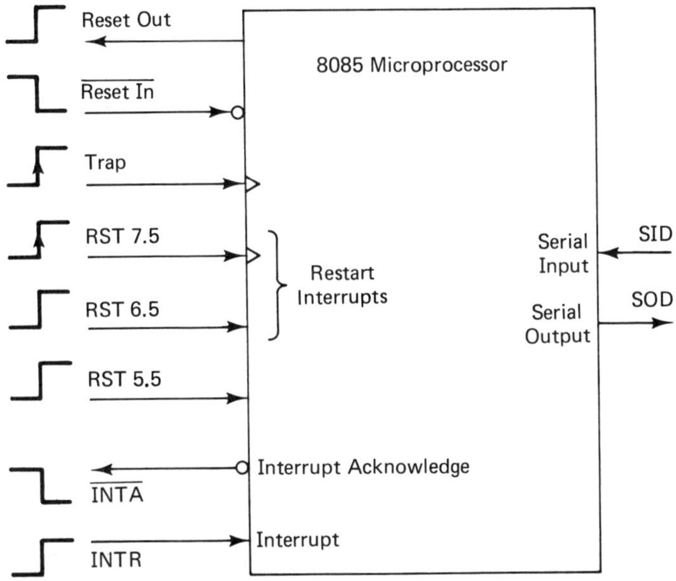

Fig 2.3. Reset, interrupt, and serial structure of the 8085.

device, which then provides the address to which the 8085 should vector. Example 2.1 will clarify the concepts of flags and interrupt vectors.

Example 2.1 Flags and Interrupts

In a particular data processing application using the 8085, an accumulator contains $(EC)_{Hex}$. Under program control, data $(CD)_{Hex}$ is added and the result is stored in the accumulator.

(a) What are the contents of various flags after addition?

(b) What will be the contents of flag bits, if the above result is rotated one position to the left through carry bit?

Table 2.1. Reset and Interrupt Definitions and Vectors.

Name	*Priority*	*Activation*	*Vectored Address*	*Maskability*
$\overline{\text{Reset In}}$	0	Low Level	0000	Nonmaskable
Trap	1	Positive Edge and Level	0024	Nonmaskable
RST 7.5	2	Positive Edge	003C	Maskable
RST 6.5	3	High Level	0034	Maskable
RST 5.5	4	High Level	002C	Maskable
INTR	5	High Level	Software controlled under acknowledge	Maskable

(c) When the above program is being executed, the trap interrupt becomes active. What are the sequence of events?

Solution

(a) *Flag Bits.* The flag bits are as shown, along with the contents of the accumulator, after the addition. Refer to Figure 2.2 for flags.

		b_7					b_3		b_0
Accumulator before addition	$= (EC)_{Hex}$	1	1	1	0	1	1	0	0
Data added	$= (CD)_{Hex}$	1	1	0	0	1	1	0	1
Result in accumulator	= (B9)	1	0	1	1	1	0	0	1

1	1	0	1	0
C	S	Z	AC	P
carry	sign	zero	auxiliary carry	parity

Carry and Auxiliary Carry are set to 1 because of overflow from bit 7 and bit 3, respectively. Sign flag is set to 1 since the bit 7 is 1. Zero flag is cleared to 0, since the accumulator is nonzero. Parity flag is cleared to 0, because of the odd number of 1s in the accumulator (odd parity).

(b) When the accumulator is rotated left through carry, b_7 shifts to C, C shifts to b_0, b_0 shifts to b_1 and so on.

Accumulator after shift rotation $(73)_{Hex} = 0\ 1\ 1\ 1\ 0\ 0\ 1\ 1$ (b_7 … b_0)

Flags:

1	0	0	1	0
C	S	Z	AC	P

(c) *Trap Interrupt.* As shown in Figure 2.1, Trap is a nonmaskable interrupt, and the micro will have to respond.

The micro will complete its present machine cycle and will store the contents of the program counter on stack and will load the program counter with the vector address 0024. It will then read the instruction at that location and start executing the program (usually called an "interrupt service routine"). The micro will return to the main program after encountering the return instruction.

Table 2.2. 8085 Instruction Set, Op Codes, and Timing Cycles (Courtesy Intel Corporation).

Mnemonic		Description	Op Code	Number of Bytes	Number of T States	Flags Effected
ACI	Data	Add immediate to A with carry.	CE	2	7	
ADC	A	Add the register contents with carry to A.	8F	1	4	
	B		88			
	C		89			
	D		8A			
	E		8B			
	H		8C			
	L		8D			
ADC	M	Add memory to A with carry.	8E	1	7	
ADD	A	Add register to A.	87	1	4	
	B		80			
	C		81			
	D		82			
	E		83			
	H		84			
	L		85			
ADD	M	Add memory to A.	86	1	7	
ADI	Data	Add immediate to A.	C6	2	7	
ANA	A	AND register to A.	A7	1	4	
	B		A0			
	C		A1			
	D		A2			
	E		A3			
	H		A4			
	L		A5			
ANA	M	AND memory to A.	A6	1	7	
ANI	Data	AND immediate A.	E6	2	7	
CALL	Addr	Call to address.	CD	3	18	
CC	Addr	Call on carry address.	DC	3	9/18	
CM	Addr	Call on minus address.	FC			
CMA		Complement A.	2F	1	4	
CMC		Complement carry.	3F	1	4	
CMP	A	Compare register with A.	BF	1	4	
	B		B8			
	C		B9			
	D		BA			
	E		BB			
	H		BC			
	L		BD			
CMP	M	Compare MEM with A.	BE	1	7	
CNC	Addr	Call on no carry.	D4	3	9/18	
CNZ	Addr	Call on no zero.	C4			
CP	Addr	Call on positive.	F4			
CPE	Addr	Call on even parity.	EC			
CPI	Data	Compare immediate with A.	FE	2	7	
CPO	Addr	Call on odd parity.	E4	3	9/18	
CZ	Addr	Call on zero.	CC			
DAA		Decimal adjust A.	27	1	4	
DAD	B	Add B&C to H&L.	09	1	10	
	D	Add D&E to H&L.	19			
	H	Add H&L to H&L.	29			
	SP	Add SP to H&L.	39			
DCR	A	Decrement register.	3D	1	4	
	B		05			

Table 2.2. *(Continued)*

Mnemonic		Description	Op Code	Number of Bytes	Number of T States	Flags Effected
	C		0D			
	D		15			
	E		1D			
	H		25			
	L		2D			
	M	Decrement memory.	35	1	10	
DCX	B	Decrement B&C.	0B	1	6	
	D	Decrement D&E.	1B			
	H	Decrement H&L.	2B			
	SP	Decrement SP.	3B			
DI		Disable interrupt.	F3	1	4	
EI		Enable interrupt.	F8	1	4	
HLT		Halt.	76	1	5	
In	Port	Input port data.	DB	2	10	
INR	A	Increment register.	3C	1	4	
	B		04			
	C		0C			
	D		14			
	E		1C			
	H		24			
	L		2C			
	M	Increment memory.	34	1	10	
INX	B	Increment B&C.	03	1	6	
	D	Increment D&E.	13			
	H	Increment H&L.	23			
	SP	Increment SP.	33			
JC	Addr	Jump on carry.	DA	3	7/10	
JM	Addr	Jump on minus.	FA			
JMP	Addr	Jump unconditional.	C3	3	10	
JNC	Addr	Jump on no carry.	D2	3	7/10	

Mnemonic		Description	Op Code	Number of Bytes	Number of T States	Flags Effected
JNZ	Addr	Jump on no zero.	C2			
JP	Addr	Jump on positive.	F2			
JPE	Addr	Jump on even parity.	EA			
JPO	Addr	Jump on odd parity.	E2			
JZ	Addr	Jump on zero.	CA			
LDA	Addr	Load A direct.	3A	3	13	
LDAX	B	Load A via B&C.	0A	1	7	
	D	Load A via D&E.	1A			
LHLD	Addr	Load H&L direct.	2A	3	16	
LXI	B	Load B&C immediate.	01	3	10	
	D	Load D&E immediate.	11			
	H	Load H&L immediate.	21			
MOV	A, A	Move register to A.	7F	1	4	
	A, B		78			
	A, C		79			
	A, D		7A			
	A, E		7B			
	A, H		7C			
	A, L		7D			
	A, M	Move memory to A.	7E			
MOV	B, A	Move register to B.	47	1	4	
	B, B		40			
	B, C		41			
	B, D		42			
	B, E		43			

	B, H		44		
	B, L		45		
	B, M	Move memory to B.	46	1	7
MOV	C, A	Move register to C.	4F	1	4
	C, B		48		
	C, C		49		
	C, D		4A		
	C, E		4B		
	C, H		4C		
	C, L		4D		
	C, M	Move memory to C.	4E	1	7
MOV	D, A	Move register to D.	57		
	D, B		50		
	D, C		51		
	D, D		52		
	D, E		53		
	D, H		54		
	D, L		55		
	D, M	Move memory to D.	56	1	7
MOV	E, A	Move register to E.	5F	1	4
	E, B		58		
	E, C		59		
	E, D		5A		
	E, E		5B		
	E, H		5C		
	E, L		5D		
	E, M	Move memory to E.	5E	1	7
MOV	H, A	Move register to H.	67	1	4
	H, B		60		
	H, C		61		
	H, D		62		
	H, E		63		
	H, H		64		
	H, L		65		
	H, M	Move memory to H.	66	1	7
MOV	L, A	Move register to L.	6F	1	4
	L, B		68		
	L, C		69		
	L, D		6A		
	L, E		6B		
	L, H		6C		
	L, L		6D		
	L, M		6E	1	7
MOV	M, A	Move register	77	1	7
	M, B	to memory.	70		
	M, C	(Address of M	71		
	M, D	is contained	72		
	M, E	in HL register)	73		
	M, H		74		
	M, L		75		
MVI	A	Move	3E	2	7
	B	immediate	06		
	C	data to	0E		
	D	register.	16		
	E		1E		
	H		26		
	L		2E		
	M	Move immediate data to memory.	36	2	10
NOP		No operation.	00	1	4
ORA	A	OR register with	B7	1	4
	B	A.	B0		
	C		B1		
	D		B2		
	E		B3		
	H		B4		

Table 2.2. *(Continued)*

Mnemonic		Description	Op Code	Number of Bytes	Number of T States	Flags Effected
	L		B5			
	M	OR memory with A.	B6	1	7	
ORI	Data	OR immediate with A.	F6	2	7	
Out	Port	Output A to port.	D3	2	10	
PCHL		H&L to program counter.	E9	1	6	
POP	B	Pop B&C from stack.	C1	1	10	
	D	Pop DE from stack.	D1			
	H	Pop HL from stack.	E1			
PUSH	B	Push BC on stack.	C5	1	12	
	D	Push DE on stack.	D5			
	H	Push HL on stack.	E5			
RAL		Rotate A left.	17	1	4	
RAR		Rotate A right with carry.	1F	1	4	
RC		Return on carry.	D8	1	6/12	
RET		Return unconditional.	C9	1	10	
RIM		Read interrupt mask.	20	1	4	
RLC		Rotate A left.	07	1	4	
RM		Return on minus.	F8	1	6/12	
RNC		Return on no carry.	D0			
RP		Return on positive.	F0			
RPE		Return on even parity.	E8			
RPO		Return on odd parity.	E0			
RRC		Rotate A right.	0F	1	4	
RST	1	Restart vectors.	CF	1	12	
	2		D7			
	3		DF			
	4		E7			
	5		EF			
	6		F7			
	7		FF			
RZ		Return on zero.	C8	1	6/12	
SBB	A	Subtract register from A with borrow.	9F	1	4	
	B		98			
	C		99			
	D		9A			
	E		9B			
	H		9C			
	L		9D			
	M	Subtract memory with borrow.	9E	1	7	
SBI	Data	Subtract immediate with borrow.	DE	2	7	
SHLD	Addr	Store HL direct.	22	3	16	
SIM		Set interrupt mask.	30	1	4	
SPHL		HL to stack printer.	F9	1	6	
STA	ADDR	Store A direct.	32	3	13	

STAX	B	Store A indirect through BC or DE.	02	1	7
	D		12		
STC		Set carry.	37	1	4
SUB	A	Subtract register from A.	97	1	4
	B		90		
	C		91		
	D		92		
	E		93		
	H		94		
	L		95		
	M	Subtract memory from A.	96	1	7
SUI	Data	Subtract immediate from A.	D6	2	7
XCHG		Exchange DE with HL.	E8	1	4
XRA	A	Exclusive OR register with A.	AF	1	4
	B		A8		
	C		A9		
	D		AA		
	E		AB		
	H		AC		
	L		AD		
	M	EXOR memory with A.	AE	1	7
XRI	Data	EXOR immediate with A.	EE	2	7
XTHL		Exchange HL with top of stack.	E3	1	16

Instruction Set

The potential of using any microprocessor depends on a thorough knowledge of the instruction set and addressing modes and how to use them in conjunction in order to accomplish a given task. Table 2.2 shows the instruction set of the 8085. A clear understanding of this set is necessary to use the 8085 effectively, and the reader is encouraged to review Table 2.2 and study the MCS 85 Family User's Manual for a detailed explanation of these instructions. The number of bytes specifies whether the instruction is 1, 2, or 3 bytes long. The number of T states provides timing information to execute any instruction. This information is necessary to compute timing in all the microcomputer-based applications. We will now study the instructional format and addressing modes of 8085, which are required to implement successfully an 8085-based system.

As shown in Figure 2.4, the instruction may be 1, 2, or 3 bytes long. The first byte is always op code. The second and third bytes may represent data or address of the data, depending on the op code and the addressing mode. Multiple-byte instructions should be stored in successive memory locations.

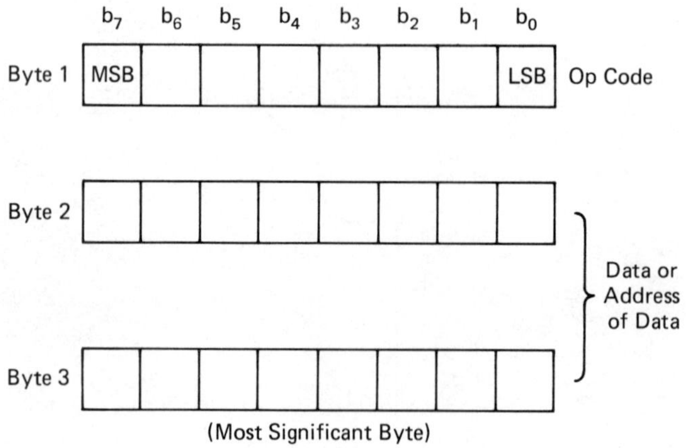

Fig 2.4. Instructional format of the 8085.

Addressing Modes

Data to be operated on is usually stored in memory. The 8085 has four distinct addressing modes to address the data stored in memory or in the internal CPU registers.

1. Register Addressing: The data to be operated is contained within CPU registers, and this addressing specifies the register or register pair where the data is located.

Example:

MOV A, B: Move contents of B register to A.
XCHG : Exchange contents of HL with DE registers.

2. Register Indirect Addressing: The address of the data is contained in a register pair.
   Example:

   MOV A, M: Move contents of location M referenced by HL register pair to A.
   LDAX B :˙ Load A with contents of location X referenced by BC register pair.

3. Immediate Addressing: The data to be operated is a part of the instruction and is contained in byte 2 or 3 depending on 8- or 16-bit data.
   Example:

   MVI A: Load A with contents of the second byte, which is 75 in this case.
   75

4. Direct Addressing: Bytes 2 and 3 of the instruction contain the direct address of the data.
   Example:

   STA A: Store accumulator A at location 20B0
   $B0_{Low}$
   20_{High}

Fortunately, the instructions and addressing modes can be clearly identified and used in conjunction in 8085-based systems without much confusion.

Example 2.2 Addressing Modes

A simple data manipulation algorithm, using the 8085 instruction set, is given below.

Location	*Mnemonic*	*Op Code*	*Address Mode*	*Comment*
2001	MVI B	06	Immediate	:Move immediate data of 00 to register B.
02	Ø Ø			
03	MOV A, B	78	Register	:Move B register to A.
04	LXI H	21	Immediate	:Load HL register with immediate data of 20A0.
05	$A0_{Low}$			
06	20_{High}			
07	INR A	3C	Register	:Increment register A.
08	MOV M, A	77	Reg Indirect	:Move A to Location M specified by HL register.
09	NOP	00	Register	
0A	INR B	04	"	Increment register B.
0B	ADD B	80	"	Add B to register A.
0C	NOP	00	"	No operation.

200D	STA A	32	Direct	Store A at location 20B0.
0E	$B0_{Low}$			
0F	20_{High}			
2010	JMP	C3	Direct	Jump to location 2007.
11	07			
12	20			

(a) What is accomplished between 2001 and 2006?
(b) What is accomplished between 2007 and 2012?
(c) What are the contents of A, B, H, L registers after the program is run once and four times?
(d) Will the program advance beyond 2012?

Solution:

(a) 2001 to 2003 B register is loaded with ØØ and is transferred to A register. That amounts to clearing A and B to all-zero condition.
2004 to 2006 H and L registers are loaded with 20 and A0 to form address vector $(20A0)_{Hex}$.

(b) 2007 and 2008 A register is incremented by 1 and is stored at location 20A0, as referenced by HL registers.
2009 to 2012 B register is incremented by 1 and is added to A, with the result in A and stored at location 20B0.
NOP instructions are just a way to generate momentary delays without modifying CPU contents.
JMP instruction at 2010, puts back the program in a loop starting at $(2007)_{Hex}$.

(c) Contents of registers A, B, H, L (for one run)
Contents of (A) → 02 (Since it gets incremented and added to B)
(B) → 01
(HL) → 20A0
Contents of registers A, B, H, L (for 4 runs)
Contents of (A) → 0E
(B) → 04
(HL) → 20A0 Unchanged

(d) *Program Loop.* The program will not advance beyond 2012 because of the indefinite loop between 2007 and 2012. Only an interrupt or reset will pull the micro out of the loop.

For a complete operating microcomputer system, in addition to the microprocessor, there should be RAM, ROM, and I/O devices. We now discuss a typical microcomputer configuration such as the SDK-85. The same discussion applies to any other 8085-based system, with few changes in the memory and I/O mapping.

2.2. 8085-BASED MICROCOMPUTER CONFIGURATION

Figure 2.5 shows the basic 8085-based microcomputer system. The 8279 is a 40-pin NMOS programmable keyboard/display interface. The receive port $R_{L0}\ldots R_{L7}$ receives key data and identifies which key it is. Ports A and B (8 bits total) generate the segment code to drive the multiplexed seven-segment display. The entire 8279 is slaved to the 8085.

Hardware Structure

The 8205 3/8 decoder decodes the selected address to provide 8-chip selects $\overline{CS0}\ldots\overline{CS7}$, which are routed to various memory and I/O devices.

The 8216 is a 4-bit bidirectional driver to buffer the data on bidirectional buses such as data buses, and effectively connects the memories and I/O devices.

The 8355/8755 is a 2K × 8 (ROM/PROM) memory and two I/O ports for user application. The system monitor and control programs usually reside in this device.

The 8155 is a 256 × 8 RAM and three I/O ports for user application. The memory part can be used for program and data storage and the I/O ports for user interface.

The 8212 is a transparent 8-bit latch, which is used to separate and latch the lower order 8 bits of the address.

2114 RAM devices (1K × 4) are used for the System Random Access Memory.

Several problems at the end of the chapter are designed to provide operating and design insight into the hardware and software features of these devices, and you are encouraged to solve them.

8085-based systems use I/O mapped I/O concepts, and the 8155 and 8755 RAM/ROM/I/O devices are very conveniently structured to respond to the memory and I/O needs of the user.

Software Structure

The I/O devices such as 8279, 8155, and 8355/8755 are characterized by internal registers that can be initialized under software control to perform various tasks. In I/O bound applications, the first few programming steps always correspond to the initialization of the hardware devices to suit the applications. We will present the discussions at the appropriate place when we introduce the applications.

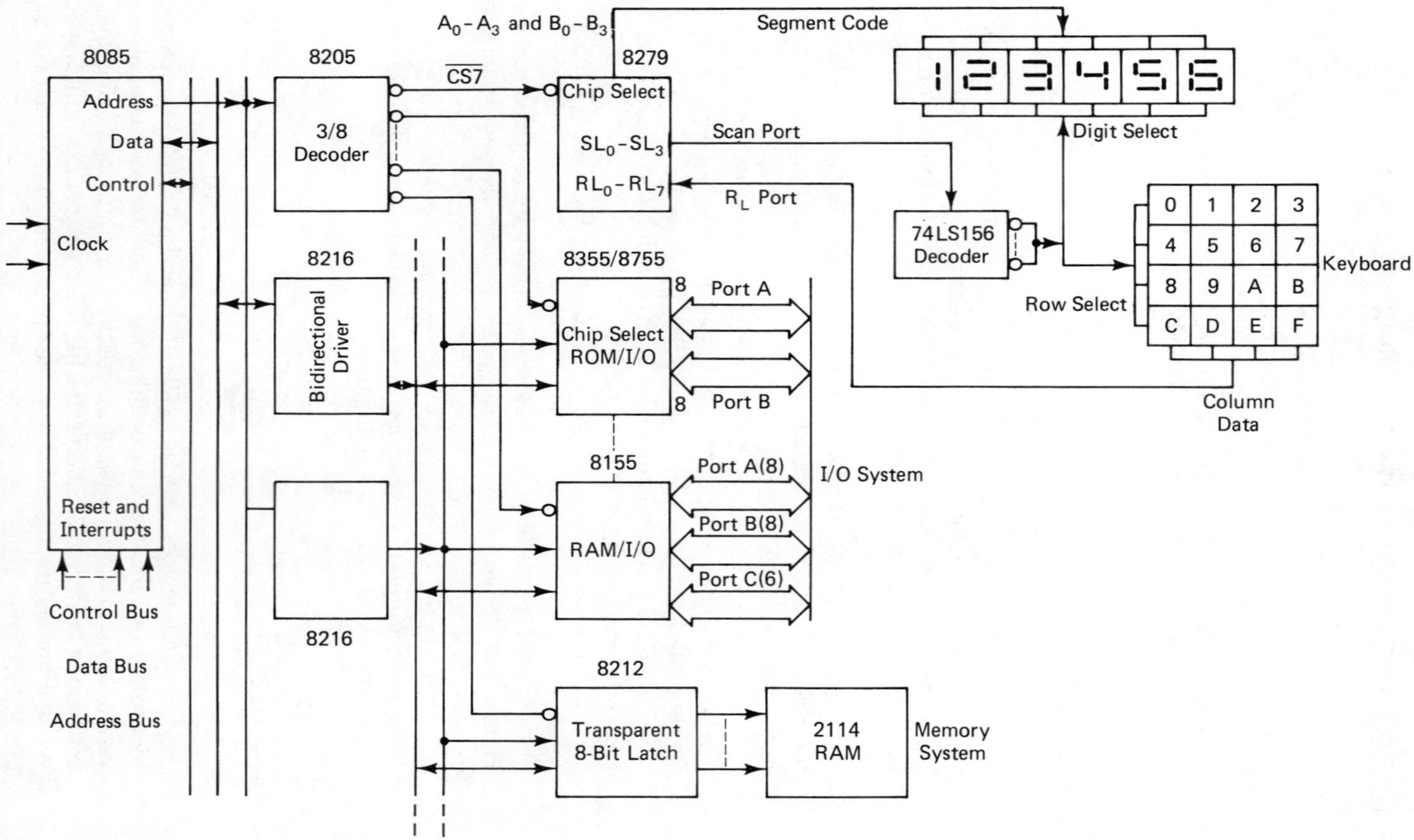

Fig 2.5. The 8085-based microcomputer system. (Courtesy Intel SDK-85 System.)

2.3. SDK-85 MICROCOMPUTER SYSTEMS

The SDK-85 single-board microcomputer as shown in Figures 2.6(a) and (b) was developed and marketed by INTEL Corporation and is convenient for learning and system applications. The concepts presented in this section should help you to gain operating experience of the SDK-85 or any other similar system. There are eight system level commands, which can be implemented through the keyboard buttons. We will now present a brief description of these functions, to allow you to quickly use the system. For details, the SDK-85 User's Manual should be consulted.

Reset Command

Activation of reset returns the control of the system to the monitor with a flashing 8085 in the display field. If the system is wandering or hung up, activation of reset should restore the system operation controlled by the monitor.

Substitute and Next Commands

Activation of "substitute memory" allows the user to examine and modify the contents of memory location. "Next" will advance to the next memory location. If new data is typed, it will be entered into the location currently being displayed in the address field (refer to Figure 2.6(b) for details).

Example (Memory Examine):

Activate keys as shown:

			Address Display	Data Display
[Subst Mem]	2 0 0 0	[Next]	[2 0 0 0]	[3E]
		[Next]	[2 0 0 1]	[7F]
Contents of Locations 2000 are 3E 2001 are 7F 2002 are 49		[Next]	[2 0 0 2]	[49]

Memory Change: Type CF

Contents of Location 2002 changed to CF			[2 0 0 2]	[CF]

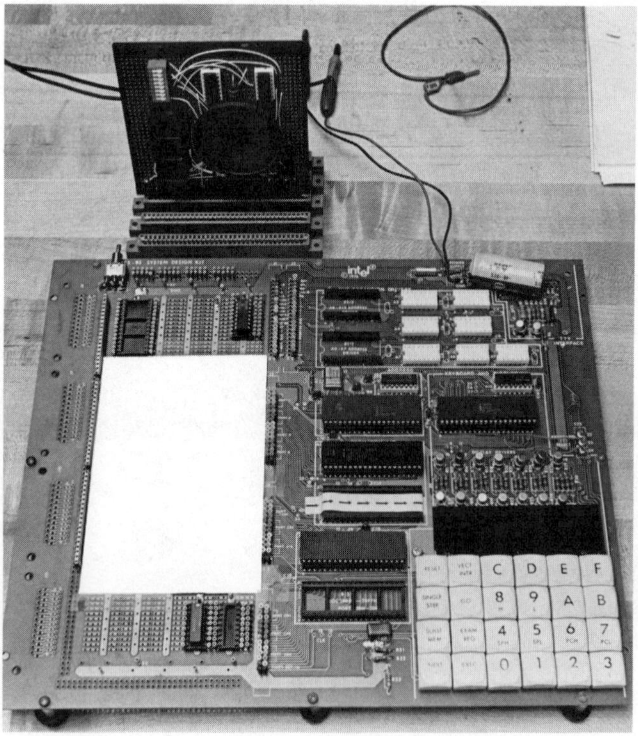

Fig 2.6 (a) SDK-85 single-board microcomputer system; (b) SDK-85 functional diagram. (Courtesy Intel Corporation.)

Examine and Change Registers

Activation of this key will allow you to examine and change the contents of all CPU registers.

Example (Register Examine and Change):

Type

[Exam Reg] [A]		[A] [29]
Contents of A are 29, which are changed to B8.	Type B8	[A] [B8]

Go and Execute

Activating GO will display the contents of the program counter in the address field, which could be modified. Activating EXEC will execute the program starting at the location specified by the program counter.

Example (Type):

		ADDRESS	DATA
[GO]		X X X X	X X
	2 0 0 0	2 0 0 0	3E
		[EXEC]	

The program starting at 2000 location is run, which is

Location	*Contents*	*Mnemonic*	*Comment*
2000	3E	MVI A	Move immediate data of 7F
01	7F	7F	into accumulator.
02	CF	RST 1	Restart 1, which returns control to monitor.

Thus, after the program is run, if A is examined it should contain 7F.

Single Step and Vector Interrupt

Activation of single step will advance the program one step at a time. The vector interrupt generates a 7.5 interrupt, which transfers control to location 003C (Fig. 2.1), which in turn branches to location 20CE in RAM memory. These are features for debugging the programs that we will use in later applications.

2.4. BUS CONCEPTS

S-100 Bus

The S-100 bus, as shown in Figure 2.7, is a microcomputer interface bus with 100 total connections, which are dedicated. The bus was originally introduced in the early 1970s to provide interface capabilities between various

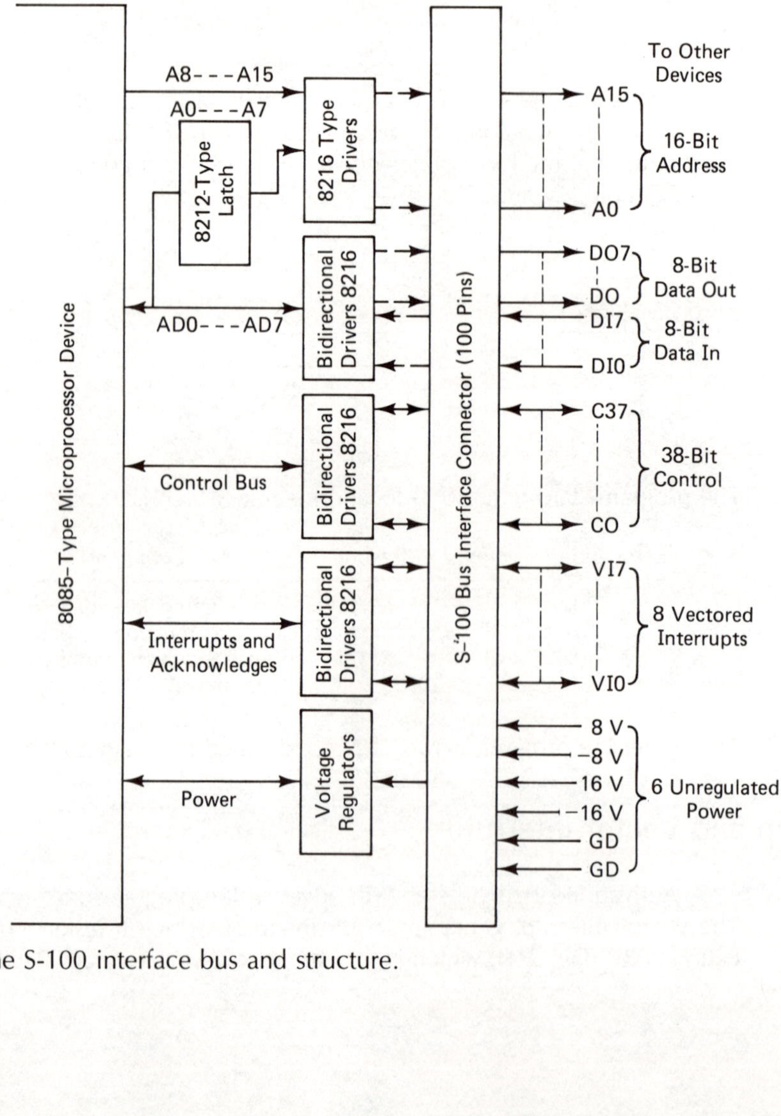

Fig 2.7. The S-100 interface bus and structure.

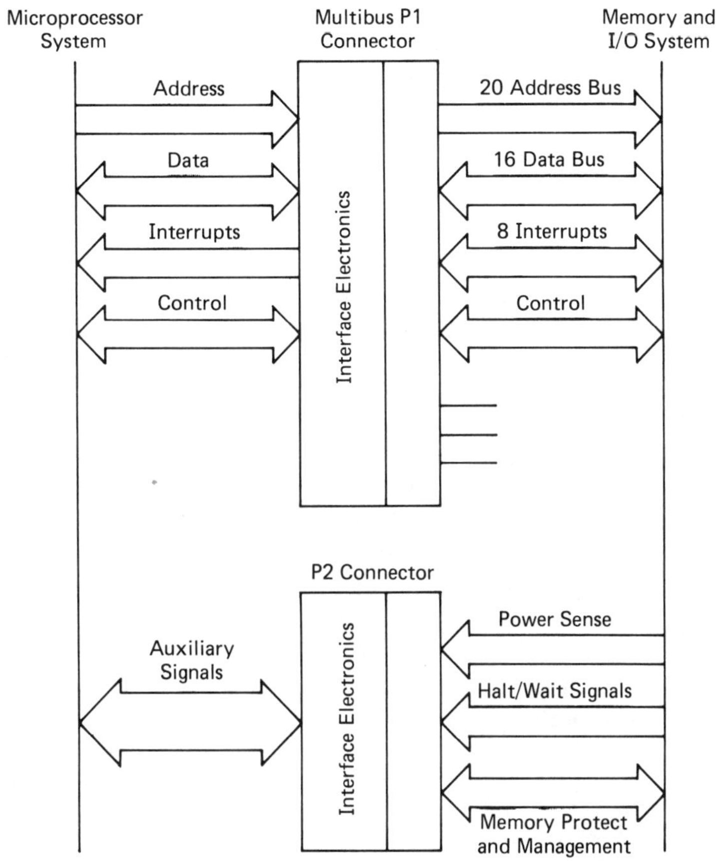

Fig 2.8. Multibus interface and structure.

devices and systems and the 8080A microprocessor. The bus has undergone several changes and has been finally standardized regarding the software and hardware characteristics. Thus, any devices and systems that are S-100 bus compatible can be interfaced to form an operating system.

It should be noted that all 100 connections need not be used for system integration. Only required signals can be effectively used. Excellent references are provided and should be consulted before interfacing to the S-100 bus. Care must be exercised for regulating the unregulated power.

Multibus

A variation of the S-100 bus is the multibus in which the interface is split between two connectors P1 and P2. P1 carries primary signals of address, data, control, and power. P2 carries secondary signals such as backup power, safety sense logic, and so on. Depending on the system requirement, S-100 or multibus configurations can be chosen. Figure 2.8 shows the multibus structure.

2.5. SUMMARY

In this chapter, the basic concepts relating to the 8085 microprocessor's architecture and instruction set have been presented. Emphasis has been placed on addressing modes and interrupt structure. In addition, a typical 8085 microprocessor-based computer system such as the SDK-85 has been introduced and studied, demonstrating real support devices such as 8205 decoders, 8212 transparent latches, 8216 bidirectional drivers, 8155 peripheral devices, and 8355 ROM and 2114-type RAMS. Also, a brief introduction was provided to the industry standard S-100 and multibus concepts.

The study of this chapter should provide enough background on the 8085 microprocessor and 8085-based microcomputer system to understand the system applications discussed in the next chapter.

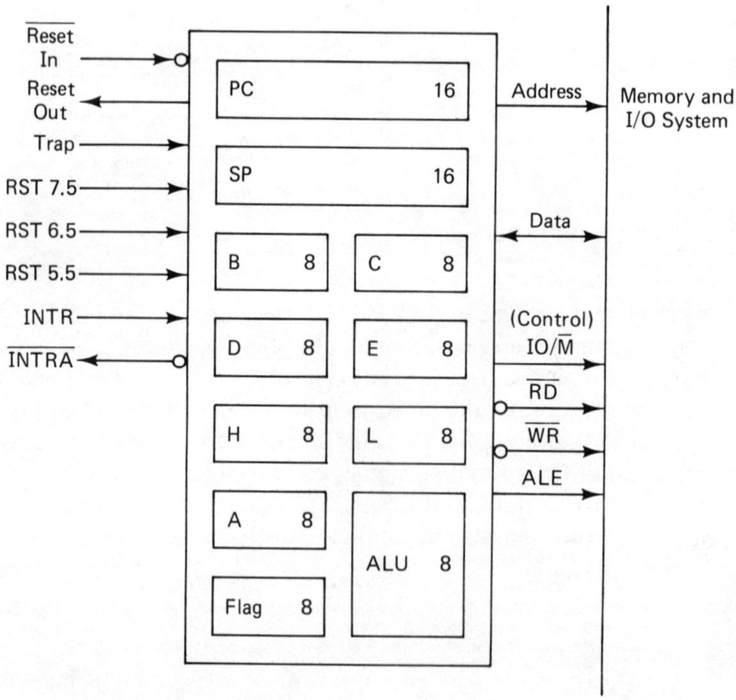

Fig 2.9. The 8085 register and bus structure.

S	Z		AC		P		CY

Fig 2.10. The flag register structure of the 8085.

Problems

2.1. Figure 2.9 shows the architecture of the 8085 and Figure 2.10 shows its flag structure.
(a) How much memory can be addressed by 8085?
(b) How much stack memory is addressable?

2.2. Stack pointer decrements each time data is pushed on to the stack and increments when the data is popped.
(a) How many bytes of stack memory are required to store all the CPU registers as shown in Figure 2.9?
(b) If the stack pointer is initialized at $(20C2)_{Hex}$, what will it contain after all the CPU registers are stacked?

2.3. A particular operation leaves the accumulator with 00001001 = $(09)_{Hex}$ data in it.
(a) What is the condition of the flag bits, as shown in Figure 2.10?
(b) If $(FF)_{Hex}$ is added to the accumulator, what is the condition of the flag bits?

2.4. Referring to Table 2.1 on reset and interrupts, explain briefly the operation of 7.5 interrupt. Will it have to be active until it is recognized?

2.5. 8085 is servicing a TV display, and 6.5 RST interrupt occurs from a slow printer, as shown in Fig 2.11.
(a) Outline the sequence of events.
(b) The television display routine takes 300 μs and has to be done at

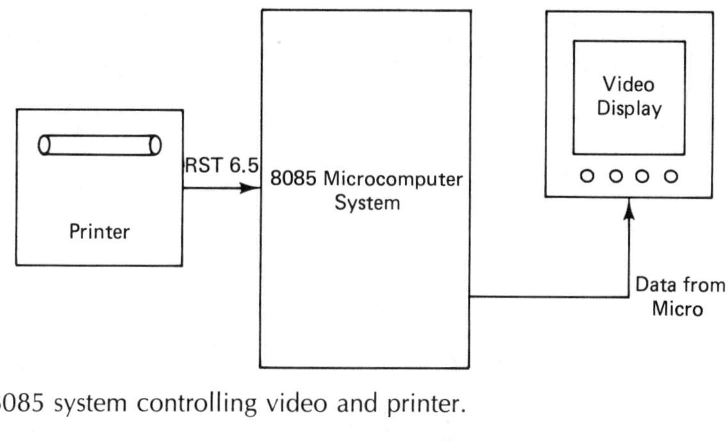

Fig 2.11. The 8085 system controlling video and printer.

least once every 1 ms. If a 6.5 RST connected routine takes 200 μs, how many times can the 8085 service a 6.5 RST interrupt without loss of display sequence?

2.6. In the above problem, specify how the TV display routine can be protected against interrupts when the routine is being actually run.

(b) Can TRAP be used by the slow printer to get the attention of the microprocessor, which is normally servicing the TV routine?

2.7. Referring to the instruction set of Table 2.2, identify how many read or write cycles have to be performed to implement the following instructions:

(a) MOV A, B

(b) MOV M, A

(c) JMP
40
40

2.8. Repeat Problem 2.7, for the following instructions:

(a) SHLD
41
40

(b) RET

(c) JNZ
42
42

2.9. Write a simple program starting at location $(2000)_{Hex}$ to add two numbers *X* and *Y* stored at locations 20A0 and 20A1 and store the result at 20A2. Show clearly all op codes and timing cycles.

2.10. Draw a flow chart and write a simple program to use DE register pair as a 0.1 S counter, which gets incremented from the all-zero condition every 0.1 s, and stops at the all-one condition.

2.11. Design a simple algorithm and write an operating program to use DE and HL register pairs as a 32-bit counter that gets incremented once every ms.

2.12. Shown in Figure 2.12 is a typical address decoding structure of an 8085-based microcomputer system, using an 8205 3/8 decoder. The memory element M0 will be addressable if chip select $\overline{CS0}$ goes low, M7 addressable if $\overline{CS7}$ goes low.

(a) The address bus of 8085 is connected to the enable and address inputs of the 8205 decoder as shown:

A15-E3, A14-E2, A13-E1, A12-A2, A11-A1, and A10-A0

What is the effective address range of each of the memory units M0...M7?

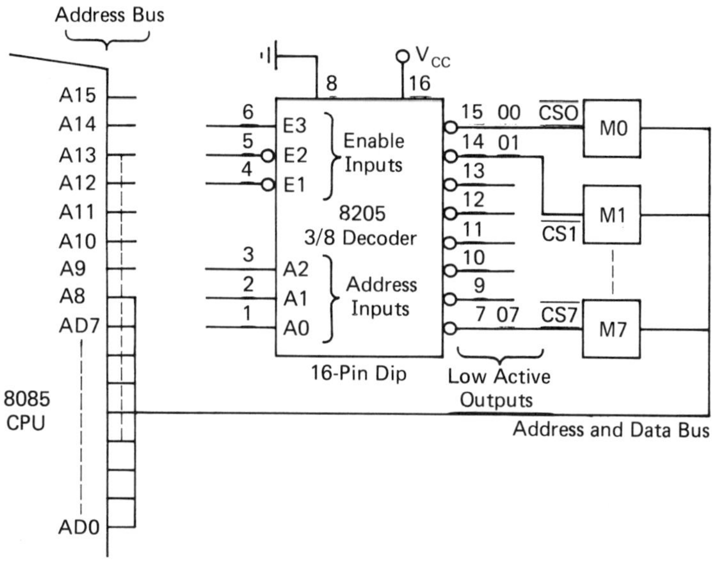

Fig 2.12. A typical 8085 address decoding structure.

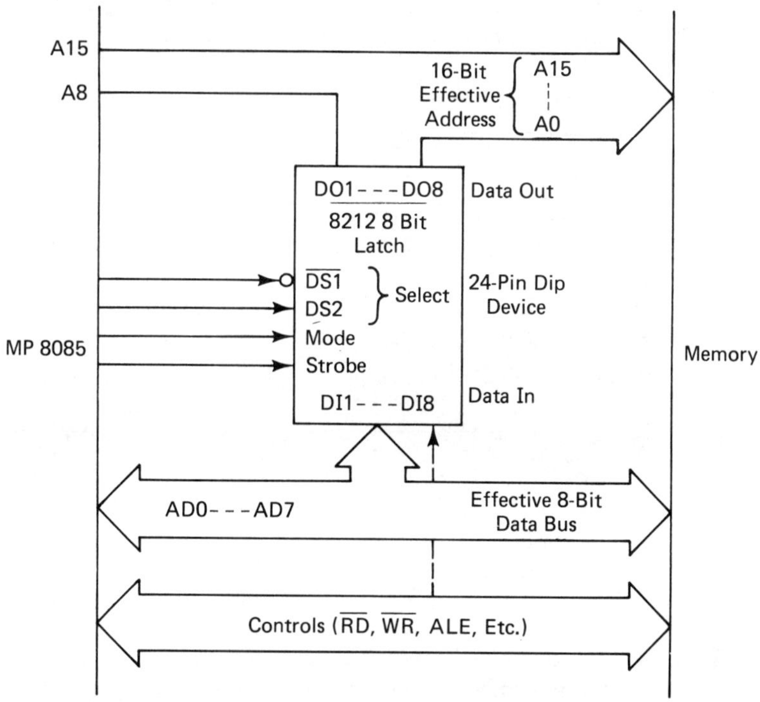

Fig 2.13. Address and data demultiplexing.

2.13. Repeat Problem 2.12, if A15 is connected to E1, A14 to E2, and A13 to E3.

2.14. The lower 8 bits of address and data are multiplexed to form an AD0...AD7 bus from the 8085. As shown in Figure 2.13, an 8212 8-bit transparent latch is used to demultiplex address and data buses.

Taking the data from the Intel Data Book, design an operating structure to provide a 16-bit effective address bus and an 8-bit effective data bus, which will interface to outside memory and I/O. Show all the control signals clearly and all the electronics necessary.

2.15. Intel 2114 1K × 4 RAMs are industry standard memory devices. Using the decoding scheme of Problem 2.12 and the address demultiplexing scheme of Problem 2.14, design an operating memory system to provide 8K × 8 effective memory. Show clearly all electronic connections and the specifics of the address range.

2.16. Using SDK-85 monitor routines of update data display (UPDDT) at 0365 and read keyboard (RDKBD) at 02E7, develop an operating program to read two numbers *X* and *Y* from the keyboard, add them, and display the result. Interpret *X* and *Y* to be binary numbers, 8 bits wide.

2.17. Develop a real time clock, using the monitor routines of the SDK-85, to count seconds, minutes, and hours, as shown:

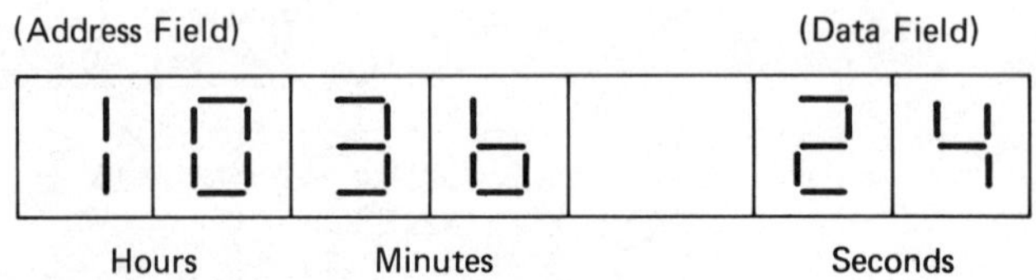

Data is to be entered using the SDK-85 keyboard. The clock should start if the VECR INTR is pressed.

2.18. Repeat Problem 2.17, with the following display format:

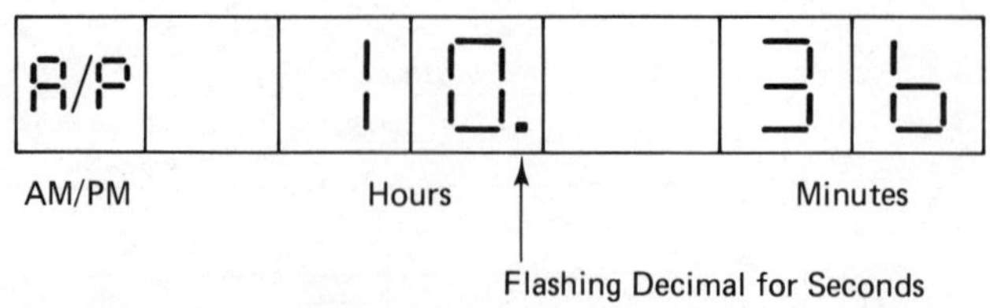

2.19. *Moving display*. Video and news industries use moving characters to display information, which can be easily done with a microcomputer system such as the SDK-85. Using monitor routines, develop an operating system that will continuously rotate the message "HELPED" as shown, with a 2-second display time.

CHAPTER THREE

8085-Based Microcomputer Applications

In this chapter we will present some practical applications using an 8085-based microcomputer such as the SDK-85. With minor modifications, these concepts are applicable for any other 8085-based system. Understanding the 8085 microprocessor and applications using the microcomputer as a logic element will greatly assist us to comprehend other derivative microprocessors and microcomputer devices such as the 8051 and 8048. This will provide enhanced system design skills for a practicing engineer.

Any microcomputer system is an operating system by itself. As such, some programs have been already developed by the manufacturer and stored in the ROM hardware (8355 for the SDK-85 microcomputer). The user's manual for SDK-85 (see Chapter Six, Table 6.1) shows some of these available program routines. In the next few examples, we will use these "monitor" routines and acquaint ourselves with the system. Using monitor routines saves the user substantial software and hardware effort.

3.1. USING MONITOR ROUTINES

One of the primary requirements of any microcomputer system is to have a convenient way of entering the data and displaying the processed data. Monitor routines called RDKBD (read keyboard) at 02E7 and UPDDT (update data display) at 036E can be used to accomplish data entry and display operations very easily as shown in the following discussions and examples.

Data Entry and Update

Most microcomputers use the fundamental operation of addition to accomplish other tasks such as multiplication, division, counting, and so on normally encountered in the processing of data. We will study the addition of digital data using the monitor routines mentioned above with the help of an example problem.

Example 3.1 8085 Software

Develop the operating software to obtain two numbers *X* and *Y* from the keyboard in hexadecimal form and display the result in the SDK-85 display (courtesy Intel SDK-85 manual).

Solution

A hexadecimal number *X* is read from the keyboard and stored in one of the internal registers of the 8085 (B register). A second number *Y* is then read from the keyboard and is added to the stored *X* number. The result is displayed in the data field of SDK-85. Figure 3.1 shows the SDK-85 memory map, and Figure 3.2 shows the flow chart. The actual listings are given in Table 3.1. Please recall from our discussion in Chapter Two that for a minimal SDK-85 system, the program was to be entered in machine code. The label is included to read and understand the programs better. If the system has an assembler (which converts the mnemonic source code into the object machine code), the program can be entered in mnemonic code.

The program listings start at $(2000)_{Hex}$, which is the first RAM location available for the user. This is shown in Figure 3.1. (The foldback memory area is used to increase the existing memory by replacing the on-board memory device with a pin-compatible memory device of twice or more memory density).

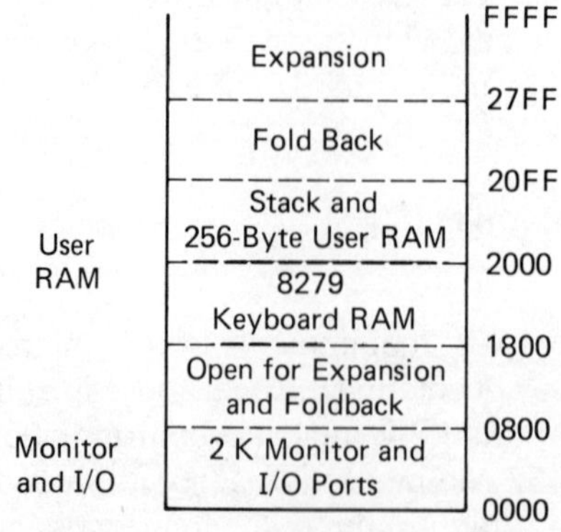

Fig 3.1. The SDK-85 minimum system memory map.

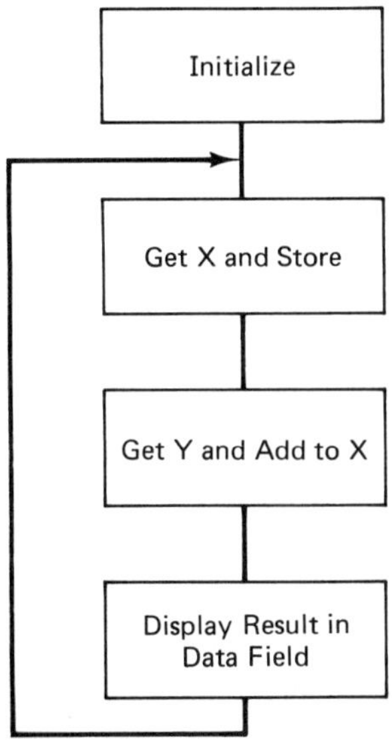

Fig 3.2. Flowchart for the addition problem of Example 3.1.

Between 2000 and 2005, the stack is initialized at 20C2, and all the interrupt masks are cleared to enable the occurrence of the interrupts. This has become necessary since the keyboard data entry routine (RDKBD) uses a 5.5 interrupt to recognize a key closure.

Between 2009 and 2012, *X* and *Y* data are obtained from the keyboard, by repeatedly calling the RDKBD subroutine at 02E7, and added together. With the result in the accumulator, the instruction at 2012 calls the UPDDT subroutine at 036E to output the result to the data display. The program is looped back by the jump instruction at 2015 to start the next addition. NOPs are included for linking any additional instructions later.

The above problem is very simple and considers *X* and *Y* to be binary numbers, with no carry. However, replacing the NOP at 2011 with DAA (decimal adjust accumulator, op code 27_{Hex}) and changing the ADD instruction at 2010 to ADC (add with carry, op code 88) will result in BCD addition of *X* and *Y* with carry.

Interrupt Handling and Timing Generation

All the physical systems operate in real time and in many instances the digital circuits generate timing information to accomplish various tasks as functions of time. In microcomputer systems, the timing information can be very

Table 3.1. The Software Listing for Addition for Example 3.1.

Location	Label	Mnemonic	Op Code	Comment
2000	Initialize	LXI SP	31	Stack pointer is loaded with $(20C2)_{Hex}$ to refer to the starting stack address.
01		C2(L)		
02		20(H)		
03		MVI A	3E	0 0 0 0 1 0 0 0 = 08 08 written into accumulator and SIM instruction performed to enable interrupts. Linkage and delay.
04		08		
05		SIM	30	
06		NOP	00	
07		NOP	00	
08		NOP	00	
09	RDKBD (X)	CALL	CD	Subroutine at 02E7 is called to read keyboard and obtain X in the accumulator.
0A		E7		
0B		02		
0C		MOV B, A	47	X in accumulator is stored at B register.
0D	RDKBD (Y)	CALL	CD	Same subroutine called to obtain Y from keyboard.
0E		E7		
0F		02		
2010		ADD B	80	X in B added to Y in A and result in A.
11		NOP	00	
12	UPDDT	CALL	CD	Subroutine at 036E is called to display the result in A in the data display field. Jump back to 0209 to start next addition.
13		6E		
14		03		
15		JMP	C3	
16		09		
17		20		

easily generated and changed under software control without having to alter any hardware.

In most microcomputer systems, the interrupts are convenient hardware signals connected to the micro to obtain its attention and divert the program. We will couple these two important concepts of timing and interrupts to generate a real-time seconds stop watch, as shown in the following example.

Example 3.2 Interrupt-Driven Stop Watch

As shown in Figure 3.3(a), the vector interrupt button of the SDK-85 generates a 7.5 interrupt, and any other key except a reset key generates a 5.5 interrupt.

Using monitor routines, develop a stop watch that can count from 0 to 99 seconds and display in the data field of the SDK-85. Pressing the vector interrupt key should stop the stop watch, and pressing any other key should restart the stop watch.

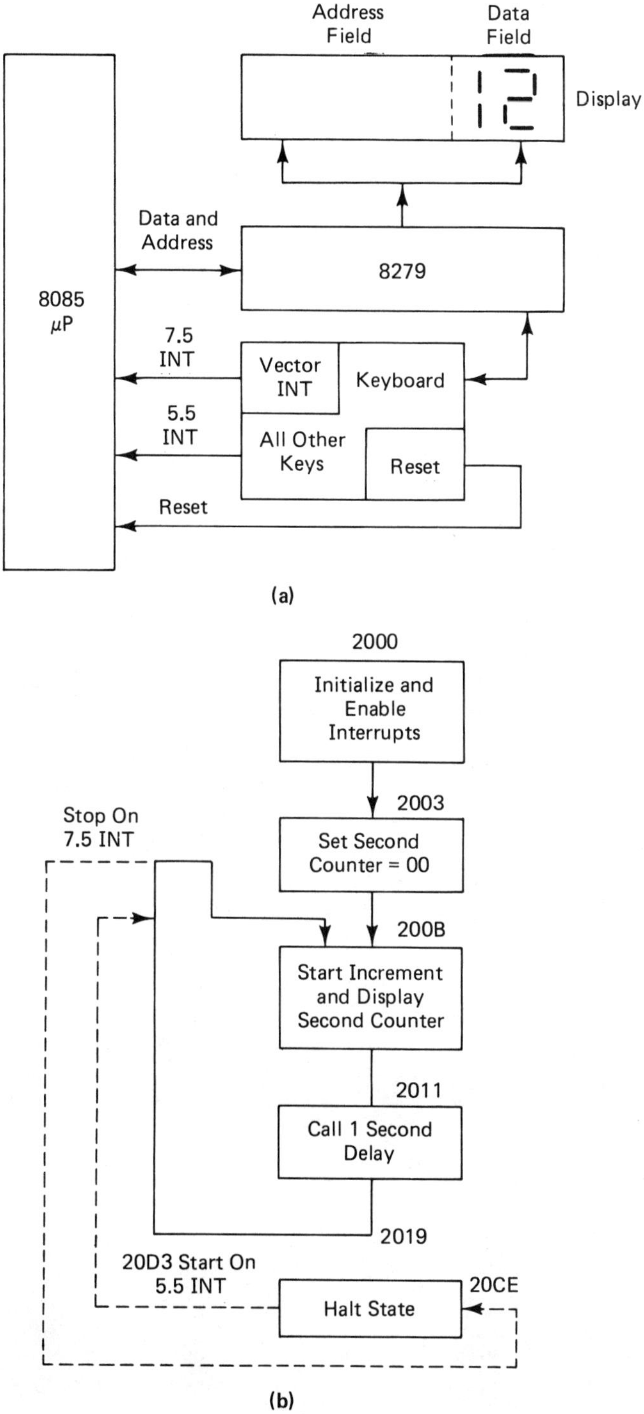

Fig 3.3. (a) Real time stop clock using the SDK-85 system and interrupt structure; (b) flow chart for the timer problem of Example 3.2.

Solution:

(a) *Concept.* One of the registers (B) is used as a *seconds counter,* which is incremented every second. A register pair such as H and L is used as a *delay counter* to generate a one second delay. An UPDDT routine is used to display the seconds counter. Figure 3.3(b) shows the flow chart, and Table 3.2 shows the actual listings.

(b) *Main Program.* Between 2000 and 200A, initialization is done with the stack set at 2080, and the seconds counter B with initial count of 00. The interrupt masks are cleared to enable the interrupts. The EI (enable interrupts) at 200B further enable the software recognition of unmasked interrupts. This interrupt enabling is necessary since our stop clock will have

Table 3.2. Actual Software Listing for Real Time Stop Clock (Example 3.2).

REAL TIME STOP CLOCK (MAIN PROGRAM)

Location	*Label*	*Mnemonic*	*Op Code*	*Comments*
2000	Initialize	LXI SP	31	Stack pointer initiated to $(2080)_{Hex}$ for stacking.
01		80		
02		20		
03	Sec:CTR	MVI B	06	Register B is the seconds counter and is initiated to 00.
04		00		
05		NOP	00	Linkage Software.
06		NOP	00	
07		NOP	00	
08		MVI A	3E	Clear interrupt masks to enable interrupts.
09		08		
0A		SIM	30	
0B	Start Count	EI	FB	Software enable of interrupts.
0C		MOV A, B	78	Seconds count in B is moved to A register, incremented, and decimal adjusted and put back in B.
0D		INR A	3C	
0E		DAA	27	
0F		MOV B, A	47	
10		PUSH B	C5	
11	UPDDT	CALL	CD	B is saved on stack, and display data routine is called to display updated seconds count in data field.
12		6E		
13		03		
14	Sec: Delay	CALL	CD	Seconds delay subroutine called to provide 1 S delay.
15		50		
16		20		
17		POP B	C1	B is restored from stack, and program jumps back to 200B to start count again.
18		JMP	C3	
19		0B		
1A		20		

REAL TIME STOP CLOCK (DELAY ROUTINE)

Location	*Label*	*Mnemonic*	*Op Code*	*Clock Cycles*	*Comments*
2050	Delay No	LDA	3A	13	Delay number N is loaded into accumulator from location 20A0. Delay counter HL pair is loaded with 00.
51		A0			
52		20			
53	Delay CTR	LXI H	21	10	
54		00			
55		00			PUSH and POP used to get timing cycles without any other effects.
56	Loop	PUSH H	E5	12	
57		POP H	E1	10	
58		PUSH H	E5	12	
	(T_{Loop})				
59		POP H	E1	10	
5A		INX H	23	6	Delay counter HL is incremented and compared to delay number N in accumulator. Program loops until required delay achieved.
5B		CMP H	BC	4	
5C		JNZ	C2	7/10	
5D		56_L			
5E		20_H			
5F		RET	C9	10	After required delay, return to main program.

INTERRUPT SERVICE ROUTINE

On pressing the vector/interrupt key, a 7.5 interrupt occurs, and the program goes to vectored interrupt location 20CE to service interrupt. On pressing any other key, a 5.5 interrupt is generated, which advances the program from halt to return, to return to counting again.

Location	Label	Mnemonic	Op Code	Comments
20CE	INT:Service (7.5)	EI	FB	Enable further interrupts.
20CF		HLT	76	
20D0		NOP	00	Program halts and advances to return (RET) on 5.5 interrupt, to start counting again.
20D1		RET	C9	

PARAMETERS

Location	Label	Value	Comments
20A0	Delay No N	$(B7)_{Hex}$	$(B7)_{Hex} = (183)_{Dec}$ to provide 1 s delay number.

to respond to the 7.5 and 5.5 interrupts from the keyboard to stop and restart the counting operation.

Between 200C to 2017, the actual incrementing of seconds counter B is taking place, with a 1-second delay. We need to transfer B to A for incrementing and decimal adjusting. The decimal adjusting can only be done on the contents of the accumulator (A register) to provide a decimal count rather than a binary count. The contents of the B register (seconds counter) are preserved on stack before going to the display and delay routines (to avoid losing them in case the B register is used in these subroutines). After the subroutines, the B register is restored, and the program jumps to 200B to start the next count.

(c) *Delay Program.* The principle centers on looping the microprocessor through a delay loop the required number of times to obtain any desired delay. Between 2056 and 205E the program takes

T_{Loop}: 64 clock cycles

The loop occurs each time the L register is incremented. For each overflow of the L register after counting (FF + 1) = 256 times, H register gets incremented once. The program is terminated with the required delay accomplished if H register is incremented N times (N is the delay number stored at 20A0). The total delay time T_{Delay} between 2050 and 205F is, therefore (considering T_{Loop} = 64):

$$T_{Delay} = 13 + 10 + (N * 256 * T_{Loop}) + 10 = 16{,}384N + 33 \text{ clock cycles}$$

With a system clock frequency of 3 MHz, each clock cycle corresponds to ⅓μs, and N = $(183)_{Decimal}$ = $(B7)_{Hex}$ to provide a 1 s delay, which is the delay number loaded into location 20A0.

(d) *Interrupt Service Routine.* In the SDK-85 system, the occurrence of a 7.5 interrupt due to pressing the vector interrupt key will take the program to location 20CE, after storing all CPU registers on stack. The interrupt service routine at 20CE enables further interrupting of the microprocessor by the EI instruction. The system will settle in halt state until 5.5 interrupt (because of pressing any other key (except reset)) advances it beyond the halt state, which will return the microcomputer to the main program. The microprocessor will restore all registers from stack and resume the main program, which results in recounting.

The important points in the above example are to initialize the stack, to generate required delays, and to respond and handle interrupts. The stack should be carefully initiated at the convenient location such that when it grows in size (toward a lesser address number), it will not be overlapping with program or data memory. Location 2080 accomplishes that. The above clock concept can be easily extended to obtain a real time clock, industrial timer, etc., and several of these problems are listed at the end of the chapter.

3.2. I/O STRUCTURE AND INTERFACE

Any microprocessor will have to communicate with outside systems to implement any operations. The outside systems may be peripherals such as printers, cassette and video terminals, or any control systems that provide signals to the microprocessor and derive signals from the microprocessor to accomplish a digital control function. As mentioned in Chapter 2, the 8085 microprocessor device communicates with the outside I/O (input and output) devices and systems through a device called programmable peripheral interface (PPI), identified as an 8155. We will present the basic features of 8155 PPI and discuss I/O applications in the next few sections.

I/O Port Configurations, 8155 PPI

As shown in Figure 3.4, the 8155 is a 40-pin integrated circuit device with 3 I/O ports, A, B, and C, a 14-bit timer and a 256 × 8 RAM section.

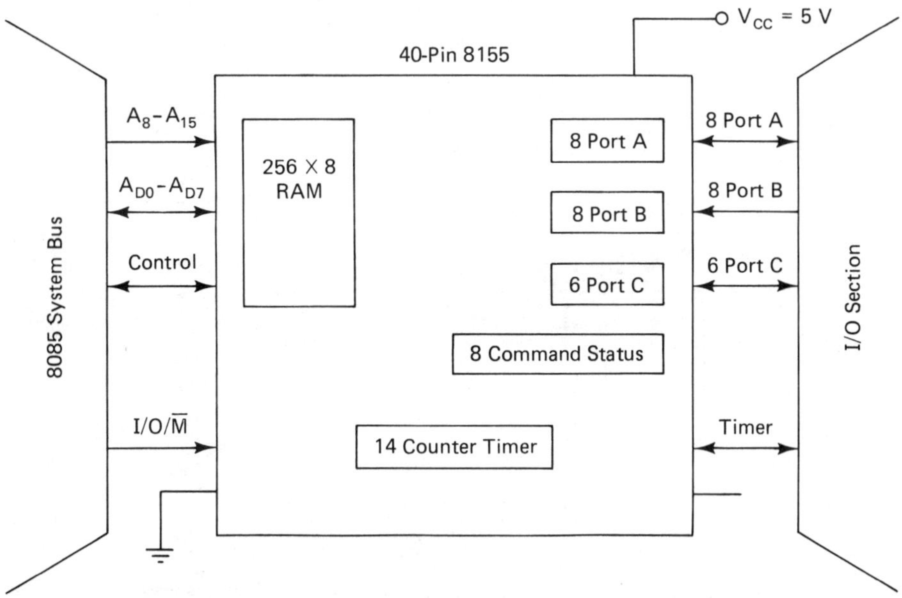

Fig 3.4. The 8155 PPI architecture and interface.

Ports A and B are 8 bits wide and can be programmed to act as input or output ports. Port C is six bits wide and can be selected to operate in a given mode under program control. The control word written into the command status register (C/S register) determines the actual mode of operation of 8155 and how ports A, B, and C should be configured as inputs or outputs. The 8085-based systems use the I/O mapped I/O concept for dealing with input and output.

Modes of Operation

Before using the 8155, it should be properly initialized by writing the appropriate control word in the C/S register, as shown in Figure 3.5. For example if the C/S register is loaded with the control word 0 0 0 0 1 1 0 0 = $(0C)_{Hex}$, it corresponds to

Port A	Input
Port B	Input
Port C	Output
Timer and Interrupt	Not used

Depending on the application, the modes of operation can be conveniently changed by changing the control word.

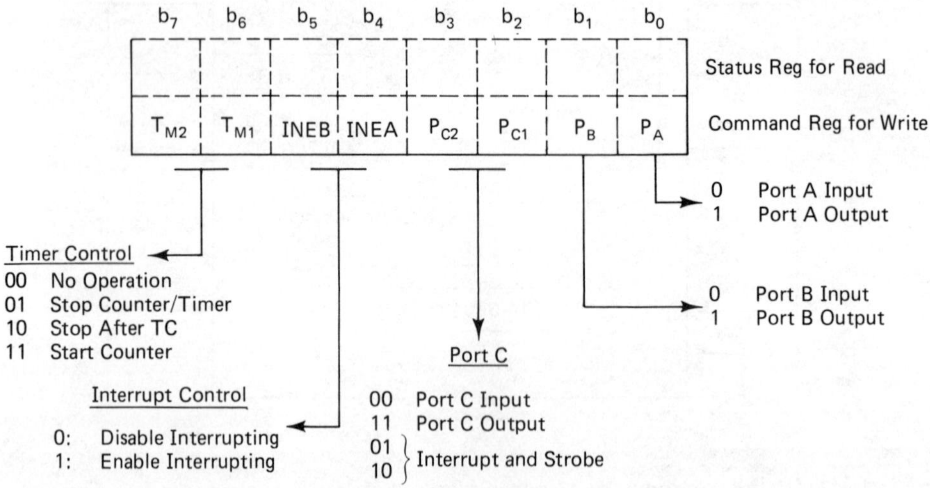

Fig 3.5. The 8155 C/S register formatting.

A Simple Interface: Data Comparison

Data comparison between two or more sources is a very widely used operation in digital control systems, especially in adjusting the response of the system. Let us suppose that X and Y digital words are coming from sensors attached to conveyor belts as shown in Figure 3.6, in an industrial process such as an auto assembly plant. Let us also suppose that the larger the value of the digital word, the faster the motion of the conveyor belt. Obviously an indication is to be provided to the process operator as to the relative speed of these belts, so that the assembly process can be conveniently controlled by the operator. This task can be very easily accomplished with the help of the SDK-85 and associated I/O ports A, B, and C. For example, ports A and B can be used as input ports to read TTL conditioned data from sensors representing X and Y digital words. Port C can be used as an output generating Z output word to drive LEDs and provide an indication to the operator.

Care should be taken to electronically buffer these I/O ports of the 8155, so as not to exceed the drive capabilities. Most of the microprocessor family of devices, such as the 8155, are of NMOS technology and can only drive a unit TTL load, per I/O interface.

An example problem follows that demonstrates the concepts of port initialization, I/O interface, and data comparison.

Example 3.3 I/O Ports and Data Comparison

The X and Y digital data from respective conveyor belts are connected to ports A and B as shown in Figure 3.6. The microprocessor should read this data and compare and turn on the LEDs as shown, driven by port C configured as output.

D_0 on if $X = Y$
D_1 on if $X < Y$
D_2 on if $X > Y$

Design and develop the necessary hardware and software to accomplish the above task.

Solution

To accomplish this data comparison and display, an interface should be developed between the SDK-85 system I/O ports and data-conditioning circuitry and the LED indicators. This is detailed in Figure 3.7. All the 8155 I/O ports are available to the outside through the J4 application connector of the SDK-85.

(a) *Hardware.* The incoming X and Y signals are buffered through the octal tristate buffers 74LS241. These devices have a high noise immunity due

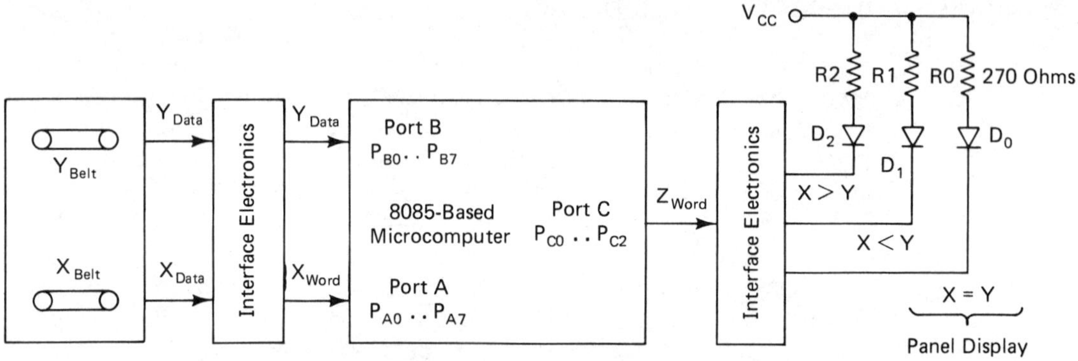

Fig 3.6. Data comparison: production belt control (Example 3.3).

to Schmitt trigger inputs and can be bussed together because of their tristate outputs. These features will help the microcomputer hardware interface very conveniently. 74LS06 open collector high current drivers are used to illuminate the LEDs.

(b) *Software Overview*. Ports A and B are configured as inputs, and port C as output. A logic 1 at port C output drives the corresponding LED on. Thus (01) at port C turns on D0, (02) turns on D1, and (04) turns on D2. *X* and *Y* words are read sequentially and compared, and the corresponding LED is turned on. The process is made repetitive, with some delay, so that the operator can actually visualize the LED read out.

Figure 3.8 shows the flowchart, and Figure 3.9 shows the I/O port map of the SDK-85 system. Table 3.3 shows the actual program listings. Between 2000 and 2005 the stack is initialized and interrupts enabled. Between 2006 and 2009, the I/O ports of the 8155 are initialized such that A and B ports are inputs, and port C is output.

The call instruction at 200A uses the same delay routine used earlier in Example 3.2 to provide a 1 s delay.

Between 200D and 2018, *Y* and *X* data are read from ports B and A and compared to each other, and the program is made to jump to appropriate routines to light up the proper LEDs. After an I/O read operation, the port contents will be in the accumulator and should be preserved before making another I/O read. The MOV B, A instruction at 200F accomplishes this task by storing *Y* data in register B before reading *X* data. Between 2019 and 202D, the appropriate LED code is sent to port C, and the program is made to jump back to 200A to provide 1 s display time and start over again.

The above program is very simple but very important and useful in control applications. In addition to lighting up LEDs, other outputs from port C can

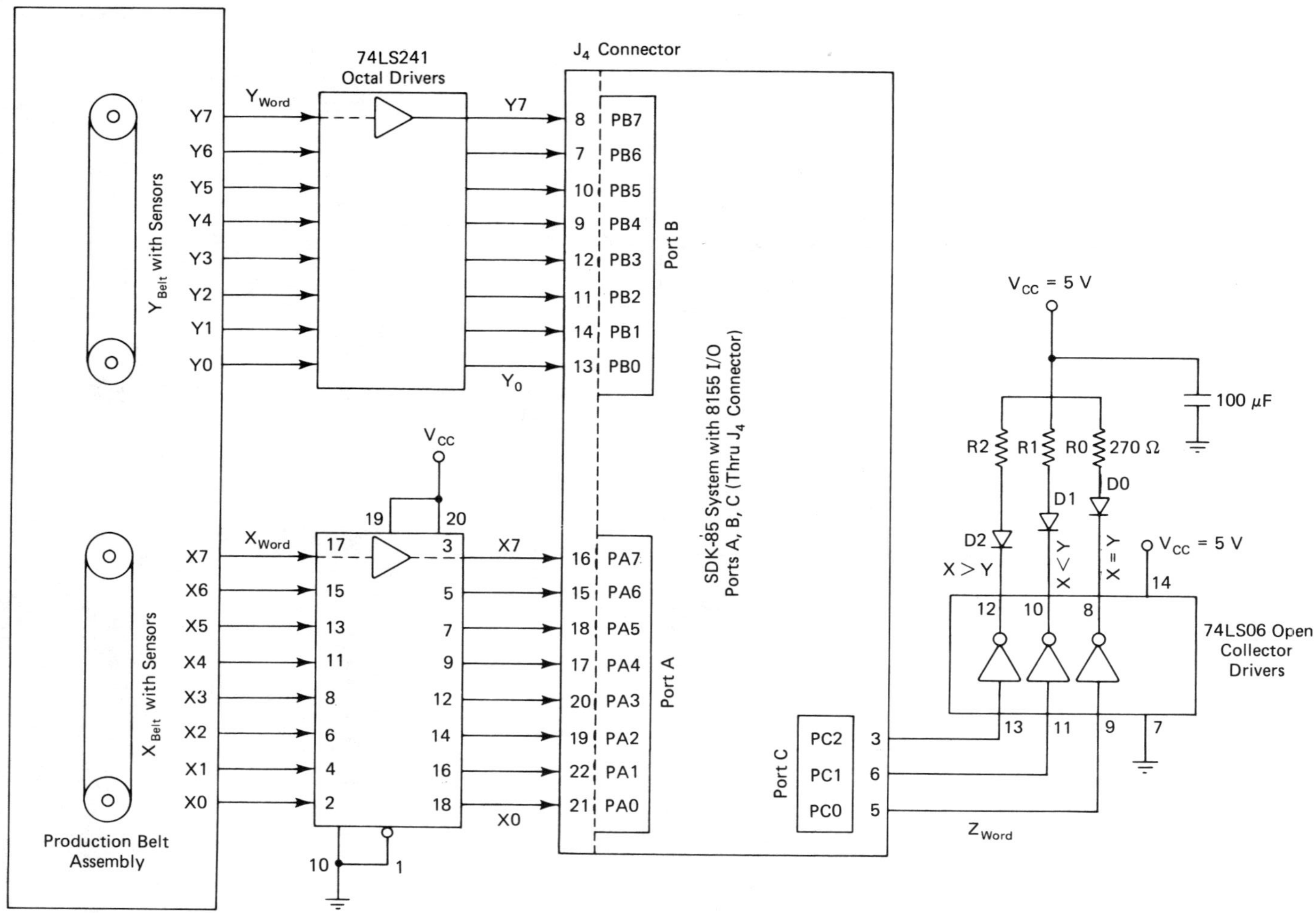

Fig 3.7. The SDK-85 microsystem I/O interface: data comparison (Example 3.3).

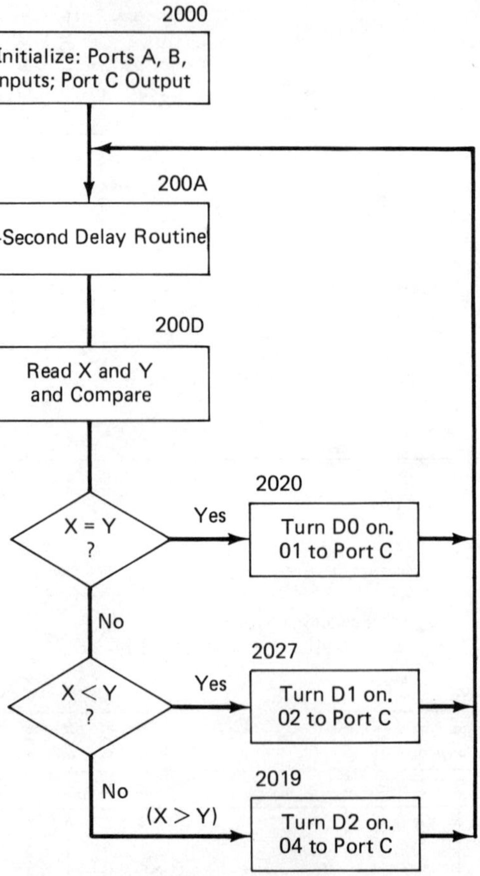

Fig 3.8. Flow chart for data comparison (Example 3.3).

LOCATION	FUNCTION		
00	Monitor ROM	Port A	
01	" "	Port B	8355 ROM
02	" "	DDRA	(Monitor)
03		DDRB	
20	User RAM	C/S Reg	
21	" "	Port A	8155 USER
22	" "	Port B	RAM
23	" "	Port C	

Fig 3.9. I/O port map of the SDK-85.

Table 3.3. Software Listings for Data Comparison (Example 3.3).

Location	*Label*	*Mnemonic*	*Op Code*	*Comment*
2000	Initialize	LXI, SP	31	Stack pointer is initialized at 20C2.
01		C2		
02		20		
03		MVI A	3E	Interrupt masks are cleared to enable interrupts.
04		08		
05		SIM	30	
06		MVI A	3E	C/S Register at (20) is loaded with 0 0 0 0 1 1 0 0 = $(0C)_{Hex}$ to make ports A and B inputs and port C output.
07		0C		
08		OUT	D3	
09		20		
0A	Delay	CALL	CD	To delay routine at 2050 for 1 second (see Example 3.2 for details).
0B		50		
0C		20		
0D	Read P_B	IN	DB	Read port B, *Y* data, and store in register B.
0E		22		
0F		MOV B, A	47	
10	Read P_A	1N	DB	Read port A, *X* data, and compare with Y data from register B ($X - Y$ accomplished).
11		21		
12		CMP B	B8	
13	$X = Y$	JZ	CA	If $X = Y$, jump to 2020 to turn on LED D0.
14		20		
15		20		
16	$X < Y$	JM	FA	If $X < Y$ jump to 2027 to turn on D1.
17		27		
18		20		
2019	Large ($X > Y$)	MVI A	3E	$X > Y$ proven. Turn on D2 LED, by outputting $(04)_{Hex}$ to port C at location (23) and jump back to 200A to start again.
1A		04		
1B		OUT	D3	
1C		23		
1D		JMP	C3	
1E		0A		
1F		20		
2020	Equal ($X = Y$)	MVI A	3E	$X = Y$ proven. Turn on D0 LED by outputting $(01)_{Hex}$ to port C and starting again.
21		01		
22		OUT	D3	
23		23		
24		JMP	C3	
25		0A		
26		20		
27	Less ($X < Y$)	MVI A	3E	$X < Y$ proven. Turn on LED D1 by outputting $(02)_{Hex}$ to port C and starting again.
28		02		
29		OUT	D3	
2A		23		
2B		JMP	C3	
2C		0A		
2D		20		

be used to accomplish different tasks such as speeding up the *X* or *Y* belts or slowing them down, stopping the process, and so on. Several problems at the end of the chapter throw light on these types of applications.

3.3. DATA HANDLING SYSTEMS

Any digital system performance depends on the flexibility with which the digital data can be handled. In addition to the arithmetic operations, data shifting, data generation, and data storage are other fundamental operations generally encountered in most of the digital systems. With its powerful instruction set and I/O features, the 8085 microprocessor lends itself as a basic digital unit in such data handling systems.

Coded Data Generation and Serialization

In control system applications, coded digital data is often generated to accomplish a given task. Also, slow peripherals and I/O devices can be very efficiently and economically controlled by a fast microcomputer with serialized data format. The 8085 is fortunately furnished with serial input (SID) and serial output (SOD) connections directly, and data serialization from parallel data and vice versa can be very easily accomplished. In addition, to improve the reliability of transmission, the digital data can be frequency coded, as shown in Figures 3.10 and 3.11. The longer tone burst in a given time interval signifies logic 1, and a shorter tone burst signifies logic 0. This type of coding has the distinct advantage of giving a relative comparison between longer and shorter tone bursts, reconstructing the original data string of 1s and 0s, and being relatively immune to noise and media property changes.

In the transmit mode, the microprocessor will generate the coded waveform at the SOD output in accordance with the digital data. In the receive mode, the micro will accept the coded waveform from I/O at its SID input and internally reconstruct the digital data. The rate at which the actual digital data is transmitted or received is referred by baud rate, which signifies the bits per second. For example, if the microprocessor is controlling a printer at 110 baud,

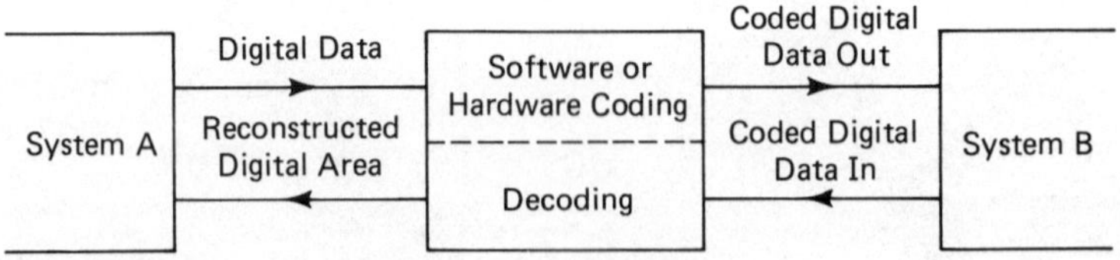

Fig 3.10. Concepts of digital data coding and decoding.

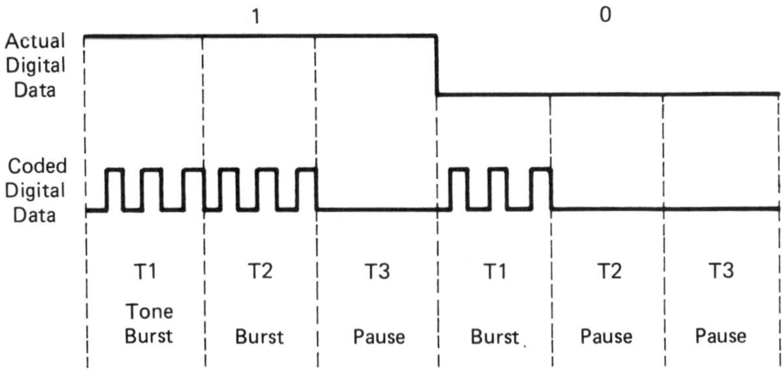

Fig 3.11. Coded digital data using burst and pause structure.

it means that the actual digital data stream is flowing at 110 bits per second, with each bit time $T_{Bit} = 1/110 = 9.09$ ms. Figure 3.12 shows the concept (courtesy INTEL Corporation's MCS 8085 User's Manual).

For coding purposes, each bit time is divided into three equal segments T1, T2, and T3. For logic 1 transmission, tone burst (square-wave-type waveform) is sent out on the SOD terminal during T1 and T2 intervals, and a pause (no waveform) is sent out during T3. For a logic 0 transmission, tone burst is sent out during T1 and pause during T2 and T3. Obviously logic 1 contains a

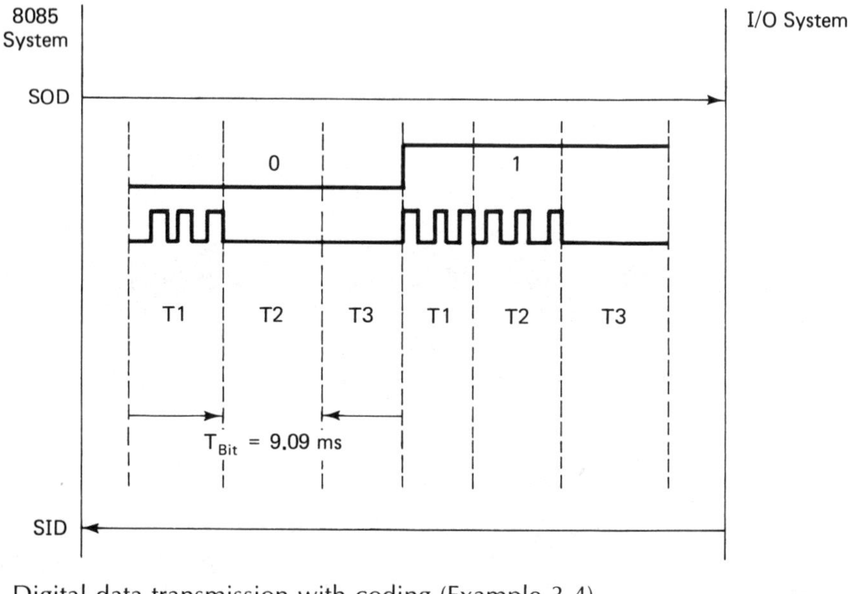

Fig 3.12. Digital data transmission with coding (Example 3.4).

longer tone burst than logic 0 and can be easily distinguished. Table 3.4 shows this relation.

Generation of tone burst is equally simple. We can alternate a 0 level and 1 level on the SOD terminal with a delay corresponding to the half period of the tone burst. This we can do a required number of times.

Example 3.4 Coded Data Generation

Using the SDK-85 microcomputer, develop the necessary algorithms to generate a coded serial waveform to represent 110-baud digital data transmission. There should be three cycles of tone frequency per unit burst time. Assume the digital word to be serialized is present in the C register. Refer to Figure 3.13 for details of the waveform.

Solution

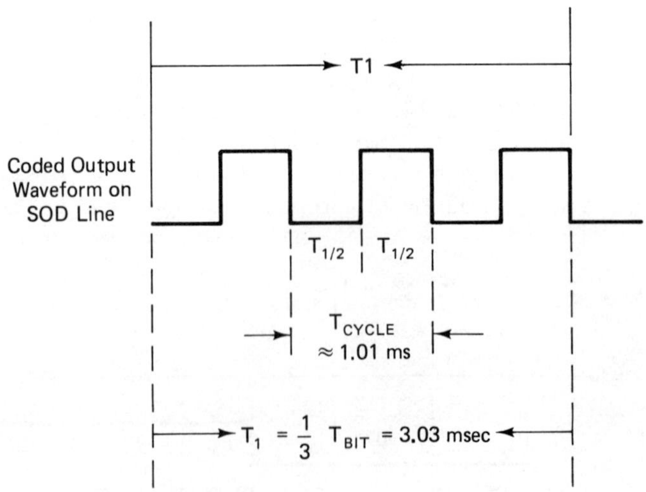

With 110 baud rate, the bit time $T_{Bit} = 1/110 = 9.09$ ms. Thus each segment $T1 = T2 = T3 = \frac{1}{3} T_{Bit} = 3.03$ ms. This would result in a tone waveform of cycle time approximately 1.01 ms, or of frequency KHz.

The generation of tone frequency reduces to alternatively outputting a high

Table 3.4. Coded Digital Data Transmission Format.

Wave Form	*T1*	*T2*	*T3*
Logic 0	Tone Burst	Pause	Pause
Logic 1	Tone Burst	Tone Burst	Pause

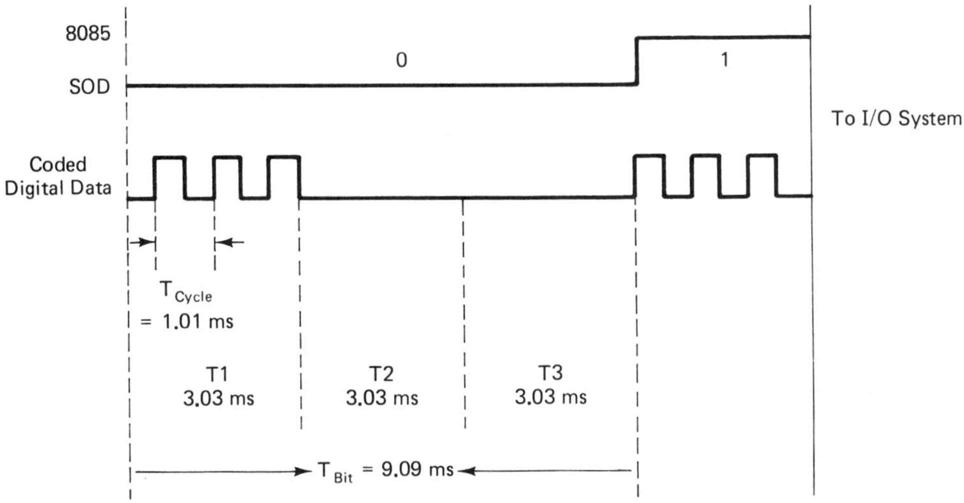

Fig 3.13. Waveform timing details (Example 3.4).

and low on SOD line with a delay of 500 μs corresponding to half-cycle time $T_{1/2}$.

To transmit a digital logic 1, a tone burst is output twice in succession during T1 and T2 and a pause during T3. To transmit a digital logic 0, tone burst is output once during T1 and pause is output during T2 and T3.

Figure 3.14 shows the flow chart, and Table 3.5 shows the actual program listing.

Between 2000 and 2007 the stack is initialized at 20C0 and register B is configured as a shift counter and is loaded with 9. This will enable us to output 8 digital data bits and a buffer 0 bit (total 9) in the coded form on the SOD line. Between 2008 and 200C, the accumulator is conditioned with $(C0)_{Hex}$, and tone burst is output on SOD during T1. Between 200D and 2016, the right-most digital data bit contained in register C is shifted into the A6 position of the accumulator. This has the effect of outputting a tone burst if A6 = 1, or a pause if A6 = 0, during T2 interval.

Between 2017 and 201A, the accumulator is cleared (thus A6 = 0), and a pause is output during T3. The last part of the program checks to see if all 9 bits of data are serialized and then returns control to the monitor of the SDK-85 via the RST 1 instruction.

Of particular interest is the burst/pause subroutine at 2020. For a three-cycle tone burst there are 6 half cycles, and this information is loaded into the D register to keep track of the number of times a 1 or 0 level is output on SOD, when SIM is executed at 2022.

Between 2023 and 2028, ½ ms delay is generated (delay loop takes 14 clock cycles at ⅓ μsec each, and the loop is run $(6B)_{Hex} = (107)_{Decimal}$ to yield 14

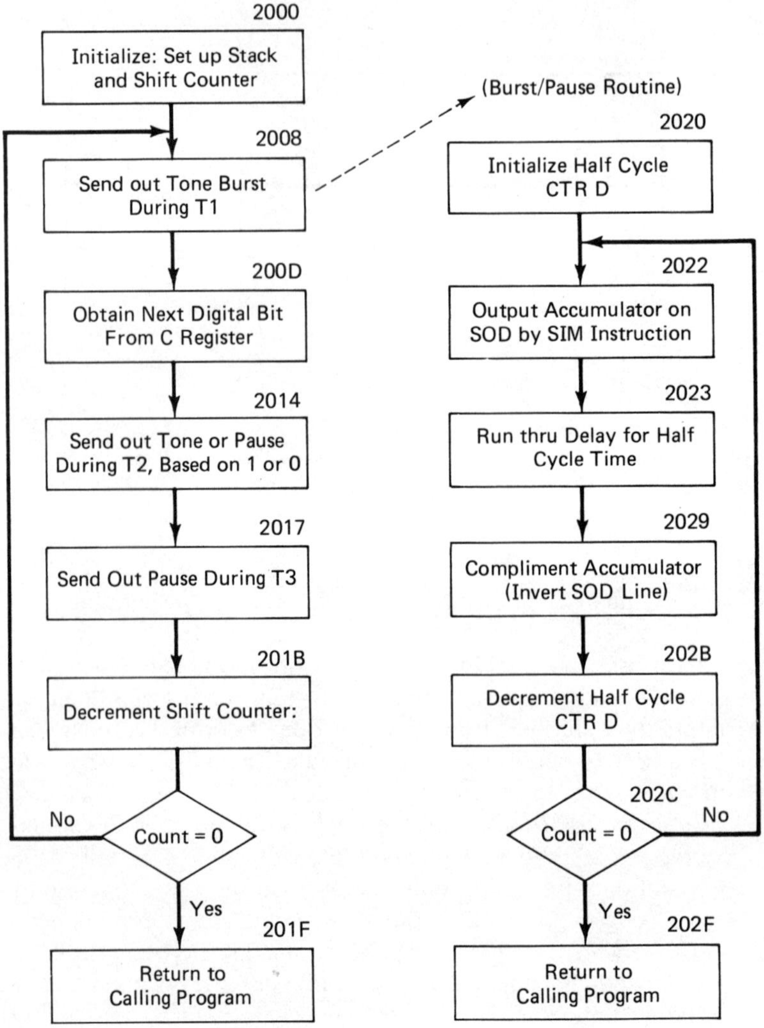

Fig 3.14. Flow chart for coded data transmission.

× ⅓ × 107 = 500 μsec to correspond to the half-cycle time of tone burst). At 2029, A7 of the accumulator is complemented, and the program is looped back to 2022 the required number of times. This has the effect of generating a near square-wave-type waveform on SOD. In our particular case, if A6 = 1 of the accumulator, the subroutine would provide 3 cycles of 1 KHz tone frequency each time it is called by the main program. Similarly if A6 = 0, the program would inhibit variations of the SOD line and hold it at a level, thus providing a pause each time it is called.

Table 3.5. Program Listings for Coded Data Generation.

Location	*Label*	*Mnemonic*	*Op Code*	*Comment*
2000	Initialize	NOP	00	Linkage software.
01		NOP	00	
02		NOP	00	Initialize stack at 20C0. Initialize B register as shift counter, with count of 9 to output 8 active bits serially and an extra 0 bit.
03		LXI SP	31	
04		C0		
05		20		
06	Code Out	MVI B	06	
07		09		
08	Start	MVI A	3E	A_7 A_6 A_5 A_4 A_3 A_2 A_1 A_0 1 1 0 0 0 0 0 0 = C0 A_6 = 1 outputs A_7 to SOD line when "SIM" is executed in the burst routine. Tone waveform is output during T1.
09		C0		
0A	Burst/Pause (T_1)	CALL	CD	
0B		20		
0C		20		
0D	Next Bit	MOV A, C	79	Data in C register is shifted one bit right, with the right-most bit shifted into carry position.
0E		RAR	1F	
0F		MOV C, A	4F	
2010		MVI A	3E	
11		01		Digital data bit in carry is shifted to A6, and 1 is put in A7. If A6 = 1, tone waveform will be output during T2. If A6 = 0, pause is output during T2.
12		RAR	1F	
13		RAR	1F	
14	Burst/Pause (T2)	CALL	CD	
15		20		
16		20		
17		XRA A	AF	

Table 3.5. *(Continued)*

Location	*Label*	*Mnemonic*	*Op Code*		*Comment*
18	Burst/Pause (T3)	CALL	CD		Accumulator cleared to 00, and a pause is output during T3.
19		20			
1A		20			
201B		DCR B	05		Shift counter is decremented. If all 8 bits and an additional 0 bit is output, program returns to monitor. Otherwise loops back to start at 2008 to shift and output next data bit.
1C		JNZ	C2		
1D	To Start	08			
1E		20			
1F		RST 1	CF		
			BURST/PAUSE SUBROUTINE		
2020	Burst/Pause	MVI D	16		D register initialized to 6 to correspond to 6 half-cycles (3 cycles).
21		06			
22	Ouput	SIM	30		A7 output to SOD if A6 = 1 of accumulator.
23	Delay CTR	MVI E	1E	Machine Cycles	E register is used as a delay counter and is loaded with 6B to generate 0.5 ms half period, corresponding to 1 KHz tone waveform.
24		6B			
25		DCR E	1D	4	
26		JNZ	C2	7/10	
27	(Delay Loop)	25			
28		20			
29		XRI	EE		A7 is complemented and is output to SOD, if D is not zero. This amounts to putting a tone waveform on SOD if A6 = 1 or a pause if A6 = 0.
2A		80			
2B		DCR D	15		
2C		JNZ	C2		
2D		22			
2E		20			
2F		RET	C9		Return

Note: If this program is to be used as a subroutine, change RST 1 at 201F to RET.

This simple code generation has a wide range of applications, and almost any wave shapes can be generated with the aid of some external electronics. Several example problems are given at the end of the chapter and you are encouraged to solve them.

Decoding of Data: Data Validation

Decoding is the complement of coding. The original data is reconstructed after a successful decoding operation on the coded data. The decoding process can be accomplished easily with the microcomputer. We will consider a simple example of reconstructing a digital data word from a serially arriving coded digital waveform on an SID input terminal of the 8085 system, as shown in Figure 3.13. The problem we are considering now is an exact complement of the previous coded data generation example. In a given bit time, T_{Bit}, if the tone burst occurs for more time than the pause, the resulting digital bit is logic 1, and vice versa, as shown.

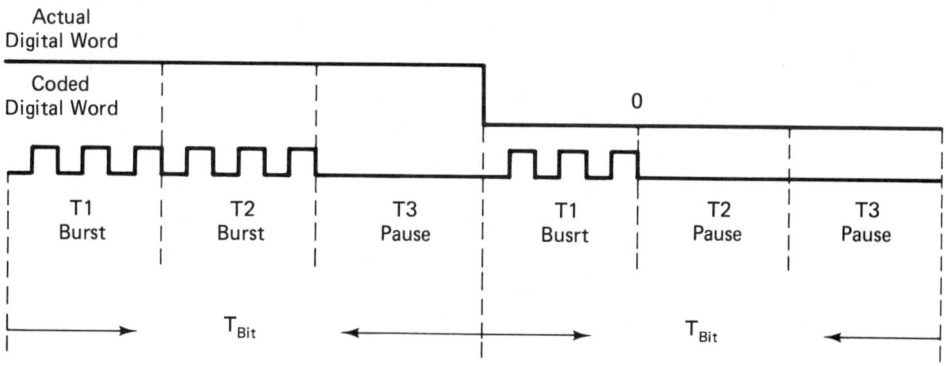

The reader is encouraged to generate his or her own software to accomplish the task. We will now present some practical applications of the coding and decoding of digital data, such as cassette recorder interface.

Data Storage: Cassette Recorder Interface

Most microcomputer systems have very limited operating memory and require a bulk storage such as floppy disk or cassette storage to store programs and data. When there is necessity for these programs, they can be conveniently loaded back into the operating memory of the microcomputer.

For an inexpensive microcomputer system, we propose to use inexpensive cassette storage and to develop the necessary software and hardware interface. A typical audio cassette can be used to store up to 100,000 bytes of

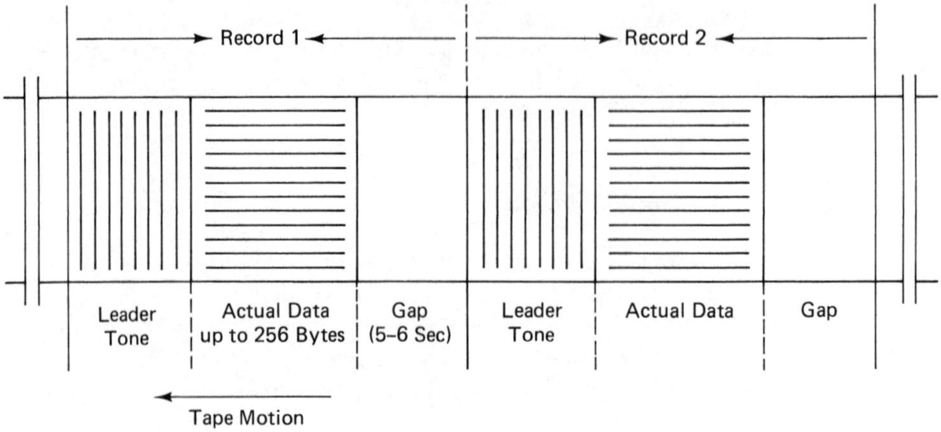

Fig 3.15. Recording format on a typical cassette tape.

memory, which is more than adequate for most applications. Although there are many ways of recording, the simplest and most efficient method is developed by INTEL Corporation,* using the coded data generation and recognition concepts of the previous section.

Figure 3.15 shows a typical recording format on a cassette tape. The recorded information is divided into blocks called "records." Each record may be up to one page (256 bytes) and is separated from the other by inter-record gaps. A complete set of information, usually called a file, may consist of several records. Each record begins with a continuous tone waveform called a leader, which indicates the beginning of a record during recording and playback operations. Also, during leader tone, the interface electronics gets conditioned.

Figure 3.16 shows the actual interface electronics required for cassette interface. The access to SOD and SID terminals is obtained through the T_X (transmit) and R_X (receive) connections of the J7 connector of SDK-85. Notice that the data gets inverted between SOD and T_X and R_X and SID. This does not cause any problems and can be ignored.

In recording mode, the digital data to be recorded on the cassette tape appears in the coded digital format (similar to the previous coded data generation example) at the SOD and T_X output of the SDK-85 microcomputer. The active bandpass filter around the A1 amplifier converts the square wave at T_X output into a near sinusoidal signal and drives the auxiliary input of the cassette recorder. For best recording results, the tape should be allowed to run in recording mode at least 10 seconds before and after the actual recording. The recording amplitude control can be adjusted to obtain proper recording with minimum distortion.

* Intel MCS 8085 Manual: Application Example 3 A1-38.

In the playback mode, the sinusoidal signal coming from the "earphone" output of the recorder is amplified by amplifiers A2 and A3 and is rectified by diodes D1 and D2. This rectified signal is RC filtered by C4 and R11 network to provide a virtual DC level V_Y. So long as the sinusoid is coming out of the recorder, V_Y is at a higher DC level than V_R at the input of the comparator amplifier A4, which ultimately presents a high level (logic 1) at the SID input of 8085. The software will examine the duration of high level and low level of the SID input and reconstruct the actual digital signal. We will now discuss details of the data recording and playback.

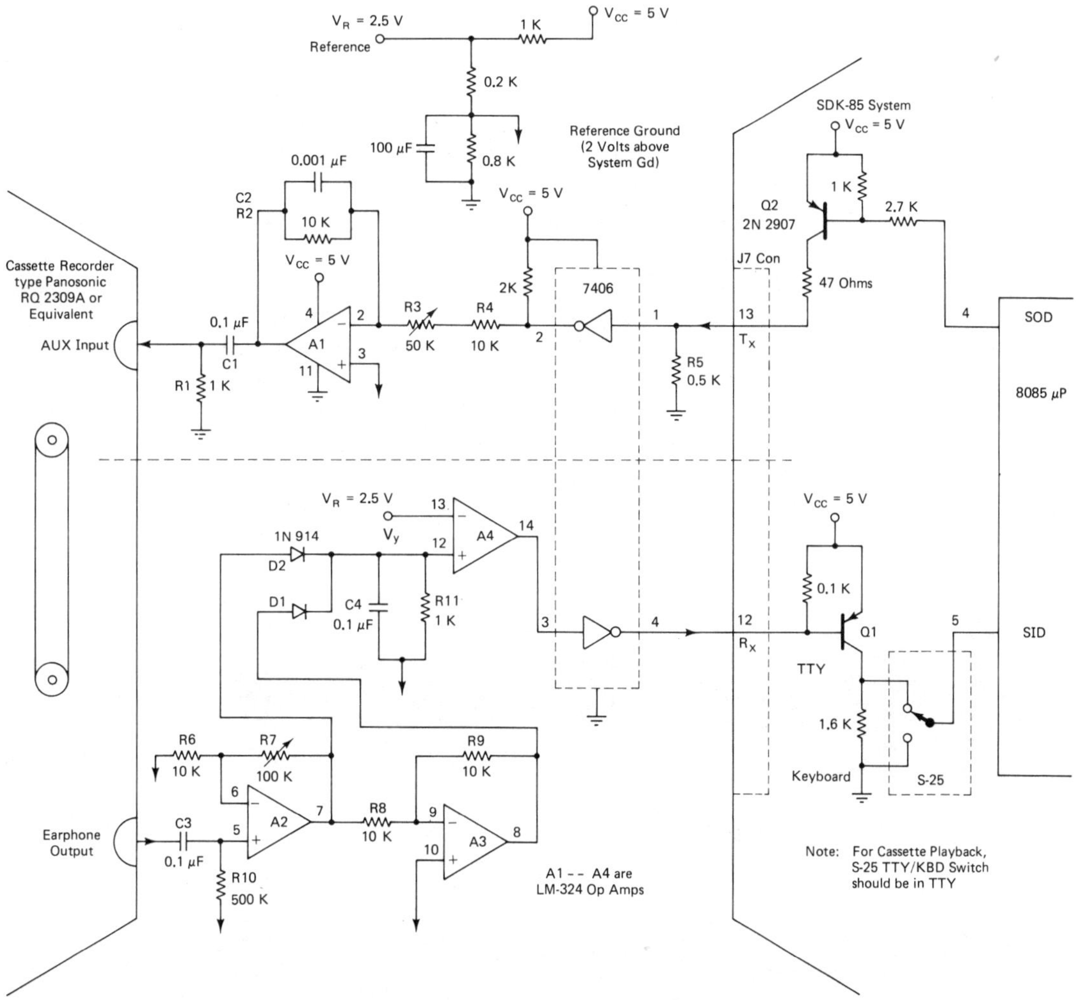

Fig 3.16. Cassette recorder interface.

Data Recording

In the recording, a block of memory is recorded sequentially, using the coded data generation technique discussed in the previous section. The HL register pair holds the address of the memory block to be recorded. By gradually incrementing HL pair and each time using the "output coded data" routine of Example 3.4, it is possible to record the required memory block. Also, register B is used to keep track of the number of bytes to be recorded. At the end of the required data recording, control can be returned to the monitor.

Figure 3.17 shows the memory formatting and Figure 3.18 shows the flow chart. Table 3.6 shows the program listings. For example, if the information starting at address $(1204)_{Hex}$ is to be recorded up to address of $(12A0)_{Hex}$ as shown in Figure 3.17, we add three bytes ahead, which actually contain the information in L, H, and B registers. This will make the recording program self-contained with the starting location for recording [$(1201)_{Hex}$ contained in H and L registers] and the number of bytes (A0 in B register). Before calling the recording program, using SDK-85 system commands (Chapter Two), H, L, and B should be loaded with proper data (H ← 12, L ← 01, and B ← A0 in this particular example).

Between 2030 and 203D, the contents of L, H, and B registers are stored at the top of the memory block to be recorded, and the stack is initialized at 20C0. Between 203E and 2048, 189 cycles of leader-tone waveform is sent out on the SOD terminal.

Between 2049 and 2053, the coded digital waveform is sent out on SOD corresponding to the entire memory block in a truly sequential manner, at 110 bits per second (baud). The byte counter B is preserved on stack, each time the Code Out routine is called, since that routine also uses B register for some other purpose.

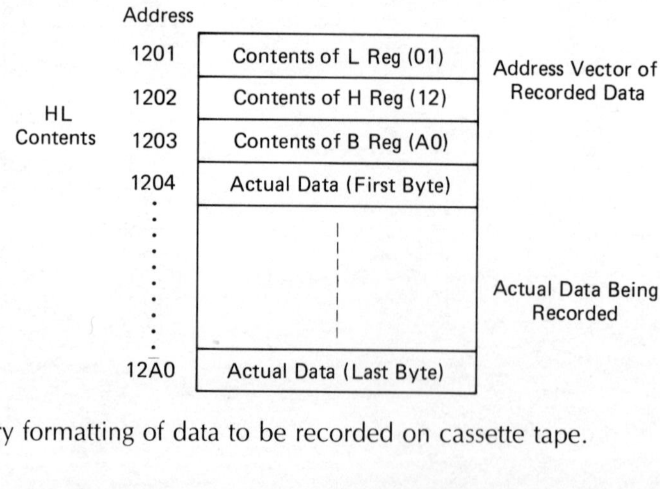

Fig 3.17. Memory formatting of data to be recorded on cassette tape.

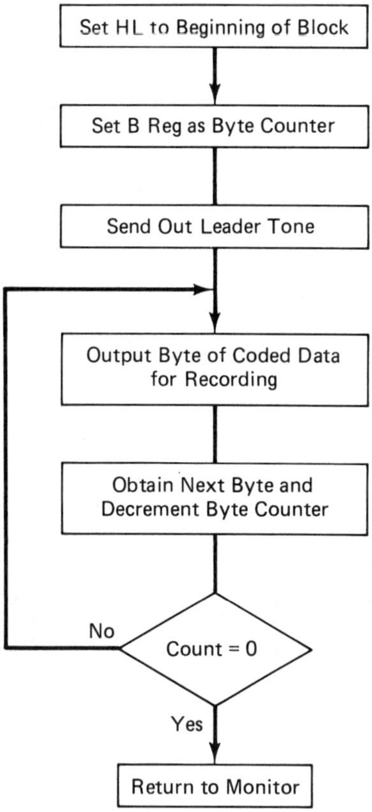

Fig 3.18. Flow chart for cassette recording software.

The control is returned to the monitor after all of the memory block is recorded.

Data Playback

As mentioned earlier, data playback and reconstruction is a complementary process to data recording and coding. In the playback mode, the sinusoidal output from the earphone output of the recorder is conditioned to form a level signal and is applied to the SID input of 8085, as shown in Figure 3.16. When there is a sinusoid at earphone output, there is a high level at SID input. Absence of sinusoid results in a low level at SID input. The software recognizes the relative duration of high and low levels at SID input in a given bit time and reconstructs the digital 1 and 0 pattern. If the duration of high level is more than low level, it is a logic 1 and vice versa.

Figure 3.19 shows the flow chart and Table 3.7 shows the program listings

Table 3.6. Program Listing for Cassette Data Recording.

Location	*Label*	*Mnemonic*	*Op Code*	*Comment*
2030	Record	NOP	00	Linkage software. Also using SDK-85 commands to load L, H, and B registers with the starting address of block and number of bytes to be recorded. First three memory locations are loaded with contents of L, H, and B registers respectively.
31		NOP	00	
32		NOP	00	
33	Top	MOV M, L	75	
34		INX H	23	
35		MOV M, H	74	
36		NOP	00	
37		INX H	23	
38		MOV M, B	70	
39		DCX H	2B	
3A		DCX H	2B	
3B		LXI SP	31	Stack initialized at 20C0.
3C		$C0_L$		
3D		20_H		
3E	Leader Set	MVI C	0E	Leader tone is generated by using subroutine burst/pause at 2020 of coded data generation of Example 3.4. Approximately $(3F)_{Hex} * 3 =$ 189 cycles of tone are generated as leader signal. (Recall that each time burst/pause is called, three cycles of tone burst are put out.)
3F		3F		
40	Leader Out	→MVI A	3E	
41		C0		
42	Burst/Pause	CALL	CD	
43		20		
44		20		
45		DCR C	0D	
46		JNZ	C2	
47		40		
48		20		
2049	Byte Out	→PUSH B	C5	Store B Register on stack. Obtain the byte from the memory block and go to Code Out routine at 2006 from Example 3.4, to output-coded digital waveform on SOD.
4A		MOV C, M	4E	
4B	Code Out	CALL	CD	
4C		06_L		
4D		20_H		
4E	Next Byte	INX H	23	Restore B and decrement B to see whether all the required number of bytes have been recorded. Otherwise loop back to byte out.
4F		POP B	C1	
2050		DCR B	05	
51		JNZ	C2	
52		49		
53		20		
54		RST 1	CF	Return control to monitor.

Note: (1) Coded data generation program—Example 3.4

(2) Change RST 1 at 201F in the code out routine to "RET" so that the program would function as subroutine.

(3) Data recording rate is 110 baud.

(4) Change 09 at location 2007 in the code out routine to 08 to correspond to actual byte shift.

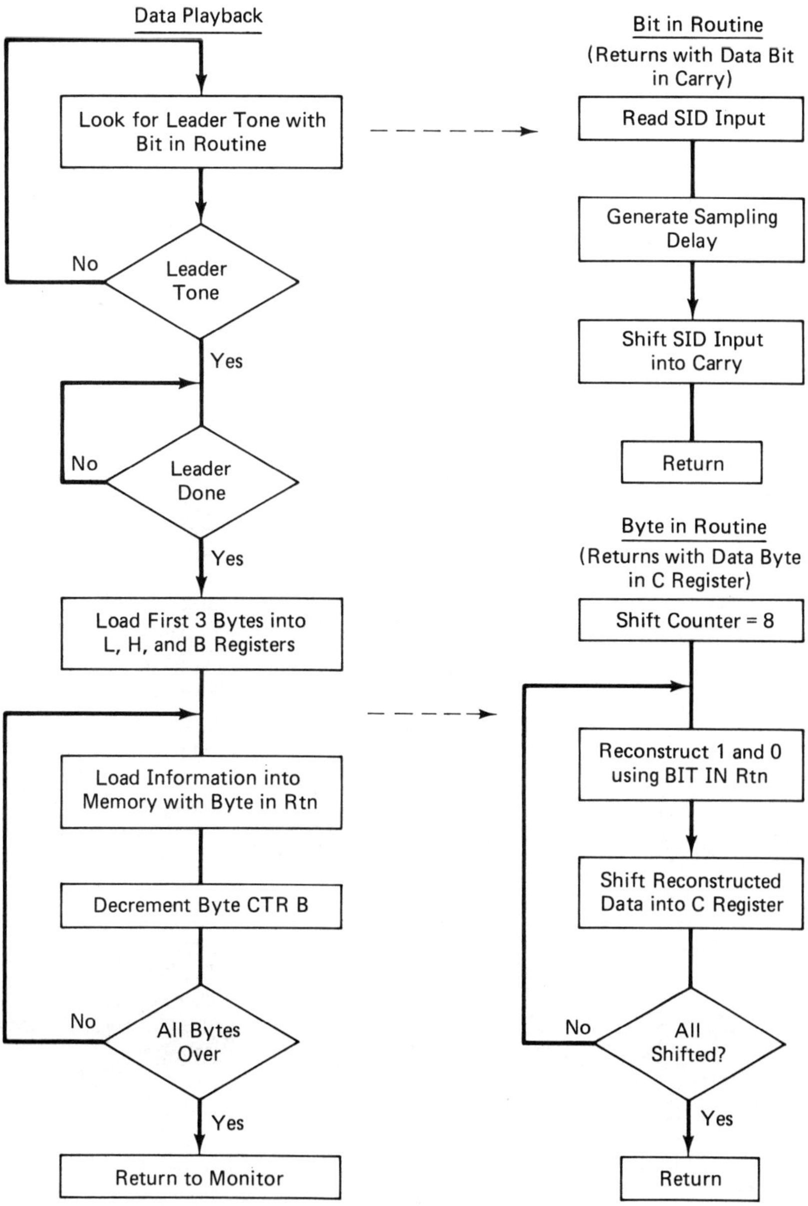

Fig 3.19. Cassette playback software flowchart with bit and byte in subroutines.

Table 3.7. Playback Routine Listings

Location	*Label*	*Mnemonic*	*Op Code*	*Comment*
2060	Playback	LXI SP	31	Stack initialized at 20C0.
61		C0		
62		20		
63	Leader Detect	CALL	CD	Bit in subroutine at 20A7 sets carry to 1 if 1 is detected at SID input, signifying occurence of leader. Program loops back until leader is detected.
64		A7		
65		20		
66		JNC	D2	
67		63		
68		20		
69	Leader Tone	CALL	CD	Leader is detected, and program loops until leader is done.
6A		A7		
6B		20		
6C		JC	DA	
6D		69		
6E		20		
6F		CALL	CD	Byte in subroutine at 2086 is called, which returns with C register filled with 8 bits (one byte) of information received on SID input terminal.
70		86		
71		20		
72		MOV L, C	69	
73		CALL	CD	First, 3 bytes are loaded into L, H, and B registers providing memory address vector in HL registers and byte counter in B register.
74		86		
75		20		
76		MOV H, C	61	
77		CALL	CD	
78		86		
79		20		
7A		MOV B, C	41	
207B	Memory Load	CALL	CD	Memory is sequentially loaded, until all required bytes are completed and the control is returned to monitor.
7C		86		
7D		20		
7E		MOV M, C	71	
7F		INX H	23	
80		DCR B	05	
81		JNZ	C2	
82		7B		
83		20		
84		RST 1	CF	
		BYTE IN SUBROUTINE LISTINGS		
86	Byte In	NOP	00	This program returns [C7 | C6 | C5 | C4 | C3 | C2 | C1 | C0] (MSB … LSB) with 1 byte of information in C register.

87		Push B	C5	B Register is stored (to save its contents from main program)
88	Shift Counter	MVI B	06	B register is reinitialized as shift counter with 08.
89		08		
8A		MVI D	16	D register is initialized to 00 and is decremented as long as the carry bit is set to 1 after calling bit in subroutine at 20A7. This has the implication of D containing a negative number with D7 = 1 so long as 1 is detected at SID.
8B		00		
8C	Code Counter	DCR D	15	
8D		CALL	Cd	
8E		A7		
8F		20		
90		JC	DA	
91		8C		
92		20		
93		INR D	14	D counter is incremented back, if "Bit In" subroutine presents a 0 in carry bit. If duration of 1, level is more than 0 at SID input, D is decremented more and is negative with most significant bit D7 = 1; otherwise D is positive and D7 = 0. Thus D7 contains SID information.
94		CALL	CD	
95		A7		
96		20		
2097		JNC	D2	
98		93		
99		20		
9A		MOV A, D	7A	D7 information is shifted into accumulator, into carry, and finally into C register.
9B		RAL	17	
9C		MOV A, C	79	
9D		RAR	1F	
9E		MOV C, A	4F	
9F		DCR B	05	Shift counter B is decremented and program loops back to 208A until all 8 bits are shifted into C register.
20A0		JNZ	C2	
A1		8A		
A2		20		
A3		POP B	C1	B of calling program is restored, and program returns to calling program.
A4		RET	C9	

BIT IN SUBROUTINE LISTINGS [This returns with (SID) value in carry]

Location	*Label*	*Mnemonic*	*Op Code*	*Clock Cycles*	*Comment*
20A7	Bit in	MVI E	1E	7	Loop counter E is loaded
A8		0B			with 0B = $(11)_{DEC}$.
A9	Loop CTR	DCR E	1D	4	Program loops 10 times
AA		JNZ	C2	7/10	to provide sampling
AB		A9			delay.
AC		20			
AD		RIM	20	4	SID information is read (A7 of ACC contains SID info).
AE		RAL	17	4	Shifted into carry and control.
AF		RET	C9	10	Back to calling program.

T_{Sample} = [(0B − 1) * 14 + 32] * ⅓ μs ≃ 58 μs

= (Time Between 20A7 and 20AF)

for the data playback, decoding, and reconstruction. Between 2063 and 2068, the program loops until a 1 is detected at SID input, signifying the presence of leader tone. Between 2069 and 206E, the program loops until the leader is done.

Main Program

Between 206F and 207A, the first three bytes read from the playback are loaded in the L, H, and B registers. This formulates an address vector in HL registers, which can be used to locate the memory where the played back information is to be stored. B register contains the number of bytes to be loaded from the tape. As an example, if the address vector in HL registers is $(1201)_{Hex}$ and B register contains (A0), then the playback routine would load information from the tape in memory starting at 1201, up to 12A0, for a total of A0 number of bytes.

Between 207B and 83, the memory is filled sequentially, and control is ultimately returned to the monitor.

Byte In Subroutine

Whenever this subroutine is called, it returns to the calling program with the reconstructed byte of information (from SID input) in the C register. The data reconstruction is accomplished by decrementing D register from 00 condition when a 1 is detected at SID input and incrementing subsequently when a 0 is detected at the SID input, as shown (refer to Figure 3.13 for details).

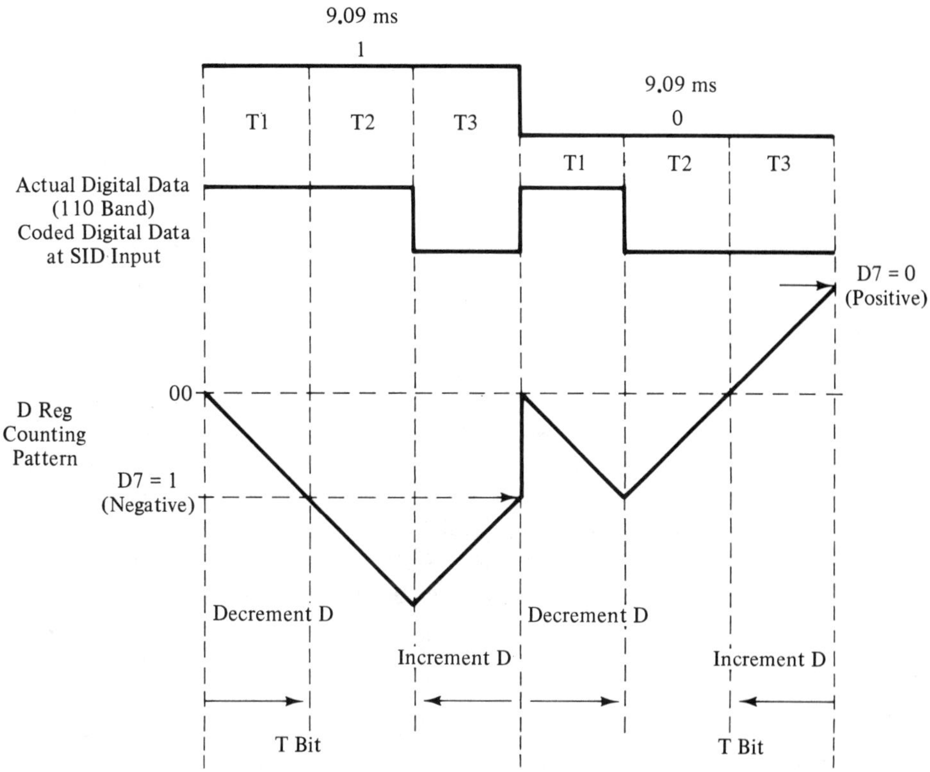

At the end of each bit time, D is negative or positive (D7 = 1 or 0) depending on whether the actual data is a 1 or 0. This is accomplished between 208C and 2099. Between 209A and 20A4, this reconstructed data is shifted into C register to form a full byte, and control is returned to the calling program.

Bit In Subroutine

Between 20A7 and 20AF, the SID input is read with a sampling loop delay and shifted into the carry flag, and the control is returned to the calling program. The loop counter E is loaded with 0B to provide an approximate sampling delay of 58 μs. For a 110-baud data, during each T1, T2, and T3 interval (3.03 ms each), SID input can be read approximately 50 times, which provides accuracy and a good sampling rate.

There are several variations of cassette recording and playback operations; for example, Kansas City Standard with error correction codes, such as "check sum," etc. All these are given as example problems at the end of the chapter, and you are encouraged to solve them as they are of practical importance and can be used with any recording mechanisms, with any microcomputer.

3.4. SYSTEM LEVEL INTERFACE AND SINGLE-CHIP MICROCOMPUTERS

The electronics industry is trying to standardize microcomputer system-level interface to peripherals and I/O, so that any microcomputer can be successfully interfaced to any I/O. One such interface standard for serial data transfer is the RS-232, which is very popular in interfacing slow I/O systems to a fast microcomputer.

In addition, for system applications, the basic microprocessor, ROM and RAM memory, and I/O ports are integrated to form a single-chip microcomputer device in order to reduce the number of devices and interconnects to improve the reliability of the system. Intel Corporation has a whole line of single-chip microcomputers such as 8021, 8022, 8048, and 8049 based on 8085 architecture.

In this section we will briefly study the RS-232 interface and 8048/49 microcomputer and use these concepts in implementing an operational system.

The RS-232 Interface

The Electronic Industries Association (EIA) standard RS-232 interface is used extensively for serial data transmission with I/O systems such as teletypes, printers, CRT displays, and instrumentation systems with baud rates between 50 baud and 19.2K baud. The interface is defined to account for 25 total connections, using a standard 25-pin D-type connector. In most cases about 6 to 8 interface signals are used, as shown in Figure 3.20. To improve noise margins over transmission distances up to about 10 meters, extended logic levels are used for RS-232, with more positive voltage than 3 volts as logic 0 and more negative voltage than -3 volts as logic 1 (negative logic sense). Fortunately, there are TTL $\rightleftarrows$ RS-232 level converters available, which we will discuss presently.

The serial data transfer on the RS-232 interface takes place in control handshaking mode. The microcomputer will initiate an RTS (request to send) control signal to the I/O, to which the I/O system will respond with CTS (clear to send) control. Then, serial data flows on the TXD (transmit data) line from computer to I/O or on the RXD (receive data) line from I/O to the computer.

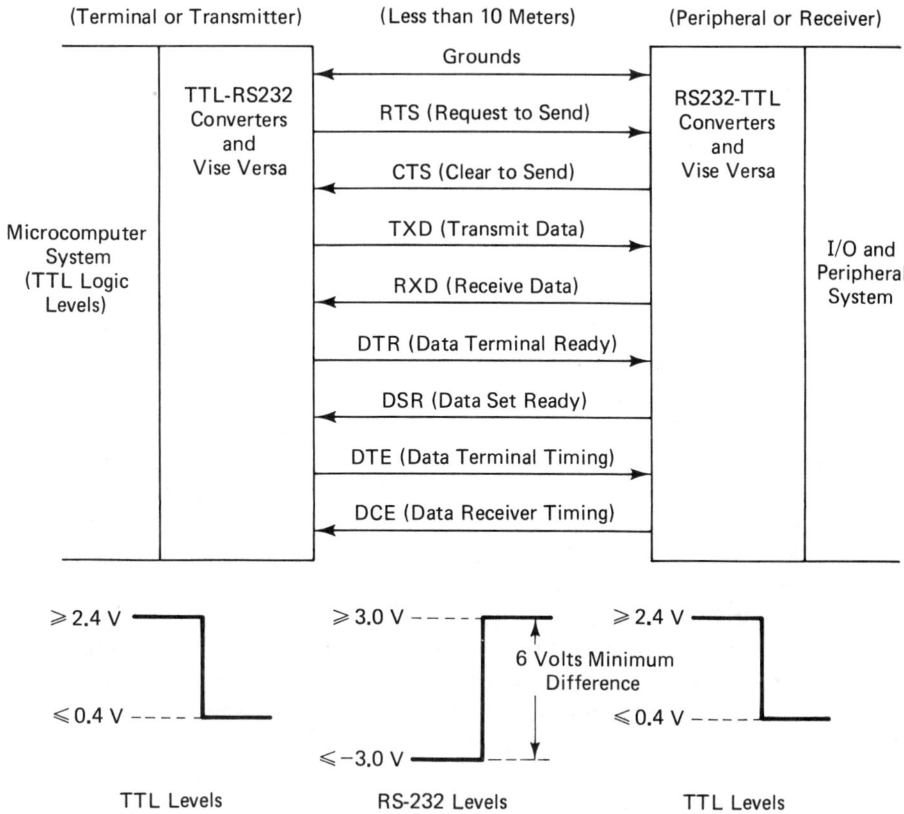

Fig 3.20. Typical RS-232 interface and logic levels.

Depending on the master timing control, the system timing information flows on the DTE (data terminal timing) line from computer to I/O or on the DCE (data receiver timing) line from I/O to computer.

Finally, two more control handshake signals are often used. The DTR (data terminal ready) from the computer signifies that the computer is establishing contact with the I/O, and DSR (data set ready) from the I/O signifies that the I/O is establishing contact with the computer channel.

At the outset, it appears that the RS-232 is too complex and inefficient. However, it is actually a very easy and standard interface, and we need to pick up the relevant signals for any given application. The hardware standardization of RS-232 and standardized signal definitions make the RS-232 interface an industry standard. You are encouraged to gain experience in implementing this interface. We will present an example after we discuss single-chip microcomputers.

Single-Chip Microcomputers

The introduction of single-chip microcomputers in the late 1970s with onboard memory and I/O features has revolutionized the system applications of microcomputers in all disciplines of electronics and controls. Almost any digital system can be implemented with single-chip micros and a few supporting devices.

8048 Architecture and Features

The INTEL 8048 is a 40-pin single-chip microcomputer device, with 1K × 8 ROM and 64 × 8 RAM and 27 I/O connections, as shown in Figure 3.21. The ROM is mask programmable at the company, with a user-supplied program. To be able to write and test programs at the user end, Intel also produces an EPROM version of the 8048, known as 8748, which is pin-to-pin compatible with 8048. In 8748, the ROM memory is replaced by user programmable and erasable ROM (EPROM) memory. The 8049 (EPROM version 8749) is similar to the 8048, except that it has double the memory capability of 2K × 8 ROM and 128 × 8 RAM and is suited for larger system applications. Table 3.8 shows the 8048 instruction set.

As can be seen from Figure 3-21 and Table 3-8, 8048 uses architecture similar to 8085, with few modifications to make the device more I/O bound. The "MCS-48 Single-Chip Microcomputers User Manual" should be consulted for details of the device and the actual machine codes.

Any bit of port 1 or 2 is individually programmable as input or output. There is no necessity to initialize the ports as input or output. The internal hardware is constructed so that the program instruction such as "In A, P" or "OUTL P, A" will automatically configure the I/O structure of the port. The data bus port is similar to port 1 or 2, except that all the bits have to be either all inputs or outputs.

In addition, a program can be branched on test, using instructions such as "JTO," etc. The register banks (R0...R7) and (R0'...R7') can be conveniently used to hold the data or address of the data, similar to the register pairs of the 8085 microprocessor. In the programmable ROM memory, the first 10 locations are dedicated for reset, interrupt, and timer interrupt vectors, as shown in Figure 3.21.

We will now integrate the concepts of RS-232 and the single-chip microcomputer in a simple data handling system in an example.

Example 3.5 System Serial Interface: Design Example

In an instrumentation system, thermal information in the form of a 4-bit word for each digit enters the microcomputer through the RS-232 interface (shown in Figure 3.22), and is to be displayed on the 7-segment display.

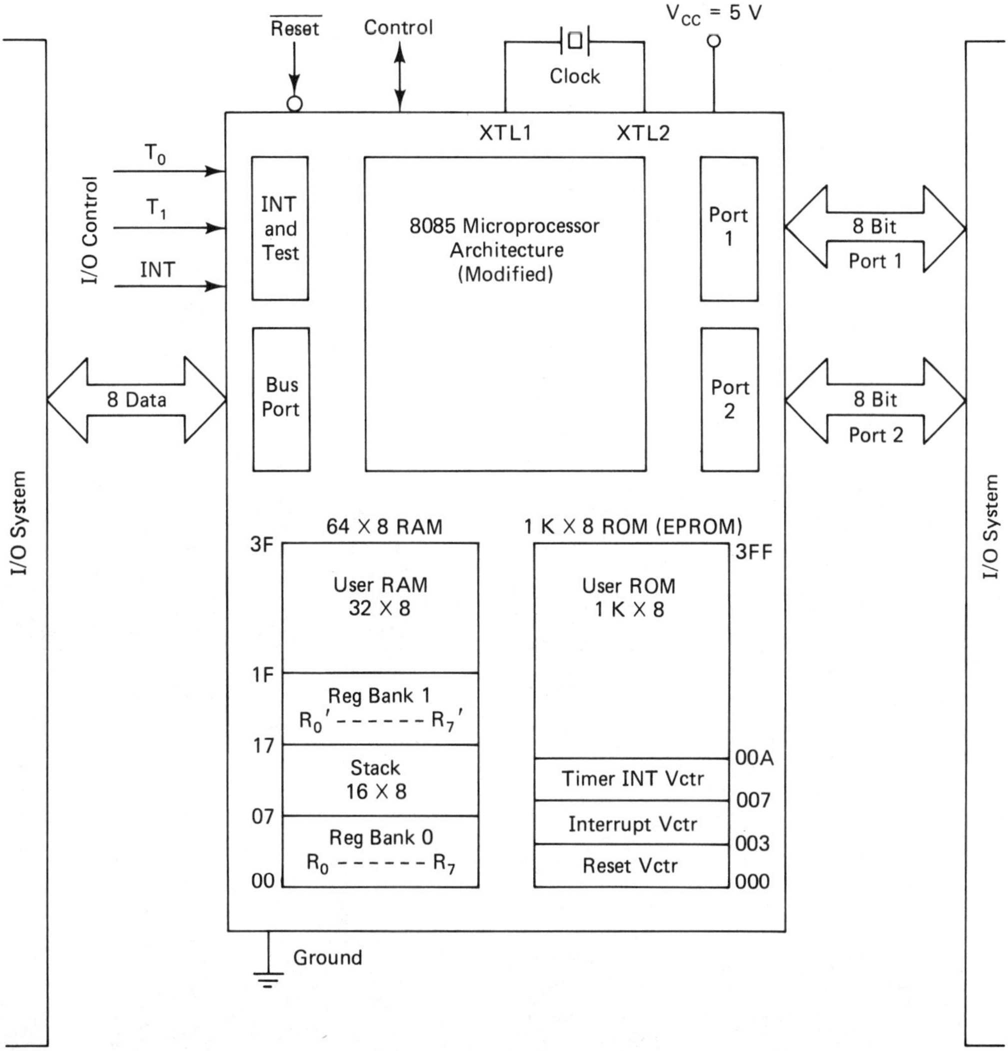

Fig 3.21. The 8048 (8748) single-chip microcomputer architecture.

Using the 8748 single-chip microcomputer and RS-232 standards, develop a complete operating system.

Solution

Figure 3.23 shows the actual system hardware and interface that will accomplish the given task. The thermal sensors are simulated with switches S0...S4. When S4 is closed, it implies that updated thermal data is available on S0...S3 and the micro should respond (data set ready).

Table 3.8. 8048/8049 Instruction Set (Courtesy of Intel Corporation).

Mnemonic	*Description*	*Bytes*	*Cycles*
ADD A, R	Add register to A	1	1
ADD A, @R	Add data memory to A	1	1
ADD A, #data	Add immediate to A	2	2
ADDC A, R	Add register with carry	1	1
ADDC A, @R	Add data memory with carry	1	1
ADDC A, #data	Add immediate with carry	2	2
ANL A, R	And register to A	1	1
ANL A, @R	And data memory to A	1	1
ANL A, #data	And immediate to A	2	2
ORL A, R	Or register to A	1	1
ORL A, @R	Or data memory to A	1	1
ORL A, #data	Or immediate to A	2	2
XRL A, R	Exclusive Or register to A	1	1
XRL A, @R	Exclusive or data memory to A	1	1
XRL A, #data	Exclusive or immediate to A	2	2
INC A	Increment A	1	1
DEC A	Decrement A	1	1
CLR A	Clear A	1	1
CPL A	Complement A	1	1
DA A	Decimal Adjust A	1	1
SWAP A	Swap nibbles of A	1	1
RL A	Rotate A left	1	1
RLC A	Rotate A left through carry	1	1
RR A	Rotate A right	1	1
RRC A	Rotate A right through carry	1	1
IN A, P	Input port to A	1	2
OUTL P, A	Output A to port	1	2
ANL P, #data	And immediate to port	2	2
ORL P, #data	Or immediate to port	2	2
INS A, BUS	Input BUS to A	1	2
OUTL BUS, A	Ouput A to BUS	1	2
ANL BUS, #data	And immediate to BUS	2	2
ORL BUS, #data	Or immediate to BUS	2	2
MOVD A, P	Input Expander port to A	1	2
MOVD P, A	Output A to Expander port	1	2
ANLD P, A	And A to Expander port	1	2
ORLD P, A	Or A to Expander port	1	2
INC R	Increment register	1	1
INC @R	Increment data memory	1	1
DEC R	Decrement register	1	1
JMP addr	Jump unconditional	2	2
JMPP @A	Jump indirect	1	2
DJNZ R, addr	Decrement register and jump	2	2
JC addr	Jump on Carry = 1	2	2
JNC addr	Jump on Carry = 0	2	2
JZ addr	Jump on A Zero	2	2

Table 3.8. (*Continued*)

Mnemonic	*Description*	*Bytes*	*Cycles*
JNZ addr	Jump on A not Zero	2	2
JT0 addr	Jump on T0 = 1	2	2
JNT0 addr	Jump on T0 = 0	2	2
JT1 addr	Jump on T1 = 1	2	2
JNT1 addr	Jump on T1 = 0	2	2
JF0 addr	Jump on F0 = 1	2	2
JF1 addr	Jump on F1 = 1	2	2
JTF addr	Jump on timer flag = 1	2	2
JNI addr	Jump on $\overline{INT}$ = 0	2	2
JBb addr	Jump on Accumulator Bit	2	2
CALL addr	Jump to subroutine	2	2
RET	Return	1	2
RETR	Return and restore status	1	2
CLR C	Clear Carry	1	1
CPL C	Complement Carry	1	1
CLR F0	Clear Flag 0	1	1
CPL F0	Complement Flag 0	1	1
CLR F1	Clear Flag 1	1	1
CPL F1	Complement Flag 1	1	1
MOV A, R	Move register to A	1	1
MOV A, @R	Move data memory to A	1	1
MOV A, #data	Move immediate to A	2	2
MOV R, A	Move A to register	1	1
MOV @R, A	Move A to data memory	1	1
MOV R, #data	Move immediate to register	2	2
MOV @R, #data	Move immediate to data memory	2	2
MOV A, PSW	Move PSW to A	1	1
MOV PSW, A	Move A to PSW	1	1
XCH A, R	Exchange A and register	1	1
XCHA, @R	Exchange A and data memory	1	1
XCHD A, @R	Exchange nibble of A and register	1	1
MOVX A, @R	Move external data memory to A	1	2
MOVX @R, A	Move A to external data memory	1	2
MOVP A, @A	Move to A from current page	1	2
MOVP3 A, @A	Move to A from Page 3	1	2
MOV A, T	Read Timer/Counter	1	1
MOV T, A	Load Timer/Counter	1	1
STRT T	Start Timer	1	1
STRT CNT	Start Counter	1	1
STOP TCNT	Stop Timer/Counter	1	1
EN TCNTI	Enable Timer/Counter Interrupt	1	1
DIS TCNTI	Disable Timer/Counter Interrupt	1	1
EN I	Enable external interrupt	1	1
DIS I	Disable external interrupt	1	1

Table 3.8. *(Continued)*

Mnemonic	*Description*	*Bytes*	*Cycles*
SEL RB0	Select register bank 0	1	1
SEL RB1	Select register bank 1	1	1
SEL MB0	Select memory bank 0	1	1
SEL MB1	Select memory bank 1	1	1
ENT0 CLK	Enable Clock output on T0	1	1
NOP	No operation	1	1

Mnemonics copyright Intel Corporation 1976.

Accumulator *Input/Output* *Registers* *Branch* *Subroutine* *Flags*
Data Moves *Time/Counter* *Control*

(a) *Data Input*. The 74165 shift register loads this thermal data when shift/$\overline{\text{load}}$ input is low. When this input is high, the shift register serializes and shifts the data on output line, as a function of the input clock on pin 2. This data output is translated to the RS-232 logic level through the MC 1488 (G1) converter and is transmitted on the RS-232 data link. On the receiving

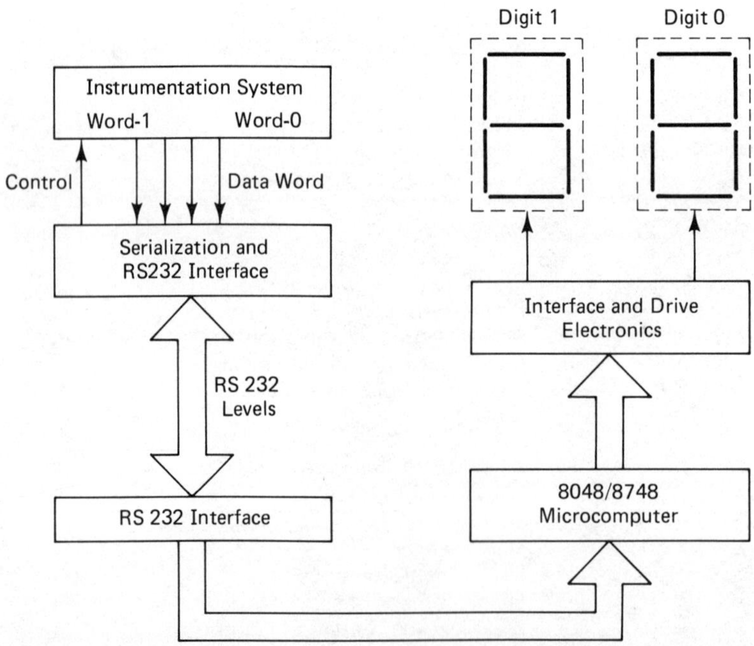

Fig 3.22. The 8048 (8748) single-chip microcomputer data serialization system with the RS-232 interface for Example 3.5.

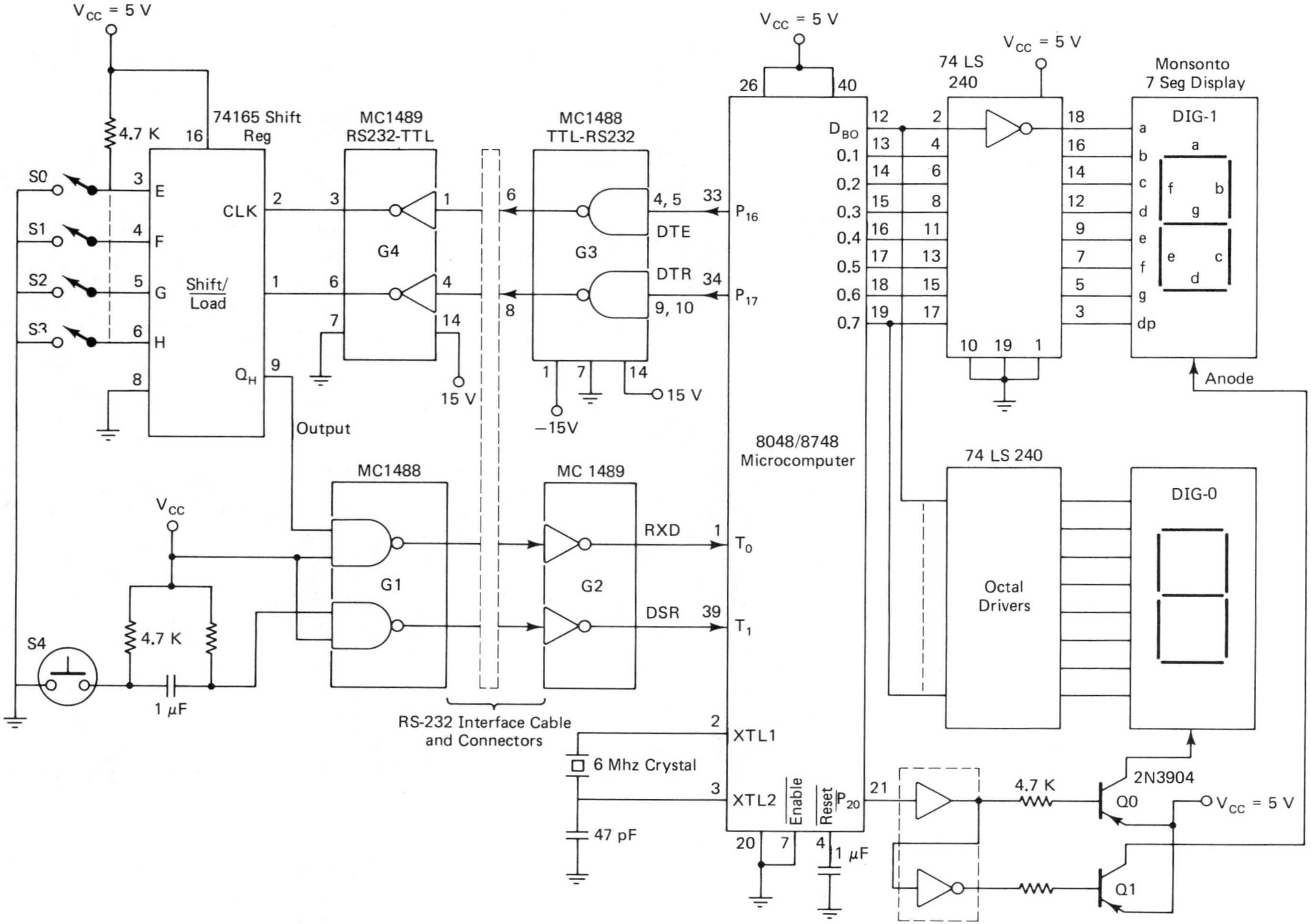

Fig 3.23. Single-chip microcomputer and RS-232 interface (Example 3.5).

end, the signal gets converted back to the TTL level through the MC 1489 (G2) and forms the RXD input (receive data) connected to T0 input of the micro. Similarly, closure of S4 is routed as DSR (data set ready) connected to the T1 input of the micro.

The corresponding handshake signal DTR (data terminal ready) is generated by the micro on its port 1, bit 7 (P17) and is routed as a shift/$\overline{\text{load}}$ control signal to the shift register. The data-timing signal DTE is generated by the micro on its P16 bit and is routed to form a shift clock for the shift register. Please refer to Figures 3.20 and 3.23 for the RS-232 interface concepts.

The RS-232 handshake occurs as shown in Figure 3.24. When S4 is activated, the DSR line goes low, signifying (new) data set is ready. The micro senses this and will pull DTR line high when it is ready to accept the data, which puts the shift register in the shift mode. Thereafter, four clock pulses are generated by the micro on the DTE line to clock the shift register, and four bits of information are received on the RXD line. The micro reads this information, reconstructs the 4-bit BCD word, stores it in the display memory, converts it into the corresponding 7-segment code, and drives the displays.

(b) *Data Display*. The data display primarily uses the scanning of the code table, which is a special handling feature of the 8048/8748, to simplify the task. Two internal registers, R0 and R1, are used to store the serial data to be displayed on digit 0 and digit 1, as shown in Figure 3.25. A table located in page 3 of the ROM/PROM memory contains the 7-segment

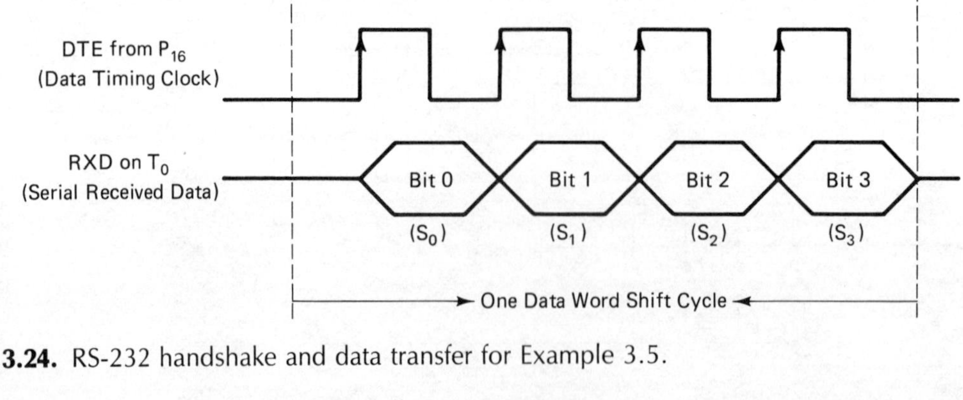

Fig 3.24. RS-232 handshake and data transfer for Example 3.5.

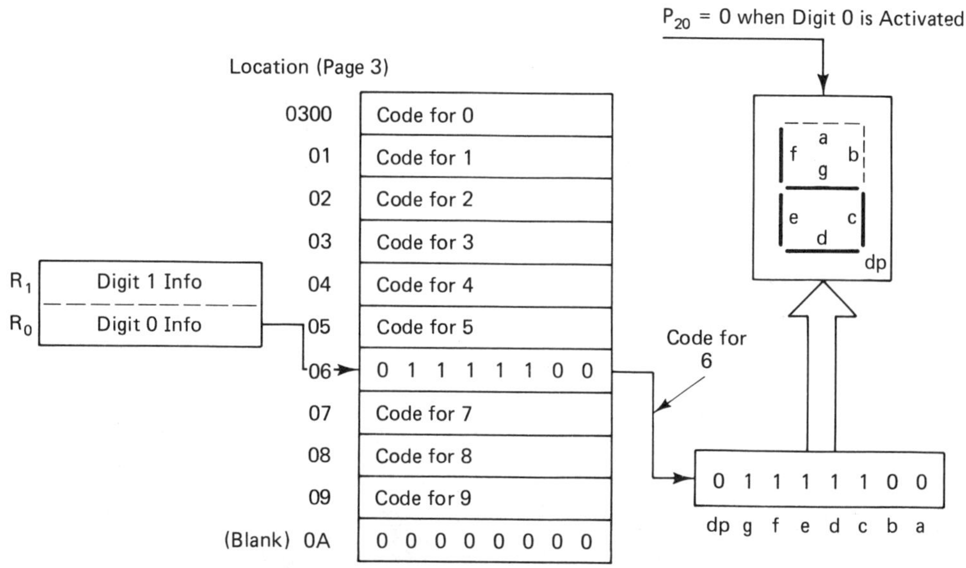

Fig 3.25. Multiplexed seven-segment display structure and interface for Example 3.5.

code of the character to be displayed. There are special instructions in the 8048 set to handle tables in page 3, which will make the task very simple. R0 and R1 are used to reference the code table.

Under software control, the code pointed by R0 or R1 is sent to the data bus, which lights up digit 0 or 1. A carry equals zero enables R0 and digit zero, and carry equals 1 enables R1 and digit 1. The carry information is brought out on port 2, bit zero (P20). The carry bit is complemented consecutively to switch between digit 0 and 1 at a fast rate, so that both digits appear to be lighted up continuously.

Because of this refresh requirement, the main program is designed to be the display program, displaying information on digits 0 and 1. When data set ready occurs from input section, the program branches to servicing the input and resuming the display program again. Figure 3.26 shows the flow chart, and Table 3.9 shows the program listing.

The program starts at location 0000, which is the vectored address for the reset input, for the 8748. Thus the system gets into the operating program soon after the reset is activated. This kind of manipulation is typical with single-chip micros. Between 0000 and 0018, the display digits 0 and 1 are flashed at a fast rate with the characters contained in R0 and R1, alternatively. The input shift register is maintained in load mode (P17 = 0). Between 001A and 0020, DSR input on T1 is checked for debounce free 0 condition (with delay 2 timing loop). If not, the program jumps to 0044, to load OTO register with FF and starts back again. If T1 is a consistent

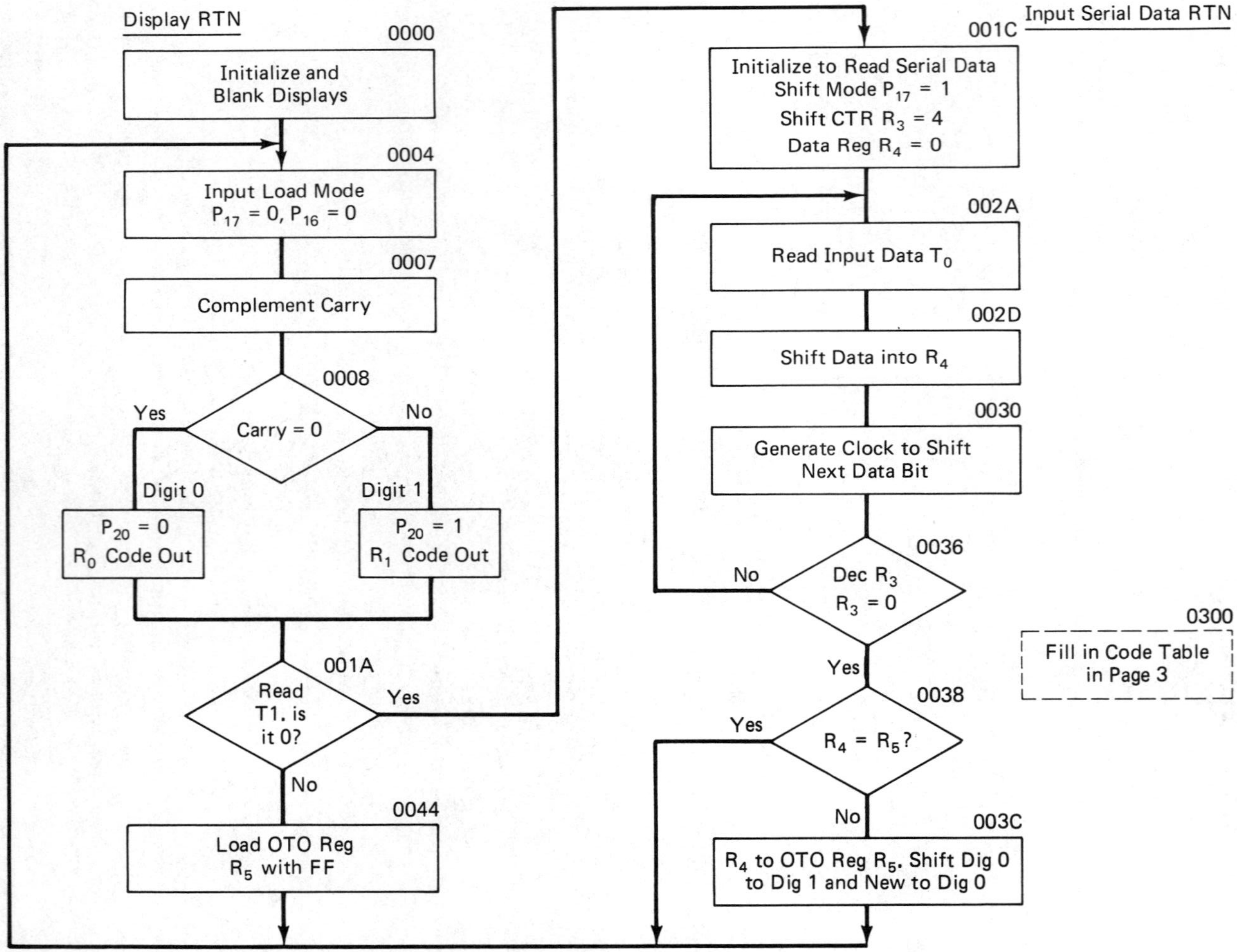

Fig 3.26. Flowchart for the RS-232 interface and single-chip microcomputer (Example 3.6).

0, the program proceeds. Between 0022 and 0035, P17 is made 1 for shift mode and clock pulses are generated to shift RXD data onto input, which is sensed and serially loaded into register R4.

Between 0036 and 0042, the 4-bit word is reconstructed in register 4, and the corresponding character is displayed on digit 0, and digit 0 character is shifted to digit 1 and the program loops back to start.

Table 3.9. 8048 Listings for RS-232 Serial Interface (Example 3.6).

Location	*Label*	*Mnemonic*	*Op Code*		*Comment*
0000	Initialize	MOV R0, #0A	B8	0A	R0 and R1 is loaded with 0A, which has location of blank code, in page 3.
02		MOV R1 #0A	B9	0A	
04	Start	CLR A	27		Input shift register is in load mode with P17 and P16 at 0.
05		OUTL P1, A	39		
06		OUTL, BUS, A	02		
07		CPL C	A7		Carry complemented.
08		JC 10	F6	10	
0A	Digit 0	MOV A, #00	23	00	P20 is made 0 to activate digit 0 if carry is 0.
0C		OUTL P2, A	3A		
0D		MOV A, R0	F8		A is loaded with R0 to display on digit 0.
0E		JMP 14	04	14	
0010	Digit 1	MOV A, #01	23	01	P20 is made 1 to activate digit 1 if carry is 1 and A is loaded with R1 to be displayed on digit 1.
12		OUTL P2, A	3A		
13		MOV A, R1	F9		
14	Display	MOV P3 A, @A	E3		A is loaded with contents of code table in page 3 and is output on data bus.
15		OUTL Bus, A	02		
16		MOV R6, #0F	BE	OF	Delay loop 1. Small delay.
18	Delay 1	DJNZ R6, 18	EE	18	
1A		JT1 44	56	44	If T1 = (DSR = 1), program jumps to 44. If T1 = 0, program checks the debounce effect and if T1 continues to be zero, program proceeds.
1C		MOV R6, #FF	BE	FF	
1E	Delay 2	DJNZ R6, 1E	EE	1E	
0020		JT1 44	56	44	
22	Serial data	MOV A, #80	23	80	P17 made 1 for shift mode.
24		OUTL P1, A	39		
25		MOV R3, #04	BB	04	Shift CTR R3 initialized to 4. Data Register R4 initialized to 0.
27		MOV R4, #00	BC	00	

Table 3.9. (*Continued*)

Location	*Label*	*Mnemonic*	*Op Code*	*Comment*
29		CLR C	97	T0 is examined and corresponding data bit is shifted into R4 (If T0 = 0, carry is cleared and if T0 = 1, carry is set to 1 and then shifted into R4.)
2A	RXD in	JNT0 2D	26 2D	
002C		CPL C	A7	
2D	Shift data	MOV A, R4	FC	
2E		RLC A	F7	
2F		MOV R4, A	AC	
0030	Clock	MOV A, #C0	23 C0	Clock signal is generated on P16, keeping P17 = 1 in shift mode, for shifting P16 data.
32		OUTL P1, A	39	
33		MOV A, #80	23 80	
35		OUTL P1, A	39	
36		DJNZ R3, 29	EB 29	R3 decremented and checked for 0 to see all 4 shifts over.
38		MOV A, R4	FC	
39		XRL A, R5	DD	If R4 = R5 signifying old data, program jumps back to start at 04.
3A		JZ 04	C6 04	
3C	Digit shift	MOV A, R4	FC	For new data, R5 is loaded with contents of R4.
3D		MOV R5, A	AD	
3E		MOV A, R0	F8	R0 shifted to R1.
3F		MOV R1, A	A9	New data in R4 shifted to R0.
0040		MOV A, R4	FC	
41		MOV R0, A	A8	
42		JMP 04	04 04	Jump to shift for next word.
44		MOV R5, #FF	BD FF	One time only (0T0) register loaded with FF and jump to start for new word. Page 3.
46		JMP 04	04 04	

7-SEGMENT CODE TABLE CONTENTS

0300	3F	Code For	0
01	06	"	1
02	5B	"	2
03	4F	"	3
04	66	"	4
05	6D	"	5
06	7D	"	6
07	07	"	7
08	7F	"	8
09	6F	"	9
0A	00	"	Blank

At 0044, 0T0 register is loaded with FF indicating that no new data has been entered during the current execution, and old data gets displayed.

Because of their importance in contemporary digital system designs, the single-chip micros should be well studied and practiced. Several example problems at the end of the chapter involving other Intel family single-chip micros such as 8021, 8022, 8049, etc. should provide insight into their applications.

3.5. SUMMARY

In this chapter, we have presented the features of an 8085 microprocessor-based computer system such as the SDK-85, which can be readily obtained and experimented with. Any other microcomputer system with proper memory map adjustment should work on all the applications presented.

Of particular interest are the examples presented on coded data generation, which are extensively used in digital data communication fields. The RS-232 interface concepts are of equal importance and can be implemented on any microcomputer and system interface.

The single-chip microcomputer discussion is of vital importance for instrumentation and system design engineers who are primarily interested in I/O applications and interface and would want to minimize the electronics hardware for dedicated applications.

Problems

3.1. A control word of $(CF)_{Hex}$ is written into the command status register of 8155.

(a) Explain how ports A, B, and C are configured.

(b) If interrupting is to be disabled and timer not used and ports A and B are to be used as inputs and port C to be used as output, what should be the control word that should be written into the C/S register?

3.2. The 8155 is connected to 8085 in the SDK-85 system, to yield the memory map as follows:

2000 to 20FF	256 bytes of RAM (memory)	
20 C/S register	21 port A	I/O
22 Port B	23 port C	I/O

Using real electronic parts such as the 8205 3/8 decoder, 8212 8-bit latch, and any other relevant parts, and obtaining data on 8085 and

8155 from the Intel Data Book, design the actual operating interface between 8085 and 8155.

3.3. In a similar system, the following is the I/O map:

E0: C/S register: E1 port A
E2: port B : E3 port C

Repeat Problem 3.2 to obtain the above I/O map. What is the corresponding memory address range?

3.4. The data comparison in Example 3.3 and Figure 3.6 can be further simplified using only one of the ports (A or B) to read both *X* and *Y* words in sequence, as shown in Figure 3.27.

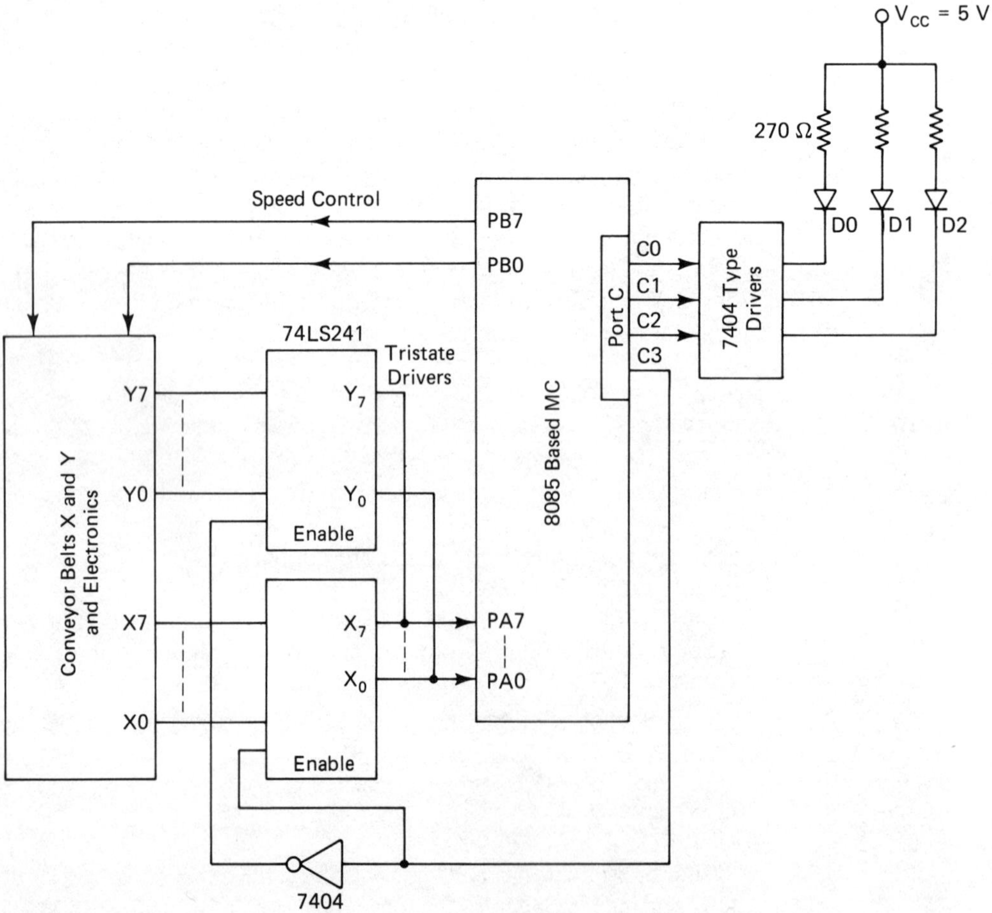

Fig 3.27. Conveyer belt interface for Problems 3.4 and 3.5a.

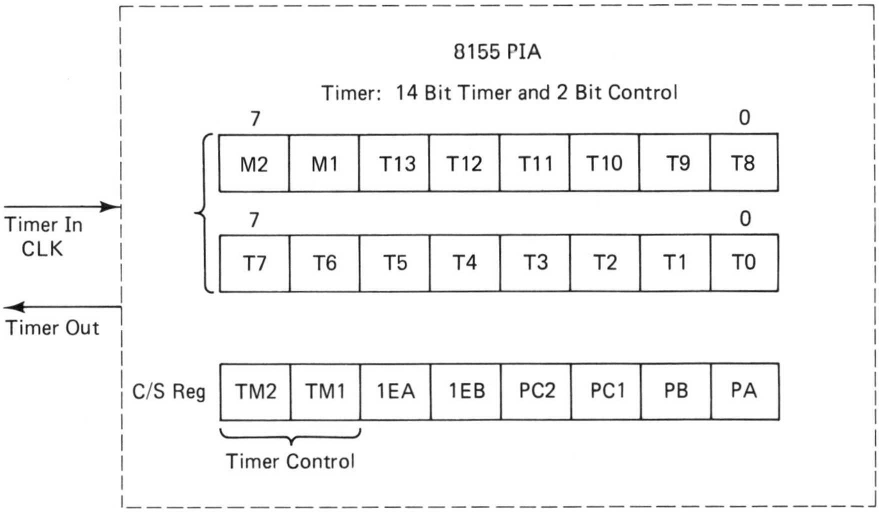

Fig 3.28. The 8155 timer section configuration and C/S register for Problems 3.6 and 3.7.

Develop the operating hardware and software to read *X* and *Y* data from conveyor belts on to port A and flash in 1 second intervals.

D0 If $X = Y$
D1 If $X > Y$
D2 If $X < Y$

3.5. The microcomputers are excellent controllers, as shown in Figure 3.27. The port B digital word has the following format:

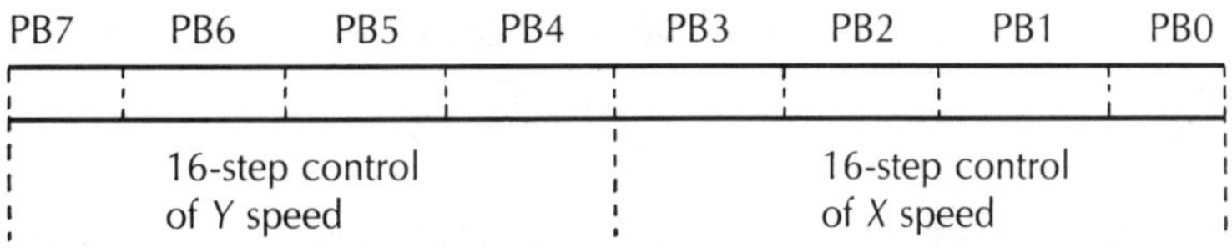

Develop the operating hardware and software so that *X* and *Y* speeds are properly adjusted to match each other.

0000 word is lowest speed
1111 word is highest speed

The input *X* and *Y* words are to be read into the micro once every 5 seconds, and speed correction is to be made accordingly.

3.6. The 8155 has a 14-bit equivalent timer and can be used for timing and counting purposes and is effectively controlled by bit 6 and bit 7 of the command/status register as shown in Figure 3.28. Obtaining data from the 8085 Family Users Manual, generate the necessary software to obtain a square wave on TIMER OUT pin of 8155, of a frequency of your choice.

3.7. (a) Repeat Problem 3.6 to obtain a square wave of 1 KHz.
(b) Modify the software to obtain 1 KHz pulses.

3.8. The timer section of 8155 as shown in Figure 3.28 may be used to count the events occurring on the timer in the clock. Design an operating system that will count events and light up LEDs from port B, as shown. LED D0 to light up after 100 events, LED D1 to light up after 200 events, and so on.

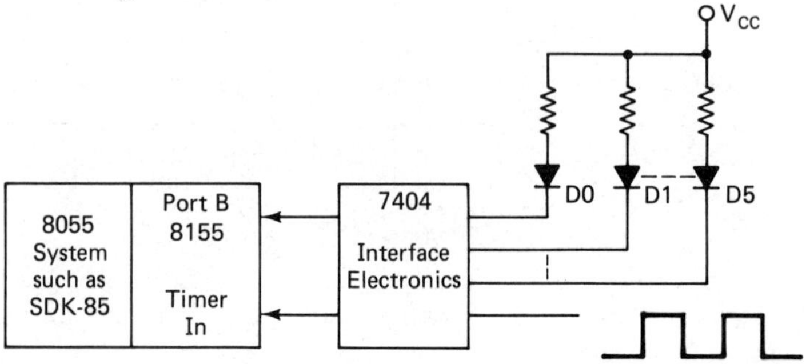

3.9. Moving display is very important. Using the micro system of your choice, develop software and hardware to have the display written from left to right (MSB to LSB) with 2 seconds delay, writing each digit. Assume the data to be displayed is present in the system memory. Assume an 8-digit 7-segment display.

3.10. Develop software routines to accomplish writing data from left to right, one digit at a time with a 2-second interval until all 8 digits are written and displayed; then blank one digit at a time with a 2-second interval until all 8 digits are blanked. The concept is as shown. Use the hardware configuration of your choice.

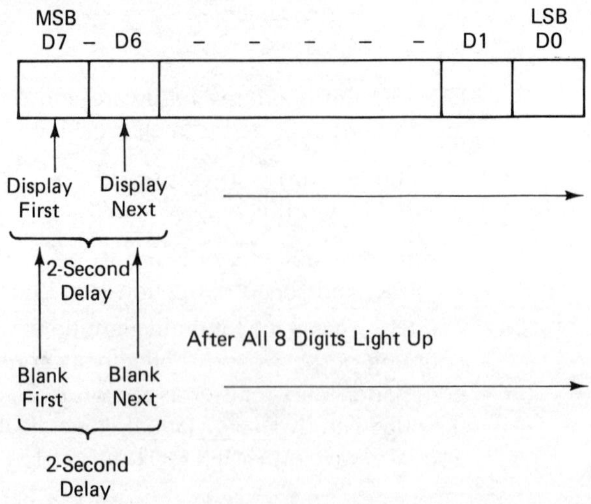

3.11. The data entry can be simulated with mechanical switches or keyboard, as shown in Figure 3.29. Consider that when a key is pressed, the corresponding column and row bits go high and the rest of them are at low level. For example:

Y_3	Y_2	Y_1	Y_0	X_3	X_2	X_1	X_0		Binary Code
1	0	0	0	0	1	0	0	→ Key 8 →	$(08)_{Hex}$
0	0	1	0	0	0	0	1	→ Key 2 →	$(02)_{Hex}$

Develop the necessary operating hardware and software to read keyboard data on to port B, generate a binary code corresponding to the key pressed, and store it in successive memory locations.

3.12. Switch Debounce: Due to vibrations, mechanical contacts produce bouncing and uncertain logic levels. Software debounce can be easily developed in which the logic state of the switch is examined periodically and if it is consistent, it is accepted; otherwise it is rejected.

Using 20 ms sampling time, observe the input data of the keyboard on port B as shown in Figure 3.29, and accept it if three consecutive samples result in the same keyboard data. Develop the necessary software routines. Shown is an example of X_0 bounce. If X_0 is consistently 1 when read three times, it is validated as 1.

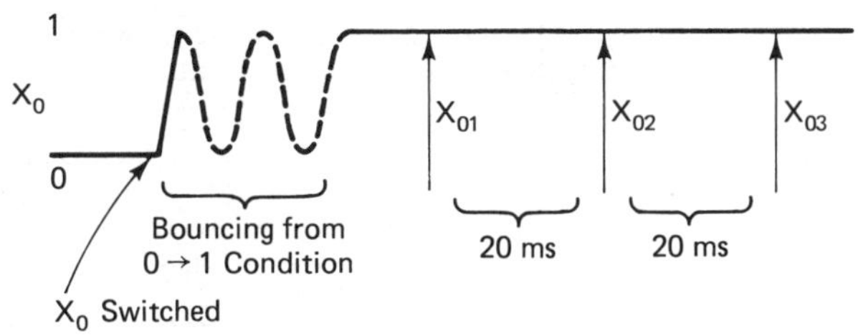

3.13. Develop the operating system with complete hardware and software to obtain information from port B through A hex keyboard interface as shown in Figure 3.29 and display it on the multiplexed 8-digit 7-segment display. The latest key pressed should be entered into LSB D0 position. D0 data should be shifted into D1, and so on.

In case of multiple key closure, reject the data, which is known as key lockout. Use the debounce routines of Problem 3.12.

3.14. Coded Data Generation: Frequency shift keying (FSK) is one way to digitally code the data for digital transmission, as shown in Figure 3.30. It is necessary to generate 9 cycles of 2 KHz square wave to represent logic 1 of digital data and 6 cycles of 1.33 KHz square wave to represent logic 0. Develop the operating hardware and software to obtain this coded digital data on the SOD output terminal. Consider that an 8-bit data word is available in C register of 8085, to be serially shifted out on SOD.

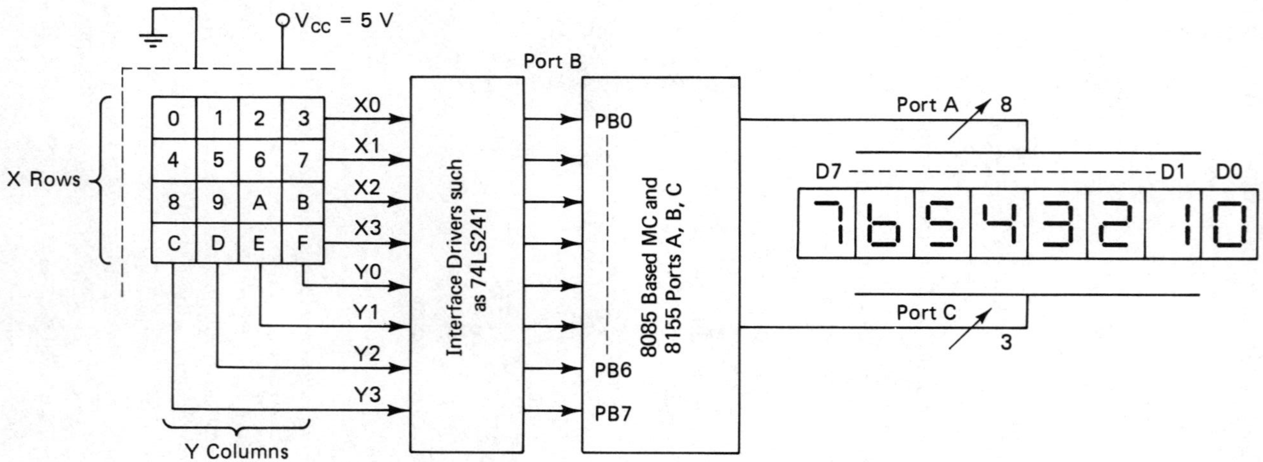

Fig 3.29. Typical interface and display for Problems 3.11, 3.12, and 3.13.

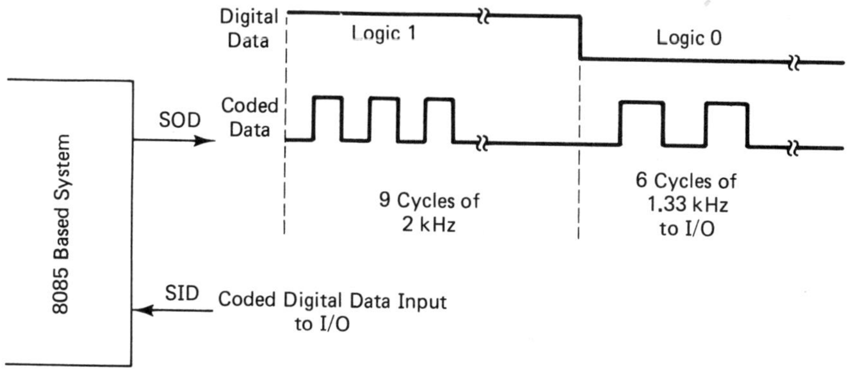

Fig 3.30. Digital coded data transmission and receiving for Problems 3.14, 3.15, and 3.16.

3.15. Any coded data should be capable of being decoded. Consider that coded digital data is entering SID input terminal as shown in Figure 3.30, with the same FSK format as Problem 3.14.

Develop and optimize software routines to reconstruct the digital data of 8 bits and store it in the D register of 8085.

3.16. Modem Interface: The coded digital data is usually converted to sinusoidal data through proper filters. Develop necessary hardware and software routines to accomplish this task.

3.17. Shown in Figure 3.16 is a typical cassette recorder interface to the SDK-85 system. Modify the system so that it is under control of port C of 8155 for remote control for On, Off, Fast Forward, Rewind, as shown. Develop the necessary software and hardware.

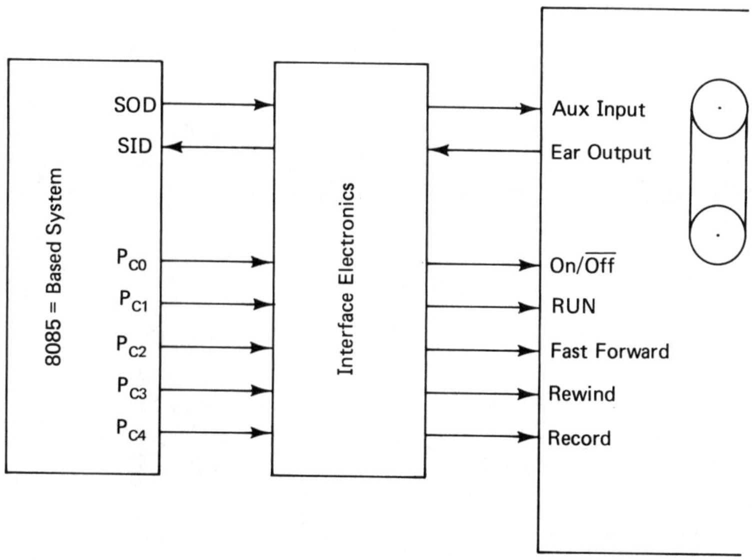

3.18. RS-232 Interface: RS-232 interface is general purpose and can be used for any serial data transmission. Using the format as shown, modify the cassette interface of Figure 3.16 so that the recorder is under the control of the micro. The Speed OK signal signifies that the recorder speed is OK and the data transfer can take place. Use all real hardware and software.

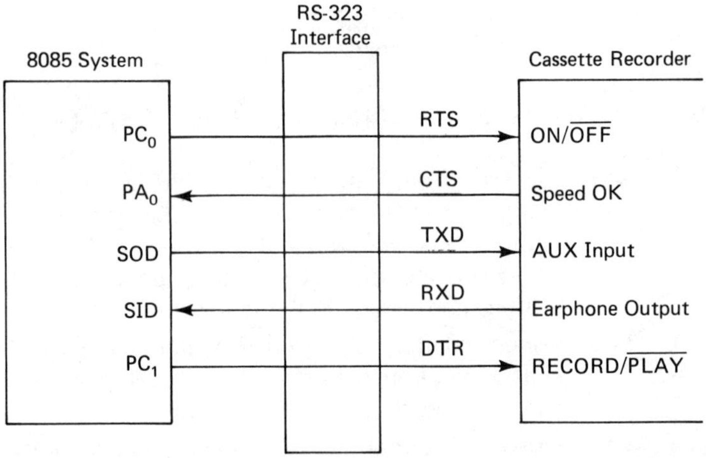

3.19. Repeat Problem 3.18., using FSK concepts for digital coding for the data.

3.20. Single-Chip Micro: Intel 8048 is an industry standard single-chip microcomputer and can be used in a multitude of applications. Develop the necessary hardware and software to produce the following waveforms, as shown: X_0 is 4 KHz square wave. (Hint: May be a counter.)

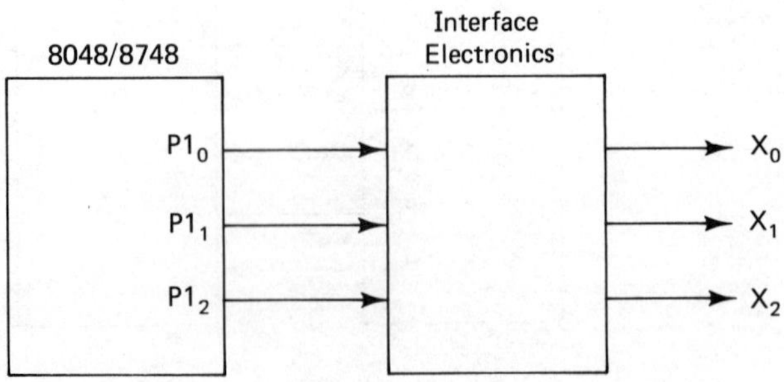

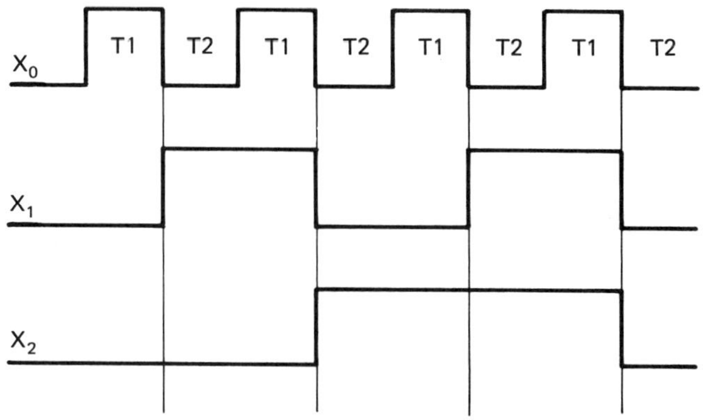

3.21. Repeat problem 3.20, where the waveforms are rectangular with

(a) T1 = 2T2

(b) T1 = 4T2

(c) T1 = 0.25T2

CHAPTER FOUR

M-6800 Microprocessor and Microcomputer System

The 6800 microprocessor developed and marketed by the Motorola Corporation is another 8-bit microprocessor fabricated with NMOS technology and contained in a 40-pin DIP package. The 6800 is extensively used in the control, communication, and auto industries because of its flexibility in the handling of I/O.

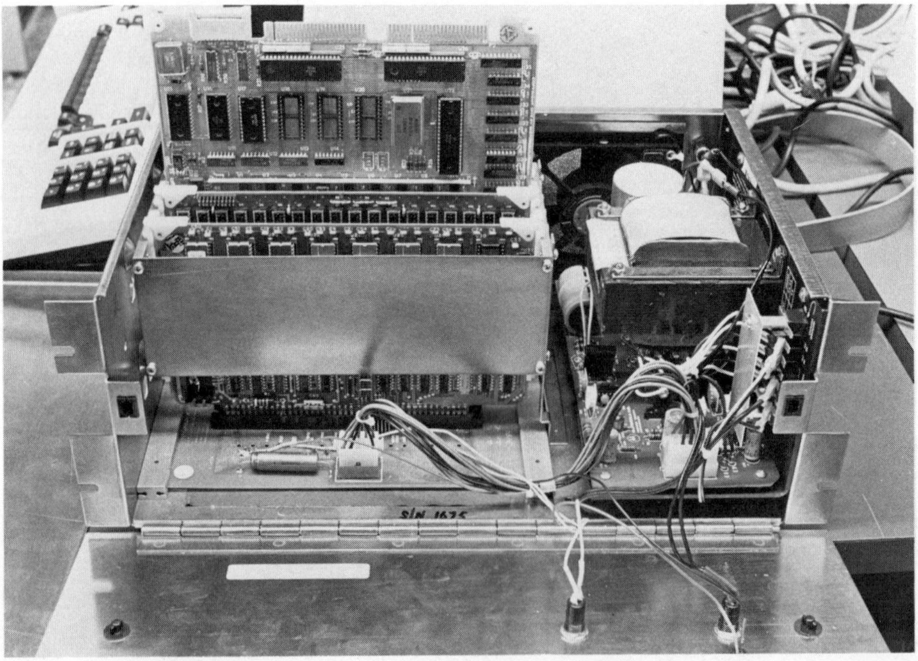

Typical 6800-based system with I/O (courtesy: Motorola Inc.).

4.1. GENERAL ARCHITECTURE

Figure 4.1 shows the architectural features of the 6800 microprocessor. The device has a much simpler structure than the 8085, but it has a more complex addressing scheme.

Registers, Flags, and Bus Structure

As shown in Figure 4.1, the 6800 consists of

16-bit program counter	PC
16-bit stack pointer	SP
16-bit index register	X
8-bit accumulator A	A
8-bit accumulator B	B
8-bit arithmetic/logic unit	ALU
8-bit condition code or flag register	CCR

The 16-bit program counter generates a 16-bit address, capable of addressing 64K locations of memory.

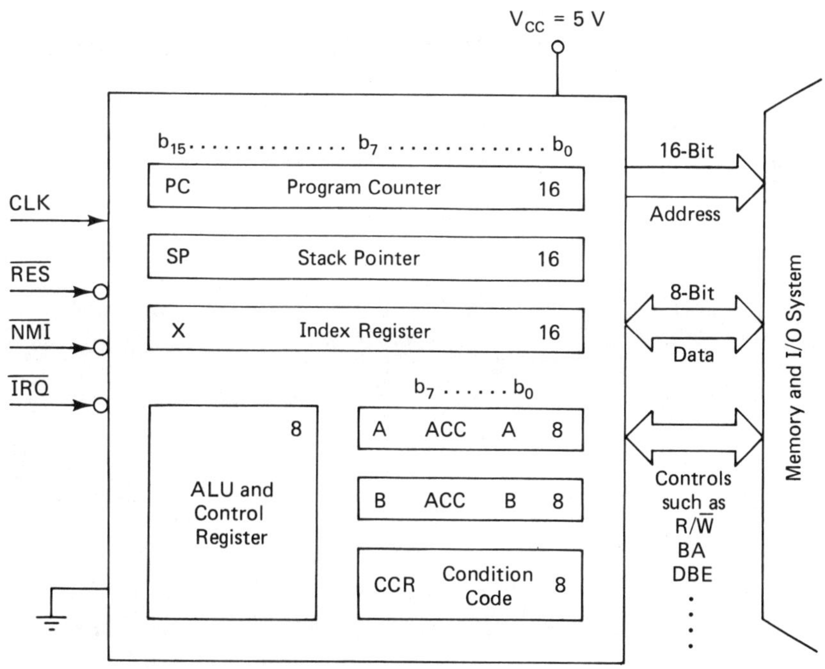

Fig 4.1. The 6800 microprocessor architecture.

The 16-bit stack pointer can set up stack anywhere in the 64K memory field.

The 16-bit index register X can be used as a general purpose storage element or as a counter. It is also used as a memory pointer in the indexed addressing mode.

The two 8-bit accumulators A and B are general purpose registers, capable of data manipulations. They can also be used as counters, data exchangers, and so on. This double accumulator feature is highly efficient and flexible in I/O bound applications, as we will see later.

The 8-bit arithmetic logic unit (ALU) is capable of all arithmetic and logical operations. The control unit generates all timing waveforms for internal data manipulations.

Flags

The condition code register (CCR) contains six effective flag bits. These are set or reset according to the previous operations performed, and the information is used in the decision-making process. Figure 4.2 shows the formatting of the CCR. You are advised to study and comprehend the CCR functions, as they will be used extensively in all the system applications.

Buses

The 16-bit unidirectional address bus can address up to 64K (actually 65,536) locations of memory, as shown in Figure 4.1.

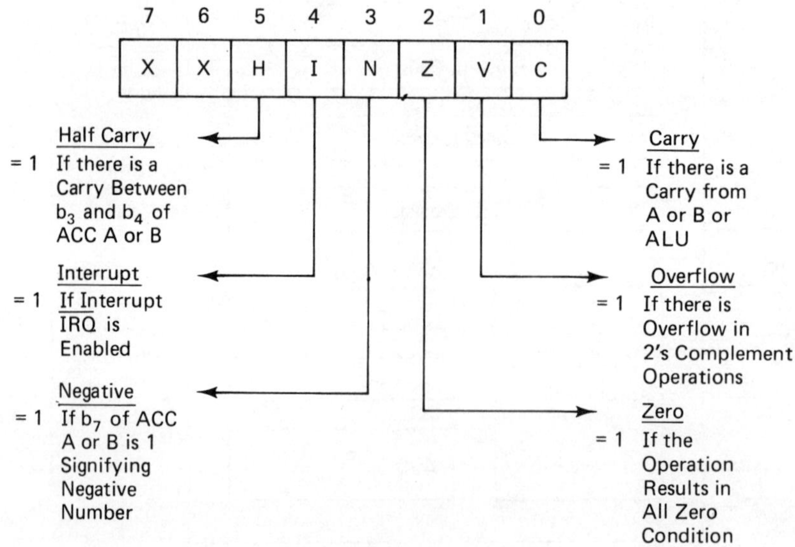

Fig 4.2. The flag structure of the condition code register.

The 8-bit bidirectional data bus communicates the data between the microprocessor and the memory. During the read cycle data flows from the memory to the microprocessor, and during the write cycle, data flows from the microprocessor to the memory.

The control bus consists of control signals such as Read/$\overline{\text{Write}}$, Halt..., etc. and controls the data flow and the buses.

Reset and Interrupt Structure

The 6800 is characterized by three hardware interrupt type signals: $\overline{\text{RES}}$ (reset), $\overline{\text{NMI}}$ (non-maskable interrupt), and $\overline{\text{IRQ}}$ (interrupt request). All are low active. On the occurrence of $\overline{\text{NMI}}$ or $\overline{\text{IRQ}}$ signals, the microprocessor will conclude the execution of the current instruction and store the CPU registers PC, X, A, B, and CCR on the stack. Then it will load the PC with the contents of the respective vectored address locations (as shown in Table 4.1) to execute the corresponding interrupt service routines (starting at the locations, as specified by the program counter). The last instruction of any interrupt service routine will be RTI (return from interrupt). On encountering RTI, the microprocessor will restore all the registers from the stack and return to the main program. Similar events occur for software interrupt (SWI).

In case of $\overline{\text{RES}}$ (reset), PC will be loaded with the contents of the reset vectored address location (Table 4.1) and the reset routine will be executed. In most cases, $\overline{\text{RES}}$ will take the system to an initialization routine contained in the monitor part of the system.

$\overline{\text{RES}}$ has the highest priority. $\overline{\text{NMI}}$, which cannot be masked, has the next priority. $\overline{\text{IRQ}}$, which can be masked by software instructions, has the lowest priority.

We will now clarify the concepts introduced above, with a few example problems.

Table 4.1. Reset and Interrupt Definitions and Vectors.

Name	*Priority (0 = highest)*	*Maskability*	*Vector Address (H = high; L = low byte)*
$\overline{\text{Reset}}$	0	Nonmaskable	FFFF ⇒ Low byte FFFE ⇒ High byte
$\overline{\text{NMI}}$	1	Nonmaskable	FFFD ⇒ Low byte FFFC ⇒ High byte
SWI	(Software)	Not Applicable	FFFB ⇒ Low byte FFFA ⇒ High byte
$\overline{\text{IRQ}}$	2	Maskable	FFF9 ⇒ Low byte FFF8 ⇒ High byte

Example 4.1 Flags

In a particular data-processing application, accumulators B and A contain $(7B)_{Hex}$ and $(CD)_{Hex}$. They are added together and stored in accumulator A.

(a) What are the contents of the condition code register (CCR), after addition?
(b) What are the contents of CCR if B is subtracted from A, with the result in A?

Solution

(a) *Addition and Flag Bits.* The contents of accumulator A are as shown before and after addition:

			b_7							b_0
A before addition	= $(CD)_{Hex}$	=	1	1	0	0	1	1	0	1
Data from B	= $(7B)_{Hex}$	=	0	1	1	1	1	0	1	1
A after addition	= $(48)_{Hex}$	=	0	1	0	0	1	0	0	0
	With carry	=	1							

CCR contents = $(21)_{Hex}$

b_5					b_0
H	I	N	Z	V	C
1	0	0	0	0	1

Half carry and carry are 1 because of overflow from b_3 and b_7. Interrupt, negative, zero, and overflow flags are all zero (interrupt is not activated, b_7 of accumulator is not 1, the contents of A are not zero, and there is no 2s complement overflow).

(b) *Subtraction and Flag Bits.*

A − B = (CD) − (7B) = $(52)_{Hex}$ = 0 1 0 1 0 0 1 0
CCR contents

H	I	N	Z	V	C	
0	0	0	0	0	0	= $(00)_{Hex}$

Example 4.2 Interrupts

As shown in Figure 4.3, the 6800 is controlling the air conditioning and the lift systems in a building. The lift system generates an interrupt whenever the

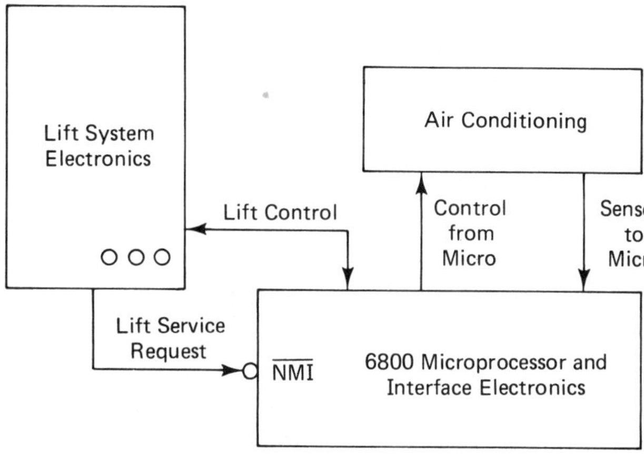

Fig 4.3. The 6800 microprocessor control and interrupt operation (Example 4.2).

lift is to be operated. The micro otherwise normally will be executing the air condition control program.

(a) Outline the sequence of events when $\overline{\text{NMI}}$ is activated.

(b) How many bytes of stack memory are required to store the CPU registers, before executing the interrupt service routine (ISR) for $\overline{\text{NMI}}$?

(c) If $\overline{\text{RESET}}$ occurs during the execution of ISR, specify the sequence of events.

Solution:

(a) *$\overline{\text{NMI}}$ Interrupt*. On the occurrence of $\overline{\text{NMI}}$ negative transition, the microprocessor concludes the execution of the current instruction, stores all its CPU registers on stack, and obtains the $\overline{\text{NMI}}$ address vector from the locations FFFD and FFFC and loads it in the program counter. It will then start executing the $\overline{\text{NMI}}$ routine at the vectored location specified by the program counter, as shown. (Refer to Table 4.1 also).

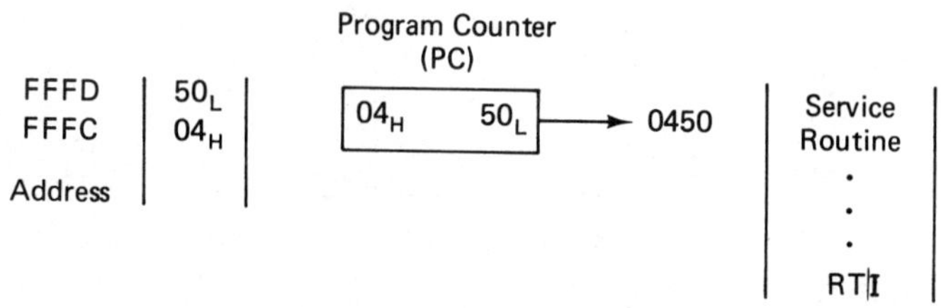

In this case, PC will be loaded with 0450, which is the location where the ISR starts. At the end of the ISR, when a return from interrupt (RTI) instruction is encountered, the micro recovers the registers from the stack and goes back to the main program it was executing before the occurrence of $\overline{\text{NMI}}$.

(b) *Stack Memory*. Referring to Figure 4.1, a total of seven stack locations are required to store PC (two bytes), X (two bytes), A, B, and CCR (one byte each). SP keeps track of the next available location on stack (SP decrements after each entry on stack).

(c) $\overline{\textit{RESET}}$. The micro suspends all its activity and obtains the RESET vectored address (Table 4.1) and starts executing the RESET routine, as shown. For example,

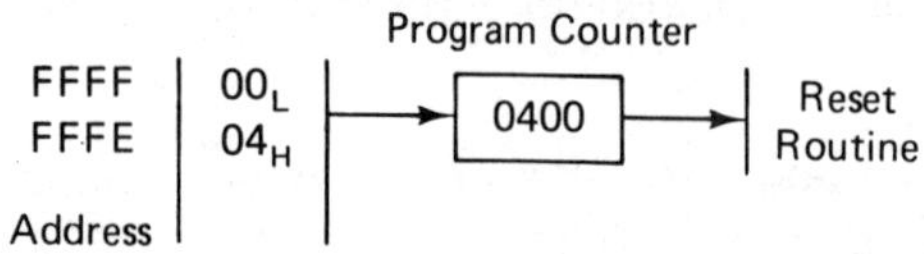

In this case the reset routine will start at 0400. There is no necessity to store any registers on stack. All these will be loaded with the default values, which the reset routine will determine. In most systems, the reset routine will be the same as the system initialization.

A study of Examples 4.1 and 4.2 should provide you with an insight into the architectural features of the 6800 microprocessor. We will now turn our attention to the instruction set and addressing modes of the 6800 family of microprocessors.

4.2. INSTRUCTION SET AND ADDRESSING MODES

The powerful manipulative power for the 6800 microprocessor comes from its flexible instruction set and associated addressing modes. Some of the instructions have the same mnemonics, but are characterized by different op codes corresponding to the different addressing modes.

Mnemonics and Op Codes

Table 4.2 shows the mnemonic and op codes for the 6800 family, along with the respective addressing modes. We suggest that you go through Table 4.2 several times to become familiar with the instruction set.

Table 4.2. M6800 IS (Courtesy of Motorola, Inc.)

MPU INSTRUCTION SET

The MC6800 has a set of 72 different instructions. Included are binary and decimal arithmetic, logical, shift, rotate, load, store, conditional or unconditional branch, interrupt and stack manipulation instructions.

MPU ADDRESSING MODES

The MC6800 eight-bit microprocessing unit has seven address modes that can be used by a programmer, with the addressing mode a function of both the type of instruction and the coding within the instruction.

Accumulator (ACCX) Addressing — In accumulator addressing, either accumulator A or accumulator B is specified. These are one-byte instructions.

Immediate Addressing — In immediate addressing, the operand is contained in the second byte of the instruction except LDS and LDX which have the operand in the second and third bytes of the instruction. The MPU addresses this location when it fetches the immediate instruction for execution. These are two or three-byte instructions.

Direct Addressing — In direct addressing, the address of the operand is contained in the second byte of the instruction. Direct addressing allows the user to directly address the lowest 256 bytes in the machine i.e., locations zero through 255. Enhanced execution times are achieved by storing data in these locations. In most configurations, it should be a random access memory. These are two-byte instructions.

Extended Addressing — In extended addressing, the address contained in the second byte of the instruction is used as the higher eight-bits of the address of the operand. The third byte of the instruction is used as the lower eight-bits of the address for the operand. This is an absolute address in memory. These are three-byte instructions.

Indexed Addressing — In indexed addressing, the address contained in the second byte of the instruction is added to the index register's lowest eight bits in the MPU. The carry is then added to the higher order eight bits of the index register. This result is then used to address memory. The modified address is held in a temporary address register so there is no change to the index register. These are two-byte instructions.

Implied Addressing — In the implied addressing mode the instruction gives the address (i.e., stack pointer, index register, etc.). These are one-byte instructions.

Relative Addressing — In relative addressing, the address contained in the second byte of the instruction is added to the program counter's lowest eight bits plus two. The carry or borrow is then added to the high eight bits.

MICROPROCESSOR INSTRUCTION SET — ALPHABETIC SEQUENCE

ABA	Add Accumulators
ADC	Add with Carry
ADD	Add
AND	Logical And
ASL	Arithmetic Shift Left
ASR	Arithmetic Shift Right
BCC	Branch if Carry Clear
BCS	Branch if Carry Set
BEQ	Branch if Equal to Zero
BGE	Branch if Greater or Equal Zero
BGT	Branch if Greater than Zero
BHI	Branch if Higher
BIT	Bit Test
BLE	Branch if Less or Equal
BLS	Branch if Lower or Same
BLT	Branch if Less than Zero
BMI	Branch if Minus
BNE	Branch if Not Equal to Zero
BPL	Branch if Plus
BRA	Branch Always
BSR	Branch to Subroutine
BVC	Branch if Overflow Clear
BVS	Branch if Overflow Set
CBA	Compare Accumulators
CLC	Clear Carry
CLI	Clear Interrupt Mask
CLR	Clear
CLV	Clear Overflow
CMP	Compare

Table 4.2. *(Continued)*

COM	Complement	ROL	Rotate Left
CPX	Compare Index Register	ROR	Rotate Right
		RTI	Return from Interrupt
DAA	Decimal Adjust	RTS	Return from Subroutine
DEC	Decrement		
DES	Decrement Stack Pointer	SBA	Subtract Accumulators
DEX	Decrement Index Register	SBC	Subtract with Carry
		SEC	Set Carry
EOR	Exclusive OR	SEI	Set Interrupt Mask
		SEV	Set Overflow
INC	Increment	STA	Store Accumulator
INS	Increment Stack Pointer	STS	Store Stack Register
INX	Increment Index Register	STX	Store Index Register
		SUB	Subtract
JMP	Jump	SWI	Software Interrupt
JSR	Jump to Subroutine		
LDA	Load Accumulator	TAB	Transfer Accumulators
LDS	Load Stack Pointer	TAP	Transfer Accumulators to Condition Code Reg.
LDX	Load Index Register	TBA	Transfer Accumulators
LSR	Logical Shift Right	TPA	Transfer Condition Code Reg. to Accumulator
NEG	Negate	TST	Test
NOP	No Operation	TSX	Transfer Stack Pointer to Index Register
ORA	Inclusive OR Accumulator	TXS	Transfer Index Register to Stack Pointer
PSH	Push Data		
PUL	Pull Data	WAI	Wait for Interrupt

ACCUMULATOR AND MEMORY		ADDRESSING MODES: IMMED			DIRECT			INDEX			EXTND			INHER			BOOLEAN/ARITHMETIC OPERATION (All register labels refer to contents)	COND. CODE REG. 5	4	3	2	1	0
OPERATIONS	MNEMONIC	OP	~	#	OP	~	#	OP	~	#	OP	~	#	OP	~	#		H	I	N	Z	V	C
Add	ADDA	8B	2	2	9B	3	2	AB	5	2	BB	4	3				A + M → A	↕	•	↕	↕	↕	↕
	ADDB	CB	2	2	DB	3	2	EB	5	2	FB	4	3				B + M → B	↕	•	↕	↕	↕	↕
Add Acmltrs	ABA													1B	2	1	A + B → A	↕	•	↕	↕	↕	↕
Add with Carry	ADCA	89	2	2	99	3	2	A9	5	2	B9	4	3				A + M + C → A	↕	•	↕	↕	↕	↕
	ADCB	C9	2	2	D9	3	2	E9	5	2	F9	4	3				B + M + C → B	↕	•	↕	↕	↕	↕
And	ANDA	84	2	2	94	3	2	A4	5	2	B4	4	3				A • M → A	•	•	↕	↕	R	•
	ANDB	C4	2	2	D4	3	2	E4	5	2	F4	4	3				B • M → B	•	•	↕	↕	R	•
Bit Test	BITA	85	2	2	95	3	2	A5	5	2	B5	4	3				A • M	•	•	↕	↕	R	•
	BITB	C5	2	2	D5	3	2	E5	5	2	F5	4	3				B • M	•	•	↕	↕	R	•
Clear	CLR							6F	7	2	7F	6	3				00 → M	•	•	R	S	R	R
	CLRA													4F	2	1	00 → A	•	•	R	S	R	R
	CLRB													5F	2	1	00 → B	•	•	R	S	R	R
Compare	CMPA	81	2	2	91	3	2	A1	5	2	B1	4	3				A − M	•	•	↕	↕	↕	↕
	CMPB	C1	2	2	D1	3	2	E1	5	2	F1	4	3				B − M	•	•	↕	↕	↕	↕
Compare Acmltrs	CBA													11	2	1	A − B	•	•	↕	↕	↕	↕
Complement, 1's	COM							63	7	2	73	6	3				$\bar{M}$ → M	•	•	↕	↕	R	S
	COMA													43	2	1	$\bar{A}$ → A	•	•	↕	↕	R	S
	COMB													53	2	1	$\bar{B}$ → B	•	•	↕	↕	R	S
Complement, 2's	NEG							60	7	2	70	6	3				00 − M → M	•	•	↕	↕	①	②
(Negate)	NEGA													40	2	1	00 − A → A	•	•	↕	↕	①	②
	NEGB													50	2	1	00 − B → B	•	•	↕	↕	①	②
Decimal Adjust, A	DAA													19	2	1	Converts Binary Add. of BCD Characters into BCD Format	•	•	↕	↕	↕	③
Decrement	DEC							6A	7	2	7A	6	3				M − 1 → M	•	•	↕	↕	④	•
	DECA													4A	2	1	A − 1 → A	•	•	↕	↕	④	•
	DECB													5A	2	1	B − 1 → B	•	•	↕	↕	④	•
Exclusive OR	EORA	88	2	2	98	3	2	A8	5	2	B8	4	3				A ⊕ M → A	•	•	↕	↕	R	•
	EORB	C8	2	2	D8	3	2	E8	5	2	F8	4	3				B ⊕ M → B	•	•	↕	↕	R	•
Increment	INC							6C	7	2	7C	6	3				M + 1 → M	•	•	↕	↕	⑤	•
	INCA													4C	2	1	A + 1 → A	•	•	↕	↕	⑤	•
	INCB													5C	2	1	B + 1 → B	•	•	↕	↕	⑤	•
Load Acmltr	LDAA	86	2	2	96	3	2	A6	5	2	B6	4	3				M → A	•	•	↕	↕	R	•
	LDAB	C6	2	2	D6	3	2	E6	5	2	F6	4	3				M → B	•	•	↕	↕	R	•
Or, Inclusive	ORAA	8A	2	2	9A	3	2	AA	5	2	BA	4	3				A + M → A	•	•	↕	↕	R	•
	ORAB	CA	2	2	DA	3	2	EA	5	2	FA	4	3				B + M → B	•	•	↕	↕	R	•
Push Data	PSHA													36	4	1	A → M_{SP}, SP − 1 → SP	•	•	•	•	•	•
	PSHB													37	4	1	B → M_{SP}, SP − 1 → SP	•	•	•	•	•	•
Pull Data	PULA													32	4	1	SP + 1 → SP, M_{SP} → A	•	•	•	•	•	•
	PULB													33	4	1	SP + 1 → SP, M_{SP} → B	•	•	•	•	•	•
Rotate Left	ROL							69	7	2	79	6	3				M	•	•	↕	↕	⑥	↕
	ROLA													49	2	1	A } C ← b_7 ← b_0	•	•	↕	↕	⑥	↕
	ROLB													59	2	1	B	•	•	↕	↕	⑥	↕
Rotate Right	ROR							66	7	2	76	6	3				M	•	•	↕	↕	⑥	↕
	RORA													46	2	1	A } C → b_7 → b_0	•	•	↕	↕	⑥	↕
	RORB													56	2	1	B	•	•	↕	↕	⑥	↕
Shift Left, Arithmetic	ASL							68	7	2	78	6	3				M	•	•	↕	↕	⑥	↕
	ASLA													48	2	1	A } C ← b_7 b_0 ← 0	•	•	↕	↕	⑥	↕
	ASLB													58	2	1	B	•	•	↕	↕	⑥	↕
Shift Right, Arithmetic	ASR							67	7	2	77	6	3				M	•	•	↕	↕	⑥	↕
	ASRA													47	2	1	A } b_7 b_0 → C	•	•	↕	↕	⑥	↕
	ASRB													57	2	1	B	•	•	↕	↕	⑥	↕
Shift Right, Logic.	LSR							64	7	2	74	6	3				M	•	•	R	↕	⑥	↕
	LSRA													44	2	1	A } 0 → b_7 b_0 → C	•	•	R	↕	⑥	↕
	LSRB													54	2	1	B	•	•	R	↕	⑥	↕
Store Acmltr.	STAA				97	4	2	A7	6	2	B7	5	3				A → M	•	•	↕	↕	R	•
	STAB				D7	4	2	E7	6	2	F7	5	3				B → M	•	•	↕	↕	R	•
Subtract	SUBA	80	2	2	90	3	2	A0	5	2	B0	4	3				A − M → A	•	•	↕	↕	↕	↕
	SUBB	C0	2	2	D0	3	2	E0	5	2	F0	4	3				B − M → B	•	•	↕	↕	↕	↕
Subract Acmltrs.	SBA													10	2	1	A − B → A	•	•	↕	↕	↕	↕
Subtr. with Carry	SBCA	82	2	2	92	3	2	A2	5	2	B2	4	3				A − M − C → A	•	•	↕	↕	↕	↕
	SBCB	C2	2	2	D2	3	2	E2	5	2	F2	4	3				B − M − C → B	•	•	↕	↕	↕	↕
Transfer Acmltrs	TAB													16	2	1	A → B	•	•	↕	↕	R	•
	TBA													17	2	1	B → A	•	•	↕	↕	R	•
Test, Zero or Minus	TST							6D	7	2	7D	6	3				M − 00	•	•	↕	↕	R	R
	TSTA													4D	2	1	A − 00	•	•	↕	↕	R	R
	TSTB													5D	2	1	B − 00	•	•	↕	↕	R	R

Table 4.2. *(Continued)*

INDEX REGISTER AND STACK POINTER OPERATIONS	MNEMONIC	IMMED OP	IMMED ~	IMMED #	DIRECT OP	DIRECT ~	DIRECT #	INDEX OP	INDEX ~	INDEX #	EXTND OP	EXTND ~	EXTND #	INHER OP	INHER ~	INHER #	BOOLEAN/ARITHMETIC OPERATION	5 H	4 I	3 N	2 Z	1 V	0 C
Compare Index Reg	CPX	8C	3	3	9C	4	2	AC	6	2	BC	5	3				$(X_H/X_L) - (M/M+1)$	•	•	(7)	↕	(8)	•
Decrement Index Reg	DEX													09	4	1	$X - 1 \rightarrow X$	•	•	•	↕	•	•
Decrement Stack Pntr	DES													34	4	1	$SP - 1 \rightarrow SP$	•	•	•	•	•	•
Increment Index Reg	INX													08	4	1	$X + 1 \rightarrow X$	•	•	•	↕	•	•
Increment Stack Pntr	INS													31	4	1	$SP + 1 \rightarrow SP$	•	•	•	•	•	•
Load Index Reg	LDX	CE	3	3	DE	4	2	EE	6	2	FE	5	3				$M \rightarrow X_H, (M+1) \rightarrow X_L$	•	•	(9)	↕	R	•
Load Stack Pntr	LDS	8E	3	3	9E	4	2	AE	6	2	BE	5	3				$M \rightarrow SP_H, (M+1) \rightarrow SP_L$	•	•	(9)	↕	R	•
Store Index Reg	STX				DF	5	2	EF	7	2	FF	6	3				$X_H \rightarrow M, X_L \rightarrow (M+1)$	•	•	(9)	↕	R	•
Store Stack Pntr	STS				9F	5	2	AF	7	2	BF	6	3				$SP_H \rightarrow M, SP_L \rightarrow (M+1)$	•	•	(9)	↕	R	•
Indx Reg → Stack Pntr	TXS													35	4	1	$X - 1 \rightarrow SP$	•	•	•	•	•	•
Stack Pntr → Indx Reg	TSX													30	4	1	$SP + 1 \rightarrow X$	•	•	•	•	•	•

JUMP AND BRANCH OPERATIONS	MNEMONIC	RELATIVE OP	RELATIVE ~	RELATIVE #	INDEX OP	INDEX ~	INDEX #	EXTND OP	EXTND ~	EXTND #	INHER OP	INHER ~	INHER #	BRANCH TEST	5 H	4 I	3 N	2 Z	1 V	0 C
Branch Always	BRA	20	4	2										None	•	•	•	•	•	•
Branch If Carry Clear	BCC	24	4	2										C = 0	•	•	•	•	•	•
Branch If Carry Set	BCS	25	4	2										C = 1	•	•	•	•	•	•
Branch If = Zero	BEQ	27	4	2										Z = 1	•	•	•	•	•	•
Branch If ⩾ Zero	BGE	2C	4	2										$N \oplus V = 0$	•	•	•	•	•	•
Branch If > Zero	BGT	2E	4	2										$Z + (N \oplus V) = 0$	•	•	•	•	•	•
Branch If Higher	BHI	22	4	2										$C + Z = 0$	•	•	•	•	•	•
Branch If ⩽ Zero	BLE	2F	4	2										$Z + (N \oplus V) = 1$	•	•	•	•	•	•
Branch If Lower Or Same	BLS	23	4	2										$C + Z = 1$	•	•	•	•	•	•
Branch If < Zero	BLT	2D	4	2										$N \oplus V = 1$	•	•	•	•	•	•
Branch If Minus	BMI	2B	4	2										N = 1	•	•	•	•	•	•
Branch If Not Equal Zero	BNE	26	4	2										Z = 0	•	•	•	•	•	•
Branch If Overflow Clear	BVC	28	4	2										V = 0	•	•	•	•	•	•
Branch If Overflow Set	BVS	29	4	2										V = 1	•	•	•	•	•	•
Branch If Plus	BPL	2A	4	2										N = 0	•	•	•	•	•	•
Branch To Subroutine	BSR	8D	8	2										See Special Operations	•	•	•	•	•	•
Jump	JMP				6E	4	2	7E	3	3				See Special Operations	•	•	•	•	•	•
Jump To Subroutine	JSR				AD	8	2	BD	9	3				See Special Operations	•	•	•	•	•	•
No Operation	NOP										01	2	1	Advances Prog. Cntr. Only	•	•	•	•	•	•
Return From Interrupt	RTI										3B	10	1	See special Operations	(10)					
Return From Subroutine	RTS										39	5	1	See special Operations	•	•	•	•	•	•
Software Interrupt	SWI										3F	12	1	See special Operations	•	S	•	•	•	•
Wait for Interrupt	WAI										3E	9	1	See special Operations	•	(11)	•	•	•	•

CONDITIONS CODE REGISTER OPERATIONS	MNEMONIC	INHER OP	INHER ~	INHER =	BOOLEAN OPERATION	5 H	4 I	3 N	2 Z	1 V	0 C
Clear Carry	CLC	0C	2	1	$0 \rightarrow C$	•	•	•	•	•	R
Clear Interrupt Mask	CLI	0E	2	1	$0 \rightarrow I$	•	R	•	•	•	•
Clear Overflow	CLV	0A	2	1	$0 \rightarrow V$	•	•	•	•	R	•
Set Carry	SEC	0D	2	1	$1 \rightarrow C$	•	•	•	•	•	S
Set Interrupt Mask	SEI	0F	2	1	$1 \rightarrow I$	•	S	•	•	•	•
Set Overflow	SEV	0B	2	1	$1 \rightarrow V$	•	•	•	•	S	•
Acmltr A → CCR	TAP	06	2	1	$A \rightarrow CCR$	(12)					
CCR → Acmltr A	TPA	07	2	1	$CCR \rightarrow A$	•	•	•	•	•	•

CONDITION CODE REGISTER NOTES:

(Bit set if test is true and cleared otherwise)

(1) (Bit V) Test: Result = 10000000?
(2) (Bit C) Test: Result = 00000000?
(3) (Bit C) Test: Decimal value of most significant BCD Character greater than nine? (Not cleared if previously set.)
(4) (Bit V) Test: Operand = 10000000 prior to execution?
(5) (Bit V) Test: Operand = 01111111 prior to execution?
(6) (Bit V) Test: Set equal to result of $N \oplus C$ after shift has occurred.
(7) (Bit N) Test: Sign bit of most significant (MS) byte of result = 1?
(8) (Bit V) Test: 2's complement overflow from subtraction of LS bytes?
(9) (Bit N) Test: Result less than zero? (Bit 15 = 1)
(10) (All) Load Condition Code Register from Stack. (See Special Operations)
(11) (Bit I) Set when interrupt occurs. If previously set, a Non-Maskable Interrupt is required to exit the wait state.
(12) (ALL) Set according to the contents of Accumulator A.

LEGEND:

OP Operation Code (Hexadecimal);
~ Number of MPU Cycles;
# Number of Program Bytes;
+ Arithmetic Plus;
− Arithmetic Minus;
• Boolean AND;
M_{SP} Contents of memory location pointed to be Stack Pointer;
+ Boolean Inclusive OR;
⊕ Boolean Exclusive OR;
$\overline{M}$ Complement of M;
→ Transfer Into;
0 Bit = Zero;
00 Byte = Zero;
H Half-carry from bit 3;
I Interrupt mask
N Negative (sign bit)
Z Zero (byte)
V Overflow, 2's complement
C Carry from bit 7
R Reset Always
S Set Always
↕ Test and set if true, cleared otherwise
• Not Affected
CCR Condition Code Register
LS Least Significant
MS Most Significant

As shown in Figure 4.4, the first byte of the instruction is always the op code. Depending on the addressing mode, the second and third bytes of the instruction may contain the data or the address of the data.

Addressing Modes

A clear understanding of the addressing modes greatly enhances the usability of the instruction set.

1. Immediate Addressing: Data to be operated are part of the instruction and are contained in byte 2 or bytes 2 and 3 (depending on 8-bit or 16-bit data).
   Example:

Mnemonic	Op Code	
LDA A	86	Load accumulator A with
#3F		immediate data of 3F.
LDX	CE	Load index register X
42_H		with immediate data
04_L		of (4204).

2. Direct Addressing: Address of the data or operand is contained in the second byte of the instruction, which is in page zero.
   Example:

ADD B	DB	Add contents of
F3		location F3 to
		accumulator B.

3. Extended Addressing: The address of data or operand is contained in the second and third bytes of the instruction.
   Example:

CMPA	B1	Compare accumulator A
43_H		with contents of
27_L		location 4327.

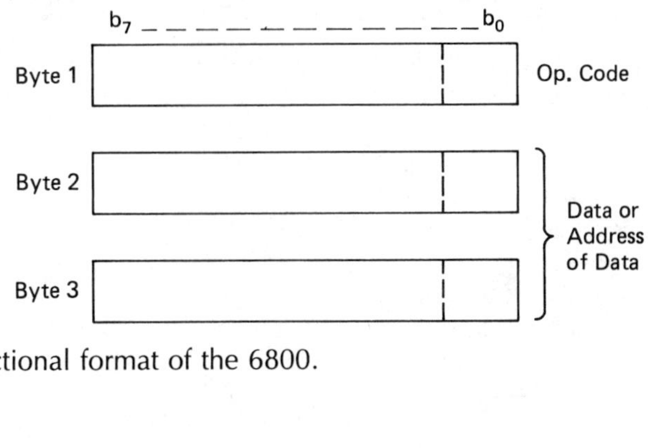

Fig 4.4. The instructional format of the 6800.

4. Indexed Addressing: The effective address of the data or operand is formulated by adding the second byte of instruction to the contents of the X index register. This addressing mode is very powerful in setting up memory tables.

   Example (Consider X register contains 4204 and accumulator A contains 3F):

STA A, X 72	A7	Contents of A are stored at effective location of (4204) + (72) = 4276:

   Thus location $(4276)_{Hex}$ contains 3F after the execution of the instruction.

5. Inherent Addressing: Single-byte instruction, always referring to a CPU register.

   Example:

DES	34	Decrement stack pointer

6. Relative Addressing: The second byte is added as an offset to the contents of the program counter to form an effective branching address. For branching back, 2's complement addition is used. All the conditional and unconditional branch instructions use this mode of addressing. It can branch 127 bytes forward or 128 bytes backward, from the current location of the program counter.

   Example (Consider that PC contains 0500):

Location	*Mnemonic*	*Op Code*	
0500	BRA	20	Relative
0501	02		
0502	LDA A	86	Immediate
0503	#37		
0504	NOP	01	Inherent
0505	NOP	01	Inherent

   When the unconditional branch instruction (BRA) is executed, the program branches to effective address given by

0502	+	02	=	0504
(current location of PC)		(offset)		(effective address)

   and executes the corresponding instruction, which is NOP in this case.

Example 4.3 6800 Software

In a data acquisition system software, the following program is being run.

Location	*Mnemonic*	*Op Code*	*Mode*	*Comment*
0500	LDX	CE	Immediate	Load X with immediate data of 0200.
01	$\#02_H$			
02	00_L			
03	LDA A	86	Immediate	Load A with immediate data of 00.
04	#00			
05	STAA, X	A7	Index	Store A at indexed location of X + 00.
06	00			
07	INCA	4C	Inherent	Increment A.
08	INX	08	Inherent	Increment X.
09	CPX	8C	Immediate	Compare X with immediate data of 0300.
0A	03_H			
0B	00_L			
0C	BNE	26	Relative	If X is not equal to 0300, branch back to 0505.
0D	F7			
0E	STA A	B7	Extended	Store A at 0350 location.
0F	03_H			
0510	50_L			
11	NOP	01	Inherent	No operation.

(a) What is being accomplished in the program?

(b) What are the contents of X and A at 0511?

Solution

(a) *The Program.* Between 0500 to 0504, X and accumulator A are loaded with immediate data of 0200 and 00.

Between 0505 and 050D, the contents of A are sequentially incremented and stored in page 2 between 0200 and 02FF, using the indexed addressing mode. Each time the program is run, A and X are incremented, and X is compared with 0300.

If X is not equal to 0300, the program is branched back (via BNE instruction at 050C) to:

050E	+	F7	=	0505
PC Current Location		Offset		(Using 2's complement addition)

The memory thus contains:

Location	*Contents*
0200	00
0201	01
02FF	FF

When X is incremented up to 0300, the program advances beyond the BNE instruction, and the contents of A are stored at location 0350.

(b) *Contents of X and A (at 0511):*
X contains 0300
A contains FF

4.3. 6800-BASED MICROCOMPUTER CONFIGURATION

As mentioned in earlier chapters, any microprocessor has to be interfaced with memory and I/O devices to form a microcomputer configuration for system applications. Figure 4.5 shows a typical 6800-based microcomputer configuration.

System Components and Structure (Figure 4.5)

128 × 8 RAM:6810

This random access memory (RAM) is for the user program and data storage. Several of these devices (24-pin NMOS dip) can be connected to the 6800 bus to expand the memory capability of the system.

1K × 8 ROM:6830

This read only memory (ROM) is mask programmable and usually contains the system operating, monitor, and other utility programs (to help initiate the microcomputer system and run such programs as keyboard data entry, etc.)

PIA (Peripheral Interface Adapter) 6821

This 40-pin NMOS devide with two programmable bidirectional ports A and B is a powerful interface device used for most of the I/O interface and applications.

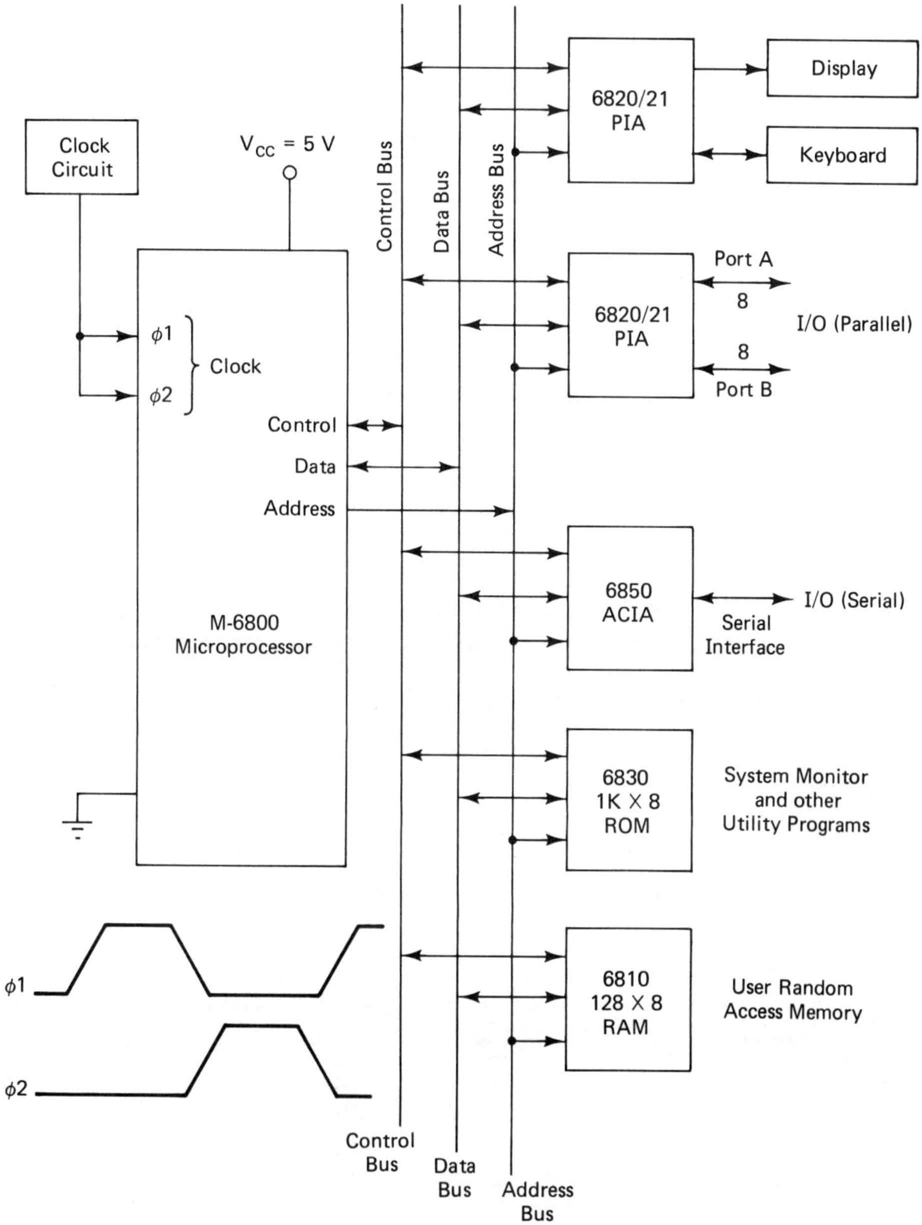

Fig 4.5. The 6800-based microcomputer configuration.

ACIA (Asynchronous Communication Interface Adapter) 6850

This 24-pin NMOS device with programmable capabilities for data specialization is used for serial data transmission, modem interface, etc.

The PIA 6821 and ACIA 6850 are powerful and sophisticated devices widely used in industry for micro interface. We will present more about these and associated applications in the next chapter.

System Timing and Control

The 6800 microprocessor operates on two-phase interlaced clock signals $\phi 1$ and $\phi 2$ as shown in Figure 4.5. The frequency of the effective clock (1 MHz for standard 6800 systems) determines the speed of the operation. Referring to Table 4.2 on the instruction set, the number of clock or MPU cycles (≅) determines the time required to fetch and execute any given instruction. For example, CLC (clear carry) requires two MPU clock cycles. This implies that on a 1-MHz clock system, it takes two μs to accomplish the clear carry operation.

The control is accomplished by bus arbitration signals such as $R/\overline{W}$ (read/write), VMA (valid memory address), BA (bus available), etc., which are generated by the microprocessor. The operating features of these signals can be obtained from the 6800 data sheets.

I/O Configuration (Input/Output)

The 6800 microcomputer system uses the "memory mapped I/O" structure, whereby any I/O location is regarded as a corresponding memory location. This has the advantage of using all the instructions to manipulate the I/O data.

Example 4.4 I/O Configuration

In a data acquisition system as shown in Figure 4.6, it is necessary to read input X_{Data} on port A (configured as input), wait for one second, multiply it by two, and output it to port B (configured as output). Consider a 1 MHz system clock. Ports A and B are located at 8008 and 800B.

Develop the operating software to accomplish the above task.

Solution

The solution is simple. It involves reading port A in one-second intervals, shifting the port A data one position left (which results in multiplication by two) and outputting it to Port B.

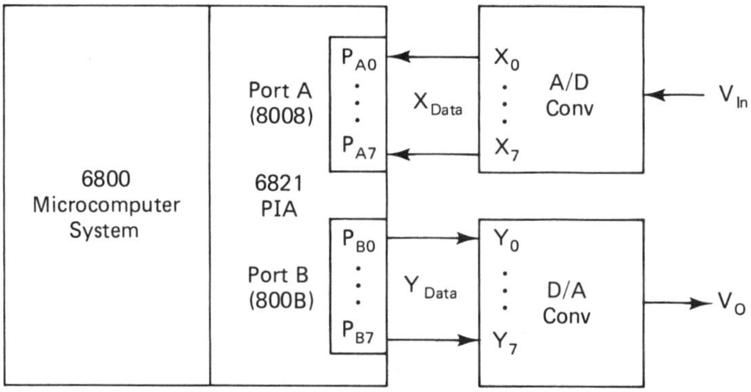

Fig 4.6. A simple data acquisition and I/O interface (Example 4.4).

(a) *Pseudo code.* This is a process (similar to flow charting) in which the required operations are specified as pseudo statements as shown. In our case, the solution of the problem can be stated as

	Program Locations
:Read Port A	0200
Go for 1 sec. delay.	0203
Initialize timing counter, for 1 sec.	0206
Decrement the counter until 1 sec.	
Go back to main program.	
:Shift port A data left, to multiply by 2	020D
:Output shifted data to port B	020F
:Go back to reading port A and repeat the process	0212

(b) *Actual Program Listings.* Table 4.3 shows the actual operating listings of the software. As shown, X data on port A is read between 0200 and 0203. X register is used to generate the required 1-second delay and is loaded with FFFF between 0203 and 0205. The delay loop between 0206 and 020C decrements X register from its initial set value of $(FFFF)_{Hex}$ to all-zero condition. Thus the loop is executed

$$(FFFF)_{Hex} = (65536)_{10} \text{ times.}$$

The NOP instructions are incorporated to obtain the required timing (each clock cycle corresponds to 1 microsecond).

$$\begin{aligned} T_{Loop} &= (65536)\ (\text{Number of clock cycles in loop}) \\ &= (65536)\ (16) = 1.04 \text{ seconds} \end{aligned}$$

Table 4.3. Listings for the Data Acquisition and I/O Configuration (Example 4.4).

Location	*Label*	*Mnemonic*	*Op Code*	*Mode*	*Comments*
0200	Port A	LDA A	B6	Extended	Load X data from port A into accumulator A.
01		80_H			
02		08_L			
03	Delay	LDX	CE	Immediate	Load delay counter (X register) with FFFF to generate 1 s approximate delay by looping that many times.
04		FF			
05		FF			*Clock Cycles*
06	→ Delay loop	NOP	01	Inherent	2
07		NOP	01	"	2 — X_{Reg} is decremented.
08	(T_{Loop})	NOP	01	"	2 — If it is not zero program loops back to
09		NOP	01	"	2 — 0206. When X reaches zero program
0A	Decrement counter	DEX	09	"	4 — advances.
0B		BNE	26	Relative	4
0C		F9			
0D	Multiply	ASLA	48	Inherent	Shift A left to cause multiplication by 2.
0E		NOP	01	"	
0F	Port B	STA A	B7	Extended	Output processed data to port B, to form Y_{Data}.
0210		80			
11		0B			
12	Repeat	JMP	7E	Extended	Repeat the operation by jumping back to 0200.
13		02			
14		00			

Note: The label and comments are included to aid the reader. For a minimal system, program should be entered in machine code along with the data and address information.

After the 1-second delay, accumulator A is shifted left (at 020D) to cause multiplication by 2. Between 020F and 0214, the contents of A are output to Port B and program jumps to 0200 to repeat the process.

Example 4.4 outlines the basic concepts of the I/O configurations and timing generations. In the next chapter, we will present details of initializing I/O ports, controlling A/D (analog to digital) and D/A (digital to analog) processes, and more.

Exerciser Bus Concepts

The exerciser or SS-50 bus was originally developed around the Motorola 6800 microprocessor. It consists of two bus structures, 50-pin and 30-pin, as shown in Figure 4.7. The 50-pin version contains all the address and control lines, whereas the 30-pin bus contains the decoded address lines (resulting in respective chip selects). The 30-pin bus is suitable for I/O type functions, and the 50-pin bus is suitable for interfacing memory and other peripherals where complete address lines are required.

4.4. SUMMARY

In this chapter, we have introduced the architectural features of the 6800 microprocessor. Of particular importance is the double accumulator structure and index addressing.

Because of the complexity of the addressing modes, an attempt has been made to substantiate with the help of example problems the distinctions between the various modes.

Also, the 6800-based microcomputer configuration is introduced along with the concepts of the memory mapped I/O and the exerciser bus.

A systematic study of this chapter will provide the required background of the 6800 microprocessor in order to comprehend the system applications presented in the next chapter.

It is highly recommended that you consult the data books on the 6800 microprocessor and the other devices discussed in this chapter. See especially the Motorola, Inc. M 6800 Microprocessor Programming Manual and Ron Bishop's *Basic Microprocessing and the 6800*, Hayden Publishing.

Problems

4.1. Figure 4.1, repeated for convenience as Figure 4.8, shows the architecture of the 6800 microprocessor.

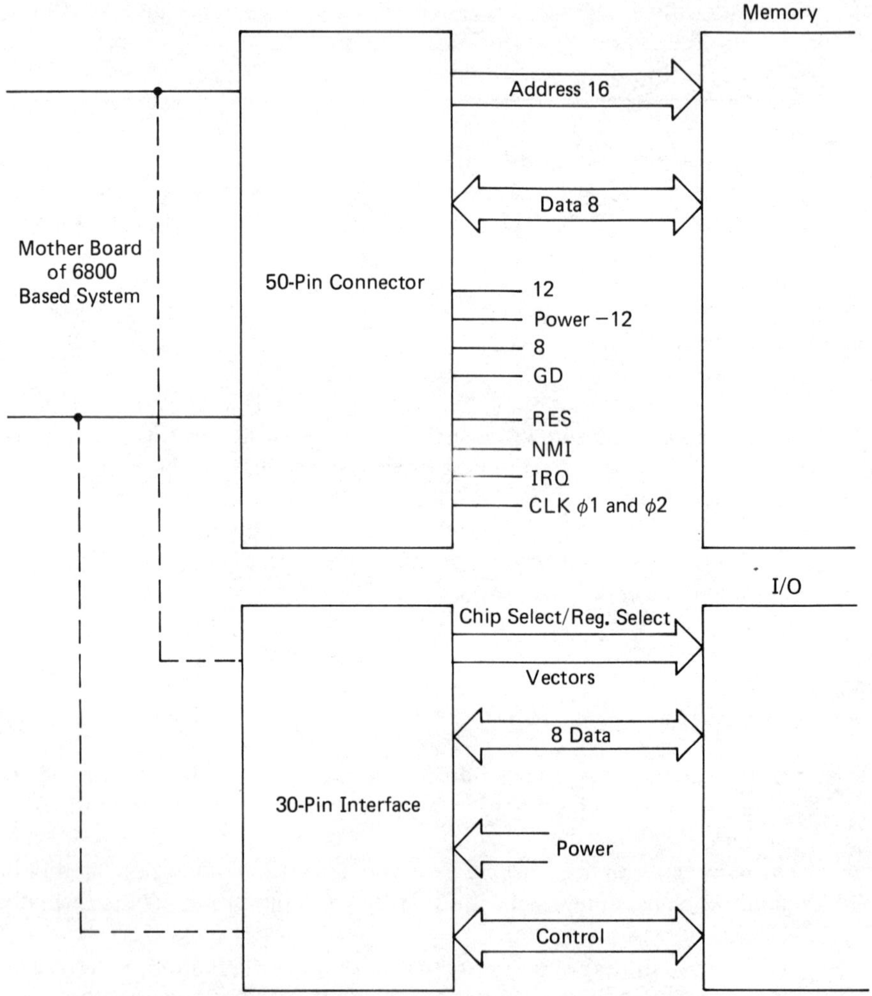

Fig 4.7. The SS-50 (exerciser) bus.

(a) What are the functional differences between the accumulators A and B, if any?

(b) Can the stack pointer be used as a counter?

4.2. In a particular application, it is required to store CCR, A, B, X, and PC on the stack.

(a) How many stack locations are required to accomplish the above task?

(b) Write a software algorithm to store the above CPU registers on the stack.

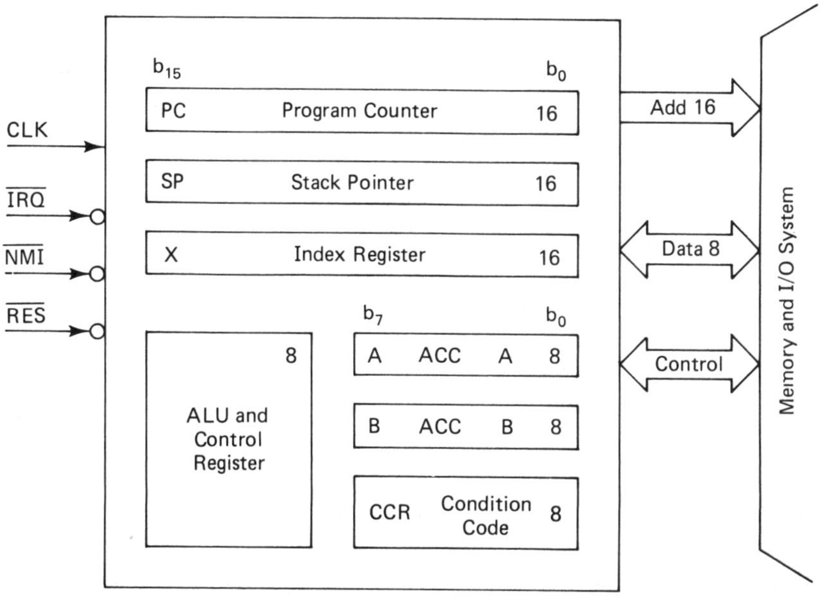

Fig 4.8. The 6800 microprocessor architecture (for Problems 4.1–4.4).

4.3. Accumulator A contains $(DE)_{Hex}$ and B contains $(79)_{Hex}$.
(a) What are the contents of the CCR if A and B are added together?
(b) Repeat (a) if B is subtracted from A.

4.4. Specify typical conditions under which the CCR contains 00.

4.5. Shown in Figure 4.9 is the ROM memory map, holding the interrupt vectors.
(a) Where will the program execution start on the power-up reset?
(b) Will the contents of the PC be saved on stack? Why?

4.6. Under a certain condition, the program is observed to start at location 0974, as identified in Figure 4.9. What is that condition?

Location	*Contents*
FFF8	37
FFF9	43
FFFA	A6
FFFB	72
FFFC	09
FFFD	74
FFFE	02
FFFF	00

Fig 4.9. The vectored memory map (for Problems 4.5–4.7).

(b) The stack pointer initially contains 0FFF. What are the contents of the stack pointer after the above condition has occurred?

4.7. In a control system application, $\overline{\text{IRQ}}$ input is used to start the process. $\overline{\text{NMI}}$ input is used to stop the system if any safety hazard is detected. The $\overline{\text{RESET}}$ input is used to initialize the microprocessor.

Conceptually develop an operating system diagram showing where the respective software programs are located. Use the information given in Figure 4.9.

4.8. Explain the brief differences between (a) extended and indexed addressing modes, and (b) immediate and direct addressing modes.

4.9. Write a software routine, in order to add the contents of locations 00A0 and 00A1 and store in the locations 00B1 and 00B0. Use only the extended addressing modes.

4.10. (a) Repeat Problem 4.9, using the indexed addressing mode only.

(b) Repeat (a) above, using the direct addressing mode.

(c) Compare (a) and (b) and compute relative speed of operation.

4.11. In computation and control system applications, the actual instructional time is very important. Develop an operating software, such that a memory table between 00A0 and 00B0 is filled with FF in the minimum possible time. Use any addressing modes of your choice.

4.12. A typical 6800-based microcomputer system is as shown in Figure 4.10. Taking the data from the manufacturer's data sheets, design an electronic interface that would address

(a) The RAM between ranges $(0000)_{\text{Hex}}$ to $(03FF)_{\text{Hex}}$. (Use the 6810-type RAM devices.)

(b) The 6830 type ROM, between the address range $(F000)_{\text{Hex}}$ to $(FFFF)_{\text{Hex}}$.

Use the decoder devices of your choice.

4.13. Repeat Problem 4.12 such that the system is expanded to have 4K × 8 RAM between $(0000)_{\text{Hex}}$ and $(0FFF)_{\text{Hex}}$. Show all the details of the drive electronics.

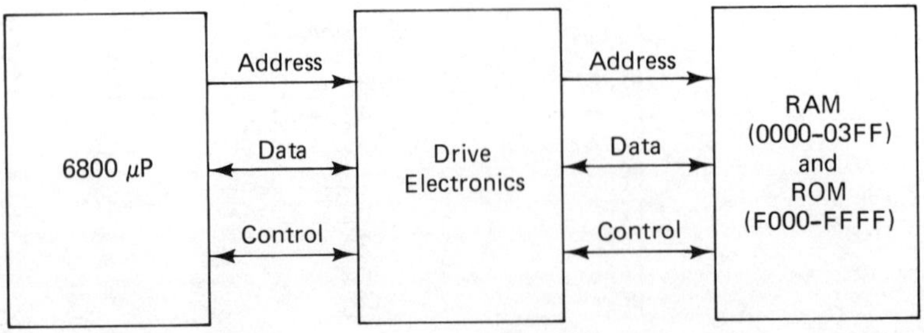

Fig 4.10. A typical 6800-based microcomputer system (Problems 4.12–4.14).

4.14. Based on Figure 4.10, show a simple decoding scheme to address I/O locations at $(8008)_{Hex}$ and $(8009)_{Hex}$.

4.15. Modify the data acquisition software of Example 4.4 and Figure 4.6, such that the sampling time is increased from 1 second to 2 seconds.

4.16. Repeat Problem 4.15 so that the sampling time is increased to 4 seconds. Also the input X_{Data} should be multiplied by 4 before being output to port B.

CHAPTER FIVE

6800-Based Microcomputer Applications

By virtue of its simple architecture and flexible addressing modes, the 6800 is well suited for system applications involving extensive I/O manipulations. Fortunately, the 6800 microprocessor is supported by equally powerful, flexible, and programmable I/O interface devices such as the 6821 PIA, 6850 ACIA, 6845 VIDEO controller, etc. We will study some of these in sufficient detail to allow us to understand system applications and develop more system designs.

5.1. INPUT/OUPUT PARALLEL INTERFACE

The 6800 architecture is well suited to handle 8-bit parallel data (1 byte). The parallel interface to any I/O device or system is accomplished through the 6821 PIA.

6821 PIA (Peripheral Interface Adapter)

As shown in Figure 5.1, the 6821 PIA is a 40-pin NMOS DIP device, consisting of two 8-bit I/O ports A and B and associated control signals CA1, CA2, CB1, and CB2. Each bit of these I/O ports is individually programmable to be input or output. Each port consists of three internal registers:

ORA and ORB (Output Registers A and B)
DDRA and DDRB (Data Direction Registers A and B)
CRA and CRB (Control Registers A and B)

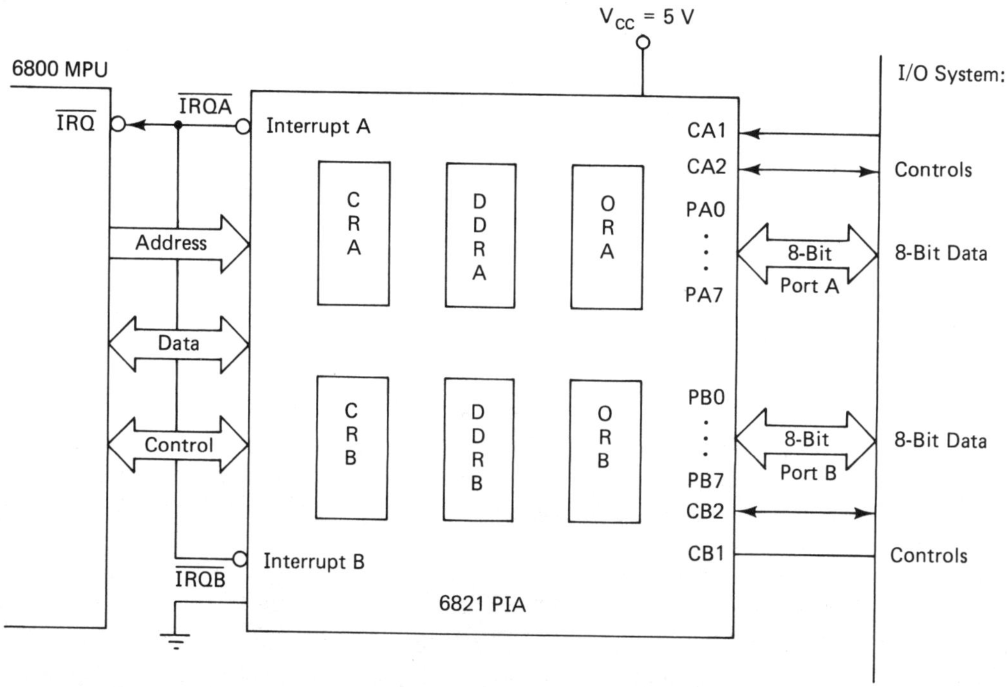

Fig 5.1. The 6821 PIA programming structure.

Output Registers (ORs)

Output registers interface with the external I/O devices and systems and are capable of driving unit TTL load.

Data Direction Registers (DDRs)

Data direction registers determine the direction of the bits of the output register.

1. 0 in DDR bit position makes corresponding port bit an input.
2. 1 in DDR bit position makes corresponding port bit an output.

As an example, if

b_7 . . . . . . b_0
0 0 0 0 1 1 1 1 = (0F)

is written into DDRA, it amounts to configuring PA7....PA4 as inputs and PA3....PA0 as outputs.

Control Registers (CRA and CRB)

Control registers determine the nature of the control lines CA1, CA2, CB1, and CB2. Figure 5.2 shows a typical structure of control register A. Depending on the application, an appropriate control word can be written into the CRA to structure CA1 and CA2. The CRB format for CB1 and CB2 is similar to CRA. Bits 6 and 7 are set by the active transitions of CA2 and CA1, when they are used as control inputs.

We will use all these features in the practical applications that follow.

Initialization of 6821

For any interface applications, the PIA should be properly initialized. For example, in a particular application, it is required to have port A as input, port B as output. The CA1 $0 \rightarrow 1$ transition has to be recognized, and the corresponding interrupt line $\overline{\text{IRQA}}$ has to be activated (pulled low). As an initialization routine,

$(00)_{\text{Hex}}$ will be loaded in DDRA to make port A input
$(FF)_{\text{Hex}}$ will be loaded in DDRB to make port B output
$(03)_{\text{Hex}}$ will be loaded in CRA to recognize $0 \rightarrow 1$ transition of CA1 and activate $\overline{\text{IRQA}}$ interrupt line.

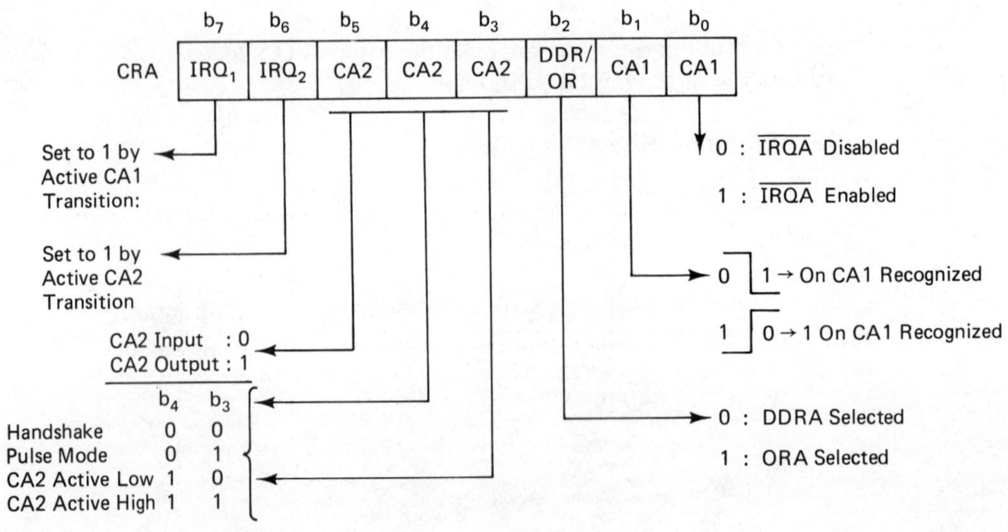

Fig 5.2. The 6821 control register (CRA) formatting.

Similarly appropriate initialization can be done depending on the application.

Design of Waveform Generation

Perhaps the most important requirement of any digital system is the capability to generate timing waveforms to accomplish different tasks at different times. Usually these waveforms are generated with the help of digital devices such as counters, shift registers, monostables, and gates. However, with a microcomputer, waveforms can be generated very easily with the greatest amount of flexibility. We will present an example problem to introduce this concept.

Example 5.1 Waveform Generation

Using port B as output, generate the timing waveforms such that

$P_{B0} \rightarrow X_0$ arbitrary clock output waveform at 1 KHz
$P_{B1} \rightarrow X_1$ clock ÷ 2 output waveform
$P_{B2} \rightarrow X_2$ clock ÷ 3 output waveform

as shown in Figure 5.3 and assume the 6800 system is operating on 1 MHz clock, and 6821 port B is located at the following addresses:

ORB/DDRB → 800A
CRB → 800B

Show all the necessary hardware and software.

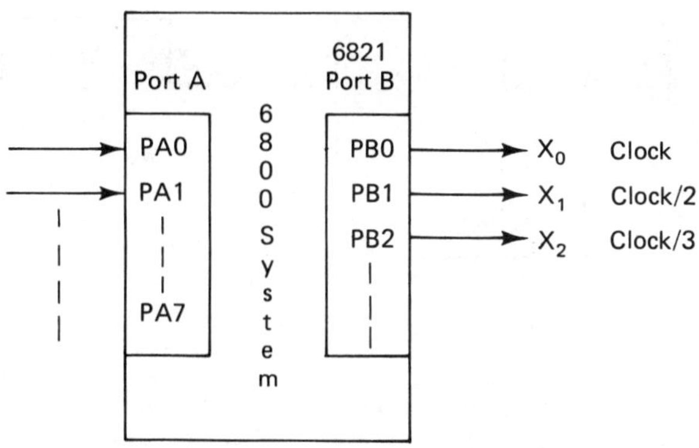

Fig 5.3. The 6800 microprocessor system generating waveforms (Example 5.1).

Solution

Figure 5.4 shows the particulars of the waveforms. It can be easily observed that the waveform pattern repeats itself every 1 × 2 × 3 = 6 clock cycles and that the digital code corresponding to the waveform changes every half cycle. Thus the concept centers on outputing the proper digital code to port B, every half cycle, as shown in Figure 5.4. The duration T1/2 of the half cycle determines the frequency of X_0 waveform. Figure 5.5 shows the flow chart and the corresponding pseudo code. Table 5.1 shows the actual operating listings.

Digital code generating the waveforms is stored in 12 memory locations (corresponding to 6 clock cycles or 12 half-clock cycles). This code is read sequentially from the memory table and is output with the required half-cycle delay. The repetitive operation of this process results in the required waveform. This method is know as the "look-up table" method and is extensively used in microcomputer systems.

(a) *Software and Listings*. The flow chart and pseudo code of Figure 5.5 outline the software requirements. In current system designs, both methods are extensively used, and the readers can choose their preference. (See Table 5.1 for the listings.)

Between 0200 to 020A, port B is configured as the output and CRB is conditioned to get access to the output register of P_B. Between 020B and 021D, the memory code table is read sequentially and is output to port B using the indexed addressing scheme. Of particular importance is the delay

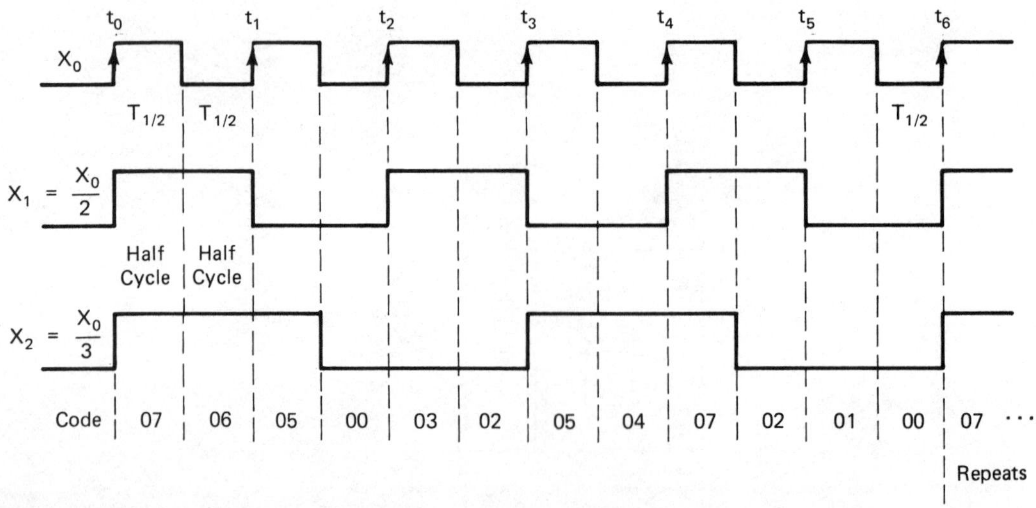

Fig 5.4. Timing waveforms generated by the 6800 (Problem 5.1).

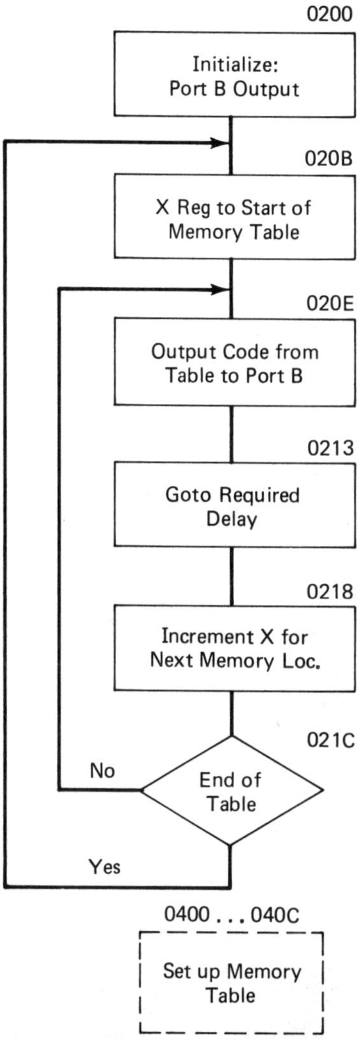

Pseudo Code

Initialize:
- Port B Output
- Set Up Memory Table with Codes
- Set Up X Reg as Memory Pointer

Output Code:
- Read Code from Table Sequentially
- Output the Code to Port B

Time Delay:
- Load a Register with Delay Number
- Decrement the Register Until Zero

Next Code:
- Increment X and Read Next Code from Table
- Continue the Process Until End of Table

Repeat:
- Re-Initialize X to Top of Table
- Repeat Output Code, Time Delay
- and Next Code Operations

Fig 5.5. The flowchart and pseudo code for waveform generation (Example 5.1).

loop (decrementing accumulator B). To obtain 1 KHz frequency for X_O, half-cycle time T1/2 has to be approximately 0.5 ms. This delay is obtained by decrementing B ($(53)_{Hex} = (83)_{Decimal}$ times), such that

$$T_{Delay} = T\tfrac{1}{2} = (53)_{Hex} * (6 \text{ timing cycles})$$

$$= (83)_{Decimal} * 6\ \mu s = 498\ \mu s$$
$$= 500\ \mu s$$

Table 5.1. Program Listings For Waveform Generation (Problem 5.1 with 6800 System).

Location	*Label*	*Mnemonic*	*Op Code*	*Address Mode*	*Comment*
0200	Initialize	LDA A	86	Immediate	00 loaded in CRB at 800B, to get access to DDRB
01		#00			
02		STA A	B7	Extended	
03		80_H			
04		$0B_L$			
05		LDX	CE	Immediate	FF loaded into DDRB at 800A to make P_B output.
06		#FF			
07		04			
08		STX	FF	Extended	04 loaded into CRB at 800B to get access to 0RB in further operations.
09		80_H			
0A		$0A_L$			
0B	Top table	LDX	CE	Immediate	X index register is loaded with the starting address of code table, which is 0400.
0C		04			
0D		00			
0E	Digital code	LDA A, X	A6	Index	Code table read sequentially using index addressing and code output to port B.
0F		00			
10	Output P_B	STA A	B7	Extended	
11		80			
12		0A			
13	Delay	LDA B	C6	Immediate	Acc B loaded with $(53)_{Hex} = (83)_{Dec}$ and decremented to zero to obtain 500 μsec half-cycle delay (T1/2).
14		$\#(53)_{Hex}$			
15	T Delay (loop to DEC B)	DEC B	5A	Inherent	Timing Cycles: 2
16		BNE	26	Relative	4
17		FD			
18	Next code	INX	08	Inherent	X incremented to read next code, until the end of the table (at 040C) is reached.
19		CPX	8C	Immediate	
1A		#04			
1B		0C			

Address	Label	Mnemonic/Data	Op Code	Mode	Comment
021C		BNE	26	Relative	If not end of table, branch back to 020E to output next code to P_B.
1D		F0			
1E		NOP	01	Inherent	No operation.
1F		NOP	01	"	
20		NOP	01	"	
21		JMP	7E	Extended	Jump back to 040B to repeat the waveform generation process.
22		04			
23		0B			

MEMORY CODE TABLE

	Location	Code	Location	Code	
Start of Table	0400	07	0407	04	
	01	06	08	07	
	02	05	09	02	
	03	00	0A	01	
	04	03	0B	00	
	05	02	0C	07	End of Table
	06	05			

When the end of the code table is reached, the process is repeated by virtue of the jump instruction at 0221.

Example 5.1 is simple but far-reaching. The "look-up table" method can be used for generating any complex waveform structures for any control system applications. Several problems at the end of this chapter are exclusively designed to illustrate more practical applications of this method.

5.2. DATA ACQUISITION SYSTEMS

All physical phenomena are basically analog (continuous) in nature. These analog signals must be converted into corresponding digital form in order to interface with microprocessor-based systems. This process is known as analog to digital (A/D) conversion. Similarly, processed digital information should be converted into the corresponding analog form in order to interface with real physical systems. This process is known as digital to analog (D/A) conversion. A typical data acquisition system consists of A/D and D/A conversions and associated digital processing, as shown in Figure 5.6.

Analog to Digital (A/D) System Interface

The principle of A/D conversion centers on generating a digital word corresponding to an analog input voltage. There are several "successive approximation" type A/D devices available that can be directly interfaced to an 8-bit microcomputer system. Figure 5.7 shows a typical operating interface of the National 0804 A/D converter IC device to the 6800 system.

The conversion clock is generated by the RC network consisting of R_c and C_c with an effective frequency f_c given by

$$f_c = \frac{0.9}{R_c C_c} \text{ Hz} \tag{5-1}$$

This clock drives the 0804 A/D converter. The analog input voltage (range $0 \rightarrow 5$ volts) is applied to the input of the A/D converter. The converter takes several conversion clock cycles and produces a digital word at its output lines D0...D7. Also, it produces an active low interrupt signal on its $\overline{\text{INTR}}$ output (pin 5), at the end of the conversion. The ouput contains valid digital data, which will remain stable in the output latch of the A/D converter until read by the micro. The next conversion can be initiated by momentarily generating a negative going transition on its $\overline{\text{WR}}$ input (Pin 3). The cycle is repetitive.

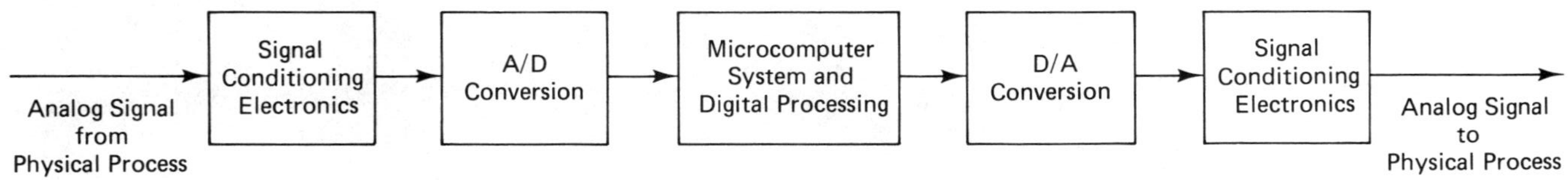

Fig 5.6. A typical data acquisition system.

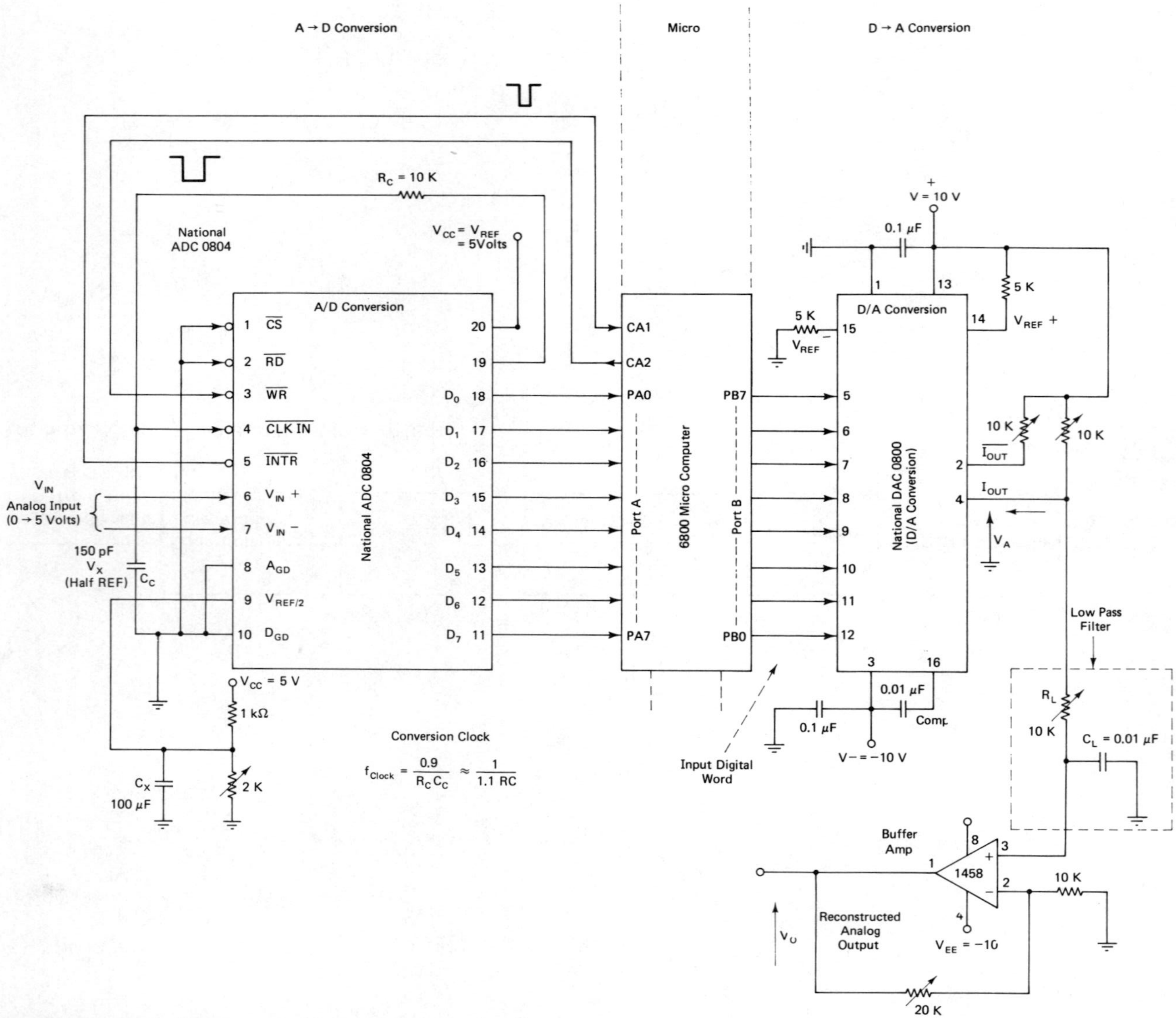

Fig 5.7. A typical A/D and D/A interface to the 6800 system.

Resolution and Digitization Error

For 8-bit digitization, there are $2^8 = 256$ possible digital words ($(00)_{Hex}$ to $(FF)_{Hex}$). For 5-volt maximum input voltage, each successive digital step corresponds to 5 volts/256 = 20 millivolts. Thus the resolution in the digitization is 20 millivolts. Also, the digitization error corresponds to one LSB (least significant bit), which in turn corresponds to 20 millivolts.

Example 5.2 Analog to Digital Conversion

In a voice digitization system, the input voice signal must be digitized and the digital data stored in one page of memory (256 bytes). Develop the complete operating hardware and software, using the M-6800 microcomputer system, under the handshake mode (8008: ORA/DDRA; 8009: CRA; 800A: ORB/DDRB; 800B: CRB).

Solution

(a) *Hardware* (refer to Figure 5.8). Input voltage V_s from the microphone amplifier setup has to be conditioned to be between $0 \rightarrow 5$ volts, to be applied to the input terminals of Figure 5.7, as V_{in}. This is accomplished by the level shift and the gain amplifier A1, as shown in Figure 5.8(a). The 6800 microcomputer system controls the A/D conversion process. The control handshake is accomplished when the 6800 system generates the pulse (on CA2) to initiate the conversion. At the end of the conversion, the A/D sends an interrupt to the micro (on CA1), to read the digitized data given to its port A. Figure 5.8(b) shows the timing waveforms.

For the values shown, the conversion clock has a frequency (using Eq. 5-1)

$$f_c = \frac{0.9}{(10K)(150pF)} = 600 \text{ KHz}. \tag{5-2}$$

The A/D converter may take up to 64 clockings to generate a digitized word. Using the sampling theorem (that the sampling rate should be at least twice that of the signal), the maximum signal frequency f_{signal} that can be digitized without loss of information is

$$f_{signal} \leq \frac{f_c}{2 \times 64} = \frac{600K}{128} = 4.6 \text{ KHz} \tag{5-3}$$

In most cases, 4.6 KHz upper audio frequency is sufficient.

(b) *Software*. The software generates a negative going pulse on CA2 to initiate the conversion as shown in Figure 5.8(b). The micro reads the digitized

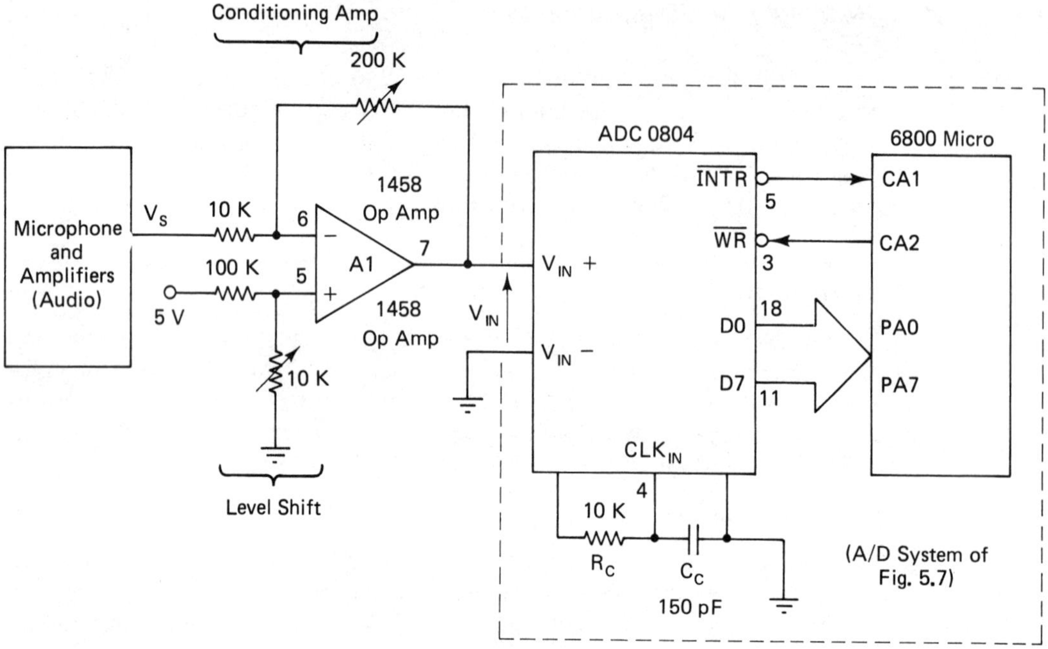

(a)

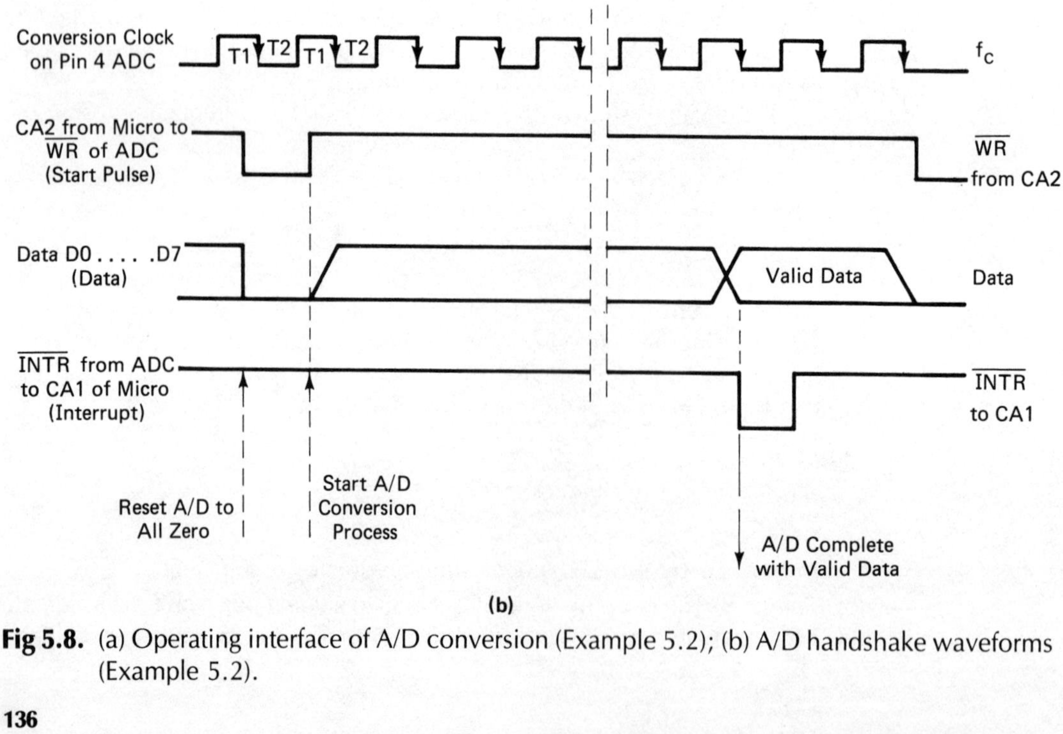

(b)

Fig 5.8. (a) Operating interface of A/D conversion (Example 5.2); (b) A/D handshake waveforms (Example 5.2).

data on port A, when CA1 interrupt is recognized. Figure 5.9 shows the flow chart and corresponding pseudo code. Table 5.2 presents the actual program listings.

Between 0200 and 021F initialization is carried out with ports A and B configured as input and output, respectively. The memory table is set up

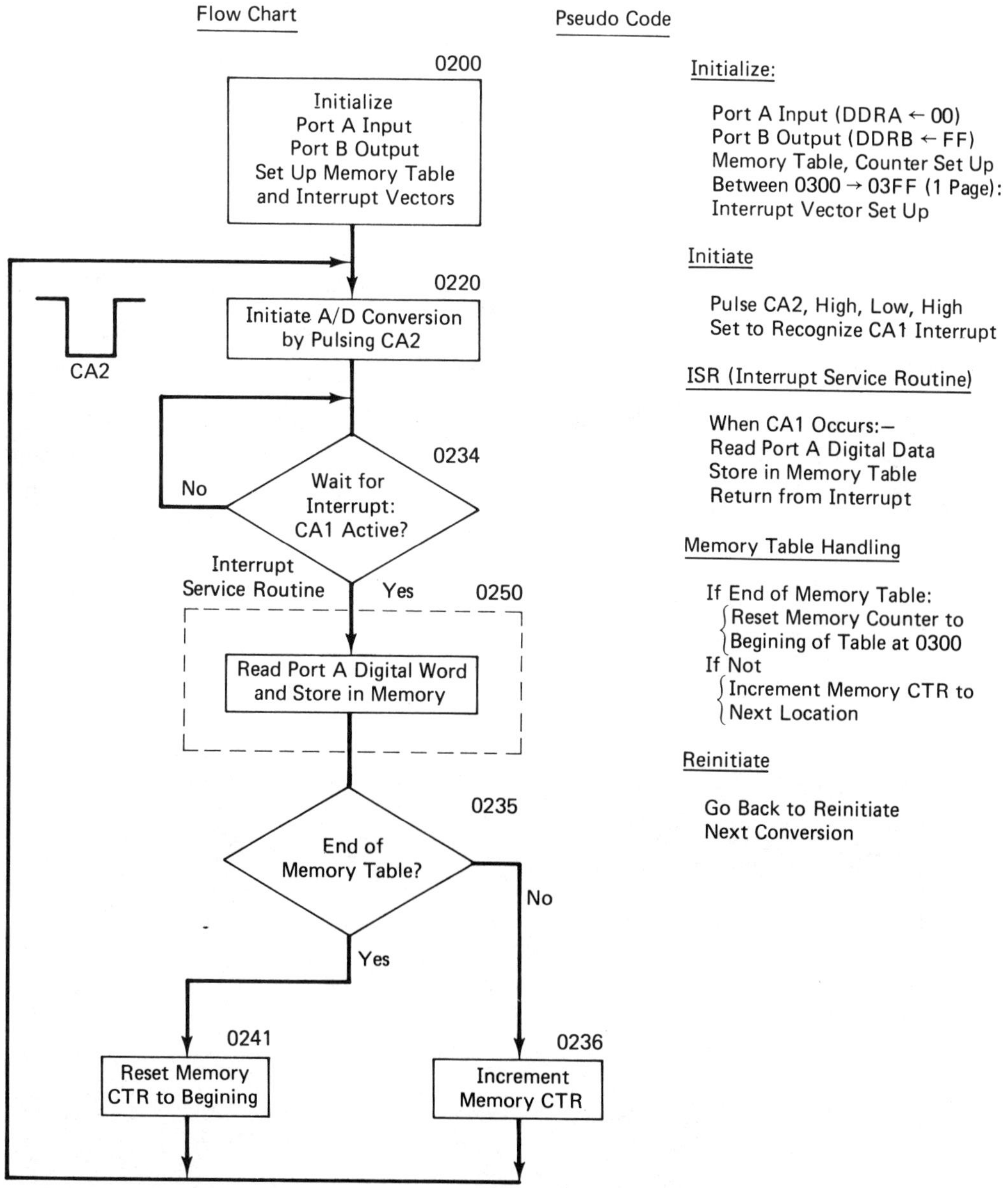

Fig 5.9. The flowchart and pseudo code for the A/D conversion (Example 5.2).

Table 5.2. Program Listings for A/D Conversion (Problem 5.2).

Location	*Label*	*Mnemonic*	*Op Code*	*Address Mode*	*Comment*
0200	Initialize	LDA A	86	Immediate	CRA and CRB are loaded with ϕϕ to get access to DDRA and DDRB (CRA at 8009, CRB at 800B).
01		#00			
02		STA A	B7	Extended	
03		80_H			
04		09_L			
05		STA A	B7	Extended	
06		80			
07		0B			
08		STA A	B7	Extended	Port A configured as input by loading 00 into DDRA and port B as output by loading FF into DDRB (DDRA at 8008, DDRB at 800A).
09		80			
0A		08			
0B		LDA A	86	Immediate	
0C		#FF			
0D		STA A	B7	Extended	
0E		80			
0F		0A			
10	Memory table	LDX	CE	Immediate	Memory table starting address of 0300 is stored at locations 0040 and 0041 (through X register).
11		$\#03_H$			
12		00_L			
13		STX	DF	Dir	
14		40			
15	Interrupt vector	LDX	CE	Immediate	Interrupt routine starting address of 0250 is loaded into the vectored locations of A000 and A001. (For the system under consideration, A000 and A001 are the vectored locations for the interrupt).
16		$\#02_H$			
17		50_L			
18		STX	FF	Extended	
19		A0			
1A		00			
1B		NOP	01	Inherent	
1C		NOP	01	Inherent	
021D		NOP	01	Inherent	Linkage Software.
1E		NOP	01	Inherent	
1F		NOP	01	Inherent	
0220	Initiate	CLI	0E	Inherent	Software interrupt mask clear. Dummy read of port A at 8008 clears any interrupt flags in the 6821 PIA.
21		LDA A	B6	Extended	
22		80			
23		08			

Address	Label	Mnemonic	Op code	Mode	Comments
24		LDA B	C6	Immediate	CB2 pulse generated by loading #34 and 3D in CRA b7 b0 0 0 1 1 0 1 0 0 CRA #34 in CRA corresponds to CA2 low: CA1 disabled #3D in CRA corresponds to CA2 high: CA1 enabled CA2  (This will initiate A/D conversion). Also, X is loaded with table address.
25		#34			
26		STA B	F7	Extended	
27		80			
28		09			
29		LDX	DE	Direct	
2A		40			
2B		NOP	01	Inherent	
2C		LDA B	C6	Immediate	
2D		#3D			
2E		STA B	F7	Extended	
2F		80			
30		09			
31		NOP [JSR]	01	Inherent	6800 system waits here until CA1 interrupt occurs. Then it goes to interrupt service routine at 0250. (*These NOPs to be replaced by JSR to 0260 for interlacing with D/A.)
32		NOP [02]	01	Inherent	
33		NOP [60]	01	Inherent	
34	Wait	WAI	3E	Inherent	
35	[From ISR]	LDX	DE	Dir	X memory pointer is read from locations 0040 and 0041 and checked to see if X equals 03FF (which corresponds to end of memory table).
36		40			
37		CPX	8C	Immediate	
38		#03			
39		FF			
023A		BEQ	27	Relative	If end of table program branches to 0241, to restart.
3B		05			
3C		INX	08	Inherent	X incremented and stored in locations 0040 and 0041 and program branches back to 0220 to start new conversion.
3D		STX	DF	Dir	
3E		40			
3F	(To 0220)	BRA	20	Relative	
0240		DF			
41	Restart	→CLR	7F	Extended	Memory table reset to starting address of 0300; as shown 0040 .... 03 } --→ 0300 0041 cleared 00 } and program branches back to 0220, to start new conversion.
42		00			
43		41			
44	(To 0220)	BRA	20	Relative	
45		DA			

Table 5.2. *(Continued)*

Location	*Label*	*Mnemonic*	*Op Code*	*Address Mode*	*Comment*
			INTERRUPT SERVICE ROUTINE		
0250	ISR	LDX	DE	Dir	Memory pointer X is restored from 0040 and 0041.
51		40			
52		LDA A	B6	Extended	Digital data from port A is read and stored in the sequential memory table location, using indexed addressing mode. X pointer stored back at 0040 and 0041.
53		80			
54		08			
55		STA A, X	A7	Ind	
56		00			
57		STX	DF	Dir	
58		40			
59		NOP	01	Inherent	
5A		RTI	3B	Inherent	Return from interrupt (joins main program at 0235)

to start at 0300. Also, the starting address of 0250 for the interrupt service routine is loaded into the revectored address locations of A000 and A001 for the 6800 system under consideration.

Between 0220 and 0233, CA2 pulse is generated to start the A/D conversion. The system goes into indefinite wait state at 0234 until CA1 interrupt occurs, at which point the program branches to 0250 for the interrupt service routine (ISR).

The ISR between 0250 and 025A reads the digital word on port A and stores it in the sequential memory locations using the indexed addressing mode. The RTI (return from interrupt) at 025A restores the program to 0235.

Between 0235 to 0245, the program checks to see whether the end of the memory table (in which digital data is stored) is reached. If not, X is incremented to refer to the next sequential table location. In case the end of the table is reached, the X register is reinitialized to the top of the table. In either case the program branches to 0220 to start the new conversion. The operation is repetitive.

It should be fairly obvious that the digitized data is stored in only one page of the memory (0300 to 03FF), which is only 256 bytes; rather small. The table is overwritten if the digitization goes beyond 256 bytes. In applications such as voice digitization, several thousands of bytes of memory are required for storing the digitized data. However, with memory becoming cheaper day by day, the A/D conversion methods and controls are becoming extremely efficient and economical and are being used extensively throughout the industry.

Digital to Analog (D/A) System and Interface

The digitized and processed data should be converted back into the corresponding analog form, as shown in Figures 5.6 and 5.7 in order to interface with the real physical process. It is usually accomplished with the help of the D/A conversion system, which produces an analog equivalent voltage (or current) at its output in proportion to the digital word at its input.

The D/A section of Figure 5.7 is repeated in Figure 5.10, for convenience. The microcomputer provides the digital word on its port B, which is accepted by the D/A (National DAC 0800) converter. The DAC 0800 then produces an output current I_{Out} in proportion to the digital input word. (The DAC 0800 family of D/A converters is complementary to the ADC-0800 series of A/D converters).

For the values shown in Figure 5.10, a full-scale amplitude of 10 volts can be obtained for the D/A output voltage V_A. V_A is then low-pass filtered through the R_LC_L network (which is also known sometimes as the holding

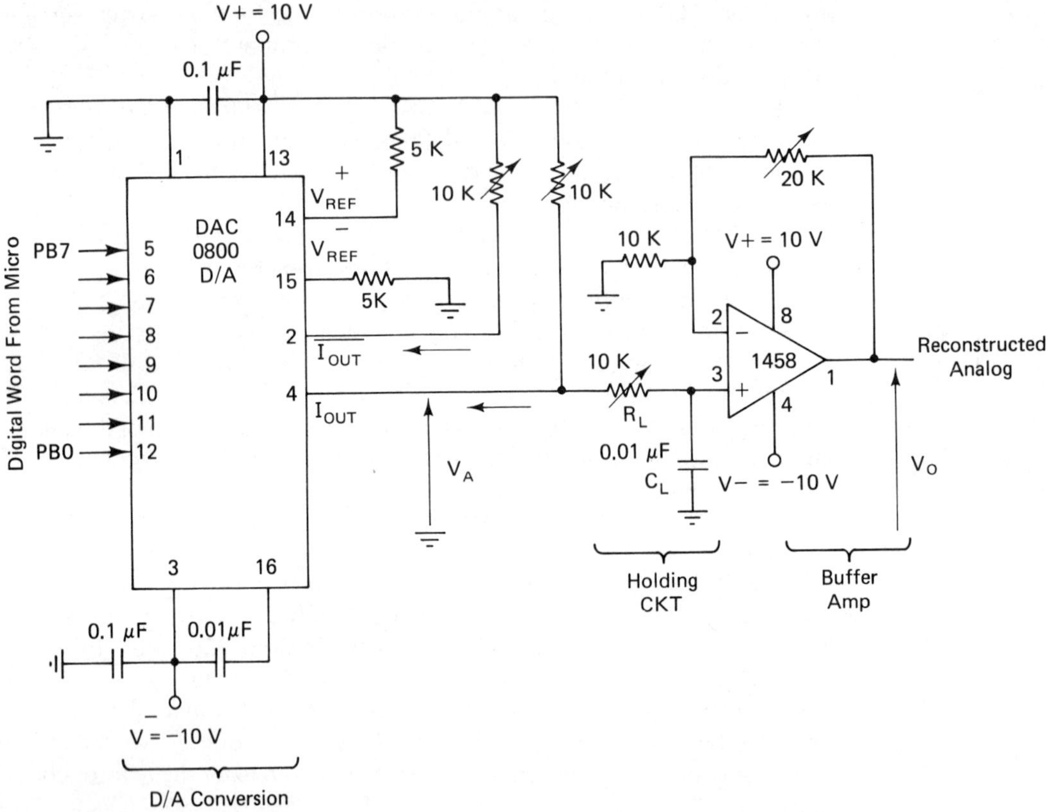

Fig 5.10. A D/A converter section of Figure 5.7 (Example 5.3).

circuit) and buffered with a 1458 type op amp with variable gain to produce reconstructed analog output V_O. The low-pass filter effectively removes switching spikes.

Example 5.3 Digital to Analog Conversion

Develop the necessary operating software and hardware to convert the digitized and stored data from Example 5.2 into the corresponding analog output, with a gain up to 4. (This program may be used as a subroutine).

Solution

The hardware of the D/A as shown in Figure 5.10 is fully operational. We assume that port B has already been configured as output, and the X register is properly initialized to index the memory table in which the digitized data is stored. (Please refer to listings between 0200 and 0210 from A/D Example

5.2 and Table 5.2.) Figure 5.11 shows the flow chart, and Table 5.3 shows the listings.

At 0260 the D/A subroutine is entered via a jump to subroutine (JSR 0260) instruction from the A/D routine example of 5.2 (listing at 0231). Between 0260 and 026C, the digital data in the memory is read into accumulator B and is multiplied up to 4 conditionally. Between 026D and 0273, the digitally processed word is output to the D/A via port B, which ultimately will be converted into the analog voltage.

Of particular importance are the SEI (set interrupt mask) and CLI (clear interrupt mask) at 0260 and 0273, which disable and enable the interrupts. This is necessary for continuous execution of the D/A routine.

The RTS (return from subroutine) at 0274 returns the program to the calling routine.

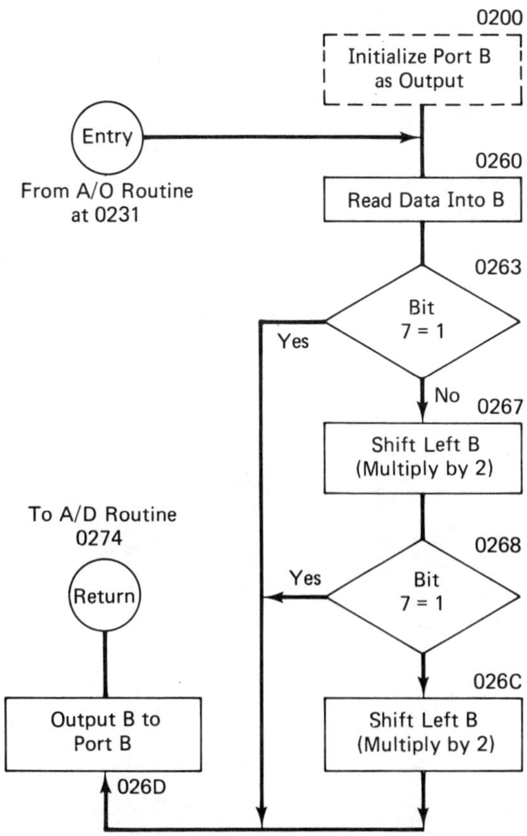

Pseudo Code

Initialize Port B as Output
Read Data from Table Into ACC B
Shift Left If MSB #1, which is Multiply by 2
Repeat Above to Multiply by Another 2
Output Processed Data to D/A Thru Port B
Return to Calling Routine

Fig 5.11. The D/A conversion flowchart and pseudo code (Example 5.3).

Table 5.3. D/A Operating Listing for Example 5.3. D/A (SUB) Routine Listings

Location	*Label*	*Mnemonic*	*Code*	*Address Mode*	*Comment*
0260	D/A conversion	SEI	0F	INH	Interrupt disabled and digital data is read from the memory table into accumulator B, using indexing.
61	Read data	LDAB, X	E6	Index	
62		00			
63		Bit B	C5	IMM	Bit 7 is checked. If it is 1, program branches to 026D to output B on to port B. Otherwise B is shifted left to effect multiplication by 2.
64		#80			
65		BNE	26	REL	
66		06			
67	Multiply 2	ASL B	58	INH	
68		Bit B	C5	IMM	Above process repeated to effect further multiplication by 2.
69		#80			
6A		BNE	26	REL	
6B		← 01			(Total multiplication up to 4.)
6C	Multiply 4	ASL B	58	INH	
6D	Output	→STA B	F7	EXT	Processed digital word in B is output to D/A conversion via port B at 800A.
6E		80			
6F		0A			
70		NOP	01	INH	Linkage software.
71		NOP	01	INH	
72		NOP	01	INH	
73		CLI	0E	INH	Interrupts enabled.
74	Return	RTS	39	INH	Return to calling program.

Note: To make this program effective as a D/A subroutine, NOP instructions in listings of A/D at 0231, 0232, and 0233 in Table 5.2 should be changed to JSR 0260.

Any type of waveform or coded signal can be easily generated using the D/A concepts. For example, if the digital table contains digital words corresponding to a sinusoid, sequentially reading the table and outputing the information results in a sinusoidal signal. Varying the delay between outputing successive digital words results in varying the frequency.

Scrambling the digital table and outputing the digital data, out of sequence, results in a scrambled waveform. This is the basis of all digital coding techniques. Several problems at the end of this chapter throw further light on the practical applications of A/D and D/A systems.

A Typical Data Acquisition System

A data acquisition system consists of the A/D and D/A subsystems integrated into an operating system. This is widely used in the industry. Voltage and current monitoring and correcting systems, digital oscilloscopes, and plotters are typical examples of data acquisition systems.

The software for such a system is already developed in the previous two examples. Proper interface of these two software routines results in an operating data acquisition system.

Example 5.4 Data Acquisition System

In a voice communication data acquisition system, it is required to continuously digitize the incoming voice signal, amplify up to a gain of 4, and reconstruct the analog output (to be displayed on the oscilloscope). Develop the complete operating system with proper software and hardware interface, using the 6800 microcomputer system.

Solution

Again, the basic system is that of Figure 5.7. To suit the present application, it has been modified as shown in Figure 5.12. The A/D converter is configured to operate in free running mode by connecting its $\overline{\text{INTR}}$ output to $\overline{\text{WR}}$ input, as shown in the figure. For details refer to Figure 5.7 and discussions on A/D and D/A systems.

The software developed in the previous examples of A/D and D/A systems have been modified to function as subroutines by incorporating RTS at appropriate places. Table 5.4 shows the operating listings for the present application. At 0280 initialize subroutine is called, which will configure ports A and B as input and output and initializes X at 0300 to refer to the beginning of the digital data table.

At 0283 the A/D conversion subroutine is called, which reads digitized data from port A and stores it in the memory table. At 0286, the D/A subroutine is called, which multiplies up to 4 the digitized data from the memory table and outputs to D/A through port B.

Table 5.4. Listings For Data Acquisition System of Example 5.4.

Location	*Label*	*Mnemonic*	*Op Code*	*Address Mode*	*Comment*
0280	Initialize	JSR	BD	EXT	Jump to initialization subroutine at 0200 (of A/D listings in Table 5.2). Instruction at 0215 to be changed to RTS.
81		02			
82		00			
83	A/D conversion	JSR	BD	EXT	Jump to A/D subroutine at 0250. Instruction at 025A to be changed to RTS (Table 5.2).
84		02			
85		50			
86	D/A conversion	JSR	BD	EXT	Jump to D/A subroutine at 0261. Instruction at 0271 to be changed to RTS (Table 5.3).
87		02			
88		61			
89		NOP	01	INH	Linkage software.
8A		NOP	01	INH	
8B		NOP	01	INH	
8C	Next	LDX	DE	DIR	X Register from locations 40 and 41 is restored and compared to see if it is incremented up to 03FF, which marks the end of digital memory table.
8D		40			
8E		CPX	8C	IMM	
8F		#03			
90		FF			
91		BEQ	27	REL	If it is the end of the table, program branches to 0298 and location 41 is cleared to 00, which amounts to making X = 0300, to refer to the top of the table, for the next run.
92		05			
93		INX	08	INH	
94		STX	DF	DIR	
95		40			
96		BRA	20	REL	If it is not the end of the table, X is incremented and stored back at 0040 and 0041.
97		03			
0298		CLR	7F	EXT	
99		00			
9A		41			
9B		NOP	01	INH	Linkage software and the program branches back to 0283 to start the next data acquisition operation.
9C		NOP	01	INH	
9D		NOP	01	INH	
9E		BRA	20	REL	
9F		E3			

Note: To make this software operational, the following modifications have to be made. Instruction at 0215 to be changed to RTS. Instruction at 025A to be changed to RTS. Instruction at 0271 to be changed to RTS. (Refer to Tables 5.2 and 5.3 of A/D and D/A routines for above changes.)

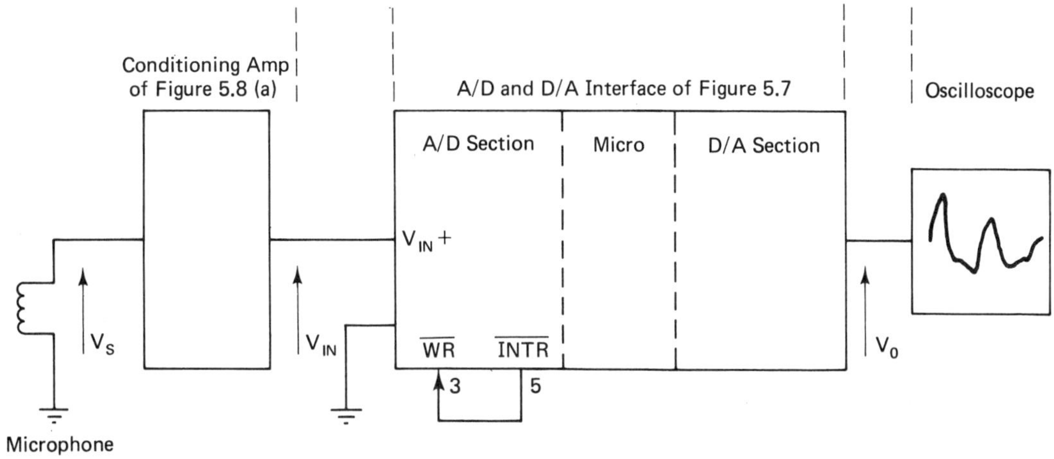

Fig 5.12. The data acquisition and monitoring system of Example 5.4.

Between 028C and 029F, X is advanced to refer to the next location in the memory table. If the end of the table is detected, X is initialized to the beginning of the table. Finally the program branches back to 0283, to start the next data acquisition operation.

5.3. INPUT/OUTPUT SERIAL INTERFACE

The microprocessor efficiently communicates with slow I/O systems (such as modems, printers, teletype, etc.) through appropriate serial interface devices. In this section we will discuss the features of one such device, the 6850 ACIA, belonging to the 6800 family, and present a serial interface example using the 6850 ACIA. This device is an industry standard and is used extensively in conjunction with other microprocessors.

6850 ACIA

The 6850 ACIA (asynchronous communications interface adapter) is a powerful serial interface device that is an industry standard. It is contained in a 24-pin dip package and is fabricated with the NMOS technology. Figure 5.13 shows the architectural features of the 6850. It converts the parallel data from the 6800 microprocessor and presents it in a serial format to the I/O. Similarly, it accepts the serial data from the I/O, converts it into the parallel data, and presents it to the microprocessor. The 6850 ACIA is completely programmable.

As shown in Figure 5.13, the ACIA consists of four 8-bit registers, four

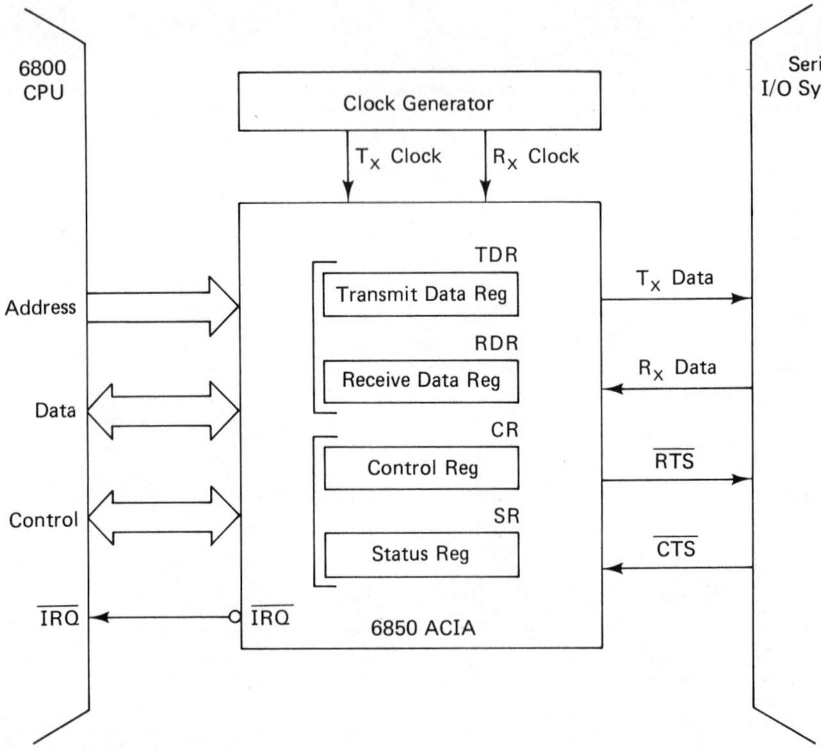

Fig 5.13. The 6850 ACIA architectural features.

I/O interface lines, and two clock lines. A brief functional description of the ACIA follows.

Transmit Mode

In the transmit mode, the TDR (Transmit Data Register) accepts and holds the 8-bit parallel data word from the microprocessor. Under software control this stored data is serialized and transmitted as serial data on the T_x (transmit data) line to the I/O system. The rate of shifting is determined by the T_x clock (transmit clock) input.

Receive Mode

In the receive mode, the RDR (receive data register) accepts the serial input data from the I/O system on the R_x (receive data) line. Under software control, this serial data is converted into the corresponding parallel 8-bit word and is stored in the RDR. At the appropriate event, the microprocessor reads this data. The rate at which the serial data is shifted into the RDR is determined by the R_x clock (receive clock).

The TDR is a "write only" register; the RDR is a "read only" register. They both share the same CPU address.

Control and Status Registers

The contents of the control register control the operation of the ACIA and the data formatting, as shown in Figure 5.14. Similarly, the contents of the status register specify the status of the data and the status of the registers of the ACIA, as shown in Figure 5.15. A clear understanding of the control and status functions is important in the understanding and application of the 6850 ACIA.

The control register is a "write only" register; the status register is a "read

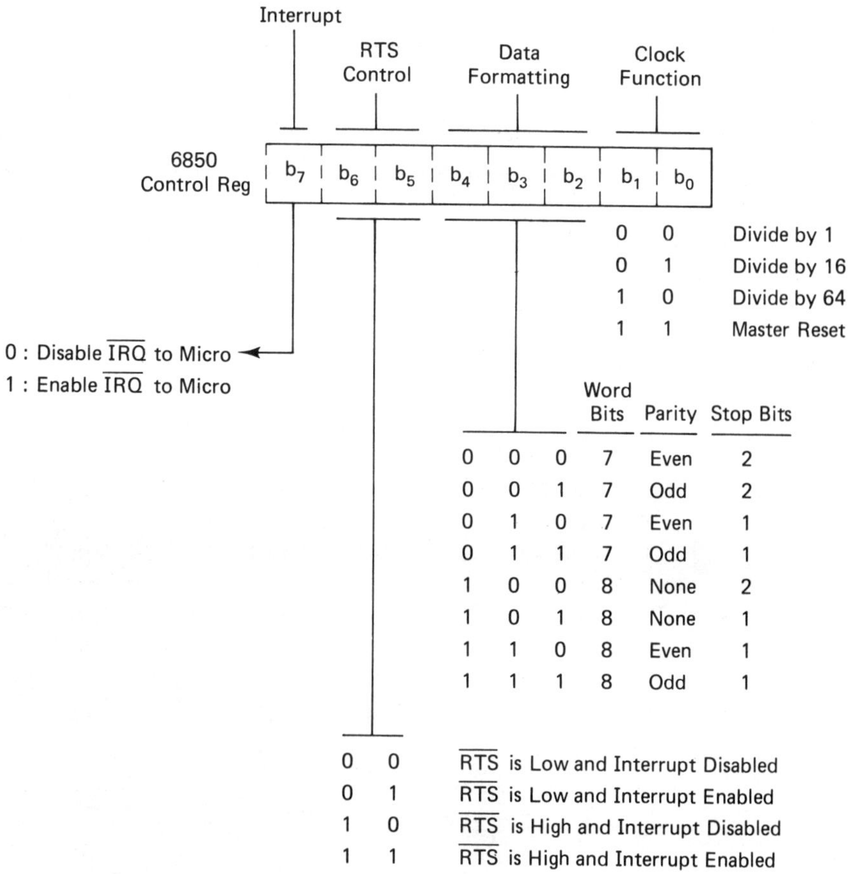

Fig 5.14. The 6850 ACIA control register formatting.

only" register. They both share the same address. To learn more about the ACIA, it is advisable to refer to the manufacturer's data sheets.

Serial Interface Example

Because of its simplicity and programmability, the 6850 ACIA is used extensively in applications involving serial interface. Example 5.5 is such an application.

Example 5.5 Serial Interface and Robotic Control

In the robotic control system of Figure 5.16, the panel keyboard sends serial data to the 6850 ACIA of the MEK 6800 microcomputer. The data configuration is shown.

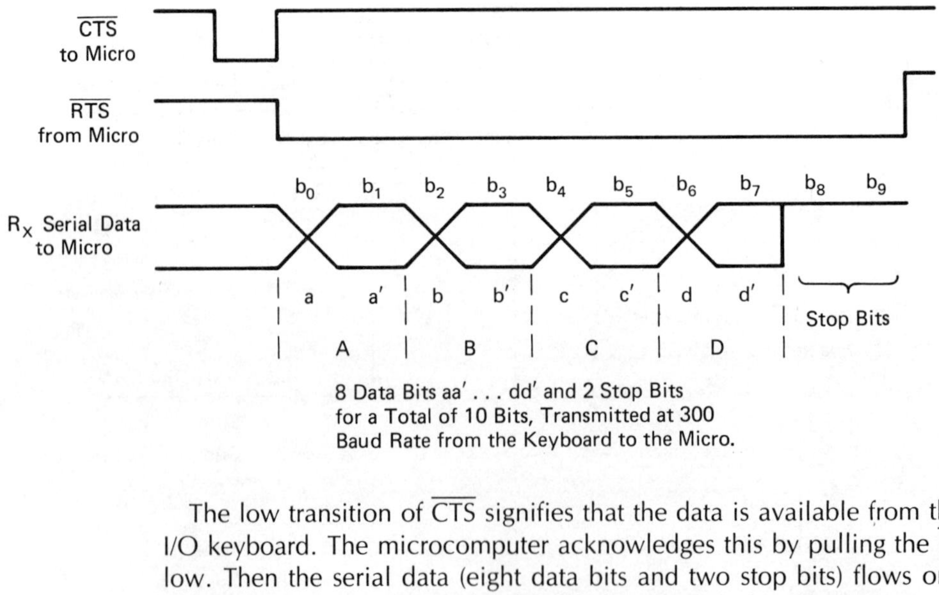

8 Data Bits aa' . . . dd' and 2 Stop Bits for a Total of 10 Bits, Transmitted at 300 Baud Rate from the Keyboard to the Micro.

The low transition of $\overline{CTS}$ signifies that the data is available from the serial I/O keyboard. The microcomputer acknowledges this by pulling the $\overline{RTS}$ line low. Then the serial data (eight data bits and two stop bits) flows on the R_x line from the keyboard. The eight data bits contain the information to run the four robotic motors A, B, C, and D. Shown below is the sequence of operations of motor A. The other motors are similar:

a a'	*Function*
0 0	No rotation
0 1	Clockwise rotation
1 0	Counter clockwise rotation
1 1	No rotation

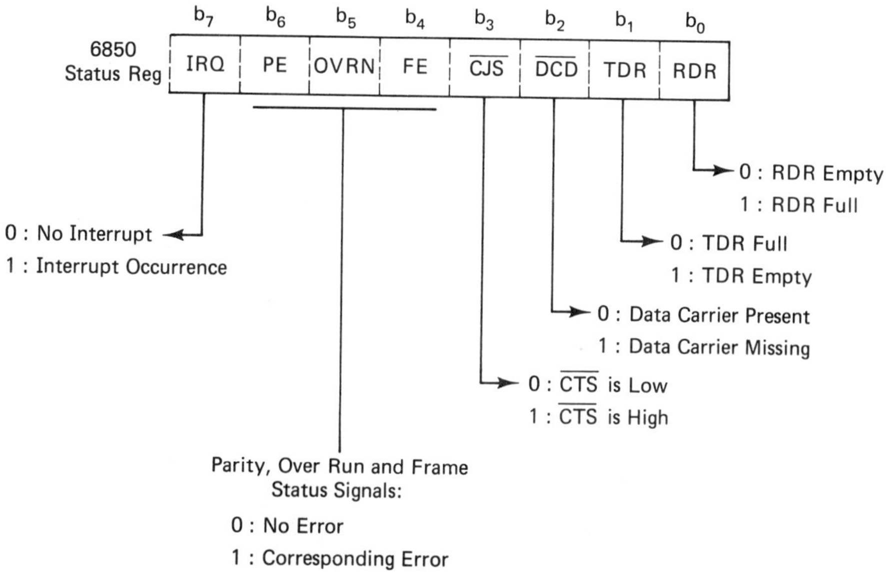

Fig 5.15. The 6850 ACIA status register structure.

Develop the necessary hardware and software to make the system of Figure 5.16 fully operational.

Solution

The hardware is self-contained in Figure 5.16. Port B of the PIA (also refer to Figure 5.1) presents the reconstructed 8-bit data word to the motor coils A, B, C, and D through the comparator drivers LM-346. Depending on the values of aa′, bb′, cc′, and dd′, the robotic motors A, B, C, D will function according to the table shown above.

(a) *Software*. The software conditions the ACIA to accept the serial data word (eight data bits and two stop bits) at 300 baud. Also it reconstructs the 8-bit parallel word and sends it to the PIA port B to run the robotic motors. Figure 5.17 shows the flow chart and Table 5.5 presents the actual operating listings. For the MEK 6800 microcomputer system the relevant I/O ports and registers are located as shown (refer to the sections on PIA and ACIA).

ORB/DDRB of PIA at location 800A
CRB of PIA at location 800B
TDR/RDR of ACIA at location 8010
CR/SR of ACIA at location 8011

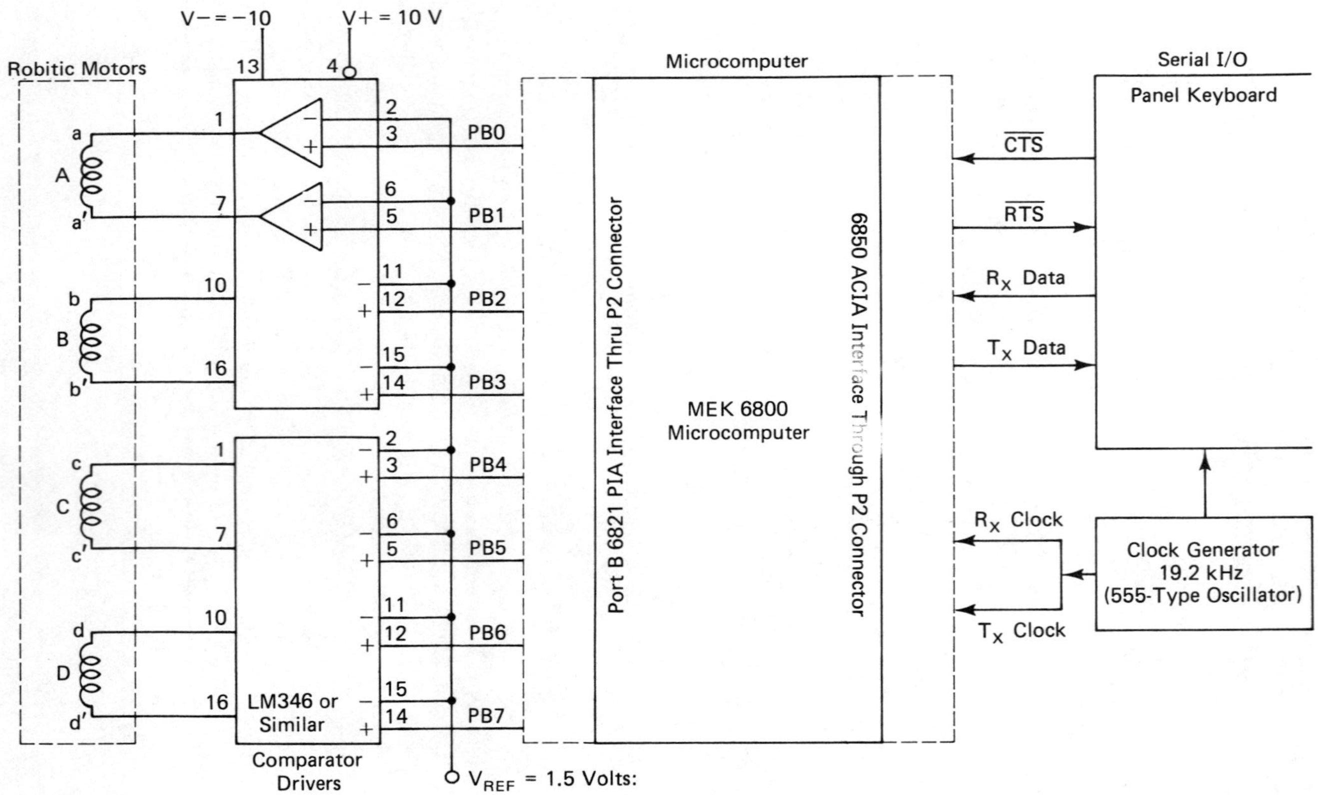

Fig 5.16. Typical ACIA serial interface and robotic control (Example 5.5).

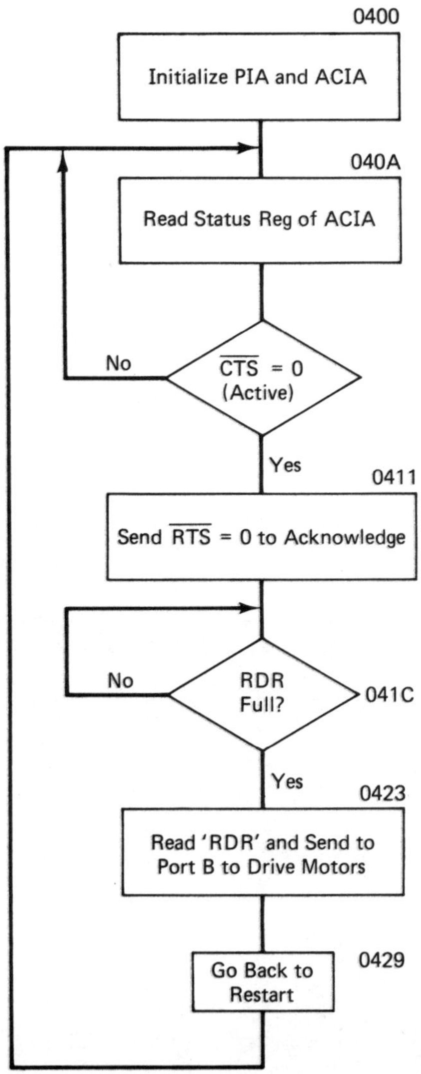

Fig 5.17. Flowchart for the serial interface and robotic control of Example 5.5.

(b) *Operating Listings.* It is assumed that port B is already configured as an output (refer to Table 5.2, listings between 0200 to 020F). Between 0400 and 0409, the ACIA is initialized to recognize the structured data of eight data bits and two stop bits at 300 baud. (refer to Figure 5.14 for control register formatting). The external R_x clock frequency of 19.2 KHz must be divided by 64 to generate the 300 Hz internal clock, to match the 300-

Table 5.5. Listings for the Serial Interface and Robotic Control (Example 5.5).

Location	Label	Mnemonic	Op Code	Address Mode	Comment
0400	Initialize	LDA A	86	IMM	Master reset of ACIA by loading 03 into the control register at 8011.
01		#03			
02		STA A	B7	EXT	
03		80			
04		11			
05	Start	LDA A	86	IMM	ACIA set to accept eight data bits and divide the clock by 64, by loading $(52)_{Hex}$ into the control register as shown. b_7 … b_0: 0 1 0 1 0 0 1 0 (RTS = 1; 8 Data; ÷64)
06		#52			
07		STA A	B7	EXT	
08		80			
09		11			
0A	CHK $\overline{CTS}$	→ LDA A	B6	EXT	Status register is checked to see if $b_3 = 0$ to signify whether $\overline{CTS} = 0$ has occurred. The program loops between 040A and 0410 until $b_3 = 0$; when $b_3 = 0$, program proceeds.
0B		80			
0C		11			
0D		AND A	84	IMM	
0E		#08			
0F		BNE	26	REL	
0410		F9			
11		NOP	01	INH	Linkage software and delay.
12		NOP	01	INH	
13		NOP	01	INH	
14		LDA A	86	IMM	

15		#12			$\overline{RTS}$ = 0 acknowledge signal sent out by loading $(12)_{Hex}$ into the control register.
16		STA	B7	EXT	
17		80			
18		11			Linkage software and delay.
0419		NOP	01	INH	
1A		NOP	01	INH	
1B		NOP	01	INH	
1C	CHK RDR	→ LDA A	B6	EXT	Status register is checked to see if b_1 = 1 to signify RDR is full. If not program loops between 041C and 0422. If b_1 = 1, program proceeds to read RDR, which contains an 8-bit parallel data word.
1D		80			
1E		11			
1F		AND A	84	IMM	
20		#01			
21		BEQ	27	REL	
22		F9			
23		LDA B	F6	EXT	RDR is read, and the contents are output to port B (at 800A) to run the robotic motors properly.
24		80			
25		10			
26		STA B	F7	EXT	
27		80			
28		0A			
29		JMP	7E	EXT	Jumps back to 0405 to start the new cycle.
2A		04_H			
2B		05_L			

Note: Port B must be configured as output (similar to Problem 5.2).

baud rate of the serial data. The control word of $(52)_{Hex}$ in the ACIA control register accomplishes this task.

Between 040A and 041B, the program checks the occurrence of $\overline{CTS} = 0$ transition and sends a $\overline{RTS} = 0$ acknowledge signal.

Between 041C and 0422, the program checks to see whether the RDR (receive data register) is full, signifying that the 8-bit parallel word has been reconstructed.

Between 0423 and 0428, the program outputs the parallel word to port B to run the robotic motors. Finally, the program jumps back to 0405 to start a new cycle.

In real robotic controls, all four motors may be spinning simultaneously, providing four degrees of motion. Detailed discussion of robotics is beyond the scope of this book, and you are encouraged to consult appropriate books on robotics.

The data transmission from the ACIA to the I/O is a similar process. TDR (transmit data register) is employed instead of the RDR. There are several example problems at the end of the chapter to help the reader to gain familiarity with the ACIA as a transmitter and receiver.

5.4. SINGLE-CHIP MICROCOMPUTER AND APPLICATIONS

There are several single-chip microcomputer devices such as 6801/68701, 6805/68705, etc., from the Motorola Corporation, with on-board RAM and ROM/EPROM. Most of these devices have architectural features similar to the 6800 microprocessor. As has been mentioned earlier, the single-chip microcomputers are well suited for I/O and system applications.

6805/68705 Single-Chip Microcomputer

The 6805/68705 family has a wide range of single-chip microcomputer devices, with varied amounts of RAM and ROM/EPROM, to suit the individual applications of the users. The EPROM version of 68705 is user programmable and well suited for developmental work. The factory mask programmable ROM version of the 6805 is well suited for the mass production of systems with fully developed designs. The 6805 and 68705 are fully pin, I/O, and memory compatible (like the 8048 and 8748 of the Intel Corporation).

Figure 5.18 shows the pin structure and Figure 5.19 shows the architecture of the 6805/68705, P_2/P_3 version. The other versions are essentially similar, with minor modifications.

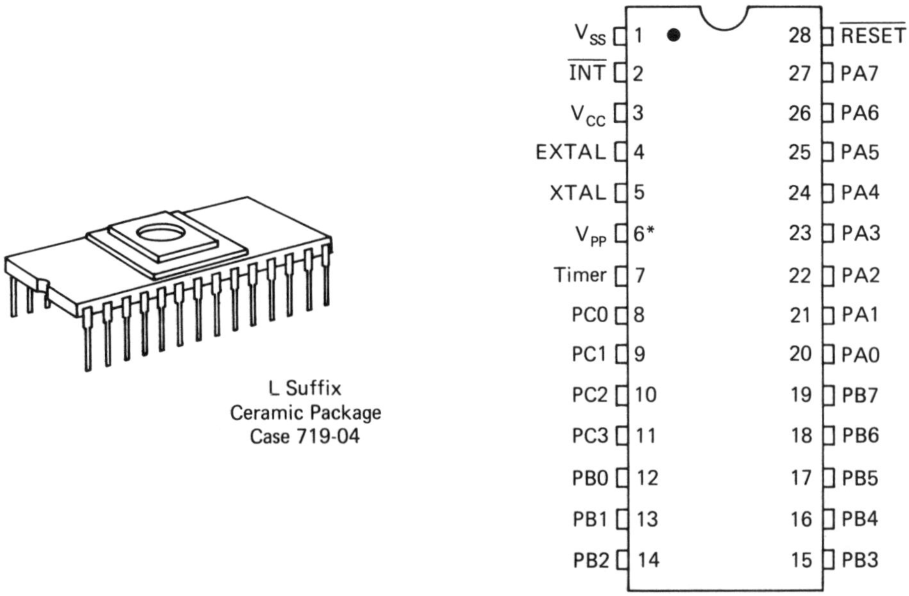

(a) 68705 Device **(b)** Pin Structure

Fig 5.18. Pin structure of the 6805/68705 microcomputer: (a) 68705 device; (b) pin structure. (Courtesy Motorola, Inc.)

Registers

The 11-bit program counter provides up to 2K memory access. The 8-bit accumulator handles byte-oriented data manipulations. Similarly, the 8-bit index register handles the data and address manipulation using the indexed scheme. The 5-bit stack pointer handles 32 bytes of stack. Finally, the 5-bit condition code register presents the status of the CPU through five flag bits [carry (C); zero (Z); negative (N); interrupt mask (I); and half carry (H)]. The architecture is essentially similar to the 6800 microprocessor.

Memory

In addition, the 6805/68705 has up to 1,912 bytes of ROM/EPROM and 128 bytes of RAM, as shown.

I/O Features

The 28-pin version of the 6805/68705 has three I/O ports (two 8-bit ports A and B and one 4-bit port C), for a total of 20 I/O lines. All these lines are

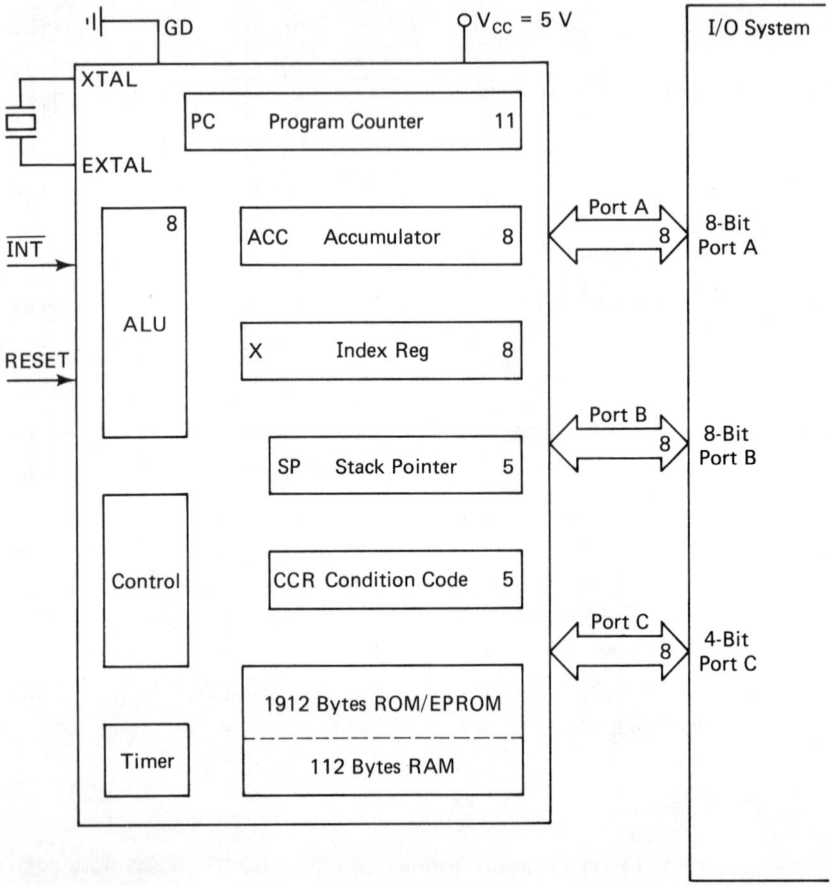

Fig 5.19. Architectural features of the 6805/68705 microcomputer (P2/P3 versions).

individually programmable as inputs or outputs. The timer section can be programmed to divide the system clock by 4, 16, 64, or 128 to provide the timing information.

Software

The instructions and software of the 6805/68705 are essentially similar to the 6800 microprocessor. In addition, there are instructions in the 6805 family to handle the bit manipulations.

Memory Map

Figure 5.20 shows the memory map of the 6805/68705 microcomputer device under consideration. The program can be easily entered into the EPROM

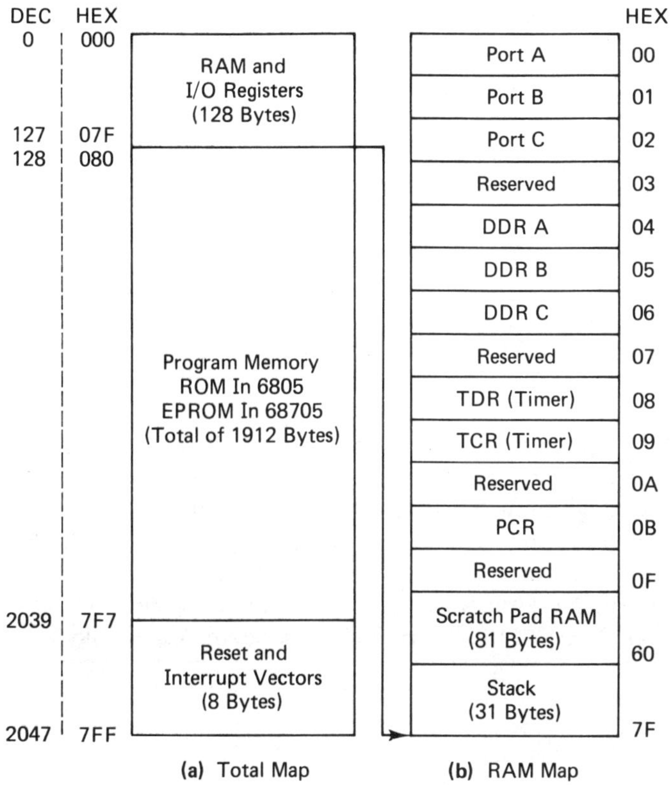

Fig 5.20. Memory map for the 6805/68705 microcomputer (P2/P3 versions).

portion of the 68705, using a simple program transfer circuit, suggested by the manufacturer. For further details, manufacturer's data and information sheets should be consulted.

Industrial Data Acquisition System

We would like to reemphasize the importance of the data acquisition concept by repeating it here and implementing it with the 68705 single-chip microcomputer. Section 5.2 should be reviewed before proceeding further.

Example 5.6 Single-Chip Micro: Data Acquisition

Develop a fully operational data acquisition system (similar to Example 5.4) using the 68705 single-chip microcomputer. You may use the hardware of Figures 5.7, 5.8, 5.10, and 5.12.

Solution

Figure 5.21 shows the operating hardware interface. The details can be obtained from Figures 5.7, 5.8, 5.10, and 5.12. The 68705 is activated with a 4 MHz crystal as shown.

Figure 5.22 shows the flow chart and Table 5.6 presents the operating listings. Between 0090 and 0099, port A is configured as the input (to accept the A/D data) and port B is configured as the output (to send the data to D/A).

Between 009A and 00A2, the A/D data is read from port A. It is shifted left twice (multiplication by 4) and sent to the D/A, connected to port B. Also the data is stored sequentially in the memory table between the locations $(20)_{Hex}$ and $(3F)_{Hex}$. Between 00A3 and 00A9, the program branches to appropriate locations to fill the memory table sequentially.

The reset vectored locations of 07FE and 07FF should be loaded with $(0090)_{Hex}$ so that the program starts at location 0090, on power up reset. Similarly, the mask option register located at 0784 should be loaded with $(0E)_{Hex}$, to allow for the crystal clock option.

The mnemonics and op codes correspond to the 68705/6805 instructions. Appropriate data sheets should be consulted.

While the program is being loaded into the 68705, V_{pp} at pin 6 should be maintained at 21 volts. To run the program, V_{pp} should be returned to 5 volts.

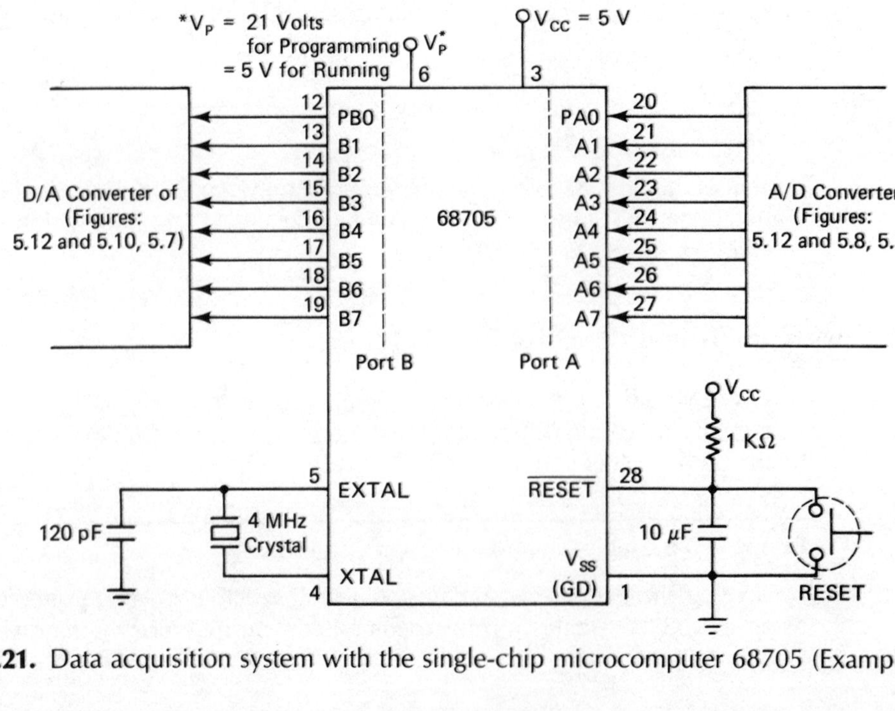

Fig 5.21. Data acquisition system with the single-chip microcomputer 68705 (Example 5.6).

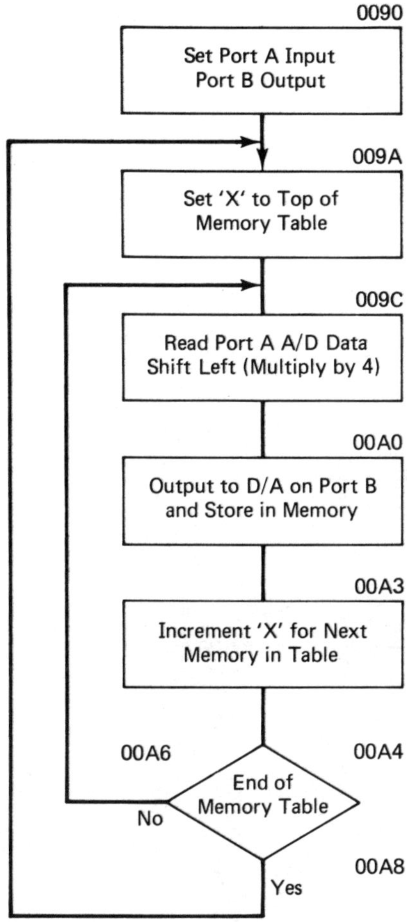

Fig 5.22. Flowchart for the data acquisition system of Example 5.6.

5.5. SUMMARY

In this chapter, we have introduced the powerful 6821 PIA and 6850 ACIA interface devices and their interaction with the 6800 microprocessor. The system consisting of the 6800, 6821, 6850, and additional memory forms a powerful and flexible microcomputer.

The usefulness of the microcomputer in the generation of timing waveforms for industrial control is discussed, illustrated by a practical application. The increasingly popular and widely used Analog ⇄ Digital conversions are introduced and implemented with the 6800 microcomputer system. These concepts are further extended to develop an operating data acquisition system.

Table 5.6. Operating Listings for Data Acquisition with 68705 (Problem 5.6).

Location	Label	Mnemonic	Op Code	Address Mode	Comment
0900		NOP	9D	INH	Linkage software.
91		NOP	9D		
92		LDA	A6	IMM	Port A configured as input by loading 00 into DDRA at location 04.
93		#00			
94		STA	B7	DIR	
95		04			
96		LDA	A6	IMM	Port B configured as output by loading FF into DDRB at location 05.
97		#FF			
98		STA	B7	DIR	
99		05			
9A	Top	→LDX	AE	IMM	Top of memory table address of 20 is loaded into X register.
9B		#20			
9C		→LDA	B6	DIR	Port A (A/D) data loaded into accumulator.
9D		00			
9E		LSL A	48	INH	Accumulator shifted left twice to provide multiplication up to 4.
9F		LSL A	48	INH	
00A0	Table	STA, X	F7	IND	Processed data stored in sequential memory location in table and is also sent to port B (D/A).
A1		STA	B7	DIR	
A2		01			
A3		INC X	5C	INH	X incremented to address next memory in table. If not the end of the table, branches back to 009C to read new A/D data.
A4		CPX	A3	IMM	
A5		#40			
A6		BNE	26	REL	
A7		F4			
A8		BRA	20	REL	At the end of the table, program branches to 009A to start new table of data.
A9		F0			

Reset	*Vector*
07FE	00_H
07FF	90_L

Mask Option	*Reg.*
0784	0E

The serial data interface concepts are introduced and implemented. The latest generation of the 6805/68705 single-chip microcomputers is discussed, and the data acquisition system is redesigned with the help of 68705.

This chapter should provide helpful background in designing systems using microcomputers based on the 6800 architecture. These concepts can be easily implemented with other microcomputer systems.

For further information refer to the Motorola Corporation, Inc. 6820/6821, 6850 ACIA, and 6805/68705 data sheets.

Problems

5.1. In a particular I/O application using the 6821 PIA, the DDRA and DDRB have been loaded with $(AA)_{Hex}$ and $(55)_{Hex}$. Identify which bits are the input and which bits are the output.

5.2. Write a brief software routine starting at location $(0200)_{Hex}$, such that P_{A0}, P_{A2}, P_{A4}, P_{A6}, P_{B1}, P_{B3}, P_{B5}, P_{B7} are configured as the inputs, and the rest of the bits are configured as the outputs.

5.3. Following the control register formatting of Figure 5.2, determine the control word

(a) to recognize CA1 negative transition and enable the corresponding interrupt,

(b) to recognize CA2 positive transition, but disable the corresponding interrupt.

5.4. Configure the control word such that

(a) Part (a) of Problem 5.3 is accomplished, together with recognizing CA2 active low transition, with interrupts disabled.

(b) Repeat (a) above, with interrupts enabled.

5.5. Generate the timing waveforms of Figure 5.23 on port A of the 6800

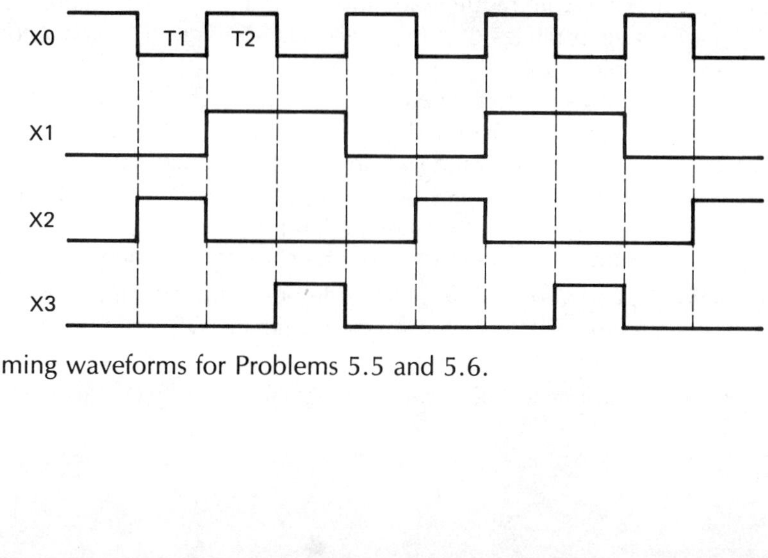

Fig 5.23. Timing waveforms for Problems 5.5 and 5.6.

system under consideration. Show clearly all your software listings and the hardware interface. Consider that T1 = T2 = 100 ms.

5.6. Repeat Problem 5.5, such that

(a) T1 = T2 is the minimum possible time on your system;

(b) T1 = 4T2 and T2 is the minimum possible time interval.

5.7. The A/D conversion is extensively used in industry. Figure 5.24 shows a simple digital scale system. As the weight is put on, the spring contracts, and the wiper moves down R1, generating more voltage V_S, which is proportional to the weight. For the values shown V_S ranges from 0.2 volts to 5 volts, as the wiper moves between A and B.

Develop the operating hardware and software, such that V_S is read in 2-second intervals, digitized and displayed. The display should indicate

2.0 pounds when V_S = 0.2 volts

50.0 pounds when V_S = 5 volts

Show clearly all the design steps and the operating listings. One decimal accuracy is acceptable.

5.8. Repeat Problem 5.7 such that the range is extended by switching a second spring parallel to the first spring (by connecting the metal bar *s*). The display now should read between 2 to 100 pounds as the wiper moves between A and B. Develop the complete operating hardware and software.

5.9. Auto scaling can be easily accomplished. Design additional hardware and software required to auto load the "s" bar in Figure 5.24, to switch between ranges of 2 to 50 pounds (Problem 5.7) and 2 to 100 pounds (Problem 5.8).

The "s" bar can be operated with the help of a solenoid, to engage (100-pound range) and disengage (50-pound range).

The system should start in the higher range (100 pounds). If the scale reading is below 50 pounds for 5 seconds consecutively, the system should go to the lower range (50 pounds)

Show all the details of your hardware design and the software listings.

5.10. Repeat Problem 5.9., with additional hardware and software to have the system operate in the following ranges: 50 pounds, 100 pounds, and 200 pounds.

5.11. Control handshake is an important feature in asynchronous applications.

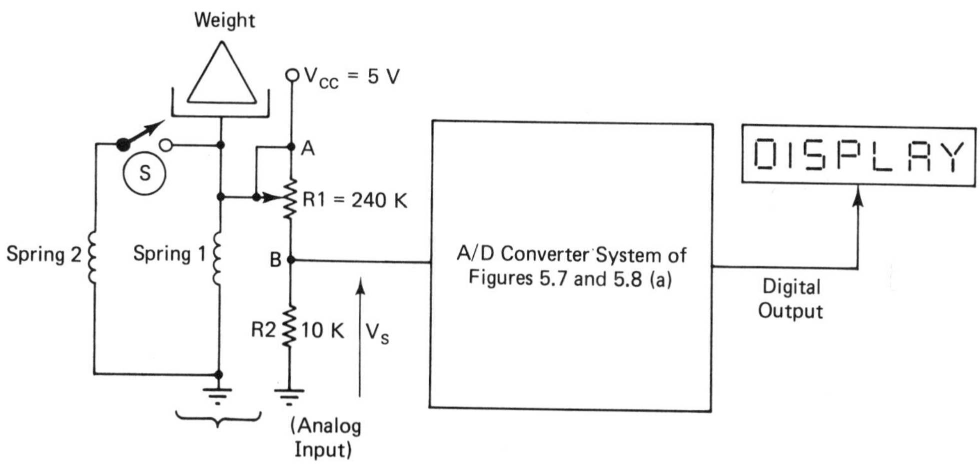

Fig 5.24. A/D conversion system for Problems 5.7–5.9.

Figure 5.25 shows an I/O system sending an active low transition on CA1 to the 6800 microcomputer system.

Develop the operating software such that the 6800 system recognizes CA1 low transition on the poling basis and generates the double pulse on CA2 ouput, with 100 microsec width.

5.12. Repeat Problem 5.11, where the system will operate on the interrupt driven mode.

5.13. Develop the necessary hardware and software to generate the waveforms of Figure 5.26, using the D/A conversion concepts of Figure 5.10. Consider that T1 = T2 = T3 = 100 μs. Consider T_O = T1.

5.14. Repeat Problem 5.13, where T1 = 2T2 = 4T3 = 400 μs. Clearly show all the operating listings and the resulting waveform.

5.15. Using the comcepts of D/A conversion, generate

$$A = 5 + 5 \sin 100t \text{ volts}$$

$$B = 5 + 5 \cos 200t \text{ volts}$$

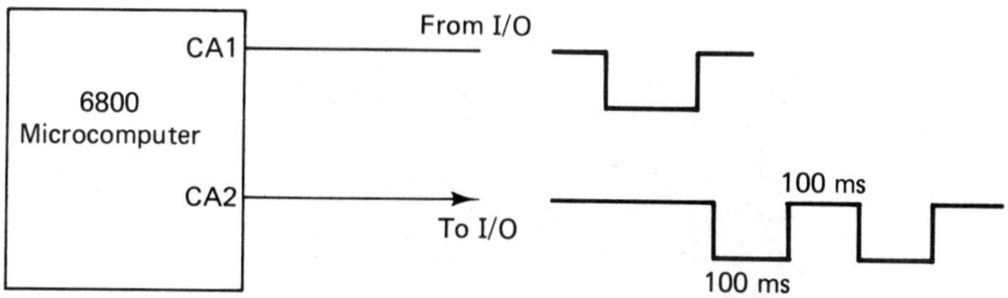

Fig 5.25. Control handshake in asynchronous applications for Problems 5.11 and 5.12.

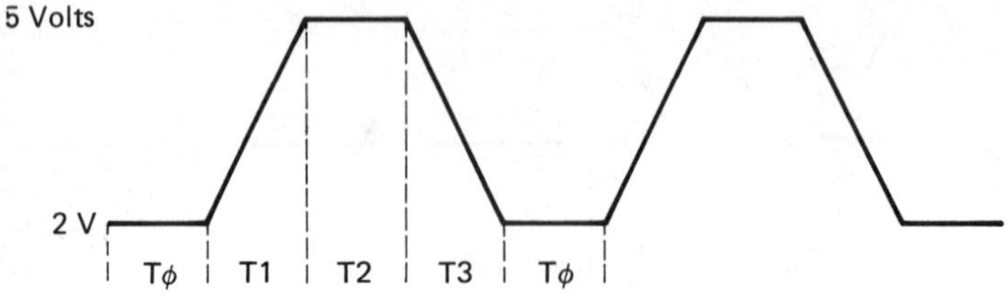

Fig 5.26. Trapezoidal waveform for Problems 5.13 and 5.14.

with at least 20 samples per cycle. Show the operating software and hardware.

5.16. In the data acquisition system of Figure 5.12, the signal voltage V_S can be approximated as

$$V_S = A_1 \sin\omega_1 t + A_2 \sin\omega_2 t + A_3 \sin \omega_3 t$$

where

$$A_1 = A_2 = A_3 = 10^{-2} \text{ volts}$$

$$\omega_1 \cong 2\omega_2 \cong 3\omega_3 \cong 6000 \text{ rad/s}$$

(a) Develop the necessary software and hardware such that V_S can be digitized and stored for 5 seconds. Show all the listings. Choose your own sampling frequency and memory range.

(b) Digitally multiply the stored data by a factor of 3 and output as V_O through the D/A converter section. Show all the hardware and software.

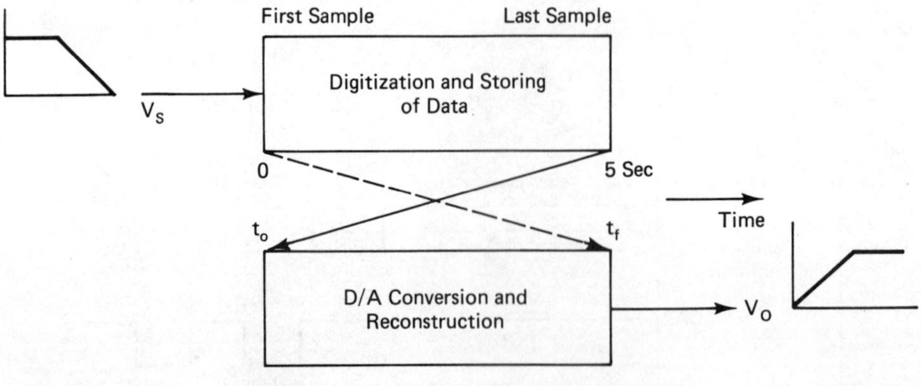

Fig 5.27. Data coding using the data acquisition concepts of Problems 5.17 and 5.18.

5.17. Data coding is very important in protecting the information. Repeat Problem 5.16, where the digitized data of V_S is reconstructed in the backward sequence as shown in Figure 5.27. The last digitized sample of V_S will be the first reconstructed analog data. Thus, V_O reconstructed voltage looks coded.

(a) Develop the complete operating software and hardware to accomplish the above task.

(b) Draw V_S and V_O waveforms, given $V_S = 5 \sin 100t + 5 \cos 200t$.

5.18. The amount of coding in Problem 5.17 is limited. We can introduce any depth of coding. Repeat Problem 5.17 such that V_O is reconstructed by taking the odd samples from the digitized data (sample 1, 3, 5, ...) and then the even samples (sample 2, 4, 6, ...) in sequence. Show all the software concepts and listings.

5.19. Using the 6850 ACIA write the control word format to

(a) Divide the clock by 16 to recognize "7-bit odd parity 1 stop bit" word; and disable the interrupt

(b) Same as (a), but with interrupt enabled.

5.20. The control words for the ACIA are as shown. In each case, identify the function being accomplished.

(a) Word 1 47

(b) Word 2 CA

5.21. Repeat Example 5.5 (and Figure 5.16) such that the data is transmitted between the control panel and the system at 110 baud instead of 300 baud.

5.22. Repeat Example 5.5 so that the system handles two robotic motors *X* and *Y* in multiplexed mode, with the serial information entering the system also in the multiplexed mode.

Show the details of the additional hardware required and complete operating software.

5.23. Using the manufacturer's data sheets, identify the functional differences between the 6805 P2, P3, and the 28-pin and 40-pin versions.

5.24. Repeat the robotic control problem of 5.21 using the 68705 single-chip microcomputer. Assume that the input information regarding the stepper codes is available as a parallel 8-bit X word that can be read by the microcomputer.

Use the hardware of your choice. Show all the hardware details and the software listings.

5.25. Repeat the data coding of Problem 5.17, using the 68705 single-chip microcomputer.

5.26. Repeat the waveform generation of Problem 5.5 with the 68705 single-chip microcomputer.

CHAPTER SIX

The 6502 Microprocessor and Microcomputer Systems

The 6502 is another 8-bit (N-channel technology, 40-pin) microprocessor, developed and marketed by MOS technology and Rockwell International. It is widely used in control systems, video games, and industrial applications. Some of the popular home computer systems such as Apple®, ATARI®, Commodore™, Pet®, Vic-20®, and board level microcomputer systems such as AIM®-65, Sym-1, and Kim-1 are all based on 6502 microprocessor and associated hardware.

We will use the Aim 65 and Apple systems format in discussing the applications. With minor modifications, the presented software and hardware can be used on any 6502-based system.

6.1. GENERAL ARCHITECTURE

Registers and Flags

As shown in Figure 6.1, the 6502 is an 8-bit microprocessor with 16-bit address and 8-bit data buses. It contains

16-bit program counter to access 64K memory locations	PC
8-bit accumulator	A
8-bit X index register	X
8-bit Y index register	Y
8-bit stack pointer (always addresses page 1)	SP
8-bit process status register (flags)	Status

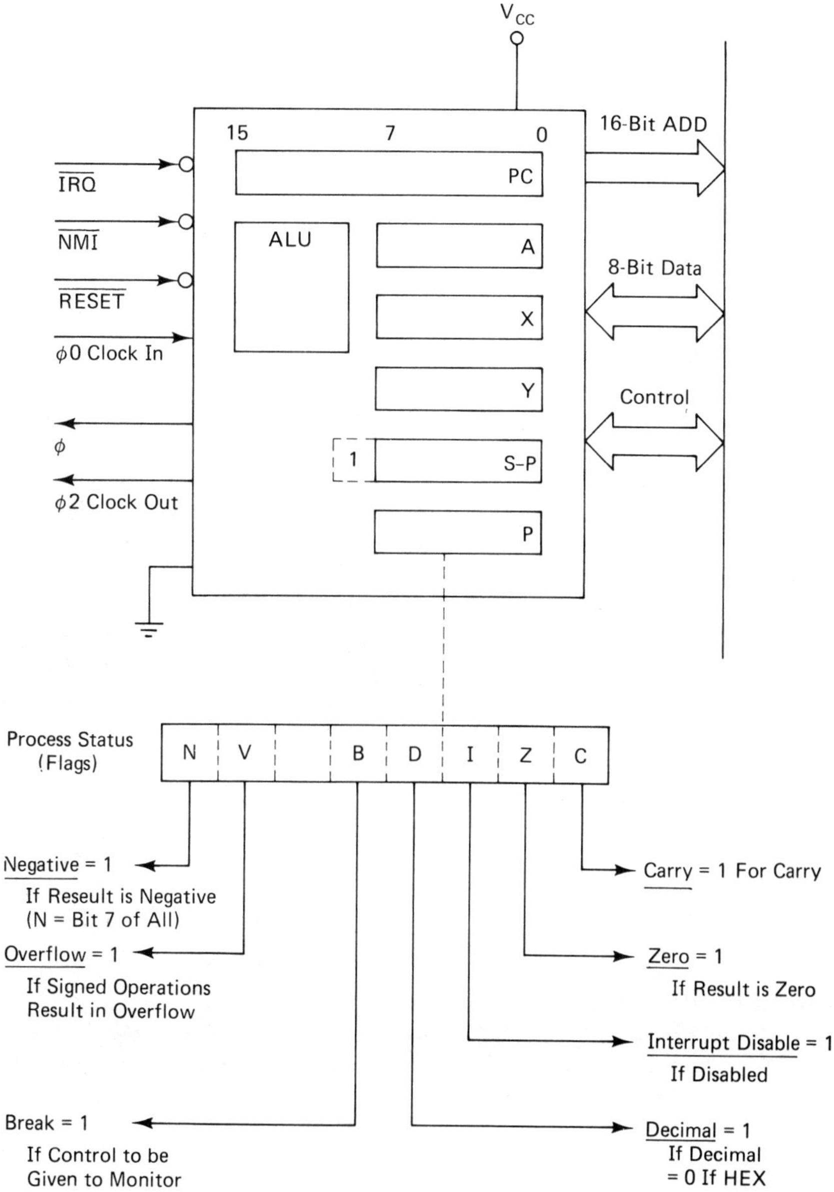

Fig 6.1. The 6502 register and flag structure.

Table 6.1. Reset and Interrupt Vectors With Specific Values for the AIM-65.

	Address	*6502 System Vectors*		*Aim 65 Values*
$\overline{\text{NMI}}$ Vector	FFFA	$\overline{\text{NMI}}$	Low Byte	02
	FFFB	$\overline{\text{NMI}}$	High Byte	A4
$\overline{\text{Reset}}$ Vector	FFFC	$\overline{\text{Reset}}$	Low Byte	BF
	FFFD	$\overline{\text{Reset}}$	High Byte	EO
$\overline{\text{IRQ}}$ Vector	FFFE	$\overline{\text{IRQ}}$	Low Byte	04
	FFFF	$\overline{\text{IRQ}}$	High Byte	A4

Reset and Interrupt Vectors

The 6502 microprocessor has a reset input $\overline{\text{reset}}$, a nonmaskable interrupt $\overline{\text{NMI}}$ (which cannot be masked), and a maskable interrupt $\overline{\text{IRQ}}$ (which can be masked under software control). All these inputs are low active. On the occurrence of any of these inputs, the microprocessor will load its program counter with the contents of vectored memory locations, as shown in Table 6.1.

After storing its registers on stack, the microprocessor will branch to these new addresses to begin the respective routines. A return from interrupt (RTI) instruction will return the micro to the main program. In Table 6.1, we have also included the vectored addresses of the AIM-65 microcomputer.

6.2. INSTRUCTION SET AND ADDRESSING MODE

The instruction set of the 6502 is characterized by different address modes (similar to 6800) for the same mnemonic.

Mnemonic and Op Codes

Tables 6.2 and 6.3 show the respective mnemonic and op codes of the 6502.

Addressing Modes

An examination of Table 6.3 shows several addressing modes for the same instruction and mnemonic. Most of these addressing modes are similar to the Motorola 6800 and can be distinguished from one another by their op codes. We present a brief explanation of these addressing modes. The first byte is always op code.

Table 6.2. Instruction Set of the 6502 (Alphabetical Sequence). (Courtesy Rockwell International.)

ADC	Add memory to accumulator with carry
AND	AND memory with accumulator
ASL	Shift left one bit (memory or accumulator)
BCC	Branch on carry clear
BCS	Branch on carry set
BEQ	Branch on result zero
BIT	Test bits in memory with accumulator
BMI	Branch on result minus
BNE	Branch on result not zero
BPL	Branch on result plus
BRK	Force break
BVC	Branch on overflow clear
BVS	Branch on overflow set
CLC	Clear carry flag
CLD	Clear decimal mode
CLI	Clear interrupt disable bit
CLV	Clear overflow flag
CMP	Compare memory and accumulator
CPX	Compare memory and index X
CPY	Compare memory and index Y
DEC	Decrement memory by one
DEX	Decrement index X by one
DEY	Decrement index Y by one
EOR	Exclusive-or memory with accumulator
INC	Increment memory by one
INX	Increment index X by one
INY	Increment index Y by one
JMP	Jump to new location
JSR	Jump to new location saving return address
LDA	Load accumulator with memory
LDX	Load index X with memory
LDY	Load index Y with memory
LSR	Shift one bit right (memory or accumulator)
NOP	No operation
ORA	OR memory with accumulator
PHA	Push accumulator on stack
PHP	Push processor status on stack
PLA	Pull accumulator from stack
PLP	Pull processor status from stack
ROL	Rotate one bit left (memory or accumulator)
ROR	Rotate one bit right (memory or accumulator)
RTI	Return from interrupt
RTS	Return from subroutine
SBC	Subtract memory from accumulator with borrow
SEC	Set carry flag
SED	Set decimal mode

Table 6.2. (*Continued*)

SEI	Set interrupt disable status
STA	Store accumulator in memory
STX	Store index X in memory
STY	Store index Y in memory
TAX	Transfer accumulator to index X
TAY	Transfer accumulator to index Y
TSX	Transfer stack pointer to index X
TXA	Transfer index X to accumulator
TXS	Transfer index X to stack pointer
TYA	Transfer index Y to accumulator

1. Immediate Addressing. The second byte of the instruction is the data itself, on which the operation has to be performed:

	Op code	Mode	
Ex: LDA #73	A9:	immediate:	load accumulator with data 73

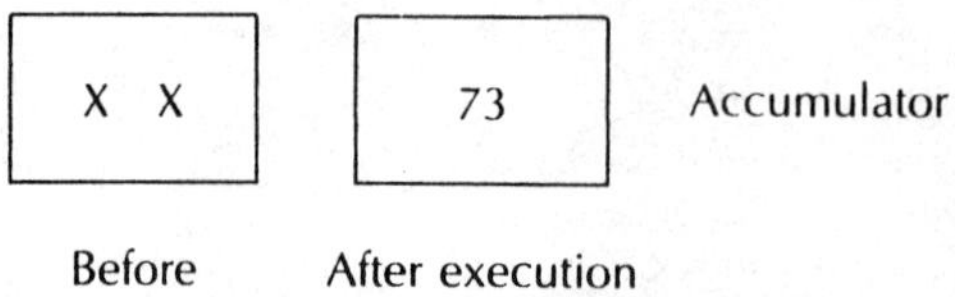

2. Absolute Addressing. The second byte contains the low byte and the third byte contains high byte of the effective address of the operand:

	Op code	Mode	
LDA A0(L) 40(H)	AD	absolute	Load accumulator with contents of location 40A0

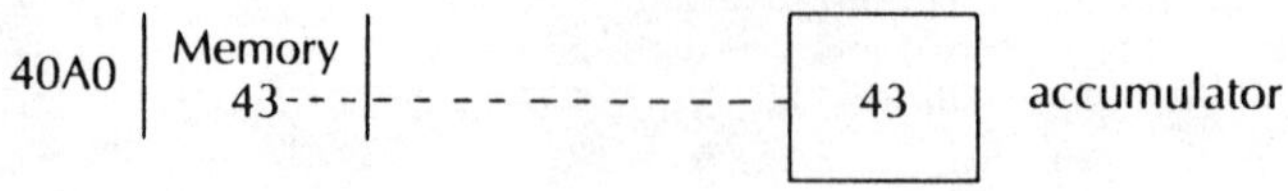

3. Zero Page Addressing. The second byte refers to the address of the operand in page zero.
   Example:

	Code	Mode	
STX 79	86	zero page:	Contents of X register are stored in location ØØ79

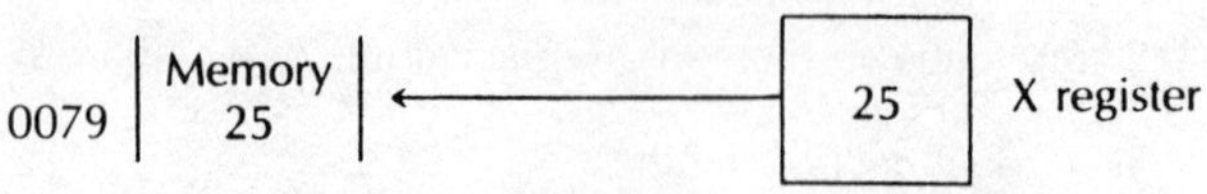

Memory after the instruction

Table 6.3. 6502 Instruction Set and Op Codes. (Courtesy Rockwell International.)

INSTRUCTION SET

INSTRUCTIONS		IMMEDIATE			ABSOLUTE			ZERO PAGE			ACCUM			IMPLIED			(IND. X)			(IND). Y			Z PAGE, X			ABS. X			ABS. Y			RELATIVE			INDIRECT			Z PAGE, Y			PROCESSOR STATUS CODES	
MNEMONIC	OPERATION	OP	n	#	OP	n	#	OP	n	#	OP	n	#	OP	n	#	OP	n	#	OP	n	#	OP	n	#	OP	n	#	OP	n	#	OP	n	#	OP	n	#	OP	n	#	7 6 5 4 3 2 1 0 N V • B D I Z C	MNEMONIC
ADC	A + M + C → A (4)(1)	69	2	2	6D	4	3	65	3	2							61	6	2	71	5	2	75	4	2	7D	4	3	79	4	3										N V • • • • Z C	ADC
AND	A ∧ M → A (1)	29	2	2	2D	4	3	25	3	2							21	6	2	31	5	2	35	4	2	3D	4	3	39	4	3										N • • • • • Z •	AND
ASL	C ← [7 0] ← 0				0E	6	3	06	5	2	0A	2	1										16	6	2	1E	7	3													N • • • • • Z C	ASL
BCC	BRANCH ON C = 0 (2)																															90	2	2							• • • • • • • •	BCC
BCS	BRANCH ON C = 1 (2)																															B0	2	2							• • • • • • • •	BCS
BEQ	BRANCH ON Z = 1 (2)																															F0	2	2							• • • • • • • •	BEQ
BIT	A ∧ M				2C	4	3	24	3	2																															M_7 M_6 • • • • Z •	BIT
BMI	BRANCH ON N = 1 (2)																															30	2	2							• • • • • • • •	BMI
BNE	BRANCH ON Z = 0 (2)																															D0	2	2							• • • • • • • •	BNE
BPL	BRANCH ON N = 0 (2)																															10	2	2							• • • • • • • •	BPL
BRK	BREAK													00	7	1																									• • • 1 • 1 • •	BRK
BVC	BRANCH ON V = 0 (2)																															50	2	2							• • • • • • • •	BVC
BVS	BRANCH ON V = 1 (2)																															70	2	2							• • • • • • • •	BVS
CLC	0 → C													18	2	1																									• • • • • • • 0	CLC
CLD	0 → D													D8	2	1																									• • • • 0 • • •	CLD
CLI	0 → I													58	2	1																									• • • • • 0 • •	CLI
CLV	0 → V													B8	2	1																									• 0 • • • • • •	CLV
CMP	A − M	C9	2	2	CD	4	3	C5	3	2							C1	6	2	D1	5	2	D5	4	2	DD	4	3	D9	4	3										N • • • • • Z C	CMP
CPX	X − M	E0	2	2	EC	4	3	E4	3	2																															N • • • • • Z C	CPX
CPY	Y − M	C0	2	2	CC	4	3	C4	3	2																															N • • • • • Z C	CPY
DEC	M − 1 → M				CE	6	3	C6	5	2													D6	6	2	DE	7	3													N • • • • • Z •	DEC
DEX	X − 1 → X													CA	2	1																									N • • • • • Z •	DEX
DEY	Y − 1 → Y													88	2	1																									N • • • • • Z •	DEY
EOR	A ⊻ M → A (1)	49	2	2	4D	4	3	45	3	2							41	6	2	51	5	2	55	4	2	5D	4	3	59	4	3										N • • • • • Z •	EOR
INC	M + 1 → M				EE	6	3	E6	5	2													F6	6	2	FE	7	3													N • • • • • Z •	INC
INX	X + 1 → X													E8	2	1																									N • • • • • Z •	INX
INY	Y + 1 → Y													C8	2	1																									N • • • • • Z •	INY
JMP	JUMP TO NEW LOC				4C	3	3																												6C	5	3				• • • • • • • •	JMP
JSR	JUMP SUB				20	6	3																																		• • • • • • • •	JSR
LDA	M → A (1)	A9	2	2	AD	4	3	A5	3	2							A1	6	2	B1	5	2	B5	4	2	BD	4	3	B9	4	3										N • • • • • Z •	LDA
LDX	M → X (1)	A2	2	2	AE	4	3	A6	3	2																			BE	4	3							B6	4	2	N • • • • • Z •	LDX
LDY	M → Y (1)	A0	2	2	AC	4	3	A4	3	2													B4	4	2	BC	4	3													N • • • • • Z •	LDY
LSR	0 → [7 0] → C				4E	6	3	46	5	2	4A	2	1										56	6	2	5E	7	3													0 • • • • • Z C	LSR
NOP	NO OPERATION													EA	2	1																									• • • • • • • •	NOP
ORA	A V M → A	09	2	2	0D	4	3	05	3	2							01	6	2	11	5	2	15	4	2	1D	4	3	19	4	3										N • • • • • Z •	ORA
PHA	A → Ms S − 1 → S													48	3	1																									• • • • • • • •	PHA
PHP	P → Ms S − 1 → S													08	3	1																									• • • • • • • •	PHP
PLA	S + 1 → S Ms → A													68	4	1																									N • • • • • Z •	PLA
PLP	S + 1 → S Ms → P													28	4	1																									(RESTORED)	PLP
ROL	← [7 0] ← [C] ←				2E	6	3	26	5	2	2A	2	1										36	6	2	3E	7	3													N • • • • • Z C	ROL
ROR	→ [C] → [7 0] →				6E	6	3	66	5	2	6A	2	1										76	6	2	7E	7	3													N • • • • • Z C	ROR
RTI	RTRN INT													40	6	1																									(RESTORED)	RTI
RTS	RTRN SUB													60	6	1																									• • • • • • • •	RTS
SBC	A − M − $\bar{C}$ → A (1)	E9	2	2	ED	4	3	E5	3	2							E1	6	2	F1	5	2	F5	4	2	FD	4	3	F9	4	3										N V • • • • Z (3)	SBC
SEC	1 → C													38	2	1																									• • • • • • • 1	SEC
SED	1 → D													F8	2	1																									• • • • 1 • • •	SED
SEI	1 → I													78	2	1																									• • • • • 1 • •	SEI
STA	A → M				8D	4	3	85	3	2							81	6	2	91	6	2	95	4	2	9D	5	3	99	5	3										• • • • • • • •	STA
STX	X → M				8E	4	3	86	3	2																												96	4	2	• • • • • • • •	STX
STY	Y → M				8C	4	3	84	3	2													94	4	2																• • • • • • • •	STY
TAX	A → X													AA	2	1																									N • • • • • Z •	TAX
TAY	A → Y													A8	2	1																									N • • • • • Z •	TAY
TSX	S → X													BA	2	1																									N • • • • • Z •	TSX
TXA	X → A													8A	2	1																									N • • • • • Z •	TXA
TXS	X → S													9A	2	1																									• • • • • • • •	TXS
TYA	Y → A													98	2	1																									N • • • • • Z •	TYA

(1) ADD 1 to "N" IF PAGE BOUNDARY IS CROSSED

(2) ADD 1 TO "N" IF BRANCH OCCURS TO SAME PAGE
ADD 2 TO "N" IF BRANCH OCCURS TO DIFFERENT PAGE

(3) CARRY NOT = BORROW

(4) IF IN DECIMAL MODE. Z FLAG IS INVALID
ACCUMULATOR MUST BE CHECKED FOR ZERO RESULT

X	INDEX X	+	ADD	M_7	MEMORY BIT 7
Y	INDEX Y	−	SUBTRACT	M_6	MEMORY BIT 6
A	ACCUMULATOR	∧	AND	n	NO. CYCLES
M	MEMORY PER EFFECTIVE ADDRESS	V	OR	#	NO. BYTES
Ms	MEMORY PER STACK POINTER	⊻	EXCLUSIVE OR		

4. Accumulator Addressing. Single-byte instruction, operating on accumulator alone
   Example:

	Code	Mode	
ASL	0A	ACC:	Contents of accumulator are shifted 1 bit left:

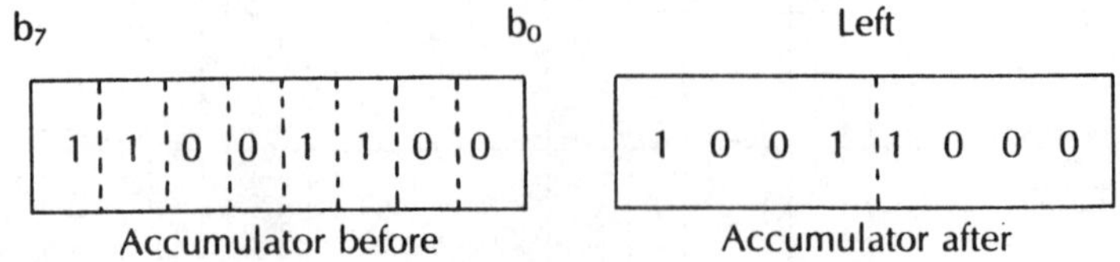

Execution of the instruction

5. Implied Addressing. Single-byte instruction, operating on the registers and flags of the 6502 microprocessor:
   Example:

	Code	Mode	
CLC	18	implied:	Clear carry flag

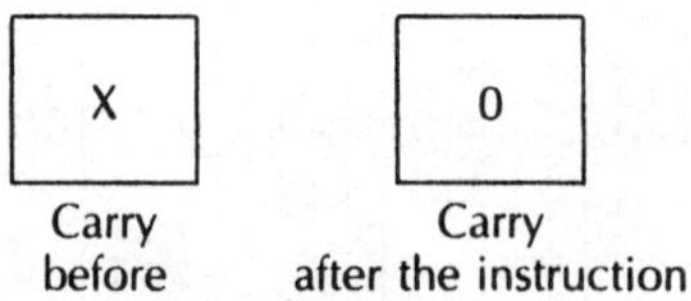

6. ABS, X: Absolute Index Addressing X. The contents of the X register are added to the address specified by the second and third bytes of the instruction, to form the effective address of the operand.
   Example:

0200 LDX	A2	Immediate: X	Register loaded with 3A.
0201 #3A			
0202 STA, X	9D	ABS, X	Contents of accumulator are stored at location of effective address 5040 + 3A = 507A.
0203 (40(L)			
0204 50(H)			

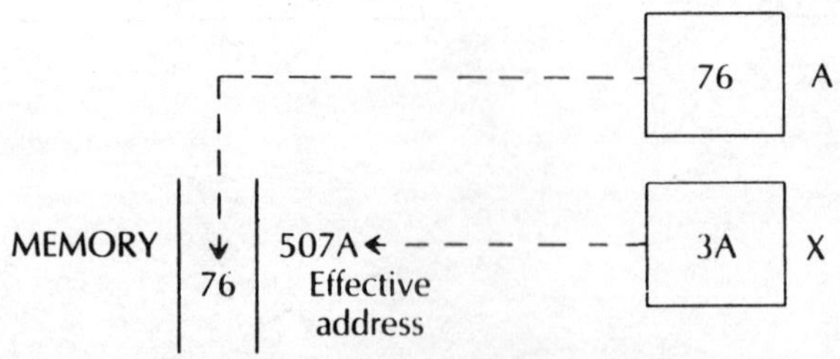

The index addressing with Y index register and zero page index addressing work the same way.

7. Relative Addressing. The second byte is added as an offset to the contents of the program counter to form the effective address. This addressing mode is extremely useful in the branch instructions.

Example:

		Code	*Mode*	
0200	BNE	D0	Relative	Branch not equal to zero
0201	03			
┌0202	CLC	18	Implied	Clear carry
0203	LDA	A9	Immediate	Load accumulator with #00
0204	#00			
└→0205	STA	85	Zero Page	Store accumulator at location A0
0206	A0			

If the condition at 0200 is met (if the result of previous operation is not zero) then the program will branch to:

0202 +	03	→ 0205
Present location of PC	Offset	

Branching can be accomplished 127 locations forward or 128 locations backward (with 2's complement addition).

8. Indirect Addressing. The effective address is the contents of the memory location addressed by the second and third byte, and the next location.

Example:

		Code	*Mode*	
0200	JMP 42_L 00_H	6C	Indirect:	Jump to location specified by contents of 0042 and 0043

Example:

0042	36_L	Effective Address 7036
0043	70_H	To which the program jumps

An indexing scheme can also be coupled with indirect addressing mode to enhance the capabilities of the data handling. The following examples will clarify the concepts of addressing modes and instruction set.

Example 6.1

In a control system application, the following software is part of the main program. We obtain op codes and timing cycles from Table 6.3.

Address Location (Contents of PC)	*Label*	*Mnemonic*	*Op Code*	*Addressing Mode*
0300	Start	LDX	A2	Immediate
01		#00		
02	Table	LDA, X	B5	Zero page, X index
03		44		
04		STA, X	95	Zero page, X index
05		A5		
06		INX	E8	Implied
07		CPX	E4	Zero page
08		08		
09		BNE	D0	Relative
0A		F7		
0B		JMP	4C	Absolute
0C		00L		
0D		03H		
0E		NOP	EA	Implied

Consider that the program is run:

(a) What are the contents of X register at 0301?

Answer: X register is loaded with immediate data #00.

(b) What is accomplished between 0302 and 030B?

Answer: Accumulator is loaded with contents of a table starting at location 44 and these contents are stored in another memory table starting at A5. X index register is used as memory pointer.

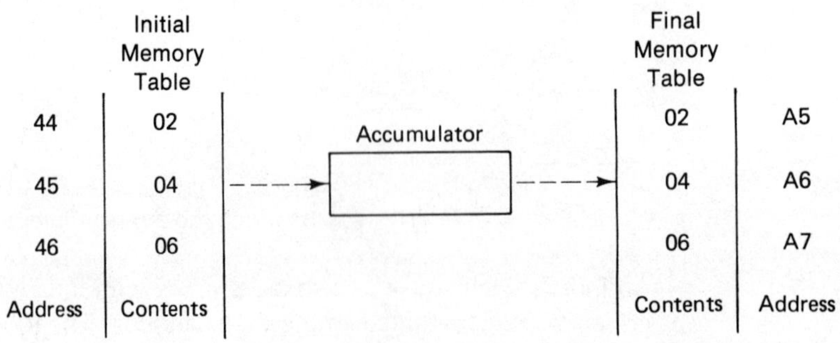

Example 6.2

(a) In the above problem, if the contents of location 08 are $(20)_{Hex}$, how long are the memory tables? Where does the branch instruction at 0309 lead to? When?

Answer: The contents of X register are compared with the contents of memory location 08, at instruction 0307. If they are not the same (the 'BNE' condition is satisfied), the program will branch back to location

```
030B + F7 = 0302
 ↙         ↘
Present   +      2's complement
program  Counter    addition
```

(F7 is a negative number 2's complement form.)

The memory tables extend from

Initial table		Final table
$(44)_{Hex}$ to $(44 + 20 - 1)_{Hex} = 63_{Hex}$	and	$(A5)_{Hex}$ to $(A5 + 20 - 1)_{Hex} = (C4)_{Hex}$

The length of memory tables $= (20)_{Hex} = (32)_{Decimal}$.

(b) Does the program advance to 030E? Why?

Answer: The program does not advance itself to 030E, since the jump instruction 030B puts the program back at 0300.

(c) If an interrupt $\overline{IRQ}$ occurs, where does the program branch to? Use the Aim-65 format. What happens if $\overline{Reset}$ occurs?

Answer: If the interrupt is not masked, the program will branch to location A404 (Refer to Table 6.1 for interrupt vector) and pick up the first byte of the instruction for interrupt subroutine and proceed.

In case of $\overline{Reset}$, the program branches to EOBF and picks up the first instruction.

6.3. 6502-BASED MICROCOMPUTER CONFIGURATION

Figure 6.2 shows a typical microcomputer based on the 6502 microprocessor. In the discussions we use the AIM-65 format. The concept is applicable to any 6502-based system, with minor modifications.

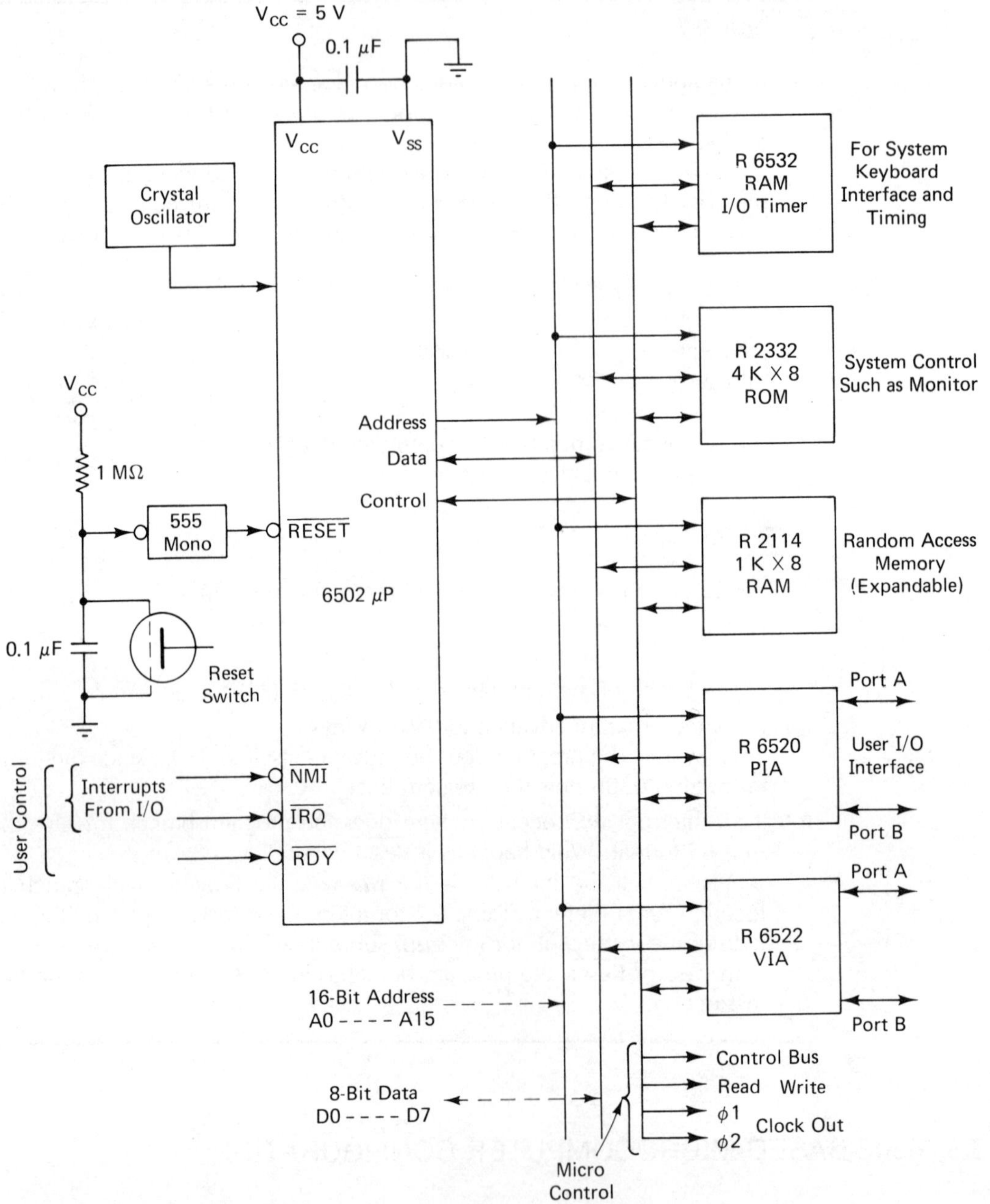

Fig 6.2. Typical 6502-based microcomputer system configuration.

System Components and Structure

1. R6532: RAM, I/O Timer (RIOT). This is a 40-pin NMOS device, which has 128 bytes of RAM, two 8-bit programmable bidirectional ports P_A and P_B, and a timer. This device can be used for I/O applications. In AIM-65, this is used to interface system ASCII keyboard to 6502.
2. R2332: ROM. This is a 4K × 8 ROM, housed in a 24-pin NMOS device, which contains system monitor and assembly programs.
3. R2114: RAM. Each 2114 is an 18-pin NMOS device with 1K × 4 static random access memory. Two of these devices in parallel provide 1K × 8 (1K bytes) of system operating memory. With proper decoding, memory can be expanded. On the AIM-65 board, one can get up to 4K × 8 memory, sufficient for most I/O applications.
4. R-6520: Peripherial Interface Adapter PIA. This is a 40-pin NMOS device that is similar and compatible with Motorola 6820 PIA. All the discussion presented there is applicable here also. It contains two bidirectional 8-bit individual programmable ports P_A and P_B with two control signals for each port. In the AIM-65, 6520 PIA is used for interfacing the 20-character display.
5. R-6522 Versatile Interface Adapter VIA. This 40-pin NMOS device, similar to 6520 PIA, has added features for I/O control. It contains two bidirectional programmable I/O ports A and B with two controls for each port, A serial data entry, and timing and counting circuitry. This device provides the basic user I/O interface in AIM-65.

System Timing and Control

1. Clock. The 6502 operates on a 1 MHz (or 2 MHz for faster versions) system clock, which is provided by crystal oscillator and waveshaping.
2. $\overline{\text{Reset}}$. This is a low active input to 6502, which will take 6502 to a prespecified address (EOBF for AIM 65) to start the reset routine. All the internal registers are cleared to default values. The reset becomes effective during power up or when the reset switch is activated.
3. Micro Control Signals. When the Read/$\overline{\text{Write}}$ (R/$\overline{\text{W}}$) line is high, the read operation is being performed, and when low, the write operation is being performed.
4. Ø1 andØ2 Clock Signals. These phase 1 and phase 2 signals at system clock frequency coordinate all timing and strobing functions in the system.
5. User Control Signals. $\overline{\text{NMI}}$ (Nonmaskable interrupt) and $\overline{\text{IRQ}}$ (interrupt request) from the user I/O branch the micro to respective vectored address locations (Table 6.1). The RDY (ready) signal going low from the user I/O will halt the micro from advancing until RDY returns high. This feature is particularly useful when slow I/O devices such as printers can halt the micro until they are ready for data transfer.

6. Address & Data Buses. The 16-bit address bus, when properly decoded, can address up to 64K locations. The data bus handles 8-bit data transfer between the 6502 micro and the memory, peripherials, and I/O.

I/O Configurations

The 6502 microprocessor uses the memory mapped I/O. We will again use a simple example problem to emphasize the properties of a microcomputer.

Example 6.3

The microcomputer in Figure 6.2 is used in the configuration as shown in Figure 6.3. The addresses of ports A and B are A001 and A000 respectively, and port A is configured as input and port B as output.

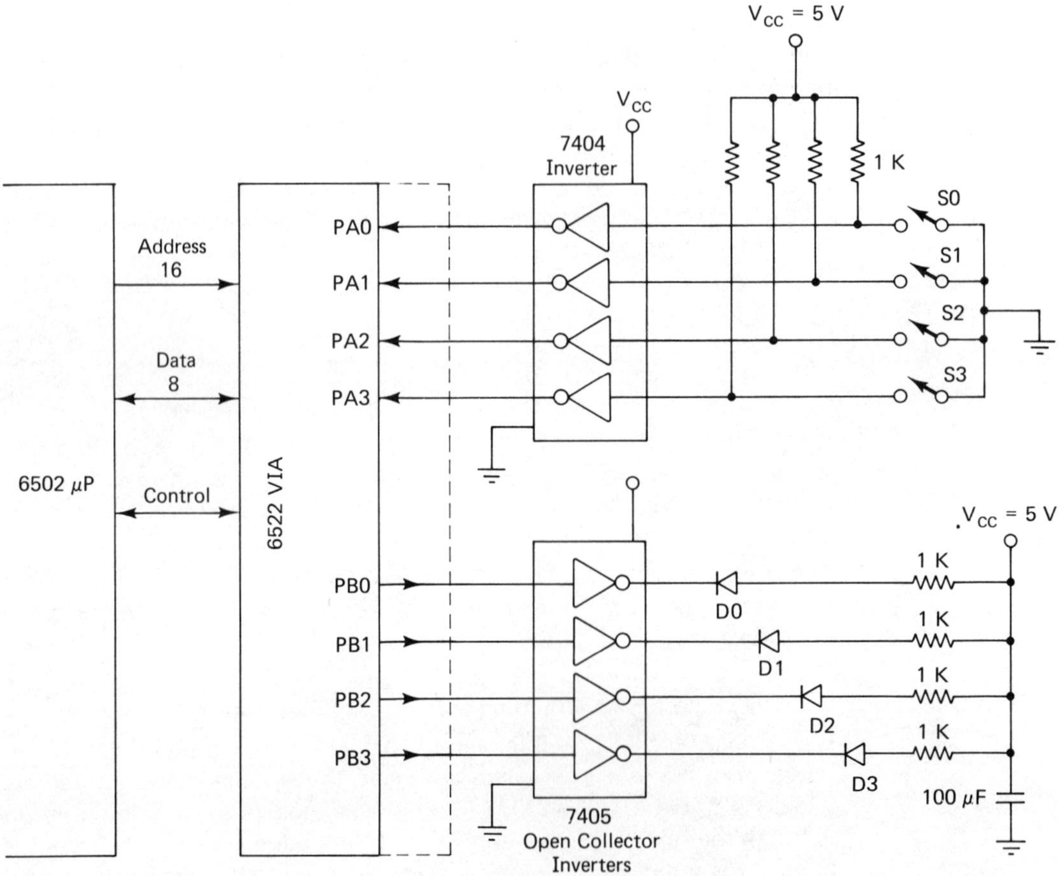

Fig 6.3. I/O interface of the 6502-based microcomputer system (Example 6.3).

(a) Develop a simple software program starting at 0200 location, to read port A, increment it by 1 and light up the corresponding LEDs on port B.
In a binary sequence (if port A reads binary 2, port B should light up D0 and D1 LEDs corresponding to binary 3).

Solution

Refer to Tables 6.2 and 6.3 for mnemonics and op codes. When the switches are closed, a logic 1 is presented at the corresponding input of port A. Our objective is to read this information into the micro, add 1 and output the resulting digital data to port B. Given is one way of accomplishing the task:

Location (Contents of Program Counter)	*Mnemonic*	*Op Code*	*Address Mode*	*Comment*
0200	CLC	18	Implied	Clear carry.
0201	LDA	AD	Absolute	Load port A into accumulator.
0202	$A0_{(H)}$*			
0203	$01_{(L)}$			
0204	ADC	69	Immediate	Add 1 to accumulator.
0205	#01			
0206	STA	8D	Absolute	Output accumulator to Port B.
0206	$A0_{(H)}$			
0207	$00_{(L)}$			
0208	JMP	4C	Absolute	Jump back to 0200 to start new cycle.
0209	$02_{(H)}$			
020A	$00_{(L)}$			
020B	NOP	EA	Implied	No operation.

* In AIM-65, format low and high byte positions, are reversed.

(b) How many read and write operations are performed while executing the LDA A001 instruction? Why?

(c) Does the program advance beyond location 020B by itself?

Solution

The microprocessor reads from location 0201 op code corresponding to LDA (AD in our case). This corresponds to one read cycle. It then performs two more read operations from locations 0202 and 0203 to obtain A0, 01. Finally the microprocessor performs one more read operation to obtain the contents of location A001. Thus there are a total of four read operations and no write operations in executing LDA A001 instruction.

No. of read = 4
No. of write = 0

The program gets into an indefinite loop between 0200 to 020A. Only a reset or interrupt occurrence will pull the microprocessor from this loop.

6.4. AN OVERVIEW OF THE AIM-65 MICROCOMPUTER

Shown in Figure 6.4 is the 6502-based microcomputer AIM-65, developed and marketed by Rockwell International. It is a complete, self-contained microcomputer system and has features of programmability in the assembly and higher-level languages such as BASIC. The 20-column alpha numeric display and DOT matrix printer provide convenient data display and print mechanisms. Figure 6.5 shows the structure of the AIM-65.

Operational Features

The operation of the AIM-65 microcomputer is controlled by 8K monitor ROM (two R-2332 devices), which contains monitor programs. The monitor provides a set of commands that simplify the use of CPU, memory, and I/O devices. The monitor programs contain a mini-assembler which converts func-

Fig 6.4. The AIM-65 single-board microcomputer with the 6502 microprocessor. (Courtesy Rockwell International.)

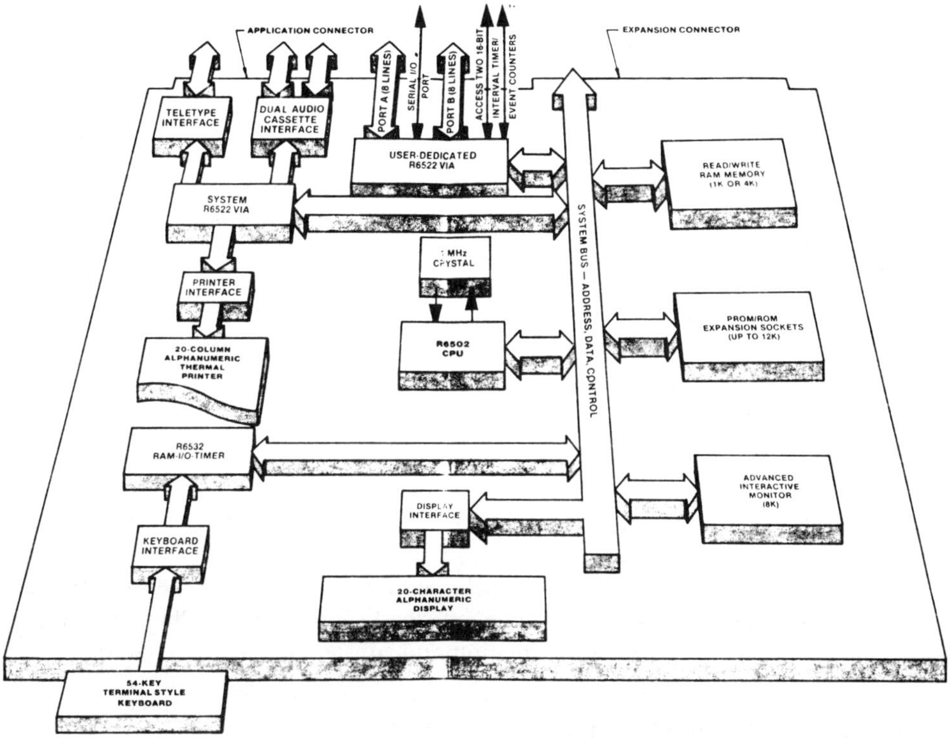

Fig 6.5. Operating model and structure of the AIM-65 microcomputer system. (Courtesy Rockwell International.)

tional mnemonic commands to machine code. In addition, the monitor programs contain routines to display and alter memory, to assemble and disassemble memory, to execute and debug programs, to load and save programs from cassette, to output data to display and printer. Because of memory mapped I/O features, the monitor resident programs controlling memory can be very conveniently used for I/O data manipulation.

Using the AIM-65 Microcomputer

We will provide a brief description of the system level commands of AIM-65, just for a start. For details the user should consult the AIM-65 users guide and operating manuals.

Power Up and Reset

On power up the reset becomes effective, and the control is transferred to the monitor. The monitor control can be recognized by the prompt on the display. During the operation, pressing the reset button always returns the AIM-65 to monitor control.

KB/TTY and Step/Run Switches

The KB/TTY switch tells AIM-65 whether the program entry is from AIM ASCII keyboard or from teletype. For keyboard data entry, this switch should be in the KB position.

The step/run switch, if in position "Step," will sequence the program in single steps, tracing the instructions and registers. This feature is extremely useful when debugging the programs.

The step/run switch in the run position will allow the programs to be executed continuously. For normal operations, this is the mode required. Thus, we proceed with the switch in run position.

Useful Monitor Commands

Proper understanding of the monitor commands will greatly help us use the microcomputer system very efficiently. Therefore, in this section we present some of the relevant information and substantiate it with example problems.

Examine and Change Memory Commands

The M command will allow us to examine the contents of memory location. The sequence of events is as follows:

Type M	After monitor prompt, AIM will respond with = sign.
⟨M⟩ =	Type the address of the memory and return. For example, typing 0200 and return will display the contents of memory locations 0200 0201 0202 0203 as shown.
⟨M⟩ =	0200 44 36 37 4F. Pressing the space bar will display the contents of next four locations.
Type space	
⟨ ⟩	0204 73 96 AC BB

Change Memory Command

After the memory contents are displayed using the M command, typing a slash (/) will put the microcomputer in write mode, where new contents can be written into addressed locations.

Example:

To load locations 0200 thru 0207 with 00, 01, 02, 03, 04, 05, 06, and 07 data:

First call M 0200 with -M- command

⟨M⟩ = 0200 44 36 37 4F

Then type / and return

⟨/⟩ 0200

Then enter the new contents and return

⟨ ⟩ 0200 00 01 02 03

Type slash / again and type new contents

⟨ ⟩ 0204 04 05 06 07

Pressing the Escape "Esc' button or the reset will return the microcomputer to monitor mode.

Examine and Change Register Commands

In the monitor mode, typing R will display the contents of the 6502 microprocessor in the following way:

```
⟨R⟩ ****  PS   AA   XX   YY   SS
    0000  04   37   00   30   FF, where
          ****  Program counter (*)
          PS    Status register   (P)
          AA    Accumulator       (A)
          XX    X index register  (X)
          YY    Y index register  (Y)
          SS    Stack pointer     (S)
```

Typing *, P, A, X, Y, or S will enable us to change the contents of the corresponding registers. Suppose we want to change the contents of program counter from ØØ to 0200. The sequence of operation would then be

Type *

AIM 65 will respond with = Sign

⟨*⟩ =

Type the desired address to be loaded into program counter and return

⟨*⟩ = 0200 return:

This will set the program counter at 0200. Similarly, any other register contents can be changed with corresponding commands.

Assemble and Disassemble Memory Commands

While all computers operate on machine code, it helps a great deal to enter the programs in higher level language such as mnemonic language (similar to assembly language). Typing I will put the microcomputer in mnemonic entry mode. The program can be easily entered using the mnemonics and proper addressing modes. Fortunately, the monitor mini-assembler understands the addressing modes by virtue of the symbols and the length of the instruction.

Example:

We will demonstrate the mnemonic entry, using load accumulator A (LDA) instruction.

LDA #73: # is interpreted to mean immediate addressing mode. (73) is loaded into accumulator

LDA 73 This is interpreted to mean zero-page addressing mode. Accumulator is loaded with contents of location 0073.

LDA 4836 This is interpreted to mean absolute addressing mode. Accumulator is loaded with the contents of location 4836.*

LDA, X 4836 This is interpreted to mean absolute indexed addressing mode. Accumulator is loaded with the contents of the effective address equal to 4836 + contents of X register.

Similarly the mini-assembler of AIM-65 understands other addressing modes.

An easy way to obtain program listings in the mnemonic code is to disassemble the memory (converting machine code in memory to mnemonics). This is conveniently accomplished using K command, as shown.

Type K; AIM-65 will respond with = sign.

Type starting address, K = 0200 in this case, and return.

AIM will respond with ⟨/⟩ sign, requesting the number of instructions to be disassembled.

Typing a number will result in that many instructions to be disassembled and the mnemonic code to be output to display and printer.

Program Entry and Execution Commands

The program counter should be initialized to the starting address of the program, using * command, as shown.

* For the convenience of the user, AIM-65 interprets 4836 as $(48)_{High}$ and $(36)_{Low}$ bytes.

Type *; AIM-65 will respond with = sign.
Type starting address and return.
⟨*⟩ = 0200
Type G and return.
AIM-65 will start executing the desired program.

Miscellaneous Commands

Printer

The printer can be turned on or off by simultaneously pressing control and print keys.

Escape

Pressing the Esc key will put the AIM-65 in monitor mode from any other mode. If a program is being executed, Esc key will lose the control, and only the activation of the reset button will restore AIM-65 monitor mode.

The commands mentioned so far are directly applicable to the AIM-65 microcomputer and allow us to get started with the software and hardware applications using the microcomputer. There are more modes of operation of the AIM-65. The reader is advised to refer the operating manuals of AIM-65.

For any other 6502 based microcomputer systems such as Apple, Commodore Pet, Sym, etc., there are similar system level commands and you can easily pick them up when you understand the concepts.

Example 6.4 (Using AIM-65 Microcomputer)

It is required to store four numbers (in Hex) 01, 02, 04, and 08 in consecutive locations in the stack memory. Develop the software and show how it can be loaded into AIM-65.

Solution

Since it is the first time, we will attempt to show how to use AIM-65 with the help of monitor commands. You are advised and encouraged to consult the operating manuals. We assume that the KB/TTY switch is in KB position, the step/run switch is in run position, and the system is just powered up and reset button activated. AIM-65 will display momentarily

'Rockwell AIM 65'

and settle in monitor mode displaying prompt ⟨.

(a) *Entering the Program in Mnemonics.* First we set the program counter to the required starting address of 0200.

Type * = 0200 and return

Next we enter the mnemonic mode of program entry with I command.

Type I and return

AIM-65 will respond 0200 and cursor. Now we are ready to enter the program. We enter the first instruction and return. The program counter automatically gets incremented to point to the address of the next instruction.

(b) *Actual Program*

Location				*Mode*	*Comment*
0200	LDA	#01	Return	Immediate	01 loaded into accumulator
0202	PHA		"	Implied	Accumulator stored on stack (stack automatically gets decremented to next position)
0203	LDA	#02	"	Immediate	Same operations as above are repeated with data 02, 04 & 08.
0205	PHA		"	Implied	
0206	LDA	#04	"	Immediate	
0208	PHA		"	Implied	
0209	LDA	#08	"	Immediate	
020B	PHA		"	Implied	
020C	BRK		"	Implied	Software return to monitor after the program is run

Now that the program entry is over, we wish to return to monitor mode. Type Esc key. AIM-65 will return to monitor displaying prompt.

Example 6.5

Disassemble and examine and then execute the program of Example 6.4 and verify the results.

Solution

When the system is in monitor mode, typing K will put AIM in disassembly mode.

Type K = 0200 and return

AIM-65 will respond with (/), requesting the number of instructions to be disassembled.

Type 09 (There are 9 instructions to be disassembled.)

If the printer is on, the number of disassembled instructions will be printed out including their op codes, as shown.

(a) *Disassembled Program*

(K) * = 0200
Ø9

	Op code	*Mnemonic*	
0200	A9	LDA	#01
0202	A8	PHA	
0203	A9	LDA	#02
0205	A8	PHA	
0206	A9	LDA	#04
0208	A8	PHA	
0209	A9	LDA	#08
020B	A8	PHA	
020C	00	BRK	

(b) *Executing the Program.* We will initiate the program counter to the start of the desired program; in our case it is 0200, and execute G and return. The program will then be executed and control will be returned to the monitor because of break (BRK) command at 020C.

(c) *Examining the Results.* Since page 1 is dedicated for stack, and the default (or reset) value of the stack pointer is (0)1FF, and since the stack pointer decrements after each pushing onto the stack operation, we would like to examine the four locations 01FC, 01FD, 01FE, and 01FF of the stack using the memory examine command M.

Type ⟨M⟩ = 01FC and return.

If our program and execution are correct, we expect to see

⟨M⟩ = 01FC 08 04 02 01

which are contents of 01FC 01FD 01FE 01FF. This clearly shows how a stack can be handled.

6.5. SUMMARY

In this chapter we have made an attempt to introduce the basics of the 6502 microprocessor, its architecture, and a typical microcomputer configuration using the 6502 processor. AIM-65 formatting is used to present real working examples to build up your confidence so that you take up more applications on your own.

If you have access to AIM-65 or any other similar 6502-based micro, you are strongly advised to study the operating manuals and use the systems. The software presented is equally applicable to all the systems, with minor modifications and proper system commands.

The instruction formatting, its usage, and addressing modes should be well understood before proceeding to the next chapter. For further information, consult the R 6500 Programming Manual, the R 6500 Hardware Manual, and the AIM 65 Users Guide, by Rockwell International.

Problems

6.1. The 6502 microprocessor has pipeline architecture with powerful index addressing modes and dedicated stack.

(a) If it is required to stack all CPU registers in a particular subroutine, how many bytes of stack memory are required?

(b) How many such subroutines can be nested without losing data?

6.2. Accumulator has (7F) in it. Data $(6E)_{Hex}$ is added to it, and the result is stored in the accumulator. What are the contents of the flag register bits N, V, B, D, I, Z, and C as shown.

Process Status Register	N	V	X	B	D	I	Z	C

6.3. Identify any word in the accumulator and any possible operation that would result in

(1) All-zero condition of the process status register.

(b) Repeat the problem, which would result in (OF) condition of the process status register.

6.4. Of all the reset and interrupt signals, which has the highest priority? Why? Pictorially identify the sequence of events when the 6502 is executing a program and $\overline{IRQ}$ becomes active (goes low) and after a while, when IRQ routine is being executed, $\overline{NMI}$ becomes active. Clearly show how stack memory is loaded and emptied.

6.5. The 6502 has the same mnemonics but different addressing modes characterized by different op codes to address and manipulate the data. What are the contents of A, X, and Y registers in each of the following cases:

```
(a) LDX       Immediate        (b) LDY   Immediate
    Ø8                             FF
    STX       Zero page            TYA   Implied
    0A                             TAX
    LDA, X    Index                DEX   Implied
    42                             TXA
    LDY       Zero page            STA   Zero page
    0A                             0B
```

6.6. Accomplish the task of Problem 6.5 using only immediate and absolute addressing modes. Can the above task be done without using immediate addressing mode? If so, how?

6.7. Relative addressing is a powerful branching operation. In the following operations,

```
(a) 0400  LDX  Immediate       (b) 0500  LDY  Immediate
      01  08                         01  0F
      02  DEX  Implied               02  DEY  Implied
      03  BNE  Relative              03  BEQ  Relative
      04  F0                         04  02
      05  NOP  Implied               05  BRA  Relative
                                     06  FB
                                     07  NOP  Implied
                                     08
```

Identify the functions being accomplished, clearly specifying where the branching instructions would branch to.

6.8. The 16-bit address bus of the 6502 can be very easily decoded and used to address memory (or I/O) as shown in Figure 6.6. Taking the information from Rockwell and logic data books, and using 2114-type 1K × 4 memories, identify the actual memory range addressed by each decoded chip select signals $\overline{CS0}$....$\overline{CS7}$.

6.9. Design a complete operating memory system with 1K × 8 memory between 0000 and 03FF, similar to Figure 6.6. Show all connections to all real electronic devices (*Note*: Data drivers should be bidirectional type).

6.10. Repeat Problem 6.9., where the RAM memory is 4K between 000 to 0FFF using 1K × 4 2114-type devices, and monitor ROM memory is 8K between E000 to FFFF using R2332-type 4K × 8 ROM devices. Show clearly all decoding logic and connections, using real electronic devices.

6.11. In a simple control system application it is required to store seven-seg-

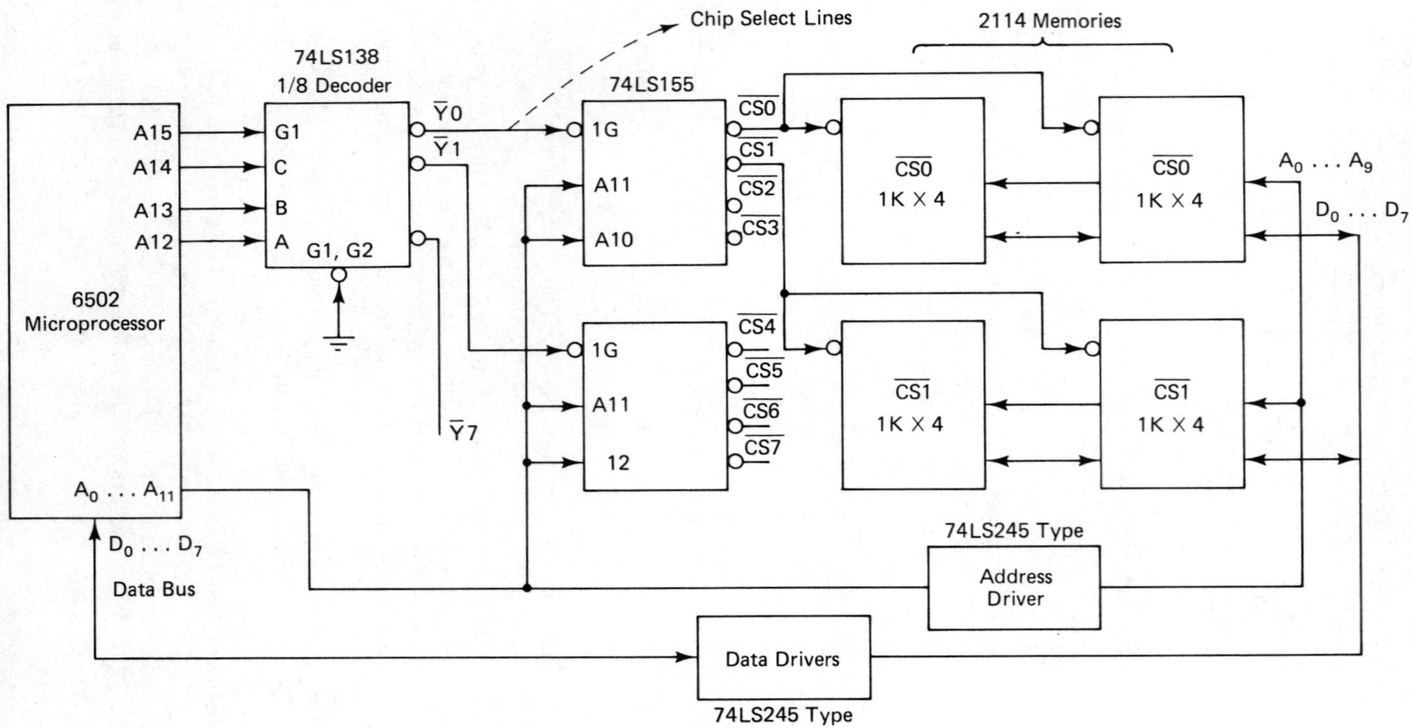

Fig 6.6. The 6502 microcomputer address decoding structure for Problems 6.8–6.10.

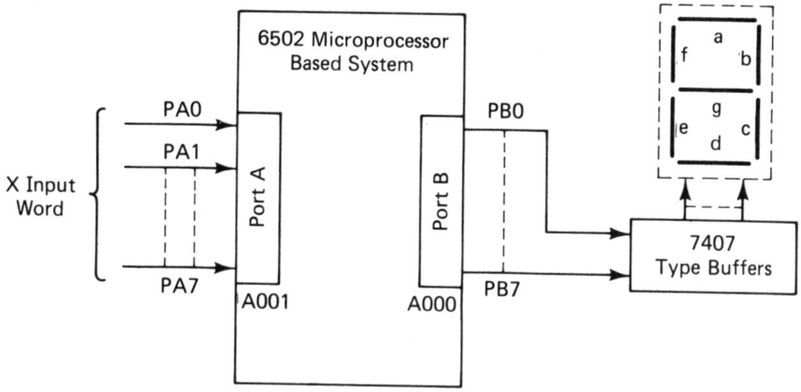

Fig 6.7. The 6502-based microcomputer system interfaced to I/O (Problems 6.13–6.15).

ment code corresponding to Hex numbers in memory starting at location 0200. The format is as shown:

D7	D6	D5	D4	D3	D2	D1	D0
dp	g	f	e	d	c	b	a

Data Word

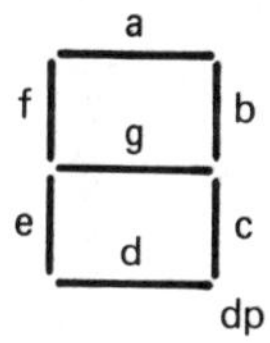

Consider that 1 lights up the segment as shown:

Location	Code	Digit	
0200	3F		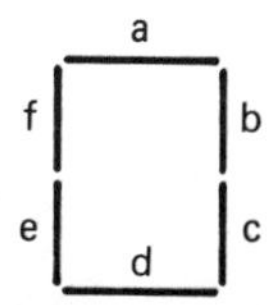
0205	6D		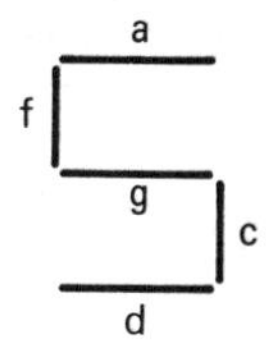
020F	71		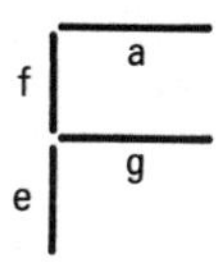

Develop the operating software that would store the codes corresponding to 0....F at locations 0200 to 020F, without using the indexed mode of addressing.

6.12. Repeat Problem 6.11., using the indexed mode and tabling methods and compare with Problem 6.11.

6.13. 6502 μP uses memory mapped I/O concepts. Consider that port A at AØØ1 is input and port B at AØØØ is output, as shown in Figure 6.7. It is necessary to count the number of 1's in input word X on port A and light up the corresponding digit on the seven-segment display on port B. The new X word is to be read in 2-second intervals. Develop the complete operating hardware and software.

6.14. Repeat Problem 6-13, in which the total number of 0's are counted in a 8-bit word X on port A.

6.15. Repeat Problem 6.13., where the X word is effectively 16 bits wide and has to be read into port A twice as low and high bytes as shown, using a multiplexer at input. Develop the complete operating hardware and software.

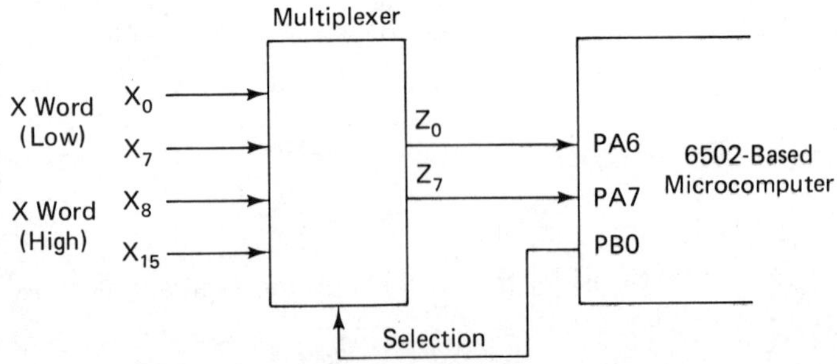

CHAPTER SEVEN

Applications of 6502-Based Microcomputer Systems

In this chapter we will discuss some practical applications using a typical 6502-based microcomputer system such as the AIM-65. The concepts (software and hardware) presented here are equally applicable on any other 6502-based system with minor modifications.

The potential of using any microcomputer system effectively depends on understanding and utilizing the user bound programs already available in the form of monitor routines. An investigative examination of the operating manuals and application notes furnished by the microcomputer manufacturer will provide this information. In the next section, we will present some applications, using monitor routines.

7.1. USING MONITOR ROUTINES

One of the many useful monitor subroutines available with AIM-65 is a display output routine called "OUTDIS," starting at location EF05 of the monitor ROM (refer to Chapter 7, Table 7.13, AIM-65 monitor subroutines, in the AIM-65 User's Guide). This will output an ASCII character in the accumulator to the output display.

Display of Information

We will use this display routine to output any ASCII coded information we want to display. Table 7.1 shows the ASCII code used in the AIM-65 system. An example problem will help us understand the concepts better.

Table 7.1. ASCII Code of Characters Used in AIM-65. (Courtesy Rockwell International)

LSD	MSD	0 000	1 001	2 010	3 011	4 100	5 101	6 110	7 111
0	0000	NUL	DLE	SP	0	@	P		p
1	0001	SOH	DC1	!	1	A	Q	a	q
2	0010	STX	DC2	"	2	B	R	b	r
3	0011	ETX	DC3	#	3	C	S	c	s
4	0100	EOT	DC4	$	4	D	T	d	t
5	0101	ENQ	NAK	%	5	E	U	e	u
6	0110	ACK	SYN	&	6	F	V	f	v
7	0111	BEL	ETB	'	7	G	W	g	w
8	1000	BS	CAN	(	8	H	X	h	x
9	1001	HT	EM	)	9	I	Y	i	y
A	1010	LF	SUB	*	:	J	Z	j	z
B	1011	VT	ESC	+	;	K	[	k	{
C	1100	FF	FS	,	<	L	\	l	|
D	1101	CR	GS	–	=	M	]	m	}
E	1110	SO	RS	.	>	N	↑	n	~
F	1111	SI	VS	/	?	O	←	o	DEL

Example 7.1 Display of Alphabet

Using the display routine at EF05, output the first 10 characters A....J of the alphabet to the display. Show all your software.

Solution

An examination of Table 7.1 reveals that

First letter A has ASCII code of $(41)_{Hex}$
Second letter B has ASCII code of $(42)_{Hex}$
Tenth letter J has ASCII code of $(4A)_{Hex}$
Eleventh letter K has ASCII code of $(4B)_{Hex}$

(a) *The Concept.* We will load $(41)_{Hex}$ into the accumulator and output it to display A. We will then increment the accumulator to display the next character B. We will repeat the process until we output $(4A)_{Hex}$ to display the tenth character J. When code $(4B)_{Hex}$ of the eleventh character K is about to be output, we will stop the process.

The system level flow chart of Figure 7.1 outlines the program flow. Table 7.2 shows the actual program. Notice that the program starts at location 0200 (page 2) as not to interfere with page 1 for stack and page 0 for user variables.

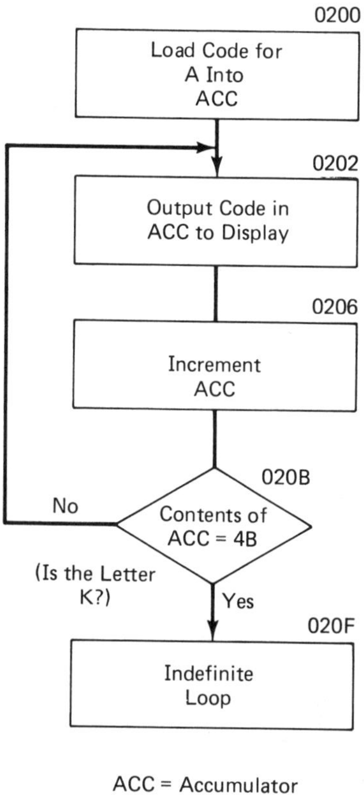

Fig 7.1. Program flow for alphabet display of Example 7.1.

(b) *Program Listing*. The program listing in Table 7.2 is the actual operational program. The labels, addressing modes, and the comments are included to benefit the reader. The program can be entered and run, using the I, M, and G commands discussed in Chapter 6. At 0200 $(41)_{Hex}$, corresponding to character A, is loaded into the accumulator. At 0202, this information is output to display, using monitor routine at EF05. Between 0205 and 0207, the operations result in incrementing the accumulator to refer to the next character. At 020B, the data in the accumulator is compared with $(4B)_{Hex}$ to see whether the program has progressed to output the eleventh character K. If not, the branching occurs to 0202 (display) to output the next character. The operation is repetitive until code in accumulator is incremented to $(4B)_{Hex}$. At that instance, the program gets out of the branch loop and advances to 020F. Between 020F and 0212, the program goes into indefinite loop. Since there are no wait type of instructions to hold the micro without doing any work, we have to do this an

Table 7.2. Actual Program Listing For Example 7.1 (AIM 65 Formatting).

Line No.	*Location*	*Label*	*Mnemonic*	*Op Code*	*Address Mode*	*Comment*
1	0200	Start	LDA	A9	Immediate	Load accumulator with data $(41)_{Hex}$, which is code for A.
2	0201		#41			
3	0202	Display	JSR*	20	Absolute	Jump to display subroutine at EF05.
4	0203		$EF_{(H)}$			
5	0204		$05_{(L)}$			
6	0205		CLC	18	Implied	Clear carry and add (01) to the accumulator, which results in incrementing accumulator by 1.
7	0206	Next	ADC	69	Immediate	
8	0207		#01			
9	0208		NOP	EA	Implied	No operation. Can be used for small delays or to use these locations for a linkage program.
10	0209		NOP	EA	Implied	
11	020A		NOP	EA	Implied	
12	020B		CMP	C9	Immediate	Compare to see whether all 10 characters have been output and code (4B) is reached in accumulator.
13	020C		#4B			
14	020D		BNE	D0	Relative	If not, branch back to location 0202. Otherwise proceed to next.
15	020E		0202**	Display		
16	020F	Loop Around	NOP	EA	Implied	Micro goes into indefinite wait loop between 020F and 0212, after all the required 10 characters have been output.
17	0210		JMP	4C	Absolute	
18	0211		$02_{(H)}$			
19	0212		$0F_{(L)}$			

* AIM-65 uses high low format.

** AIM-65 automatically calculates displacements to branch to given location.

indirect way. Only an interrupt or reset would pull the micro out of the loop.

(c) *Result.* If your program entry and operation of AIM-65 is correct, you should expect to see

A B C D E F G H I J

on the display panel.

Perhaps while observing the results you may have wished to see the letters actually being written, instead of appearing at one shot. This can be easily accomplished by incorporating extra delay in the main program.

Time Delay Generation

Any register or memory can be loaded with a given number and made to count up or down to reach a predetermined value. This sequence of operations takes a certain number of machine cycles, which in turn manifests itself as a time delay. This is the general principle used in generating delays. We will illustrate with an example problem.

Example 7.2 Time Delay

Generate a time delay under software control. Consider the operating clock of the 6500 microprocessor 1MHz (each machine clock cycle = 1 μs).

(a) Show the delay generation concept.

(b) Show the actual program listing and calculate delay. Consider that this delay subroutine will be called by a main program such as the alphabet display program of Example 7.1.

Solution

(a) The concept centers on using one of the registers such as X register as a long counter and another register such as Y register as a short counter and inner looping them to count, as shown in the flow chart of Figure 7.2. This kind of inner looping allows us to generate larger time loops and delays.

(b) Table 7.3 shows the actual program listing. It is always a good programming practice to store the microprocessor registers to be used in the subroutine, so that their contents relevant to the main calling program are saved and are readily available for registration.

Between program locations 0250 to 0252, a monitor subroutine is used to store X and Y registers on stack.

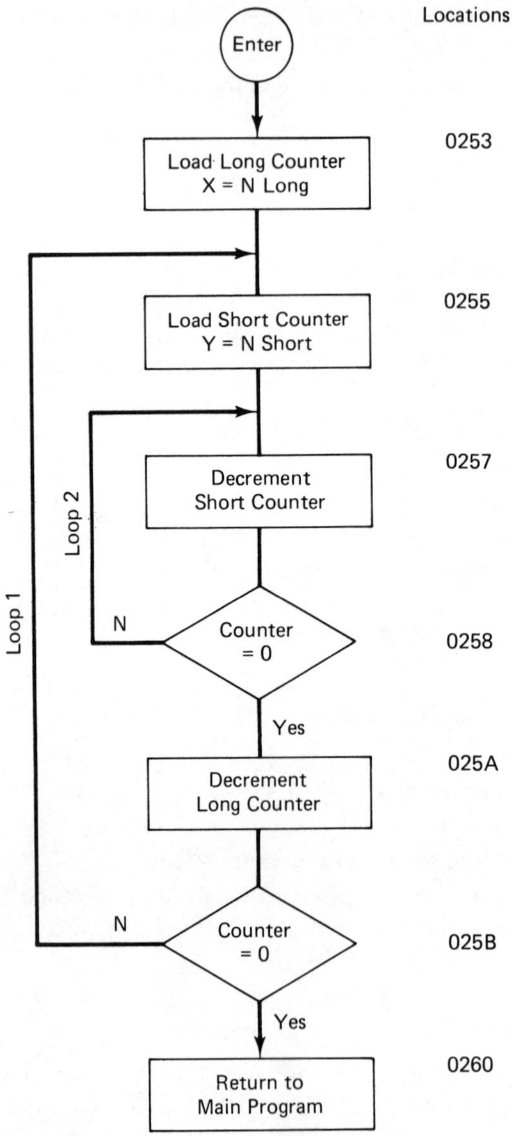

Fig 7.2. Flowchart relating to the time delay of Example 7.2.

Between 0253 and 0256, the long counter X and short counter Y are loaded with contents of locations 0A (N_{Long}) and 0B (N_{Short}). These numbers can be changed to obtain different values of delays.

Between 0257 and 0259, short counting loop L_2 is entered, and between 0255 and 025C, long counting loop L_1 is entered.

At 025D, monitor subroutine called PLXY at EBAC is used to restore *X*

Table 7.3. Actual Listing for Delay Routine—AIM-65 Format (Example 7.2).

Program Location	Label	Mnemonic	Op Code	Address Mode	Number of Clocks		Comments
0250	PSXY	JSR	20	Absolute	6		Jump to monitor subroutine at EB9E to push X and Y on stack (save X and Y).
0251		EB(H)					
0252		9E(L)				T1	
0253		LDX	A6	Zero page	3		Load X and Y from contents of locations 0A and 0B respectively, (N_{Long}) and (N_{Short}).
0254		0A					
0255	Loop 1	LDY	A4	Zero page	3		
0256		0B				T2	
0257	Loop 2	DEY	88	Implied	2		Decrement X and enter into short counter loop 2.
0258	L2	BNE	D0	Relative	3		
0259	L1	(0257)				T3	
025A		DEX	CA	Implied	2	T4	Decrement X and enter into long counter loop 1.
025B		BNE	D0	Relative	3		
025C		(0255)					
025D	PLXY	JSR	20	Absolute	6		Jump to monitor subroutine at EBAC to pull X and Y from stack (restore X and Y).
025E		EB(H)				T5	
025F		AC(L)					
0260		RTS	60	Implied	6		Return to the main calling program.

and *Y* values from stack. At 0260 the program returns to the main program via the return from subroutine (RTS) instruction.

(c) *Delay Calculations*. Table 7.3 lists the number of clock cycles to execute each instruction and linear times T1, T2, T3, T4, and T5 are required to execute corresponding groups of instructions. Assuming that the contents of 0A and 0B correspond to N_{Long} and N_{Short} (*Note*: These can be between $(00)_{Hex}$ to $(FF)_{Hex}$ each):

$$\underset{\text{Short Loop 2 Delay}}{T_{L2}} = N_{Short} * T_3 \ \mu s \tag{1}$$

$$\underset{\text{Long Loop 1 Delay}}{T_{L1}} = N_{Long} [T_2 + T_{L2} + T_4] \ \mu s \tag{2}$$

$$\underset{\text{Total Delay}}{T_{Total}} = T_1 + T_{L1} + T_5 \ \mu s \tag{3}$$

Note T1 and T5 contain time to execute the subroutines as well. For a 1 MHz clock system such as AIM-65, each clock cycle corresponds to 1 μs. For example, if

$$N_{Short} = (F0)_{Hex} = (240)_{Decimal}$$

$$N_{Long} = (64)_{Hex} = (100)_{Decimal}$$

with

$$T_2 = 3 \ \mu s$$

$$T_3 = 5 \ \mu s \qquad \text{(From Table 7.3)}$$

$$T_4 = 5 \ \mu s$$

Using equations 1 and 2, we obtain

$$T_{L2} = (240) * 5 = 1200 \ \mu s = 1.2 \text{ ms}$$

$$\boxed{T_{L2} = 1.2 \text{ ms}}$$

$$T_{L1} = 100 * [3 + 1200 + 5] = 0.1208 \text{ s}$$

$$\boxed{T_{L1} = 0.1208 \text{ s}}$$

Approximating T1 and T5 to be small, we get

$$T_{Total} = T_{L1} = 0.12 \text{ s}$$

$$\boxed{T_{Total} = 0.12 \text{ s}}$$

Thus any amount of delay can be generated by software inner looping methods.

Try to incorporate this delay loop in the alphabet display example (7.1) by replacing NOP instructions at 0208...020A with a JSR 0250 to call the delay program and observe the results.

Several example problems are listed at the end of the chapter to generate monostables, counters, etc., and you are encouraged to solve them.

7.2. INPUT/OUTPUT INTERFACE

In order to use the microcomputer effectively as a programmable and flexible digital system, we should interface the outside electronic devices and systems to provide the input/output (I/O) capability to the microcomputer. In 6502-based systems, this is usually accomplished through the 6522 VIA (versatile interface adapter), which is a 40-pin I/O bound programmable interface device. All the electronic signals in and out of the VIA are TTL compatible with unit TTL load. For heavy current loads, these I/O lines may require to be buffered. It is similar but more sophisticated than 6820 PIA studied earlier.

We will now discuss this VIA in enough detail to enable us to use it for our I/O applications.

6522 Versatile Interface Adapter (VIA)

As shown in Figure 7.3, the VIA consists of

(a) Two parallel individually programmable 8-bit I/O ports A and B.
(b) Corresponding control signals CA1, CA2 for port A, and CB1, CB2 for port B.
(c) Serial data entry through CB1 and CB2

The VIA communicates with the 6502 microprocessor via the address, data, and control buses as shown in Figure 7.3. The registers of 6522, which are considered as memory locations by 6502 μP, actually control the operation of the I/O ports, the timer, and counter section of the VIA. We will now present a brief description of these registers.

Data Direction and Output Registers (DDR and OR)

DDRA and ORA for port A, and DDRB and ORB are for port B.

A 1 or 0 in the DDR bit position makes the corresponding bit in the output register an output or input respectively.

Example:

If DDRA is loaded with F0, PA0 → PA3 will be configured as inputs and PA4 → PA7 will be configured as outputs for the output register ORA:

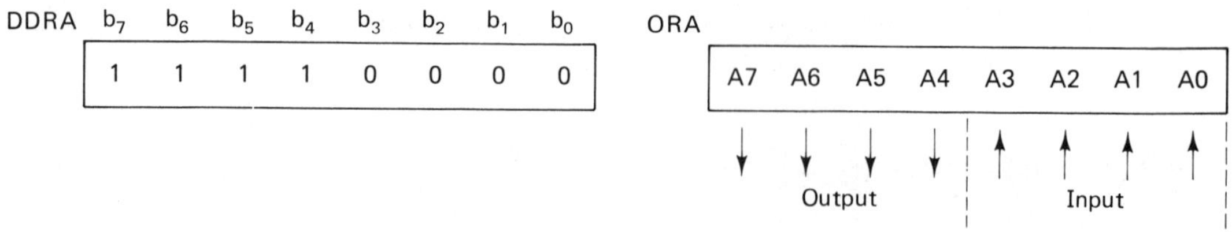

Peripheral Control Register (PCR)

The information written in this register by the microprocessor controls the operation of the control I/O lines CA1, CA2, CB1, and CB2. The CA and CB operations are similar. When the transitions on these lines are recognized, the corresponding flag bits in the interrupt flag register (IFR) are set. Reading the IFR, the micro will learn the occurrence of these control I/O lines. Figure 7.4 shows the formatting of PCR. We show the operation for CB1 and CB2. The same is applicable for CA1 and CA2, with the corresponding bits taking the same values.

Interrupt Enable/Flag Registers (IER/IFR)

These registers will work in conjunction with PCR and ACR (auxiliary control register, which will be discussed later) to handle the interrupts. Figure 7.5 shows IER/IFR structure.

Interrupts Enabled

If b7 of IER is a 1, then 1 in any bit position of IER will enable the corresponding signal line to set the bits in the IFR and activate $\overline{IRQ}$ to the microprocessor.

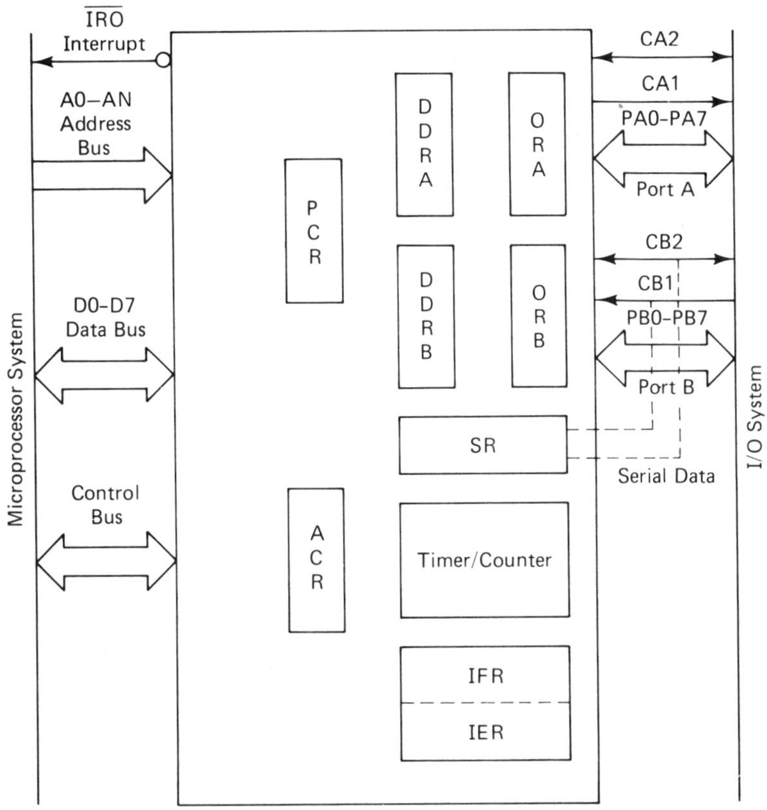

Fig 7.3. Versatile interface adapter (VIA) for the 6522 programming structure.

Interrupts Disabled

If b7 of IER is a zero, then a 1 in any bit position of IER will disable the corresponding interrupt inputs and inhibit them from setting any flags in the IFR and activating $\overline{IRQ}$ to the micro.

We would like to put these concepts to use before we proceed any further. Some example problems should help us handle the sophisticated VIA. Figure 7.6 shows the memory map of 6522, as seen by 6502 μP in AIM-65. 6522 VIA data sheets should be consulted to obtain familiarity with other registers such as ACR, SR, etc.

Typical Control System Interface

Microcomputers such as AIM-65 can be very effectively used in any control system applications with control handshake. Handshake refers to es-

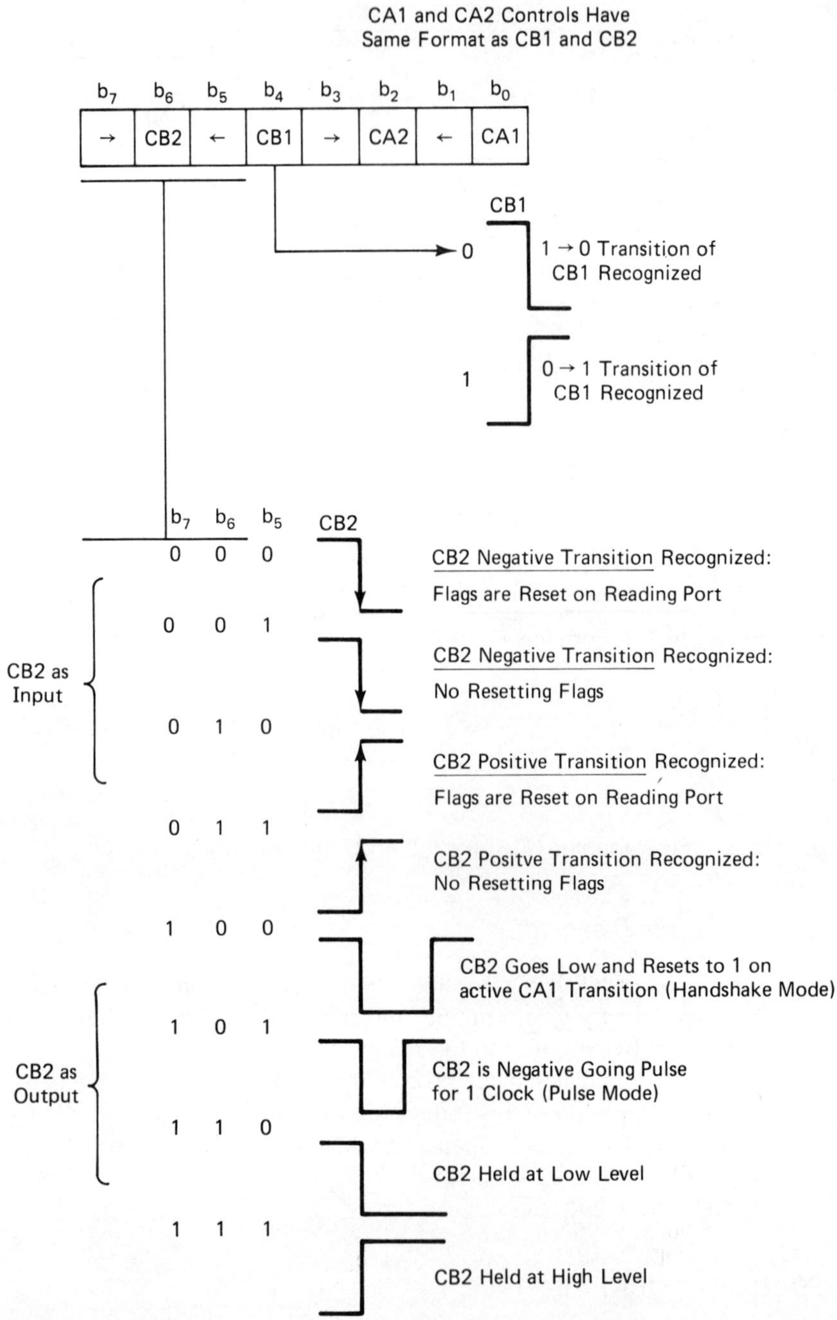

Fig 7.4. VIA PCR control formatting.

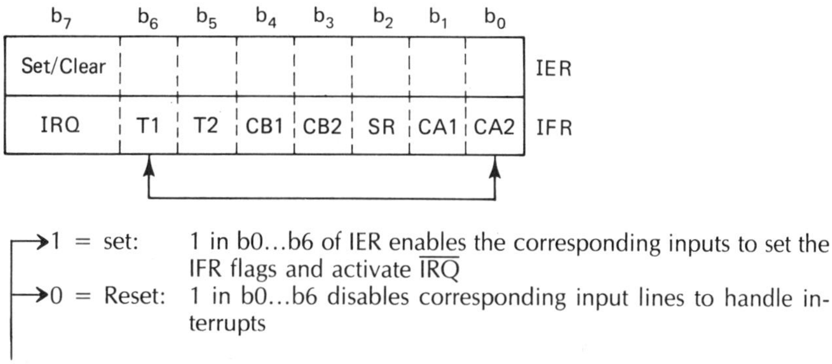

When enabled, these signals will set the bits in IFR and activate $\overline{IRQ}$.

Fig 7.5. Basic IER/IFR structure of the VIA.

tablishing a mutual communication in response to a request from I/O to the micro, or vice versa. We will present an example problem concerning furnace control to clarify these concepts.

Example 7.3 Furnace Control

In addition to running a main program such as the display alphabet of Example 7.1, the AIM-65 microcomputer is used to control a furnace, on interrupt basis, as shown in Figure 7.7.

When the furnace gets overheated, it sends a high level signal to CBI input. Develop the operating system such that the micro will respond to the CBI interrupt, shut off the power to the system VIA CB2 control signal, and flash a warning signal for 10 times.

Location	*Registers of 6522 VIA*	
A000	ORB:	Output register B
A001	ORA:	Output register A
A002	DDRB:	Data DRN register B
A003	DDRA:	Data DRN register A
A004 → AA0A	Timers and shift register	
A00B	ACR:	Auxiliary control register
A00C	PCR:	Peripheral control register
A00D	IFR:	Interrupt flag register
A00E	IER:	Interrupt enable register
A00F	ORA:	Output register A., with no handshake

Fig 7.6. Memory map of the 6522 in the AIM-65.

Solution

We have chosen to turn off the power to the furnace through the 2N 2713 transistor relay driver circuit, opening the relay contacts when CB2 goes high. We have also chosen port B, PB0...PB3 signals as outputs used to flash the LED indicators on the furnace panel. Figure 7.7 shows the actual operating electronics interface and system.

CB2 going high presents high level at the output of gate G5, which turns off the transistor, cutting down the current supply to the relay coil. This will disable the relay and open the contacts of the relay to shut off power to the furnace. A logic 1 at PB0...PB3 turns on the panel LED lamps, and logic 0 would turn them off. To get a flashing effect, we will turn them on and off with intermittent delay. Figure 7.8 shows the flow chart, and Table 7.4 shows the actual program listings.

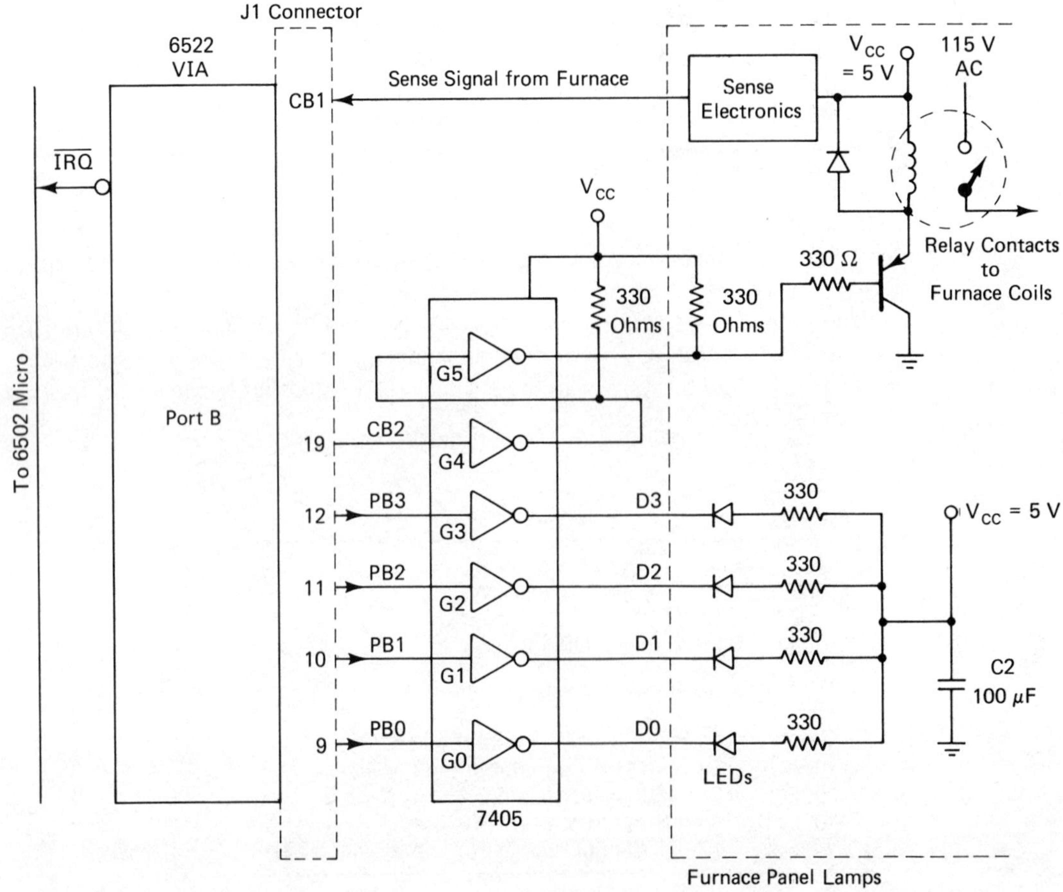

Fig 7.7. The AIM-65 microcomputer furnace control for Example 7.3.

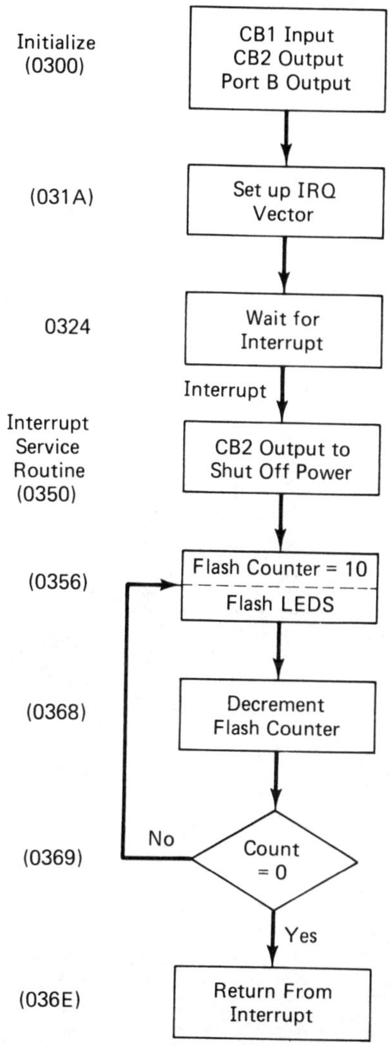

Fig 7.8. Flowchart for furnace control (Example 7.3).

(a) *Initialization.* Between 0303 and 0307 the peripheral control register (PCR) of VIA 6522 is loaded with #D0 to recognize 0 → 1 transition on CB1 and to configure CB2 as output at 0 level.

Between 0308 and 0311, the interrupt enable register (IER) is conditioned to recognize only CBI interrupt activation, which will in turn activate $\overline{IRQ}$ interrupt input to 6502.

Between 0312 and 0316, Port B is configured as output, by writing all 1s in the DATA direction register for port B (DDRB).

Table 7.4. Program Listing for Furnace Control (Example 7.3).

Program Location	Label	Mnemonic	Op Code	Address Mode	Comment
0300	Initialize	NOP	EA	Implied	No operation.
01		NOP	EA		
02		CLI	58	Implied	Enable Interrupts.
03		LDA	A9	Immediate	PCR at A00C loaded with
04		#D0			1 1 0 1 0 0 0 0 = D0 CB2 CB1 CA2 CA1
05		STA	8D	Absolute	to recognize 0 → 1 on CB1 and set CB2 = 0 (Refer to
06		A0			Figure 7.4).
07		0C			
08		LDA	A9	Immediate	IER at AØØE loaded with
09		#6F			0 1 1 0 1 1 1 1 = 6F
0A		STA	8D	Absolute	CB1
0B		AØ			to disable all other interrupts except CB1.
0C		0E			
0D		LDA	A9	Immediate	IER at A00E loaded with
0E		#90			1 0 0 1 0 0 0 0 = 90
0F		STA	8D	Absolute	CB1
0310		AØ			to enable CB1 interrupt.
11		ØE			
12		LDA	A9	Immediate	DDRB at AØØ2 loaded with FF to make port B output.
13		#FF			
14		STA	8D	Absolute	
15		A0			
16		02			
17		STA	8D	Absolute	All 1s output to output port B to establish steady
18		AØ			condition. Furnace on. LEDs on.
19		00			
1A	IRQ Vector	LDA	A9	Immediate	IRQ service routine address of 0350 is loaded into the
1B		#50			AIM-65.
1C		STA	8D	Absolute	This is done by loading (03_H 50_L) into the vectored
031D		A4			address locations of A405 & A404.
1E		04			
1F		LDA	A9	Immediate	
0320		#03			
21		STA	8D	Absolute	On $\overline{IRQ}$ occurrence (when CB1 is activated), program
22		A4			goes to 0350.
23		05			

Address	Label	Mnemonic/Operand	Op code	Mode	Comments
25		NOP	EA		occurs.
26		NOP	EA		
27		JMP	4C	Absolute	
28		03			
29		24			
2A	Monitor	BRK	00	Implied	Program termination.
			INTERRUPT SERVICE ROUTINE		
0350		SEI	78	Implied	Set interrupt mask and disable further interrupts.
51		LDA	A9	Immediate	CB2 set to 1 output to turn off furnace, by loading FØ in PCR at AØØC.
52		#FØ			
53		STA	8D	Absolute	
54		AØ			
55		OC			
56	Flash Ctr	LDX	A2	Immediate	X register used as flash counter and loaded with $(0A)_{Hex} = (10)_{Dec}$.
57		$\#0A_{Hex}$			
58	Flash	→ LDA	A9	Immediate	Turn off LEDs by outputing 0s on port B.
59		#00			
5A		STA	8D	Absolute	
5B		AØ			
5C		ØØ			
5D		JSR	20		Jump to delay subroutine at 0250 (see Example 7.2)
5E		02(H)			
035F		50			
60		LDA	A9	Immediate	Turn on LEDs by outputing 1s on port B.
61		#0F			
62		STA	8D	Absolute	
63		A0			
64		00			
65		JSR	20	Absolute	
66		02			
67		50			
68	Decrement	DEX	CA	Implied	Decrement flash counter. If not zero branch back to 0358 to start flashing LEDs again.
69		BNE	D0	Relative	
6A		(0358)			
6B		NOP	EA	Implied	No operation.
6C		NOP	EA		
6D		NOP	EA		
6E		CLI	58		Enable further interrupt by clearing interrupt mask and return from interrupt to main program.
6F		RTI	40		

Between 0317 and 0319, all 1s are output to turn the LED indicators on. At the same time the CB2 control line goes low, as configured at 0303 to 0307. This will turn the furnace on by turning on Q transistor (Figure 7.7) and activating the power relay coil. We want to start the interrupt service routine at address 0350. This information is loaded into the AIM-65 vectored $\overline{IRQ}$ address of A404 and A405 (Chapter 6, Table 6.1). When interrupt occurs, program automatically branches to location 0350. The corresponding instructions are between 031A and 0323.

Between 0324 and 0329, the microcomputer goes into a dummy loop, waiting for the interrupt to occur.

(b) *Interrupt Service Routine*. When the furnace temperature exceeds the set safety limit, a 0 → 1 transition occurs at CB1, which will be recognized as a valid interrupt, and the program branches to the 0350 location, from the dummy loop.

At 0350 the interrupt mask is set to disable any further interrupts. This is a standard practice in handling interrupts.

Between 0351 and 0355, CB2 is configured as a high level output, which turns off relay and cuts furnace power.

At 0356, X register is considered as flash counter and loaded with $(0A)_{Hex}$ corresponding to $(10)_{Decimal}$.

Between 0358 and 036A, alternate 1s and zeros are output on port B, with a delay subroutine in between (same type of delay subroutine of Example 7.2). This has the effect of flashing the LEDs on the panel.

Between 0368 and 036A, the flash counter X is decremented each time the LEDs are flashed and checked to see if 10 flashings have been accomplished. If not, the program branches back to 0358 to continue flashing. After the required number of flashings, the program advances to 036B. At 036E the interrupt mask is cleared to enable further interrupts. The RTI instruction returns the program from interrupt to 032A location, where it has left the main program.

In our case, the BRK instruction at 032A returns the control of the monitor.

The above example problem is extremely important and shows how to initialize ports and how to handle port controls and interrupts. You are urged to understand and practice these concepts before proceeding further. The NOP instructions are for delay or program linkage.

7.3. POSITION CONTROL SYSTEMS

In most industrial applications, position control is very important, especially in automatic assembly lines, in sorting and filling and distribution type of operations. Also in graphics and plotter operations, the basic concept is digitization and position location along X and Y axes. With the relative ease, flexibility, and reliability associated with the microprocessors, the digitally controllable stepper motors under the microprocessor control are becoming more and more popular. We will now study some of the basic properties of a stepper motor control and interface.

Stepper Motor Control and Interface

There are several companies such as Superior Electric, Rapidsyn (Dana) industries, Air Pax, etc. manufacturing these stepper motors at very competitive prices. They are usually specified in terms of angular rotation per step of the shaft. A 1.8° rotation per step implies that for a full 360° revolution, 200 discrete steps or positions can be obtained.

Each time the digital activation on the motor changes in a given sequence, it is considered as one step. The stepper motor is capable of rotating clockwise (forward) and counter clockwise (backward), depending upon the sequencing of the digital word activating the motor winding.

A linearly attached gearing mechanism to the motor rotating shaft results in a linearized motion control. Some of the Airpax digital linear stepper motors have a resolution of 2 mils (0.002 inches) per step, which is sufficient for most of the industrial position controls. Figure 7.9 shows some of these stepper motors.

Microprocessor Control

We can control the movement of the stepper motor very conveniently with the help of a microcomputer. For example, the information regarding how many steps the motor should turn, whether it should turn clockwise or counterclockwise etc., can be input into port A of 6522 VIA. In real industrial environments, this information may be coming from sensors attached to the industrial process.

Because of inductive loading, the stepper motors require some special drive circuits. Shown in Fig. 7.10(a) is a typical drive circuitry for Superior Electric 1.8° substep stepper motor, interfaced to AIM-65. The transistor drivers Q0, Q1, Q2, and Q3 supply the required drive currents to the coils W0, W1, W2, and W3. The diodes D0, D1, D2, and D3 prevent the inductive transients of the coils. The series resistances RS0, RS1, RS2, and RS3 restrict the current through each coil when activated.

Figure 7.10(b) shows the sequence of activation of the above stepper motor. When the coils are activated in downward sequence, the stepper rotates in the clockwise direction. Each time the coil code changes, the stepper moves through a substep of 1.8°. As can be seen, the code repeats itself after four

Fig 7.9. Typical stepper motors. (Courtesy Airpax.)

substeps, which can be interpreted as resulting in 4 × 1.8° = 7.2° angular rotation.

If the coils are activated in the upward sequence, the stepper rotation will be in the counterclockwise direction.

Example 7.4 Stepper Motor Control

In the circuit of Figure 7.10, using the Superior Electric 1.8° substep stepper motor, P_{A0} thru P_{A5} provide the information regarding the number of full steps (7.2° = full step) to be rotated. P_{A6} and P_{A7} provide directional information as shown.

P_{A7}	P_{A6}	*Operation*
0	0	No rotation
0	1	Clockwise
1	0	Counterclockwise
1	1	Reset to home position

A 0 → 1 transition on CA1 provided by the optical sensing signifies home position.

Develop a complete operating system, with software and hardware fully functional.

Solution

(a) *The Concept.* We will read port A input information and then go to appropriate routines to control the stepper. Port B is configured as output and drives the stepper coils. The stepper activation code is output on port B in proper sequence with proper delay to rotate the stepper through a given number of steps in the given direction, as determined by the port A input word. Figure 7.11 shows the system level flow chart and Table 7.5 shows the actual program listings.

(b) *Main Program.* Between 0400 and 040A, Port A is configured as input, and port B is configured as output. Between 040B and 0414, the peripheral control register (PCR) and the interrupt enable register (IER) are conditioned to recognize CA1 interrupt transition. Between 0418 and 042A, input port A is read, stored, and examined, and the program branches to the appropriate routine depending on the condition of PA7 and PA6.

(c) *Clockwise and Counterclockwise Routines.* Between 0440 and 0444, the last 6-bit information of port A is transferred into the Y register, which acts as step counter. Between 0445 and 0453, the contents of the code table (code table is contained between locations 00 and 06, as shown) are output in the forward sequence using the index mode of addressing, to rotate the motor one full step of 7.2° in the clockwise direction. The delay routine developed in Example 7.2 is used here as a delay subroutine with delay parameters adjusted to yield 2 ms.

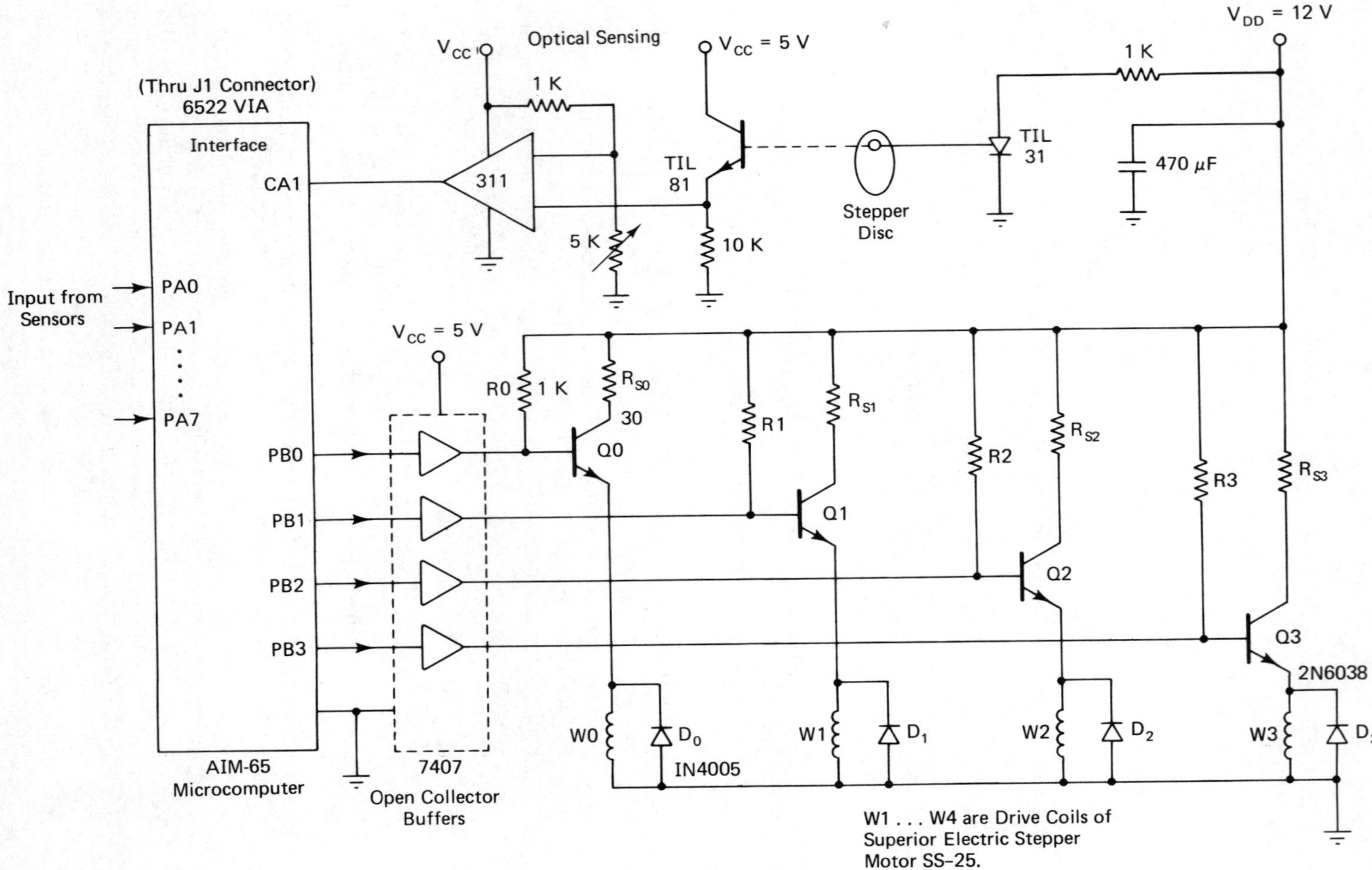

Fig 7.10. (a) The AIM-65 and stepper motor interface; (b) stepper motor code table (for Superior electric motor).

Forward ↓ Backward ↑

Sequence	W3	W2	W1	W0	Hex Code
0	0	0	1	1	03
1	0	1	1	0	06
2	1	1	0	0	0c
3	1	0	0	1	09
4	0	0	1	1	03

Fig. 7.10(b). Stepper Motor Code Table (Superior Electric Motor)

This delay is required to let the stepper coils to respond to the new code. For any given stepper motor, the manufacturer's data sheets should be consulted to get the required delay. Between 0454 and 0456, the step counter is decremented, and the program is branched back to rotate through one more step, until the motor rotates through the required number of steps. Then the control is returned to the monitor via the BRK instruction.

The counterclockwise routine between 0460 and 046A essentially is similar to the clockwise routine, except that the X pointer is initialized to the end of the code table at 0465, and the code is output in the backward sequence.

(d) *Reset Home Routine.* As shown in Figure 7.10(a), the TIL 31 and 81 infra red LED and phototransistor combination provide a signal when light from LED passes to the phototransistor through the registration hole in a disk attached to the stepper motor shaft. Between 0480 to 048E, the stepper is stepped through effective clockwise rotation. After each stepper advancement, the interrupt flag register (IFR) is examined for the occurrence of 0 → 1 transition on CA1, which suggests the home position of the stepper motor. If CA1 transition is not detected, the program branches back to 0480 to step further. If CA1 transition is detected, program control is transferred to the monitor, and the stepper continues to stay at the home position. Figure 7.12 shows the actual code table stored in the memory.

It looks as though we have gone through a very tedious exercise. The importance of the stepper motor in the digital and microcomputer field resulted in an elaborate presentation of the material. You are urged to understand this problem completely. Several practical problems are presented at the end of the chapter to help introduce many applications.

We can certainly use our systems approach to develop complex system designs in a simple way. This concept will be applied to implement a graphics system, using the *XY* plotting technique with the help of two stepper motors X_{Stepper} and Y_{Stepper}.

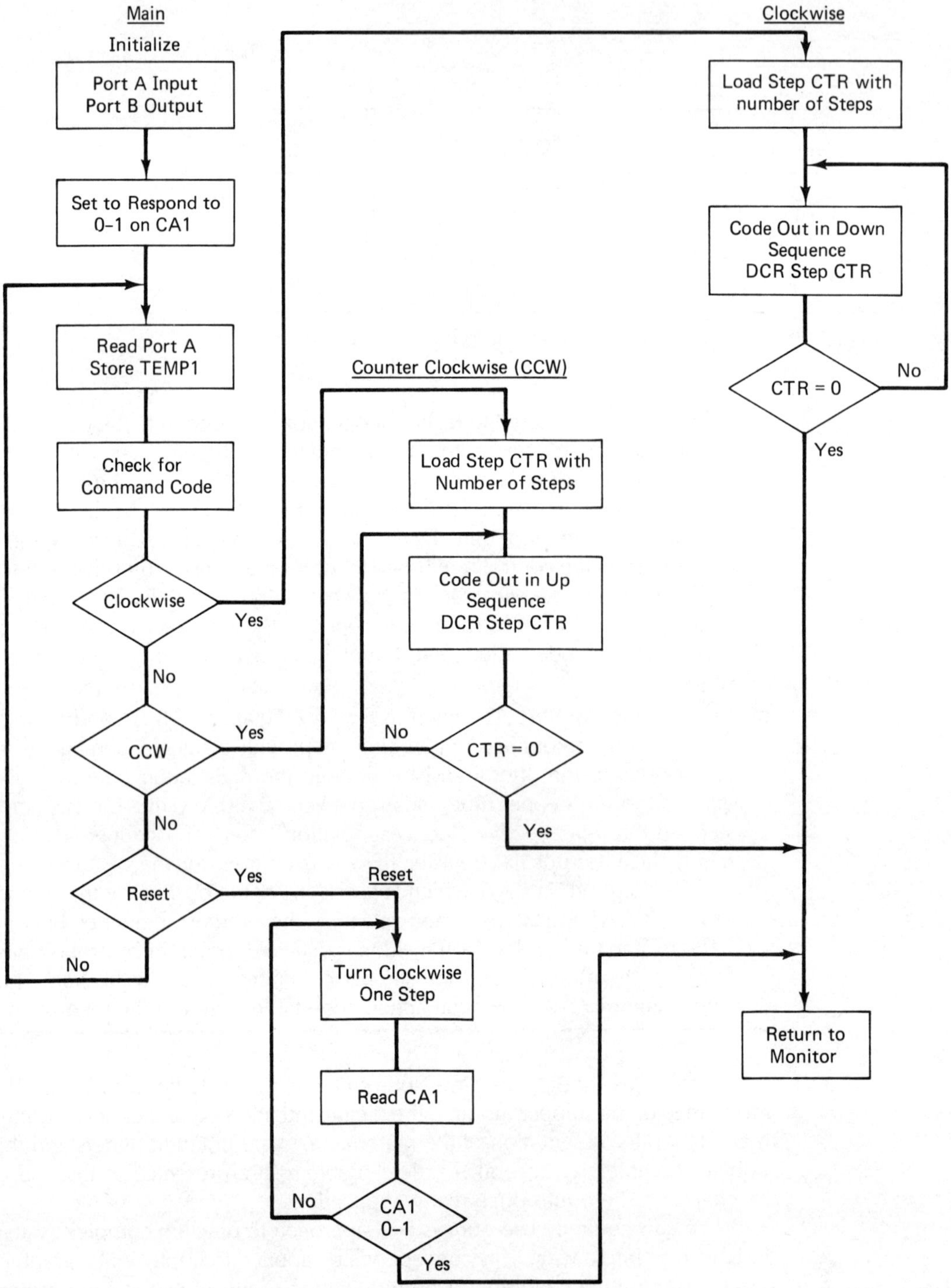

Fig 7.11. Flowchart for stepper motor control (Example 7.4).

STEPPER CODE TABLE IN MEMORY

Memory Location	*Stepper Coils* W_4	W_3	W_2	W_1	*Hex Code*
00 and 01	0	0	1	1	(03)
02	0	1	1	0	(06)
03	1	1	0	0	(0C)
04	1	0	0	1	(09)
05 and 06	0	0	1	1	(03)

Note: The memory locations 00 thru 06 are loaded with (03), (06), (0C), (09), and (03) Hex as shown.

Fig 7.12. Stepper motor code table in memory.

Plotter Interface: *XY* Graphics Control

Figure 7.13 shows a simple and practical *XY* plotter interface using two stepper motors *X* and *Y*. A linearized attachment to teath gear results in a linear motion as the stepper shaft rotates, as shown in Figure 7.14. Such an arrangement is made in Figure 7.13 to move the *Y* arm back and forth in the *X* direction

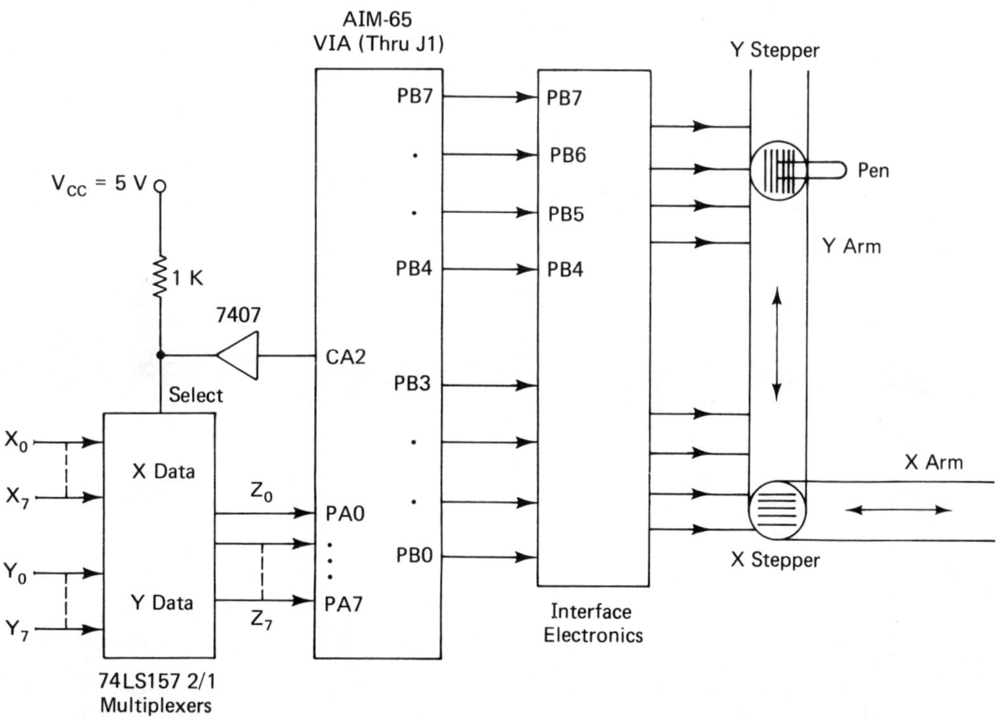

Fig 7.13. *X, Y* plotter interface to the AIM-65.

Table 7.5. Stepper Motor Control Listings (Example 7.4).

Program Location	Label	Mnemonic	Op Code	Address Mode	Comments
0400	Initialize	LDA	A9	Immediate	Port A made input by loading ØØ in DDRA at AØØ3
01		#00			
02		STA	8D	Absolute	
03		A0			
04		03			
05		LDA	A9	Immediate	Port B made output by loading FF in DDRB at AØØ2.
06		#FF			
07		STA	8D	Absolute	
08		AØ			
09		02			
0A		NOP	EA	Implied	
0B		LDA	A9	Immediate	PCR at AØØC is set to recognize 0 → 1 transition on CA1 and set flag in IFR (Refer to Figures 7.4 to 7.6).
0C		#01			
0D		STA	8D	Absolute	
0E		A0			
0F		0C			[0 0 0 0 0 0 0 1] PCR = $(01)_{Hex}$ (bit 0: CA1)
0410		LDA	A9	Immediate	CA1 interrupt enabled to set corresponding flag in IFR, by writing #82 in IER
11		#82			
12		STA	8D	Absolute	
13		A0			[1 0 0 0 0 0 1 0] IFR = $(82)_{Hex}$ (bit 1: CA1)
14		0E			
15		NOP	EA	Implied	Delay or linkage software.
16		NOP	EA	Implied	
17		NOP	EA	Implied	
18	Read	LDA	AD	Absolute	Read Port A at A001 and store it in temporary location 0A.
19		A0			
1A		01			
1B		STA	85	Zero Page	
1C		0A			
1D		AND	29	Immediate	Mask out $P_{A0}...P_{A5}$ and keep only P_{A7} and P_{A6}.
1E		#C0			
1F		CMP	C9	Immediate	Compare to see the condition of P_{A7} and P_{A6} and branch to proper routines. If
20		#40			

Address	Label	Mnemonic	Op code	Mode	Comments
21	(To clockwise)	BEQ	F0	Relative	P_{A7} P_{A6}
22		(0440)			0 1 → $(40)_{Hex}$ clockwise RTN at 0440
23		CMP	C9	Immediate	
24		#80			1 0 → $(80)_{Hex}$ counterclockwise RTN at 0460
25	(To counterclockwise)	BEQ	F0	Relative	
26		(0460)			1 1 → $(CO)_{Hex}$ Reset RTN at 0480
27		CMP	C9	Immediate	0 0 Jump back to 0418 to read again.
28		#C0			
29	(To reset)	BEQ	F0	Relative	
2A		(0480)			
2B		NOP	EA	Implied	
2C		NOP	EA	Implied	
2D		JMP	4C	Absolute	
2E		04			
2F		18			

CLOCKWISE ROUTINE

Address	Label	Mnemonic	Op code	Mode	Comments
0440		LDA	A5	Zero Page	Get port A data from location 0A.
41		0A			
42		AND	29	Immediate	Get only last 6-bit information and put it in Y register to act as step counter.
43		#3F			
44		TAY	A8	Implied	
45	← (from 0456)	LDX	A6	Zero Page	X register is used as pointer to refer to stepper activation code table and output the code to port B. X is loaded from location 0B.
46		OB			
47	Code table ← (from 0453)	LDA, X	B5	Index	
48		00			
49		STA	8D	Absolute	
4A		A0			
4B		00			
4C		JSR	20	Absolute	Delay routine with parameters adjusted to yield 2 msec delay.
4D		02			
4E		50			
4F		INX	E8	Implied	X is incremented to get code data in forward sequence. Program branches back to 0447 until all 5 code words are output. End value of X is stored in location 0C.
50		CPX	E4	Zero Page	
51		OC			
52		BNE	D0	Relative	
53	To code table	(0447)			
54		DEY	88	Implied	Step counter is decremented. Program branches back to 0445 to step the motor again, until the required number of steps are over.
55		BNE	D0	Relative	
56		(0445)			
57		NOP	EA	Implied	

Table 7.5. *(Continued)*

Program Location	*Label*	*Mnemonic*	*Op Code*	*Address Mode*	*Comments*
58		NOP	EA	Implied	Linkage and delay.
59		NOP	EA	Implied	
5A		BRK	00	Implied	Return to monitor.
		COUNTERCLOCKWISE ROUTINE			
0460		LDA	A5	Zero page	Get port A data from location 0A.
61		0A			
62		AND	29	Immediate	Get last 6-bit information and put it in Y register to make it step counter.
63		#3F			
64		TAY	A8	Implied	
65		→ LDX	A6	Zero page	Activation code table is scanned backward by initializing X pointer to the end of the table location and using index address to output to port B.
66		0C			
67		→ LDA, X	B5	Index	
68		00			
69		STA	8D	Absolute	
6A		A0			
6B		00			
6C	(To delay)	JSR	20	Absolute	Delay with parameters adjusted to yield 2 ms delay.
6D		02			
6E		50			
6F		DEX	CA	Implied	X is decremented to output to port B. All five code words in backward sequence.
0470		CPX	E4	Zero page	
71		0B			
72		BNE	D0	Relative	
73		(0467)			
74		DEY	88	Implied	Step counter decremented and program loops back to 0465 until the required number of steps are over.
75		BNE	D0	Relative	
76		(0465)			
77		NOP	EA	Implied	Linkage or delay.
78		NOP	EA	Implied	
79		NOP	EA	Implied	
7A		BRK	00	Implied	Return to monitor.

MEMORY LOCATIONS & CONTENTS

Temp 1	0A	Contents of port A
Temp 2	0B	00 Beginning of code table
Temp 3	0C	06 End of code table

RESET HOME ROUTINE

Address	Branch	Instruction	Op code	Mode	Comments
0480		→LDX	A6	Zero page	Code table initialized to the beginning for clockwise rotation, and the code is output to port B in sequence.
81		0B			
82		→LDA, X	B5	Index	
83		00			
84		STA	8D	Absolute	
85		AØ			
86		Ø0			
87	(To delay)	JSR	20	Absolute	2 ms delay.
88		02			
89		50			
8A		INX	E8	Implied	Loop back to code table to get next code word.
8B		CPX	E4	Zero page	
8C		0C			
8D		BNE	D0	Relative	
8E		(0482)			
8F		LDA	AD	Absolute	The interrupt flag register is examined to see if Bit b1 is set, implying CA1
0490		A0			
91		0D			
92		Bit	24	Zero page	Active transition has occurred (home position). Location 0D should be preloaded with hex data (01). If not, branch back to beginning to start one more full step.
93		0D			
94		BNE	D0	Relative	
95		(0480)			
96		NOP	EA	Implied	
97		NOP	EA	Implied	
98		NOP	EA	Implied	Linkage or delay.
99		BRK	00	Implied	Back to monitor.

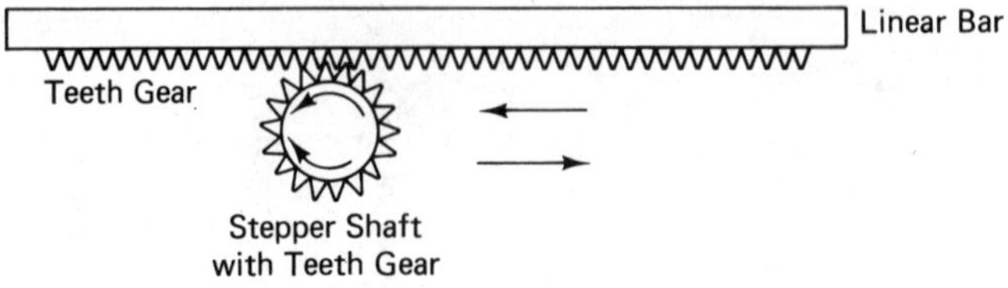

Fig 7.14. Obtaining linear motion by teeth gear arrangement to stepper shaft.

as $X_{Stepper}$ rotates and to move the pen up and down in the Y direction as the $Y_{Stepper}$ rotates.

In the actual graphics system, the X and Y motions are implemented in sequential order, one at a time. Port B drives X and Y stepper ($P_{B0}...P_{B3}$ $X_{Stepper}$ and $P_{B4}...P_{B7}$ $Y_{Stepper}$). When $CA_2 = 0$, input multiplexer switches the X input data to port A of VIA. The micro reads this information and rotates X stepper accordingly, which results in moving the Y arm in the X direction. Similarly $C_{A2} = 1$ connects the Y input to the port A, and the micro moves the pen in the Y direction to the appropriate position. Thus successive X and Y motions result in a plot being drawn in the XY plane. The stepper motor software and routines developed for Example 7.4 can be used in the graphics interface under consideration, with few modifications. The stepper motor code table of Figure 7.12 is modified as shown in Figure 7.15 to accommodate X and Y steppers. The first 6 locations (00 to 05) correspond to X stepper, and the last 6 locations (07 to 0C) correspond to Y stepper.

Location	b_7	b_6	b_5	b_4	b_3	b_2	b_1	b_0		
00	0	0	1	1	0	0	1	1	$(33)_H$	
01	0	0	1	1	0	0	1	1	$(33)_H$	
02	0	0	1	1	0	1	1	0	$(36)_H$	
03	0	0	1	1	1	1	0	0	$(3C)_H$	X Stepper Code
04	0	0	1	1	1	0	0	1	$(39)_H$	
05	0	0	1	1	0	0	1	1	$(33)_H$	
06	0	0	1	1	0	0	1	1	$(33)_H$	
07	0	0	1	1	0	0	1	1	$(33)_H$	
08	0	1	1	0	0	0	1	1	$(63)_H$	
09	1	1	0	0	0	0	1	1	$(C3)_H$	Y Stepper Code
0A	1	0	0	1	0	0	1	1	$(93)_H$	
0B	0	0	1	1	0	0	1	1	$(33)_H$	
0C	0	0	1	1	0	0	1	1	$(33)_H$	
0D										
	Activates Y Stepper				Activates X Stepper					
	$(W_{Y3}$	W_{Y2}	W_{Y1}	$W_{Y0})$	$(W_{X3}$	W_{X2}	W_{X1}	$W_{X0})$		

Fig 7.15. Stepper code table for X and Y steppers.

The lower nibble $b_0 \ldots b_3$ drives the *X* stepper and the upper nibble $b_4 \ldots b_7$ drives the *Y* stepper. An inactive code of 0011 is presented to *Y* stepper when *X* stepper is activated and is presented to *X* stepper when *Y* stepper is activated, as shown in Figure 7.15. This adjustment has become necessary since the same port B drives both the steppers.

Figure 7.16 and Table 7.6 show the flow chart and the actual listings for the graphics interface. Between 0500 to 0509, ports A and B are configured as input and output respectively. Between 050A and 051F, temporary locations 2 and 3 at 0B and 0C are loaded with 00 and 06, which correspond to the beginning and ending addresses of the stepper code table for *X* (Figure 7.15).

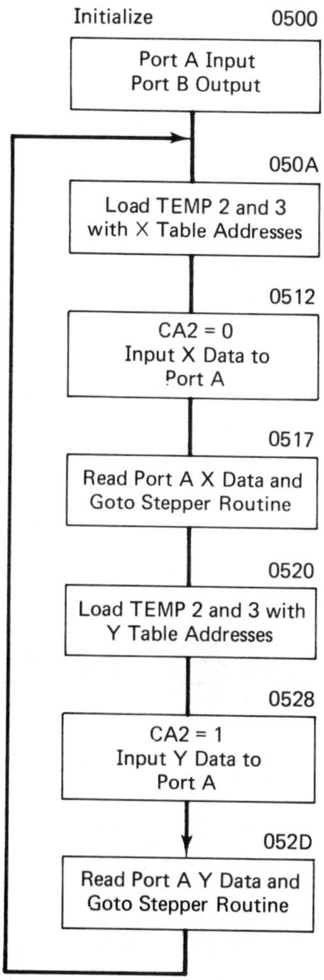

Fig 7.16. *X, Y* graphics interface flowchart.

Table 7.6. *XY* Graphics Interface Listings.

Location	*Label*	*Mnemonic*	*Op Code*	*Address Mode*	*Comment*
0500	Initialize	LDA	A9	Immediate	Port A configured as input and port B as output by writing ØØ in DDRA at AØØ3 and FF in DDRB at AØØ2.
01		ØØ			
02		STA	8D	Absolute	
03		AØ			
04		Ø3			
05		LDA	A9	Immediate	
06		#FF			
07		STA	8D	Absolute	
08		AØ			
09		Ø2			
0A	*X* stepper	LDA	A9	Immediate	Beginning and end addresses 00 and 06 of *X* code table are loaded into temporary locations 0B and 0C.
0B		ØØ			
0C		STA	85	Zero page	
0D		0B			
0E		LDA	A9	Immediate	
0F		06			
0510		STA	85	Zero page	
11		0C			
12		LDA	A9	Immediate	CA2 configured as 0 level output. This switches X data to port A.
13		0C			
14		STA	8D	Absolute	
15		A0			
16		0C			
17		LDA	AD	Absolute	X data on port A is read.
18		A0			
19		01			
1A		NOP	EA	Implied	
1B		NOP	EA	Implied	
1C		NOP	EA	Implied	

Address	Label	Instruction	Op code	Mode	Comments
051D	(To stepper)	JSR	20	Absolute	Jump to the stepper motor control (please read note at the end of the listing)[1] routine at 0418.
1E		04			
1F		18			
20	Y stepper	LDA	A9	Immediate	Beginning and end addresses 06 and 0C of *Y* code table loaded into temporary locations 0B and 0C.
21		#06			
22		STA	85	Zero page	
23		0B			
24		LDA	A9	Immediate	
25		#0C			
26		STA	85	Zero page	
27		0C			
28		LDA	A9	Immediate	CA2 configured as 1 level output. This switches *Y* data to port A.
29		#0E			
2A		STA	8D	Absolute	
2B		A0			
2C		0C			
2D		LDA	AD	Absolute	*Y* data on port A is read.
2E		A0			
2F		01			
30		NOP	EA	Implied	
31		NOP	EA		
32		NOP	EA		Linkage and delay.
33		JSR	20	Absolute	Jump to stepper motor control routine at 0418.[1]
34	(To stepper)	04			
35		18			
36		JMP	4C	Absolute	Restart the cycle by jumping to 050A.
37		05			
38		0A			

[1] Change the NOP instructions at 042B, 0457, 0477, and 0497 to RTS to have the program operation.

X input data is read into the micro. The stepper subroutine starting at 0418 (Example 7.4 and Table 7.5) will use all this information and rotate the *X* stepper through the required number of steps, which moves *Y* arm.

Between 0520 0535, the temporary locations are loaded with *Y* code table addresses, and *Y* input information is read on to port A. The stepper subroutine starting at 0418 now rotates the *Y* stepper through the required number of steps, which moves the pen. The program keeps looping around by the jump instruction at the end.

Several example problems are presented at the end of the chapter to familiarize you to the other important features of the 6522 VIA, such as timer and shift register-based applications and other I/O interface characteristics. You are encouraged to solve them to gain more experience.

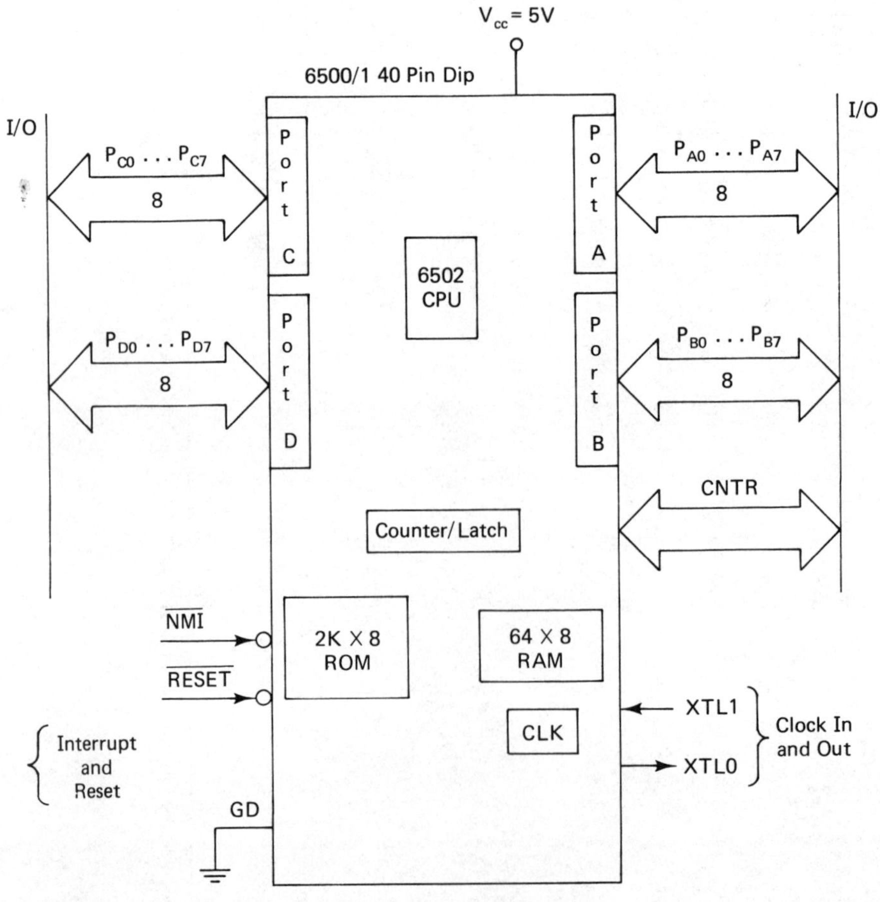

Fig 7.17. The 6500/1 single-chip microcomputer structure.

7.4. SINGLE-CHIP MICROCOMPUTERS

As we have seen earlier, the single-chip microcomputer devices are particularly suitable for I/O bound applications and control systems. As such, the 6500/1 single-chip micro from Rockwell, along with its emulator device 6500/1E, is extremely popular in such applications. With its 32 I/O lines with individual programmability, 6500/1 is very widely used in high speed and video applications.

6500/1 and 6500/1E Single-Chip Microcomputers

The 6500/1 microcomputer as shown in Figure 7.17 has a similar architecture and instruction set as the 6502 microprocessor and is suitable for dedicated I/O applications. The 2K × 8 ROM is mask programmable at the factory, containing the user programs and data. The four I/O ports A, B, C, and D are individually programmable as inputs or outputs. The 64 × 8 RAM is available for user variables and stack. Figure 7.18 shows the effective memory map.

The 6500/1EB, the backpack emulator device as shown in Figure 7.19, is intended as a developmental aid and is functionally identical to the 6500/1 microcomputer. The ROM portion is brought outside, and the address bus is

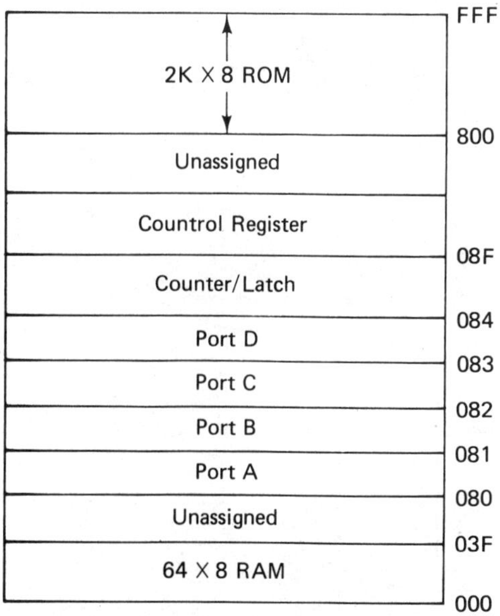

Fig 7.18. The 6500/1 microcomputer memory map.

Table 7.7. Program Listing for Traffic Control (Example 7.5).

TRAFFIC LITE CONTROL—MAIN PROGRAM: 6500/1

Location	*Label*	*Mnemonic*	*Op Code*	*Mode*	*Comment*
0800	Initialize	LDX	A2	Immediate	Stack pointer initialized to 3F, by loading *X* with 3F and transferring to stack pointer.
01		#3F			
02		TXS	9A	Implied	
03	Code pointer	LDX	A2	Immediate	X register used as code pointer and initialized to top of table at 08.
04		#08			
05		LDA, X	B5	Indexed	
06		00			
07	Code out	STA	85	Zero page	Code read from table in sequence and output to port A at (80).
08		80			
09		STX	86	Zero page	*X* pointer stored at 0A and to delay subroutine at 0850 for 10 s and *X* pointer restored from 0A.
0A		0A			
0B	Delay	JSR	20	Absolute	
0C		50_{Low}			
0D		08_{High}			
0E		LDX	A6	Zero page	
0F		0A			
10	Decrement	DEX	CA	Implied	*X* pointer decremented. If not end of table, branches to 0805 to output next code.
11		BNE		Relative	
12		F2			
13		NOP	EA	Implied	
14		JMP	4C	Absolute	If end of table, jumps to 0803 to reinitialize the pointer.
15		03_{Low}			
16		08_{High}			

CODE TABLE

Location		Contents	Location		Contents
0008	...	82	0004	...	28
0007	...	92	0003	...	29
0006	...	92	0002	...	29
0005	...	42	0001	...	24

10-SECOND DELAY ROUTINE 6500/1E

Address	Instruction	Code	Mode	Timing Cycles	Notes
0850	LDX	A2	Immediate	2	
51	IF				
52	STX	86	Zero page	3	
53	0B				
54	LDX	A2	Immediate	2	Counter 2 (Loop 3 target); T_{L3} begins
55	#FF				
56	LDY	A0	Immediate	2	Counter 1 (Loop 2 target); T_{L2} begins
57	#FF				
58	DEY	88	Implied	2	Loop 1 target; T_{L1} begins
59	BNE	D0	Relative	3	T_{L1} ends
5A	FD				Loop 1
5B	DEX	CA	Implied	2	
5C	BNE	D0		3	T_{L2} ends
5D	F8				Loop 2
5E	DEC 0B	C6 0B	Zero page	5	
60	BNE	D0	Relative	3	T_{L3} ends
61	F2				Loop 3
62	NOP	EA	Implied	2	
63	RTS	60	Implied	6	

Y Register Counter 1
X Register Counter 2
OB Location Counter 3

Reset	Vector
FFC	00_{Low}
FFD	08_{High}

After power on, address vector 0800 will be picked up from vectored reset locations of FFC and FFD and program execution will start at 0800.

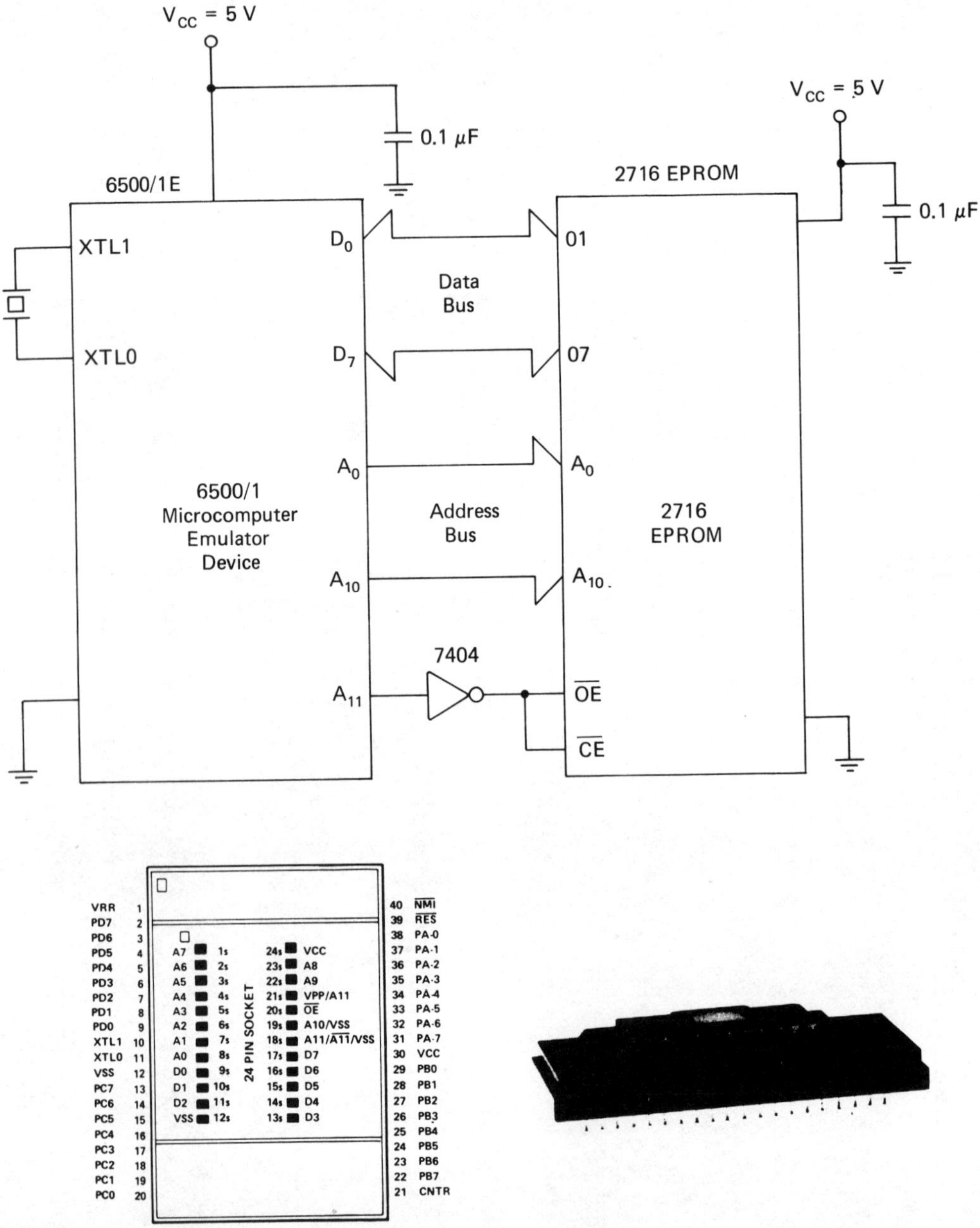

R6500/1EB Pin Configuration

Fig 7.19. (a) The 6500/1E emulator and the 2716 EPROM configuration; (b) physical structure of the 6500/1EB backpack device with the 2716 plugged in. (Courtesy Rockwell International.)

provided to address the external ROM/PROM device. The industry standard 2716 EPROM device, loaded with user programs, directly fits into the back connector.

Traffic Light Controller Design and Interface

We will now present an operating example of a simple traffic light structure controlled by the 6500/1EB microcomputer emulator device in conjunction with 2716 EPROM. We will introduce the concept with an example problem.

Example 7.5 Single-Chip Micro 6500/1—Traffic Controller

A simulated traffic control system is as shown in Figure 7.20, where G, Y, R, and W lights correspond to green, yellow, red, and walk signs, A refers to avenue, and S corresponds to street. Logic 1 turns on the light and 0 turns off the light. Using the 6500/1E single-chip microcomputer system of Figure 7.19, develop the operating software and hardware. The system should stay in each state for 10 seconds.

Solution

The system hardware is as shown in Figure 7.21. The system will be functional as desired, if the light code of Figure 7.20(b) is sequentially output to

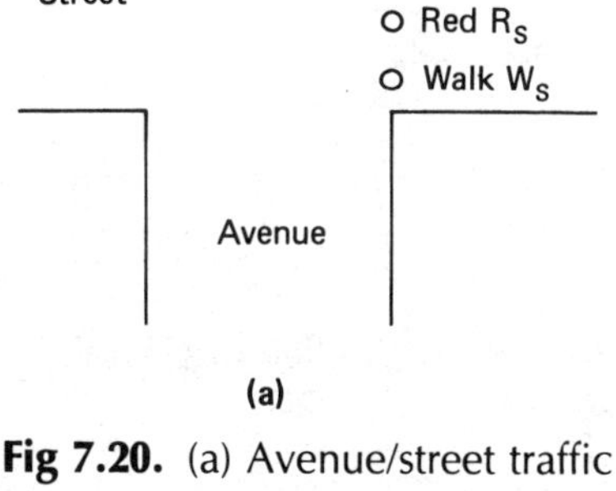

(a)

Avenue Lights				Street Lights				
G_A	Y_A	R_A	W_A	G_S	Y_S	R_S	W_S	Code
1	0	0	0	0	0	1	0	82
1	0	0	1	0	0	1	0	92
1	0	0	1	0	0	1	0	92
0	1	0	0	0	0	1	0	42
0	0	1	0	1	0	0	0	28
0	0	1	0	1	0	0	1	29
0	0	1	0	1	0	0	1	29
0	0	1	0	0	1	0	0	24

(b)

Fig 7.20. (a) Avenue/street traffic light system; (b) truth table expressing relation.

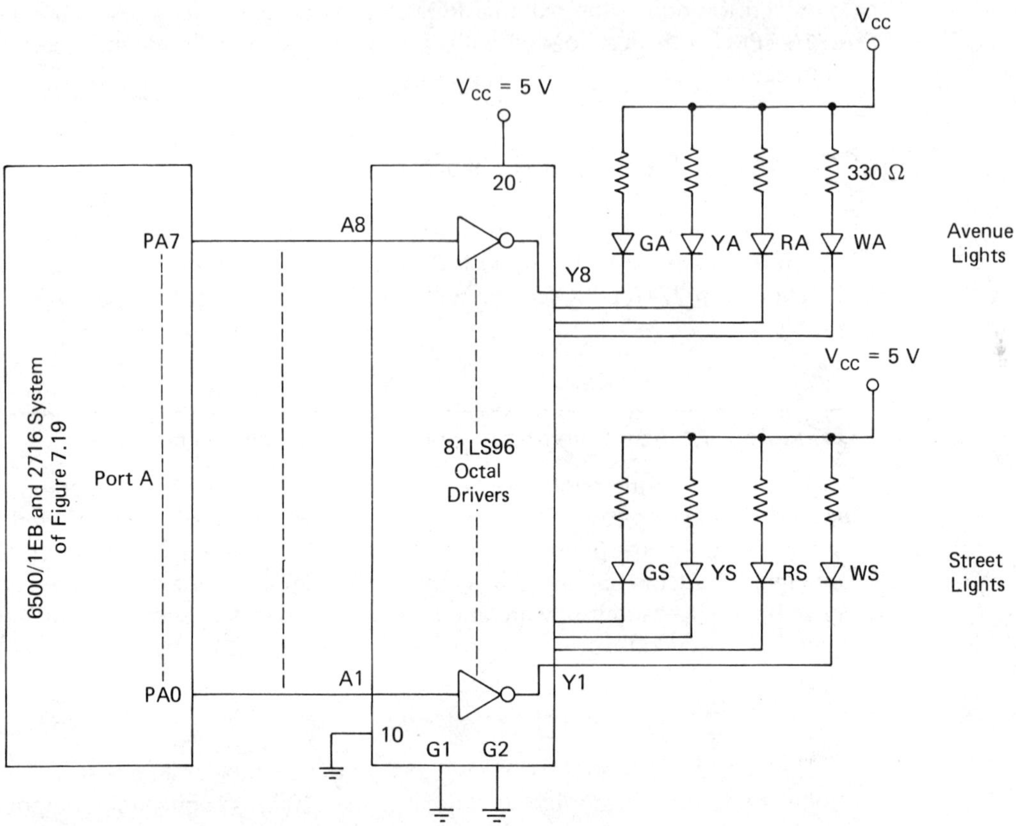

Fig 7.21. Traffic light control system with the 6500/1EB microcomputer.

port A, with a 10 s interval between successive codes. For example:

Code	$(82)_{Hex}$	turns on	avenue green and street red
	$(92)_{Hex}$	turns on	avenue green and walk and street red
		⋮	
	$(24)_{Hex}$	turns on	avenue red and street yellow

The reader should verify that walking through codes $(82)_{Hex}$...$(24)_{Hex}$ sequentially indeed corresponds to a real traffic light pattern.

(a) *Pseudo Code.* Using the pseudocode that we have studied in Chapter 5, the software can be expressed in the following statements:

Initialize code table

			Code
Top of table	08	....	82
	07	....	92
Bottom of table	01	....	24

→ Initialize code pointer (X) to top of table: $X = 08$
  → Output code from pointed location
  Go for 10 s delay
  Decrement code pointer to get new code
If not the end of table, keep outputting code in sequence
If end of table, reinitialize pointer X to top of table

(b) *Actual Listings.* Table 7.7 shows the actual listings. As can be observed, the instructions of the 6500/1E are basically similar to the 6502 CPU. The major difference is in handling the I/O ports. In 6500/1 microcomputer devices, there are no data direction registers. Any word can be output on any port, just like storing a word in a memory location. If the port is to be used as an input, it has to be preconditioned by first writing $(FF)_{Hex}$ into it.

At 0800, stack is initialized at the highest available RAM address of 3F. At 0803, X register is used as the code pointer and is initialized to 08, corresponding to the top of the code table. Between 0805 and 0812, the code table is read sequentially (with a 10 s delay between each code) and is output to port A. This has the effect of turning the traffic lights on and off in the required sequence. When the end of the table is reached, the JMP instruction at 0814 reinitializes the code pointer X to the top of the table to start a new cycle. Since the X register is to be used in the delay routine, it is stored at (0A) before jumping to subroutine and is restored after the subroutine.

(c) *Delay Routine.* Y, X and location 0B are used as counter 1, counter 2, and counter 3, which are interlooped between 0850 and 0861 as shown. With 1 MHz clock, the loop delays:

Loop 1 TL1 $= (FF)_{Hex} * 5 = 1275\ \mu s$
Loop 2 TL2 $= (FF)_{Hex} * [T_{L1} + 7] = 0.3269$ sec
Loop 3 TL3 $= (1F)_{Hex} * [T_{L2} + 10] = 10.13$ s
Total delay between 0850 and 0863 $= T_{L3} + 13\ \mu s = T_{L3} = 10.13$ s

Thus delay routine yields approximately 10 s.

(d) *Reset Vector.* The vectored locations of FFD and FFC for reset are loaded with (08_H 00), which corresponds to the starting address of the traffic control routine.

As can be seen, complex problems can be handled very easily with single-chip microcomputers, using minimum hardware.

7.5. SUMMARY

In this chapter, we have discussed the applications of 6502-based microcomputer system such as AIM-65. All the concepts and programs presented are applicable to any other 6502-based systems such as Apple, VIC-20, SYM, etc.

Particular emphasis is given to the usage of the powerful interface device 6522 VIA, which is industry standard for the 6500-based systems. The stepper motor control examples are meant to provide the reader with insight into the position control and associated robotics, which is an expanding field under micro control.

The graphics interface is meant to integrate microcontrol concepts in obtaining a system level function.

The traffic light control example is particularly designed to introduce single-chip microcomputer 6500/1 and a practical example of how effectively they can be integrated to realize an operating system.

The examples studied with respect to other microprocessors can be easily implemented with 6502 microprocessor-based systems.

The problems at the end of the chapter should provide a much better insight into other applications.

Problems

7.1. Figure 7.22 shows some useful monitor routines of the AIM-65 system. Using these, develop operating software to output the following message onto display:

Number	*Name of Monitor Subroutine*	*Location*	*Registers Effected*	*Description*
1	Blank	E83E	A	Outputs a blank to display/printer.
2	Equal	E7D8	A	Outputs = to display.
3	Outdis	EF05	A, X, Y	Outputs ASCII CHR in A to display.
4	PHXY	EB9E	—	Pushes X and Y to stack.
5	PLXY	EBAC	XY	Pulls X and Y from stack.
6	READ	E93C	A	Reads keyboard and puts the ASCII code in A.

Fig 7.22. AIM-65 monitor routines (Problems 7.1–7.5).

MICROCOMPUTER GREAT

7.2. Repeat Problem 7.1, such that the information flashes at 1-second intervals.

7.3. Develop the operating software using the monitor routines of Figure 7.22 to shift the displayed information to the left at a rate of 1 digit per second, as shown.

MICROCOMPUTER GREAT
MICROCOMPUTER GREAT

L ←- - - -
Shift Left

7.4. The basis for any video game is the moving display of information, providing an optical illusion. Using the monitor routines of your choice, develop the operating software to move:

(a) = sign from left to right at 0.2-5 intervals to create the impression that it is continuously moving.

(b) Repeat (a) where = sign moves from right to left.

7.5. Repeat Problem 7.4 such that the = sign moves from left to right and then from right to left.

7.6. Develop the operating software so that the time information can be entered through the keyboard, and the system will act as a real time clock as shown in Figure 7.23, displaying information continuously and updating the display every second.

7.7. Many commercial signs display time and temperature information alternatively, which can be easily accomplished with a microcomputer system. Develop the operating software of the 6502-based system to

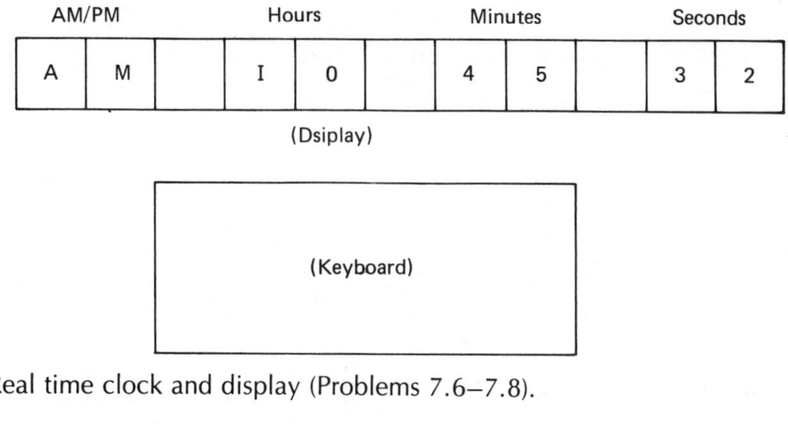

Fig 7.23. Real time clock and display (Problems 7.6–7.8).

display time and temperature information alternatively at 5-second intervals. Display time for 5 seconds and temperature for 5 seconds in the following format

AM 10 45 32
and
Temperature 30°C

The time and temperature information initially can be entered through the keyboard.

7.8. Repeat Problem 7.7, with the time and temperature information continuously rotating from right to left, as shown, with a 1-second shift interval.

--TIME TEMPERATURE--

ROTATIONAL SHIFT

7.9. Shown in Figure 7.24 is a typical I/O interface of a 6502-based system such as Aim-65, using the 6522 VIA. Develop the operating hardware and software using real devices to read the information from port A in BCD format, and display the information on a multiplexed 7-segment display connected to port B. Port A should accept bounce-free input data in 1-second intervals, from *X* input through proper interface electronics. Port B (P_{B0}—P_{B6}) should furnish the 7-segment code corresponding to the digit being displayed. P_{B7} should be used to switch between digit 0 digit 1 at least 20 times a second, to provide the optical illusion of continuous display.

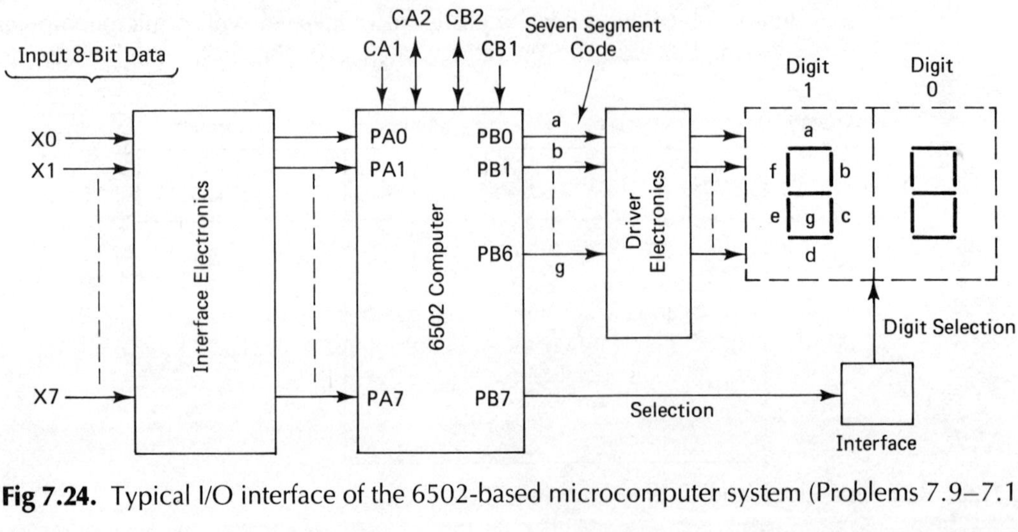

Fig 7.24. Typical I/O interface of the 6502-based microcomputer system (Problems 7.9–7.13).

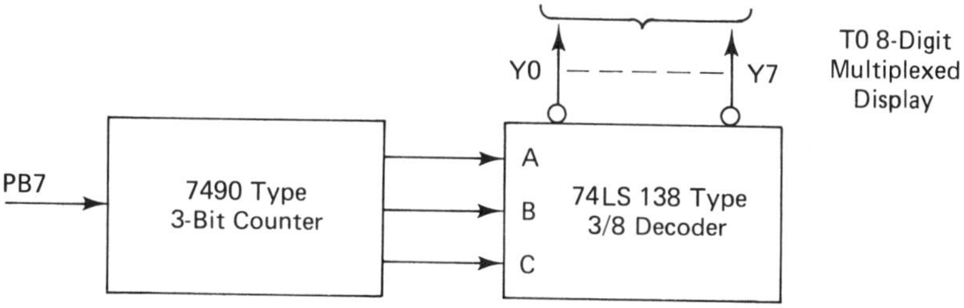

Fig 7.25. Expanding the output drive capability to eight digits.

7.10. Repeat Problem 7.9 so that the output display can be extended to 8 multiplexed digits, and P_{B7} is used as a digit advancement clock as shown in Figure 7.25. This type of concept is used whenever there is a limitation of I/O connections and external hardware required.

7.11. *Furnace Controllers.* The $X_0...X_7$ data of Figure 7.24 is coming from temperature sensors from a furnace. The X data is BCD and should be read in 5-second intervals. If the temperature reading is more than 80° for more than 1 minute, power to the furnace should be stopped by pulling CA2 line low. Develop the operating software and hardware.

7.12. Repeat Problem 7.11 to set an alarm connected to CB2 output as shown, at 500 Hz.

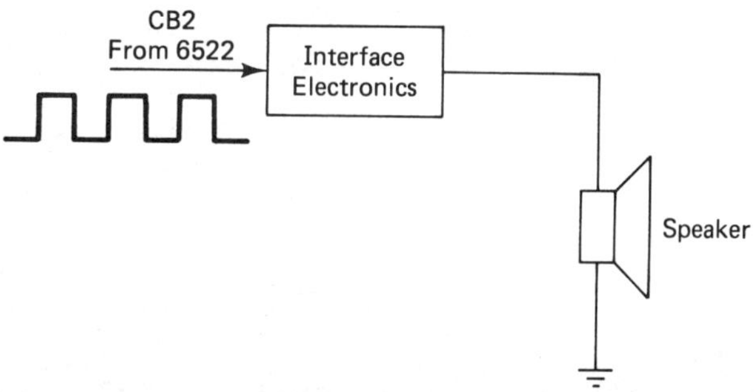

7.13. *Interrupt Handling.* Slow systems interact with fast microprocessor systems through interrupts. In Figure 7.24, CA1 input is to be initialized as a low active interrupt signal from an I/O system, as shown:

Develop a software routine such that negative transition from I/O on CA1 is recognized as interrupt, and the display of Figure 7.24 flashes all zeros in 1-second intervals as an interrupt service routine. After 10 flashings, the system should return to its original program.

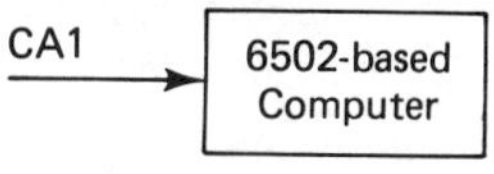

7.14. Repeat Example 7.4 such that the stepper turns 360° in clockwise direction, waits for 10 seconds and rotates in the counterclockwise direction for 360°. The operation should be repetitive.

7.15. Repeat Problem 7.14 using the 6500/1E single-chip microcomputer.

7.16. Redesign the graphics system studied with the help of single-chip microcomputer.

CHAPTER EIGHT

Z-80 Microprocessor and Microcomputer Systems

Developed and marketed by the Zilog Corporation, the Z-80 is one of the most flexible 8-bit microprocessors and is widely used in the industry. It has architectural features similar to the Intel 8085 processor and indexing features similar to the 6800 and 6502 microprocessors. In addition, part of the instruction set of the Z-80 is compatible with the 8085 microprocessor at the machine code level. Many of the word processing systems and home computer systems use the Z-80 microprocessor (e.g., Sinclair 81, TRS 80®).

8.1. GENERAL ARCHITECTURE OF THE Z-80

The Z-80 is fabricated with the enhanced NMOS technology and is contained in a 40-pin dip. Figure 8.1 shows the basic architectural features and the bus structure of the Z-80 microprocessor.

Registers, Flags, and Bus Structure

Registers

As shown in Figure 8.1, the Z-80 consists of:

16-bit program counter	PC
16-bit stack pointer	SP

16-bit index register X	1X
16-bit index register Y	1Y
Six 8-bit registers (with alternates) paired as:	BC (B′C′) DE (D′E′) HL (H′L′)
8-bit refresh register	R
8-bit accumulator (with alternate)	A (A′)
8-bit flag register (with alternate)	F (F′)
8-bit arithmetic logic unit	ALU

The 16-bit program counter can address up to 65,536 (64K) memory locations. The 16-bit stack pointer can set up the stack anywhere within the

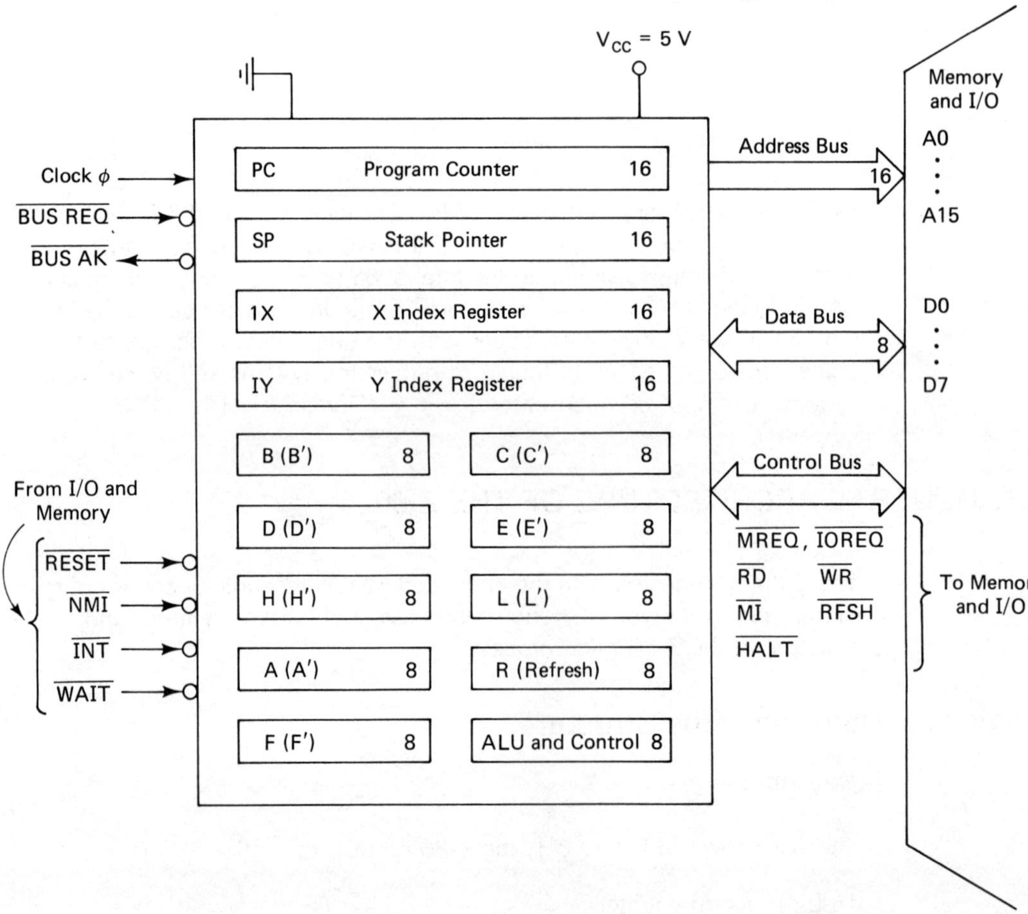

Fig 8.1. The Z-80 programming structure with registers and buses (courtesy Zilog Corporation).

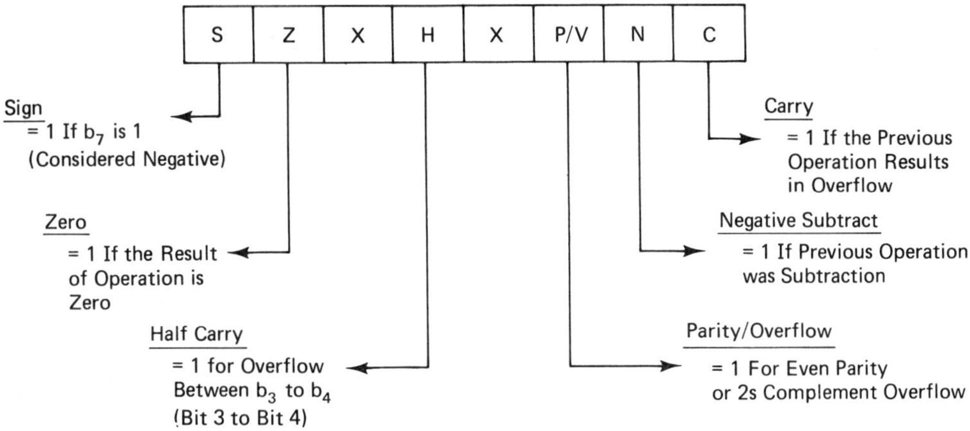

Fig 8.2. The Z-80 flag register format (courtesy Zilog Corporation).

64K memory space. The 16-bit index registers help set up the memory tables and help the index addressing within the 64K memory space.

The six general purpose registers B, C, D, E, H, and L and their alternates B′, C′, D′, E′, H′, and L′ can be used for the operand storage and manipulation within the processor. They can also be operated in pairs to obtain a 16-bit format for indirect addressing and counting operations.

The 8-bit accumulator and the ALU handle the byte-oriented data manipulations. The 8-bit refresh register generates a refresh address to handle the dynamic RAMS.

In addition, there is an interrupt register I, which holds the high byte of the interrupt vector address.

Flags

The flag register F has six effective flag bits, as shown in Figure 8.2. These bits are set, because of certain operations, as defined in Figure 8.2. The flag bits help the decision-making process. They make the program branch to a different location under software control.

Bus Structure

The Z-80 microprocessor consists of 16-bit address bus A0...A15, 8-bit data bus D0...D7, and the associated control bus, as shown in Figure 8.1. The 16-bit address bus is capable of addressing up to 65,536 (64K) memory locations. The 8-bit data bus provides the byte-wide bidirectional data transfers between the Z-80 microprocessor and the external memory and I/O. The control bus generates the necessary timing and control signals.

Reset and Interrupt Vectors

The Z-80 interrupt structure is very flexible and well-suited for the present applications. The interrupt and the reset signals are as shown in Figure 8.1.

The $\overline{\text{NMI}}$ (nonmaskable interrupt) is nonmaskable and negative edge-triggered. On the occurrence of the $\overline{\text{NMI}}$ signal, the execution of the present instruction is completed, and the program counter is stored on the stack. The microprocessor jumps to the vectored location of $(0066)_{\text{Hex}}$ to execute the $\overline{\text{NMI}}$ service routine. A RETN (return from nonmaskable interrupt) at the end of the $\overline{\text{NMI}}$ service routine will restore the main program.

The $\overline{\text{INT}}$ (interrupt) is a maskable interrupt, capable of operating in three modes. The DI and EI instructions disable and enable the $\overline{\text{INT}}$ interrupt. The instructions for the interrupt mode (IM0, IM1, and IM2) set the Z-80 microprocessor to one of the three modes, which are identified as MODE 0, MODE 1, and MODE 2. In all these modes, the microprocessor concludes the current instruction and stores the program counter on the stack. It then goes to the corresponding interrupt service routine.

Mode 0. The Z-80 responds to the $\overline{\text{INT}}$ by generating an $\overline{\text{IORQ}}$ signal. The Z-80 then expects the instructions to be placed on the data bus by the corresponding I/O device. It reads that instruction and starts executing the interrupt service routine.

Mode 1. The Z-80 automatically branches to location $(0038)_{\text{Hex}}$ and starts executing the interrupt service routine.

Mode 2. The Z-80 accepts the lower byte of the address from the I/O devices and couples it with the higher byte of the address from the I register to form a 16-bit address vector. Then it starts executing the interrupt service routine from the vectored address location.

In all the above cases, an appropriate RET (return) instruction will restore the main program.

$\overline{\text{RESET}}$ is a low-level active signal of the highest priority and cannot be masked. On the occurrence of the $\overline{\text{RESET}}$, the program counter and the I and R registers are cleared to an all-zero condition. Thus, the reset vectored address is $(0000)_{\text{Hex}}$. In addition MODE 0 is set for the interrupts. $\overline{\text{RESET}}$ is usually used to get the system started or restarted.

Example 8.1 Z-80 Architecture

In a particular peripheral control application, the accumulator contains $(\text{EC})_{\text{Hex}}$. Under program control, data $(\text{CE})_{\text{Hex}}$ is added, with the result in the accumulator.

(a) What are the values of the various flags in the flag register, after the addition?

(b) When the above addition program is being run, $\overline{\text{NMI}}$ interrupt occurred. Outline the sequence of events.

(c) Suppose the stack pointer contains $(0FFF)_{Hex}$. As a part of the interrupt service routine, all the CPU registers are stored on the stack. What is the new value of the stack pointer?

(d) Is there a better way of storing the CPU registers?

Solution

Refer to Figure 8.3 for the pictorial representation of the results.

(a) *Flags*. The addition and the corresponding values of the flags are as shown in Figure 8.3(a). Because of the overflow from bit 7 and bit 3, the carry (C) and half carry (H) are set to 1. Because bit 7 is 1, the sign (S) flag is set to 1.

The zero (Z) and the parity (P/V) flags are reset to 0, since the accumulator is nonzero and contains odd numbers of 1's. The N flag is reset, since the previous operation was not a subtraction.

(b) $\overline{\textit{NMI}}$. This interrupt is nonmaskable. The sequence of events is as shown in Figure 8.3(b). The Z-80 concludes the current instruction, pushes the PC on stack, and branches to the NMI vectored location of $(0066)_{Hex}$. It will start executing the interrupt service routine (ISR). The last instruction of the ISR will be RETN (return from nonmaskable interrupt), which restores the PC from the stack and returns the micro to the main program.

(c) *Storing on the Stack*. Refer to Figure 8.3(c). It requires 14 bytes to store the PC, 1X, 1Y, BC, DE, HL, and AF on the stack. The stack pointer gets decremented to 0FF1, to point the next available stack location.

(d) *Storing CPU Registers*. The contents of the CPU registers A, F, BC, DE, and HL can be exchanged with their alternates A′, F′... by using the exchange (EX, AF, and EXX) instructions. This amounts to storing the main registers in their alternates. This is considered an efficient way of saving the CPU registers and servicing the interrupts.

Example 8.1 provides insight into the architectural features of the Z-80 and should be well understood before proceeding further.

8.2. INSTRUCTION SET AND ADDRESSING MODES

The instruction set of the Z-80 is very powerful and contains most of the 8080/8085 instructions as subsets (about 78 instructions at machine code

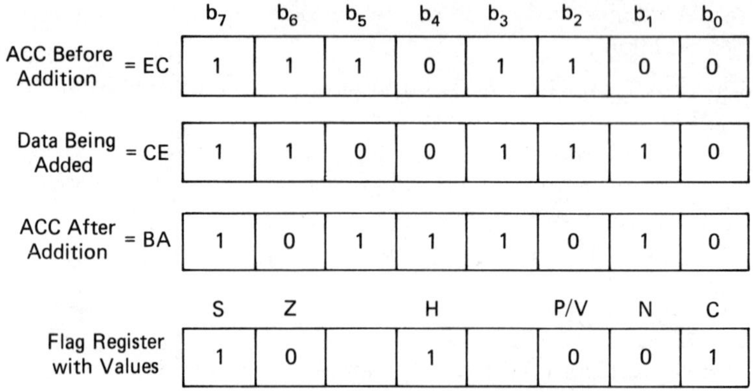

(a) Addition and Flag Register Values

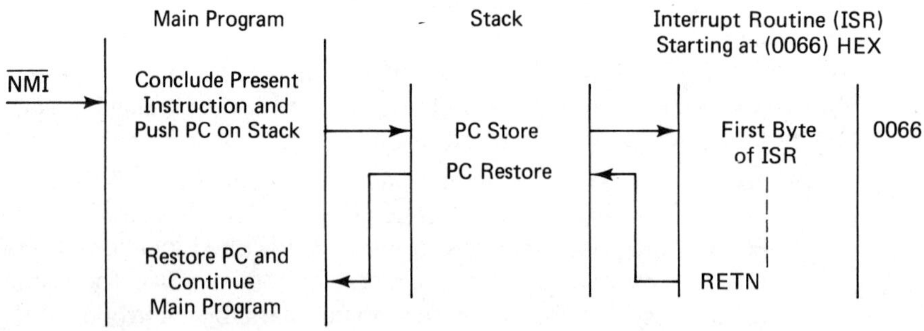

(b) Sequence of Events in $\overline{NMI}$ Service Routine

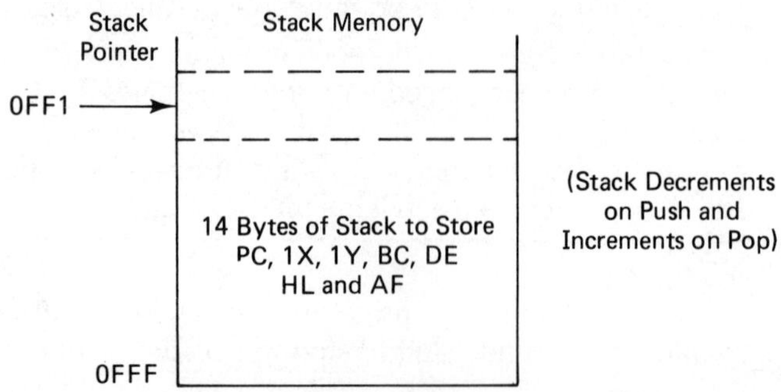

(c) Stack Memory Structure

Fig 8.3. Flag and stack structure of the Z-80 (Example 1).

level). The Z-80 contains 80 additional instructions. These are used for indexing and bit manipulations, similar to the 6800. Thus the Z-80 combines the processing power of the 8080 (8085) and the 6800 types of processors.

Mnemonics and Op Codes

Tables 8.1 and 8.2 show the mnemonics and the details of the Z-80 op codes. Depending on the addressing mode, the instruction may be up to four bytes long. The first byte is always an op code, as shown in Figure 8.4. The other bytes correspond to the data or the address of the data. We urge you to examine the instruction set (Tables 8.1 and 8.2) before proceeding any further. Table 8.2 also provides the 8080/8085 instruction equivalence.

Addressing Modes

The Z-80 instruction set uses different addressing modes, which we will introduce now.

Implied (Implicit or Register) Addressing

This is a single-byte instruction, which operates on the internal registers of the CPU.

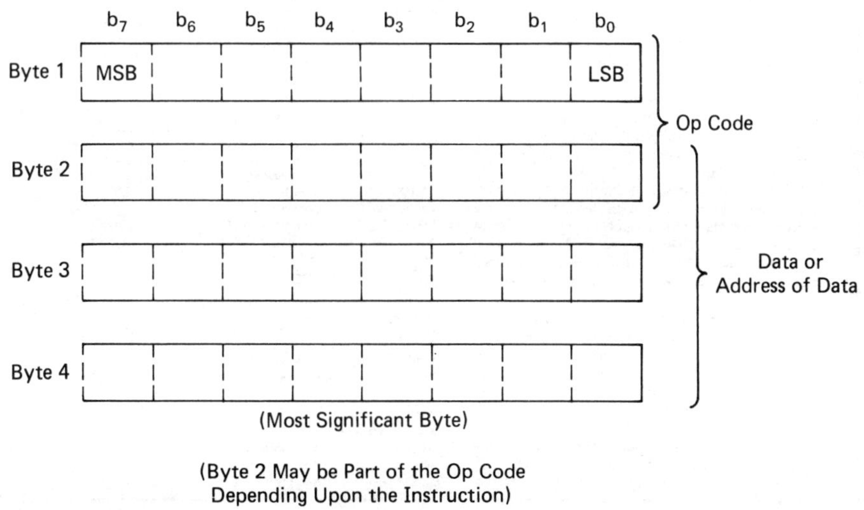

Fig 8.4. The instructional set of the Z-80.

Table 8.1. Mnemonic Codes of the Z80 microprocessor. (Reproduced by permission © 1981 Zilog, Inc. This material shall not be reproduced without written consent of Zilog, Inc.)

Software capabilities of the Z80

Able to execute over 150 different instructions, including all 78 of the 8080A command set, the Z80 features seven basic families of instructions: load-and-exchange, block-transfer-and-search, arithmetic and logic, bit-manipulation (set, reset and test), jump, call-and-return, input/output, and basic μP-control commands. In all, the Z80 can recognize 696 op codes —244 are the codes of the 8080A.

Load instructions move data internally between μP registers or between the registers and external memory. All these instructions must specify a source location, from which data are to be moved, and a destination location. Block-transfer instructions permit any block of memory to be moved to any other location. Search commands let any block of external memory be examined for any 8-bit character. Once the character is found, the instruction is terminated.

The ALU instructions operate on data held in the accumulator and other general-purpose registers or external memory. Results are held in the accumulator, and appropriate flags are set. Bit-manipulation commands allow any bit in the accumulator, any general-purpose register or any external memory location to be set, reset or tested with a single instruction. Jump, Call and Return instructions are used to transfer between various locations in the program.

I/O instructions permit a wide range of transfers between external memory locations or general-purpose Z80 registers and external I/O devices. In either case, the port number is provided on the lower eight bits of the address bus during any I/O operation. Also, the basic μP-control commands include such instructions as setting or resetting the interrupt-enable flip-flop or setting the mode of interrupt response.

In addition to the seven addressing modes of the 8080—direct, register, register indirect, modified page Ø, extended, implied and immediate—the Z80 has three more addressing modes: relative, indexed, and bit addressing—that can be used.

A special byte-call instruction lets the Z80 program proceed to any of eight locations in page Ø of the memory. This modified page Ø addressing allows a single byte to specify a complete 16-bit address, which saves memory space.

Relative addressing lets the Z80 use the byte following the op code to specify a displacement from the current program-counter value. The displacement value is in 2's-complement form, which permits up to a +127 or −128 byte displacement. Extended addressing includes two bytes of address in the instruction.

Index registers can also be used as part of the address. In the indexed addressing mode, a byte of data following the op code is a displacement value that must be added to the specified index register (the op code indicates which register) to form a memory pointer. Also available is an implied addressing mode in which the op code uses the contents of one Z80 register or more as the operands. The last addressing mode lets the Z80 access any memory location or μP register and permits any bit to be set, reset or tested.

Mnemonic	Description
8-bit load instructions	
LD r, r'	Load register r with r'
LD r, n	Load register r with n
LD r, (HL)	Load r with location (HL)
LD r, (IX+d)	Load r with location (IX+d)
LD r, (IY+d)	Load r with location (IY+d)
LD (HL), r	Load location HL with r
LD (IX+d), r	Load location IX+d from register r
LD (IY+d), r	Load location IY+d from register r
LD (HL), n	Load location HL with value n
LD (IX+d), n	Load location IX+d with n
LD (IY+d), n	Load location IY+d with n
LD A, (BC)	Load AC with location BC
LD A, (DE)	Load AC with location DE
LD A, (nn)	Load AC with location nn
LD (BC), A	Load location BC with AC
LD (DE), A	Load location DE with AC
LD (nn), A	Load location nn with AC
LD A, I	Load register A from I
LD A, R	Load AC with register R
LD I, A	Load register I with AC
LD R, A	Load register R with AC
16 bit load instructions	
LD dd, nn	Load registers dd with nn
LD IX, nn	Load register IX with nn
LD IY, nn	Load register IY with nn
LD HL, (nn)	Load L with contents of location nn and H with (nn+1)
LD dd, (nn)	Load registers dd with location nn
LD IX, (nn)	Load IX with location nn
LD IY, (nn)	Same but for IY
LD (nn), HL	Load location nn with HL
LD (nn), dd	Load location (nn) with register pair dd
LD (nn), IX	Same but for IX
LD (nn), IY	Same but for IY
LD SP, HL	Load stack pointer from HL
LD SP, IX	Load stack pointer from IX
LD SP, IY	Load stack pointer from IY
PUSH qq	Load register pair qq onto stack
PUSH IX	Load IX onto stack
PUSH IY	Load IY onto stack
POP qq	Load register pair qq with top of stack
POP IX	Load IX with top of stack
POP IY	Load IY with top of stack
Exchange, transfer and search instructions	
EX DE, HL	Exchange contents of DE & HL
EX AF, A' F'	Exchange contents of AF & A' F'
EXX	Exchange all six general purpose registers with alternates
EX (SP), HL	Exchange stack pointer contents with HL contents
EX (SP), IX	Same but use IX register
EX (SP), IY	Same but use IY register
LDI	Load (HL) into DE, increment DE and HL, decrement BC
LDIR	Same but loop until (BC) = O
LDD	Load location (PE) with location (HL) and decrement DE, HL and BC
LDDR	Same but loop until (BC) = O
CPI	Compare contents of AC with (HL), set Z flat if =, increment HL and decrement BC
CPIR	Same but repeat until BC = O
CP s	Compare operand s with AC
CPD	Same as CPI but decrement HL
CPDR	Same as CPIR but decrement HL
8-bit arithmetic and logic instructions	
ADD A, r	Add contents of r to AC
ADD A, n	Add byte n to AC
ADD A, (HL)	Add contents of HL to AC

ADD A, (IX+d)	Add location (IX+d) to AC
ADD A, (IY+d)	Same but (IY+d)
ADC A, s	Add with carry operand s to AC
SUB s	Subtract contents of r, n, HL, IX+d or IY+d from AC
SBC s	Same but also subtract carry flag
AND s	Logic AND of operand s and AC
OR s	Same but OR with AC
XOR s	Same but EX-OR with AC
INC r	Increment register r
INC (HL)	Increment location (HL)
INC (IX+d)	Same but use (IX+d)
INC (IY+d)	Same but use (IY+d)
DEC m	Decrement operand m

16-bit Arithmetic instructions

ADD HL, ss	Add register pair ss to HL
ADC HL, ss	Same but include carry flag
SBC HL, ss	From HL subtract contents of ss and carry flag
ADD IX, pp	Add register pair pp to IX
ADD IY, rr	Same but use rr and IY
INC ss	Increment register pair ss
INC IX	Increment IX register
INC IY	Same but IY register
DEC ss	Decrement register pair ss
DEC IX	Same but IX register
DEC IY	Same but IY register

General purpose arithmetic & control instructions

DAA	Decimal adjust accumulator
CPL	Complement (AC)
NEG	Complement (AC) and add 1
CCF	Complement carry flag
SCF	Set carry flag = 1
NOP	No operation
HALT	Halt, wait for interrupt or reset
DI	Disable interrupts
EI	Enable interrupts
IM0	Set μP to interrupt mode 0
IM1	Set μP to interrupt mode 1
IM2	Set μP to interrupt mode 2

Rotate and shift instructions

RLCA	Rotate AC left
RLA	Same but include carry flag
RRCA	Rotate AC right
RRA	Same but include carry flag
RLC r	Rotate register r left
RLC (HL)	Rotate location (HL) left
RLC (IX+d)	Same but location (IX+d)
RLC (IY+d)	Same but location (IY+d)
RL m	Same as any RLC but include carry flag
RRC m	Same as RLC but shift right
RR m	Same as RL m but shift right
SLA s	Shift left (any RLC register)
SRA s	Same but shift right and keep MSB
SRL s	Same as SLA but shift right
RLD	Simultaneous 4-bit rotate from AC_L to L, L to H and H to AC_L
RRD	Simultaneous 4-bit rotate from AC_L to H, H to L and L to AC_L

Bit set, reset and test instructions

BIT b, r	Test bit b of register r
BIT b, (HL)	Test bit b of location (HL)
BIT b, (IX+d)	Test bit b of location (IX+d)
BIT b, (IY+d)	Test bit b of location (IY+d)
SET b, r	Set bit b in register r to 1
SET b, (HL)	Same but use contents of location HL
SET b, (IX+d)	Same but use contents of location IX+d
SET b, (IY+d)	Same but use contents of location IY+d
RES b, s	Reset bit b of operand m

Jump, c all and return instructions

JP nn	Unconditional jump to location nn
JP cc, nn	If condition cc True, do a JP nn otherwise continue
JR e	Unconditional jump to PC+e
JR C, e	If C = 0 continue. If C = 1 do JR e
JR NC, e	Reverse of JR c, e
JR Z, e	If Z = 0 continue. If Z = 1 do JR e
JR NZ, e	Reverse of JR Z, e
JP (HL)	Load PC from (HL)
JP (IX)	Load PC from (IX)
JP (IY)	Load PC from (IY)
DJNZ, e	Decrement register B and jump relative if B = 0
CALL nn	Unconditional call subroutine at location nn
CALL cc, nn	Call subroutine at location nn if condition cc is True
RET	Return from subroutine
RET cc	If cc false continue, otherwise do RET
RETI	Return from interrupt
RETN	Return from nonmaskable interrupt
RST p	Store PC in stack, load 0 in PC_H and restart vector in PC_L

Input/output instructions

IN A, n	Load AC with input from device n
IN r, (C)	Load r with input from device C
INI	Store contents of location specified by C in address specified by HL, decrement B and increment HL
INIR	Same but repeat until B = 0
IND	Same as INI but decrement HL too
INDR	Same as INIR but decrement HL too
OUT n, A	Load output port (n) with AC
OUT (C), r	Load output port (C) with register r
OUTI	Load output port (C) with location (HL) and increment HL and decrement B
OTIR	Same but repeat until B = 0
OUTD	Same as OUTI but decrement HL
OTDR	Same as OTIR but decrement HL

Notes

b represents a 3-bit code that indicates position of the bit to be modified

cc represents a 3-bit code that indicates which of eight condition codes are to be used

d is an 8 bit offset value

dd refers to register pairs BC, DC, HL or the stack pointer

e represents a signed two's complement number between -126 and +129

m is an 8 bit number

n is an 8 bit number

nn refers to two 8 bit bytes

p represents one of eight restart vector locations on page 0

pp refers to register pairs BC, DE, the IX register or the stack pointer.

qq refers to register pairs AF, BC, DE or HL

r or r' refers to registers A, B, C, D, E, H or L or their alternates

rr refers to register pairs BC, DE, the IY register or the stack pointer

s refers to either the r registers, the n data word or the contents of locations specified by the contents of the HL, IX+d or IY+d registers

ss refers to register pairs BC, DE, HL or the stack pointer

Table 8.2. Z80 Op Codes and the 8080 Instruction Equivalence. (Reprinted from *Programming the Z80*, by Rodney Zaks, by permission of Sybex, Inc. © 1980 Sybex, Inc.)

Z80 INSTRUCTION CODES

(The literal d is shown as 05 in the object code.)

OBJ CODE	SOURCE STATEMENT	
8E	ADC	A,(HL)
DD8E05	ADC	A,(IX+d)
FD8E05	ADC	A,(IY+d)
8F	ADC	A,A
88	ADC	A,B
89	ADC	A,C
8A	ADC	A,D
8B	ADC	A,E
8C	ADC	A,H
8D	ADC	A,L
CE20	ADC	A,n
ED4A	ADC	HL,BC
ED5A	ADC	HL,DE
ED6A	ADC	HL,HL
ED7A	ADC	HL,SP
86	ADD	A,(HL)
DD8605	ADD	A,(IX+d)
FD8605	ADD	A,(IY+d)
87	ADD	A,A
80	ADD	A,B
81	ADD	A,C
82	ADD	A,D
83	ADD	A,E
84	ADD	A,H
85	ADD	A,L
C620	ADD	A,n
09	ADD	HL,BC
19	ADD	HL,DE
29	ADD	HL,HL
39	ADD	HL,SP
DD09	ADD	IX,BC
DD19	ADD	IX,DE
DD29	ADD	IX,IX
DD39	ADD	IX,SP
FD09	ADD	IY,BC
FD19	ADD	IY,DE
FD29	ADD	IY,IY
FD39	ADD	IY,SP
A6	AND	(HL)
DDA605	AND	(IX+d)
FDA605	AND	(IY+d)
A7	AND	A
A0	AND	B
A1	AND	C
A2	AND	D
A3	AND	E
A4	AND	H
A5	AND	L

OBJ CODE	SOURCE STATEMENT	
E620	AND	n
CB46	BIT	0,(HL)
DDCB0546	BIT	0,(IX+d)
FDCB0546	BIT	0,(IY+d)
CB47	BIT	0,A
CB40	BIT	0,B
CB41	BIT	0,C
CB42	BIT	0,D
CB43	BIT	0,E
CB44	BIT	0,H
CB45	BIT	0,L
CB4E	BIT	1,(HL)
DDCB054E	BIT	1,(IX+d)
FDCB054E	BIT	1,(IY+d)
CB4F	BIT	1,A
CB48	BIT	1,B
CB49	BIT	1,C
CB4A	BIT	1,D
CB4B	BIT	1,E
CB4C	BIT	1,H
CB4D	BIT	1,L
CB56	BIT	2,(HL)
DDCB0556	BIT	2,(IX+d)
FDCB0556	BIT	2,(IY+d)
CB57	BIT	2,A
CB50	BIT	2,B
CB51	BIT	2,C
CB52	BIT	2,D
CB53	BIT	2,E
CB54	BIT	2,H
CB55	BIT	2,L
CB5E	BIT	3,(HL)
DDCB055E	BIT	3,(IX+d)
FDCB055E	BIT	3,(IY+d)
CB5F	BIT	3,A
CB58	BIT	3,B
CB59	BIT	3,C
CB5A	BIT	3,D
CB5B	BIT	3,E
CB5C	BIT	3,H
CB5D	BIT	3,L
CB66	BIT	4,(HL)
DDCB0566	BIT	4,(IX+d)
FDCB0566	BIT	4,(IY+d)
CB67	BIT	4,A
CB60	BIT	4,B
CB61	BIT	4,C
CB62	BIT	4,D

OBJ CODE	SOURCE STATEMENT	
CB63	BIT	4,E
CB64	BIT	4,H
CB65	BIT	4,L
CB6E	BIT	5,(HL)
DDCB056E	BIT	5,(IX+d)
FDCB056E	BIT	5,(IY+d)
CB6F	BIT	5,A
CB68	BIT	5,B
CB69	BIT	5,C
CB6A	BIT	5,D
CB6B	BIT	5,E
CB6C	BIT	5,H
CB6D	BIT	5,L
CB76	BIT	6,(HL)
DDCB0576	BIT	6,(IX+d)
FDCB0576	BIT	6,(IY+d)
CB77	BIT	6,A
CB70	BIT	6,B
CB71	BIT	6,C
CB72	BIT	6,D
CB73	BIT	6,E
CB74	BIT	6,H
CB75	BIT	6,L
CB7E	BIT	7,(HL)
DDCB057E	BIT	7,(IX+d)
FDCB057E	BIT	7,(IY+d)
CB7F	BIT	7,A
CB78	BIT	7,B
CB79	BIT	7,C
CB7A	BIT	7,D
CB7B	BIT	7,E
CB7C	BIT	7,H
CB7D	BIT	7,L
DC8405	CALL	C,nn
FC8405	CALL	M,nn
D48405	CALL	NC,nn
C48405	CALL	NZ,nn
F48405	CALL	P,nn
EC8405	CALL	PE,nn
E48405	CALL	PO,nn
CC8405	CALL	Z,nn
CD8405	CALL	nn
3F	CCF	
BE	CP	(HL)
DDBE05	CP	(IX+d)
FDBE05	CP	(IY+d)
BF	CP	A
B8	CP	B
B9	CP	C
BA	CP	D
BB	CP	E
BC	CP	H
BD	CP	L
FE20	CP	n
EDA9	CPD	
EDB9	CPDR	

OBJ CODE	SOURCE STATEMENT	
EDB1	CPIR	
EDA1	CPI	
2F	CPL	
27	DAA	
35	DEC	(HL)
DD3505	DEC	(IX+d)
FD3505	DEC	(IY+d)
3D	DEC	A
05	DEC	B
0B	DEC	BC
0D	DEC	C
15	DEC	D
1B	DEC	DE
1D	DEC	E
25	DEC	H
2B	DEC	HL
DD2B	DEC	IX
FD2B	DEC	IY
2D	DEC	L
3B	DEC	SP
F3	DI	
102E	DJNZ	e
FB	EI	
E3	EX	(SP),HL
DDE3	EX	(SP),IX
FDE3	EX	(SP),IY
08	EX	AF,AF'
EB	EX	DE,HL
D9	EXX	
76	HALT	
ED46	IM	0
ED56	IM	1
ED5E	IM	2
ED78	IN	A,(C)
ED40	IN	B,(C)
ED48	IN	C,(C)
ED50	IN	D,(C)
ED58	IN	E,(C)
ED60	IN	H,(C)
ED68	IN	L,(C)
34	INC	(HL)
DD3405	INC	(IX+d)
FD3405	INC	(IY+d)
3C	INC	A
04	INC	B
03	INC	BC
0C	INC	C
14	INC	D
13	INC	DE
1C	INC	E
24	INC	H
23	INC	HL
DD23	INC	IX
FD23	INC	IY
2C	INC	L
33	INC	SP
DB20	IN	A,(n)

Table 8.2. *(Continued)*

OBJ CODE	SOURCE STATEMENT	
EDAA	IND	
EDBA	INDR	
EDA2	INI	
EDB2	INIR	
C38405	JP	nn
E9	JP	(HL)
DDE9	JP	(IX)
FDE9	JP	(IY)
DA8405	JP	C,nn
FA8405	JP	M,nn
D28405	JP	NC,nn
C28405	JP	NZ,nn
F28405	JP	P,nn
EA8405	JP	PE,nn
E28405	JP	PO,nn
CA8405	JP	Z,nn
382E	JR	C,e
302E	JR	NC,e
202E	JR	NZ,e
282E	JR	Z,e
182E	JR	e
02	LD	(BC),A
12	LD	(DE),A
77	LD	(HL),A
70	LD	(HL),B
71	LD	(HL),C
72	LD	(HL),D
73	LD	(HL),E
74	LD	(HL),H
75	LD	(HL),L
3620	LD	(HL),n
DD7705	LD	(IX+d),A
DD7005	LD	(IX+d),B
DD7105	LD	(IX+d),C
DD7205	LD	(IX+d),D
DD7305	LD	(IX+d),E
DD7405	LD	(IX+d),H
DD7505	LD	(IX+d),L
DD360520	LD	(IX+d),n
FD7705	LD	(IY+d),A
FD7005	LD	(IY+d),B
FD7105	LD	(IY+d),C
FD7205	LD	(IY+d),D
FD7305	LD	(IY+d),E
FD7405	LD	(IY+d),H
FD7505	LD	(IY+d),L
FD360520	LD	(IY+d),n
328405	LD	(nn),A
ED438405	LD	(nn),BC
ED538405	LD	(nn),DE
228405	LD	(nn),HL
DD228405	LD	(nn),IX
FD228405	LD	(nn),IY
ED738405	LD	(nn),SP
0A	LD	A,(BC)
1A	LD	A,(DE)
7E	LD	A,(HL)
DD7E05	LD	A,(IX+d)
FD7E05	LD	A,(IY+d)
3A8405	LD	A,(nn)
7F	LD	A,A
78	LD	A,B
79	LD	A,C
7A	LD	A,D
7B	LD	A,E
7C	LD	A,H
ED57	LD	A,I
7D	LD	A,L
3E20	LD	A,n
ED5F	LD	A,R
46	LD	B,(HL)
DD4605	LD	B,(IX+d)
FD4605	LD	B,(IY+d)
47	LD	B,A
40	LD	B,B
41	LD	B,C
42	LD	B,D
43	LD	B,E
44	LD	B,H
45	LD	B,L
0620	LD	B,n
ED4B8405	LD	BC,(nn)
018405	LD	BC,nn
4E	LD	C,(HL)
DD4E05	LD	C,(IX+d)
FD4E05	LD	C,(IY+d)
4F	LD	C,A
48	LD	C,B
49	LD	C,C
4A	LD	C,D
4B	LD	C,E
4C	LD	C,H
4D	LD	C,L
0E20	LD	C,n
56	LD	D,(HL)
DD5605	LD	D,(IX+d)
FD5605	LD	D,(IY+d)
57	LD	D,A
50	LD	D,B
51	LD	D,C
52	LD	D,D
53	LD	D,E
54	LD	D,H
55	LD	D,L
1620	LD	D,n
ED5B8405	LD	DE,(nn)
118405	LD	DE,nn
5E	LD	E,(HL)
DD5E05	LD	E,(IX+d)
FD5E05	LD	E,(IY+d)
5F	LD	E,A
58	LD	E,B
59	LD	E,C
5A	LD	E,D

OBJ CODE	SOURCE STATEMENT	
5B	LD	E,E
5C	LD	E,H
5D	LD	E,L
1E20	LD	E,n
66	LD	H,(HL)
DD6605	LD	H,(IX+d)
FD6605	LD	H,(IY+d)
67	LD	H,A
60	LD	H,B
61	LD	H,C
62	LD	H,D
63	LD	H,E
64	LD	H,H
65	LD	H,L
2620	LD	H,n
2A8405	LD	HL,(nn)
218405	LD	HL,nn
ED47	LD	I,A
DD2A8405	LD	IX,(nn)
DD218405	LD	IX,nn
FD2A8405	LD	IY,(nn)
FD218405	LD	IY,nn
6E	LD	L,(HL)
DD6E05	LD	L,(IX+d)
FD6E05	LD	L,(IY+d)
6F	LD	L,A
68	LD	L,B
69	LD	L,C
6A	LD	L,D
6B	LD	L,E
6C	LD	L,H
6D	LD	L,L
2E20	LD	L,n
ED4F	LD	R,A
ED7B8405	LD	SP,(nn)
F9	LD	SP,HL
DDF9	LD	SP,IX
FDF9	LD	SP,IY
318405	LD	SP,nn
EDA8	LDD	
EDB8	LDDR	
EDA0	LDI	
EDB0	LDIR	
ED44	NEG	
00	NOP	
B6	OR	(HL)
DDB605	OR	(IX+d)
FDB605	OR	(IY+d)
B7	OR	A
B0	OR	B
B1	OR	C
B2	OR	D
B3	OR	E
B4	OR	H
B5	OR	L
F620	OR	n
ED8B	OTDR	

OBJ CODE	SOURCE STATEMENT	
EDB3	OTIR	
ED79	OUT	(C),A
ED41	OUT	(C),B
ED49	OUT	(C),C
ED51	OUT	(C),D
ED59	OUT	(C),E
ED61	OUT	(C),H
ED69	OUT	(C),L
D320	OUT	(n),A
EDAB	OUTD	
EDA3	OUTI	
F1	POP	AF
C1	POP	BC
D1	POP	DE
E1	POP	HL
DDE1	POP	IX
FDE1	POP	IY
F5	PUSH	AF
C5	PUSH	BC
D5	PUSH	DE
E5	PUSH	HL
DDE5	PUSH	IX
FDE5	PUSH	IY
CB86	RES	0,(HL)
DDCB0586	RES	0,(IX+d)
FDCB0586	RES	0,(IY+d)
CB87	RES	0,A
CB80	RES	0,B
CB81	RES	0,C
CB82	RES	0,D
CB83	RES	0,E
CB84	RES	0,H
CB85	RES	0,L
CB8E	RES	1,(HL)
DDCB058E	RES	1,(IX+d)
FDCB058E	RES	1,(IY+d)
CB8F	RES	1,A
CB88	RES	1,B
CB89	RES	1,C
CB8A	RES	1,D
CB8B	RES	1,E
CB8C	RES	1,H
CB8D	RES	1,L
CB96	RES	2,(HL)
DDCB0596	RES	2,(IX+d)
FDCB0596	RES	2,(IY+d)
CB97	RES	2,A
CB90	RES	2,B
CB91	RES	2,C
CB92	RES	2,D
CB93	RES	2,E
CB94	RES	2,H
CB95	RES	2,L
CB9E	RES	3,(HL)
DDCB059E	RES	3,(IX+d)
FDCB059E	RES	3,(IY+d)

Table 8.2. *(Continued)*

OBJ CODE	SOURCE STATEMENT	
CB9F	RES	3,A
CB98	RES	3,B
CB99	RES	3,C
CB9A	RES	3,D
CB9B	RES	3,E
CB9C	RES	3,H
CB9D	RES	3,L
CBA6	RES	4,(HL)
DDCB05A6	RES	4,(IX+d)
FDCB05A6	RES	4,(IY+d)
CBA7	RES	4,A
CBA0	RES	4,B
CBA1	RES	4,C
CBA2	RES	4,D
CBA3	RES	4,E
CBA4	RES	4,H
CBA5	RES	4,L
CBAE	RES	5,(HL)
DDCB05	RES	5,(IX+d)
FDCB05	RES	5,(IY+d)
CBAF	RES	5,A
CBA8	RES	5,B
CBA9	RES	5,C
CBAA	RES	5,D
CBAB	RES	5,E
CBAC	RES	5,H
CBAD	RES	5,L
CBB6	RES	6,(HL)
DDCB05B6	RES	6,(IX+d)
FDCB05B6	RES	6,(IY+d)
CBB7	RES	6,A
CBB0	RES	6,B
CBB1	RES	6,C
CBB2	RES	6,D
CBB3	RES	6,E
CBB4	RES	6,H
CBB5	RES	6,L
CBBE	RES	7,(HL)
DDCB05BE	RES	7,(IX+d)
FDCB05BE	RES	7,(IY+d)
CBBF	RES	7,A
CBB8	RES	7,B
CBB9	RES	7,C
CBBA	RES	7,D
CBBB	RES	7,E
CBBC	RES	7,H
CBBD	RES	7,L
C9	RET	
D8	RET	C
F8	RET	M
DO	RET	NC
CO	RET	NZ
FO	RET	P
E8	RET	PE
EO	RET	PO
C8	RET	Z

OBJ CODE	SOURCE STATEMENT	
ED4D	RETI	
ED45	RETN	
CB16	RL	(HL)
DDCB0516	RL	(IX+d)
FDCB0516	RL	(IY+d)
CB17	RL	A
CB10	RL	B
CB11	RL	C
CB12	RL	D
CB13	RL	E
CB14	RL	H
CB15	RL	L
17	RLA	
CB06	RLC	(HL)
DDCB0506	RLC	(IX+d)
FDCB0506	RLC	(IY+d)
CB07	RLC	A
CB00	RLC	B
CB01	RLC	C
CB02	RLC	D
CB03	RLC	E
CB04	RLC	H
CB05	RLC	L
07	RLCA	
ED6F	RLD	
CB1E	RR	(HL)
DDCB051E	RR	(IX+d)
FDCB051E	RR	(IY+d)
CB1F	RR	A
CB18	RR	B
CB19	RR	C
CB1A	RR	D
CB1B	RR	E
CB1C	RR	H
CB1D	RR	L
1F	RRA	
CB0E	RRC	(HL)
DDCB050E	RRC	(IX+d)
FDCB050E	RRC	(IY+d)
CB0F	RRC	A
CB08	RRC	B
CB09	RRC	C
CB0A	RRC	D
CB0B	RRC	E
CB0C	RRC	H
CB0D	RRC	L
OF	RRCA	
ED67	RRD	
C7	RST	00H
CF	RST	08H
D7	RST	10H
DF	RST	18H
E7	RST	20H
EF	RST	28H
F7	RST	30H
FF	RST	38H
DE20	SBC	A,n

OBJ CODE	SOURCE STATEMENT	
9E	SBC	A,(HL)
DD9E05	SBC	A,(IX+d)
FD9E05	SBC	A,(IY+d)
9F	SBC	A,A
98	SBC	A,B
99	SBC	A,C
9A	SBC	A,D
9B	SBC	A,E
9C	SBC	A,H
9D	SBC	A,L
ED42	SBC	HL,BC
ED52	SBC	HL,DE
ED62	SBC	HL,HL
ED72	SBC	HL,SP
37	SCF	
CBC6	SET	0,(HL)
DDCB05C6	SET	0,(IX+d)
FDCB05C6	SET	0,(IY+d)
CBC7	SET	0,A
CBC0	SET	0,B
CBC1	SET	0,C
CBC2	SET	0,D
CBC3	SET	0,E
CBC4	SET	0,H
CBC5	SET	0,L
CBCE	SET	1,(HL)
DDCB05CE	SET	1,(IX+d)
FDCB05CE	SET	1,(IY+d)
CBCF	SET	1,A
CBC8	SET	1,B
CBC9	SET	1,C
CBCA	SET	1,D
CBCB	SET	1,E
CBCC	SET	1,H
CBCD	SET	1,L
CBD6	SET	2,(HL)
DDCB05D6	SET	2,(IX+d)
FDCB05D6	SET	2,(IY+d)
CBD7	SET	2,A
CBD0	SET	2,B
CBD1	SET	2,C
CBD2	SET	2,D
CBD3	SET	2,E
CBD4	SET	2,H
CBD5	SET	2,L
CBD8	SET	3,B
CBDE	SET	3,(HL)
DDCB05DE	SET	3,(IX+d)
FDCB05DE	SET	3,(IY+d)
CBDF	SET	3,A
CBD9	SET	3,C
CBDA	SET	3,D
CBDB	SET	3,E
CBDC	SET	3,H
CBDD	SET	3,L
CBE6	SET	4,(HL)

OBJ CODE	SOURCE STATEMENT	
DDCB05E6	SET	4,(IX+d)
FDCB05E6	SET	4,(IY+d)
CBE7	SET	4,A
CBE0	SET	4,B
CBE1	SET	4,C
CBE2	SET	4,D
CBE3	SET	4,E
CBE4	SET	4,H
CBE5	SET	4,L
CBEE	SET	5,(HL)
DDCB05EE	SET	5,(IX+d)
FDCB05EE	SET	5,(IY+d)
CBEF	SET	5,A
CBE8	SET	5,B
CBE9	SET	5,C
CBEA	SET	5,D
CBEB	SET	5,E
CBEC	SET	5,H
CBED	SET	5,L
CBF6	SET	6,(HL)
DDCB05F6	SET	6,(IX+d)
FDCB05F6	SET	6,(IY+d)
CBF7	SET	6,A
CBF0	SET	6,B
CBF1	SET	6,C
CBF2	SET	6,D
CBF3	SET	6,E
CBF4	SET	6,H
CBF5	SET	6,L
CBFE	SET	7,(HL)
DDCB05FE	SET	7,(IX+d)
FDCB05FE	SET	7,(IY+d)
CBFF	SET	7,A
CBF8	SET	7,B
CBF9	SET	7,C
CBFA	SET	7,D
CBFB	SET	7,E
CBFC	SET	7,H
CBFD	SET	7,L
CB26	SLA	(HL)
DDCB0526	SLA	(IX+d)
FDCB0526	SLA	(IY+d)
CB27	SLA	A
CB20	SLA	B
CB21	SLA	C
CB22	SLA	D
CB23	SLA	E
CB24	SLA	H
CB25	SLA	L
CB2E	SRA	(HL)
DDCB052E	SRA	(IX+d)
FDCB052E	SRA	(IY+d)
CB2F	SRA	A
CB28	SRA	B
CB29	SRA	C
CB2A	SRA	D

Table 8.2. *(Continued)*

OBJ CODE	SOURCE STATEMENT	
CB2B	SRA	E
CB2C	SRA	H
CB2D	SRA	L
CB3E	SRL	(HL)
DDCB053E	SRL	(IX+d)
FDCB053E	SRL	(IY+d)
CB3F	SRL	A
CB38	SRL	B
CB39	SRL	C
CB3A	SRL	D
CB3B	SRL	E
CB3C	SRL	H
CB3D	SRL	L
96	SUB	(HL)
DD9605	SUB	(IX+d)
FD9605	SUB	(IY+d)
97	SUB	A
90	SUB	B
91	SUB	C
92	SUB	D
93	SUB	E
94	SUB	H
95	SUB	L
D620	SUB	n
AE	XOR	(HL)
DDAE05	XOR	(IX+d)
FDAE05	XOR	(IY+d)
AF	XOR	A
A8	XOR	B
A9	XOR	C
AA	XOR	D
AB	XOR	E
AC	XOR	H
AD	XOR	L
EE20	XOR	n

(Courtesy of Zilog Inc.)

Z80 to 8080 EQUIVALENCE

Z80	8080	Z80	8080	Z80	8080
ADC A, (HL)	ADC M	EX (SP), HL	XTHL	OR n	ORI [B2]
ADC A, n	ACI [B2]	HALT	HLT	OR r	ORA r
ADC A, r	ADC r	IN A, (n)	IN [B2]	OR (HL)	ORA M
ADD A, (HL)	ADD M	INC BC	INX B	OUT (n), A	OUT [B2]
ADD A, n	ADI [B2]	INC DE	INX D	POP AF	POP PSW
ADD A, r	ADD r	INC HL	INX H	POP BC	POP B
ADD HL, BC	DAD B	INC r	INR r	POP DE	POP D
ADD HL, DE	DAD D	INC SP	INX SP	POP HL	POP H
ADD HL, HL	DAD H	INC (HL)	INR M	PUSH AF	PUSH PSW
ADD HL, SP	DAD SP	JP C, nn	JC [B2] [B3]	PUSH BC	PUSH B
AND n	ANI [B2]	JP M, nn	JM [B2] [B3]	PUSH DE	PUSH D
AND r	ANA r	JP NC, nn	JNC [B2] [B3]	PUSH HL	PUSH H
AND (HL)	ANA M	JP nn	JMP [B2] [B3]	RET	RET
CALL C, nn	CC [B2] [B3]	JP NZ, nn	JNZ [B2] [B3]	RET C	RC
CALL M, nn	CM [B2] [B3]	JP P, nn	JP [B2] [B3]	RET M	RM
CALL NC, nn	CNC [B2] [B3]	JP PE, nn	JPE [B2] [B3]	RET NC	RNC
CALL nn	CALL	JP PO, nn	JPO [B2] [B3]	RET NZ	RNZ
CALL NZ, nn	CNZ [B2] [B3]	JP Z, nn	JZ [B2] [B3]	RET P	RP
CALL P, nn	CP [B2] [B3]	JP (HL)	PCHL	RET PE	RPE
CALL PE, nn	CPE [B2] [B3]	LD A, (DE)	LDAX	RET PO	RPO
CALL PO, nn	CPO [B2] [B3]	LDA, (nn)	LDA [B2] [B3]	RET Z	RZ
CALL Z, nn	CZ [B2] [B3]	LD DE, nn	LXID [B2] [B3]	RLA	RAL
CCF	CMC	LD SP, nn	LXI SP, [B2] [B3]	RLCA	RLC
CP r	CMP r	LD (BC), A	STAX B	RRA	RAR
CP (HL)	CMP M	LD (DE), A	STAX D	RRCA	RRC
CPL	CMA	LD (HL), r	MOV M, r	RST P	RST P
CP n	CPI [B2]	LD (nn), A	STA [B2] [B3]	SBC A, (HL)	SBB M
DAA	DAA	LD (nn), HL	SHLD [B2] [B3]	SBC A, n	SBI [B2]
DEC BC	DCX B	LD A, (BC)	LDAX B	SBC A, r	SBB r
DEC DE	DCX D	LD BC, nn	LXIB [B2] [B3]	SCF	STC
DEC HL	DCX H	LD HL, (nn)	LHLD [B2] [B3]	SUB n	SUI [B2]
DEC r	DCR r	LD HL, nn	LXI H [B2] [B3]	SUB r	SUB r
DEC SP	DCX SP	LD r, (HL)	MOV r, M	SUB (HL)	SUB M
DEC (HL)	DCR M	LD r, n	MVI r, [B2]	XOR n	XRI [B2]
DI	DI	LD r, r'	MOV r1, r2	XOR r	XRA r
EI	EI	LD SP, HL	SPHL	XOR (HL)	XRA M
EX DE, HL	XCHG	NOP	NOP		

Example:

Mnemonic	Op Code	
INC A	3C	Increment register A
LD E, B	58	Load E with the contents of B

Immediate Addressing

This is multibyte instruction, in which the data is contained in the instruction itself.

Example:

LD 1X, nn 73_L $2B_H$	DD21	Load immediate data of $(2B73)_{Hex}$ into the index register X.
Add A, n 36	C6	Add immediate data of $(36)_{Hex}$ to the accumulator

Register Indirect Addressing

The address of the data or operand is contained in one of the register pairs of the CPU.

Example:

DEC (HL)	35	Decrement the memory location specified by the (HL) register pair

Extended (Absolute or Direct) Addressing

This is multibyte instruction, where the absolute address of the data is contained in the higher bytes of the instruction.

Example:

LD A, (nn) 73_L 46_H	3A	Load the accumulator with the contents of location $(4673)_{Hex}$

Relative Addressing

This is two-byte instruction, where the second byte is added as an offset to the program counter to form the effective address of the data or operand. This addressing mode is extremely useful in the branch instructions.

Example:

P.C.			
0132	JR e	18	Jump (relative) to the effective address of P.C. + offset = 0134 + 36 = 016A
0133	36		
0134			
⋮	⋮		

Indexed Addressing

This is multibyte instruction, where the offset (or displacement) specified by the highest byte is added to the contents of the index registers (X or Y as specified in the op code), to form the effective address of the data or operand. This has a 2-byte op code.

Example (suppose 1X has F000 in it):

CP (1x + d) 33	DDBE	The accumulator is compared with the operand specified by the effective address 1x + d: F000 + 33 = F033

The accumulator is thus compared with the contents of the location F033. The indexed addressing mode is very powerful in setting up the memory tables and handling the blocks of data.

Bit Addressing

This is an added facility. Coupled with the other addressing modes, this can test and manipulate any bit.

Example:

BIT 7, L	CB7D	Bit 7 of reg L is tested. The zero flag is set if the bit tested is 0.

The bit addressing can also be coupled with the indexed and register indirect addressing modes.

Modified Page Zero Addressing

This refers to one of the eight locations in the zero page, corresponding to the restart vectors:

Example:

RST, 08	CF	Restart at location $(0008)_{Hex}$ (which has an op code of CF)

A clear understanding of these addressing modes will help us handle the Z-80 very efficiently. The data book(s) on the Z-80 by Zilog and other manufacturers should be consulted, to obtain more familiarity with the instruction set and the addressing modes.

Example 8.2 Z-80 Instructions

Table 8.3 shows a part of the software in a particular processing application.

(a) What is being accomplished between $(3000)_{Hex}$ and $(3013)_{Hex}$?
(b) What are the contents of the memory locations $(4000)_{Hex}$ $(4001)_{Hex}$...?
(c) How many times is the loop executed?

Consider initially that X register contains $(4000)_{Hex}$.

Solution

(a) *Function Accomplished.* The contents of the accumulator are sequentially loaded into the indexed memory table, starting at location $(4000)_{Hex}$.
(b) *Memory Contents.* Initially the accumulator is loaded with FF, which is loaded into location 4001. Thereafter, the decremented accumulator is

Table 8.3. Z-80 Software for Processing (Example 8.2).

Location	*Mnemonic*	*Op Code*	*Add Mode*	*T States*	*Comment*
3000	NOP	00	IMP	4	No Operation.
01	NOP	00	IMP	4	
02	NOP	00	IMP	4	
03	→LD A, n	3E	IMM	7	Load immediate data
04	FF				FF into A.
05	→INC 1X	DD23	IMP	10	Increment X register.
07	LD (1x + d), A	DD77	IND	19	Store A at location specified by 1x + d.
09	00				
0A	DEC A	3D	IMP	4	Decrement A.
0B	CP n	FE	IMM	7	Compare A with immediate data 85.
0C	85				
0D	JR NZ	20	REL	7/12*	If A #85, branch back to 3005.
0E	F6				
0F	NOP	00	IMP	4	No operation.
3010	NOP	00	IMP	4	"
11	NOP	00	IMP	4	"
12	NOP	00	IMP	4	"
13	JP	C3	EXT	10	Jump to 3003 to start new cycle.
14	03_L				
15	30_H				

* 7 states if condition not met; 12 states if condition is met.

stored at sequentially incremented (indexed memory) locations. The following shows the concept:

Location	Contents
4000	Don't Know
4001	FF
4002	FE
4003	FD
⋮	⋮

(c) *Loop Execution*. Between 3005 and 300E, the program goes into a loop until the accumulator is decremented to $(85)_{\text{Hex}}$. If the accumulator is not equal to $(85)_{\text{Hex}}$, the conditional and relative jump instruction at 300D loops the program back to 3005. Thus the program loops $(\text{FF})_{\text{Hex}} - (85)_{\text{Hex}} = (7\text{A})_{\text{Hex}} = (122)_{\text{Decimal}}$. The loop is executed 122 times.

8.3. Z-80 TIMING AND I/O STRUCTURE

Timing is very important in any processing and control applications. The Z-80 microprocessor has very well-defined instructional timing and I/O formating, which are suitable to any contemporary processing and control applications.

Instructional Timing

The instruction fetch and the execution are divided into several machine cycles. Each machine cycle is further subdivided into several timing cycles or states (T states). Each T state corresponds to one clock-time period. The data books on Z-80 provide the details of the timing states and the machine cycles required for each instruction. As design engineers, we should be aware of this important timing information and use it to our advantage.

Example 8.3 Z-80 Timing

Consider software Table 8.3 of Example 8.2. The Z-80 operates on a 2 MHz clock.

(a) Find the loop time T_{Loop} taken by the processor to execute the program between 3005 and 300E.

(b) Find the total time, T_{Total}, to run the program between 3000 and 3015.

Solution

(a) *Loop Time T_{Loop}.* Each T state corresponds to 0.5 μs at 2 MHz clock. From Table 8.3, we observe that the Z-80 takes 52 such T states to execute the loop (once between 3005 and 300E). Thus $T_1 \rightarrow 52$ T states = 26 μs (time to execute loop once). From Example 8.2, part c, we know that the loop is executed 122 times.

$$T_{Loop} = (\text{no. of times loop is executed}) * (\text{time to execute loop once})$$

$$\boxed{T_{Loop} = 122 * 26 = 3172\ \mu\text{sec} = 3.17\ \text{ms}}$$

(b) Total Time T_{Total}. From Table 8.3, we observe that there are 45 T states (22.5 μs), besides the loop. Thus,

$$\boxed{T_{Total} = T_{Loop} + 22.5\ \mu\text{s} = 3194.5\ \mu\text{s} = 3.194\ \text{ms}}$$

I/O Configuration

The Z-80 microprocessor uses the I/O mapped I/O concept. It is provided with one of the best I/O instruction sets (please refer to Tables 8.1 and 8.2 and Z-80 data sheets) of any 8-bit microprocessor. There are byte-oriented and block-oriented I/O instructions, which handle the I/O data transfers very efficiently.

The Z-80 microprocessor communicates to the outside world through the peripheral devices such as Z-80 PIO, 8255 PPI, and so on, as shown in Figure 8.5. We will attempt an example problem to obtain familiarity with the I/O instructions. The details of initializing these peripheral devices will be discussed in the next chapter.

Example 8.4 Z-80 I/O Configuration

Figure 8.5 shows a simple Z-80-based I/O system, controlling the smoke and fire alarm system in an office building. Consider that the peripheral devices have already been properly initialized.

Port A at I/O location (0) is the input port
Port B at I/O location (1) is the output port

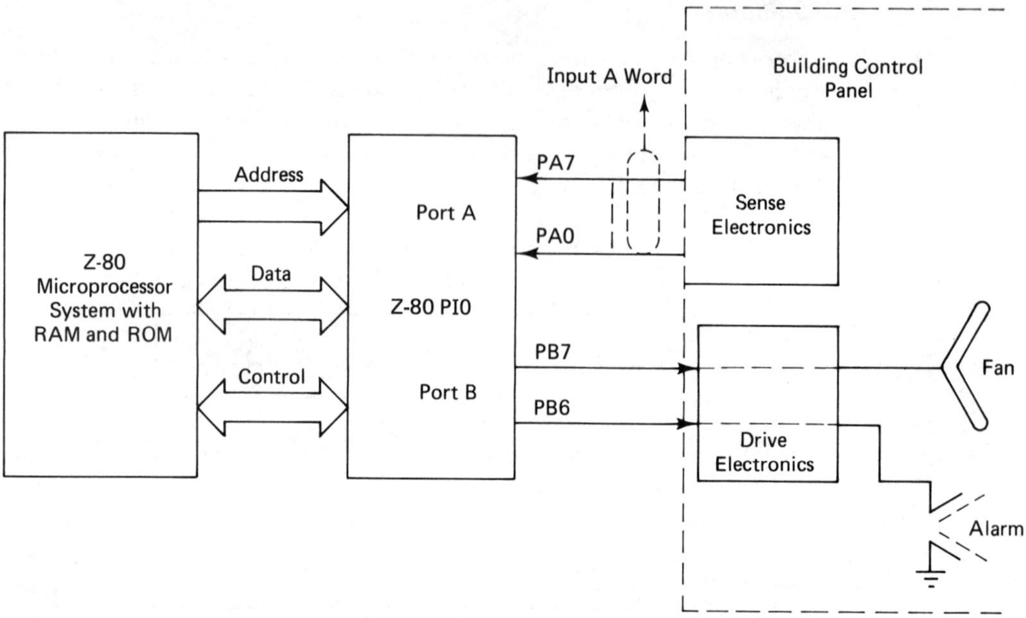

Fig 8.5. A simple Z-80 base I/O system for the alarm system of Example 4.

Develop the operating system such that the exhaust fan will be turned on if the input A word exceeds the accepted smoke level, and the fire alarm will be turned on if the A word exceeds the dangerous smoke level.

Solution

(a) *Hardware.* The system hardware is as shown in Figure 8.5. We will not worry about the details of the sense and drive electronics, which can be easily designed. However, we will assume:

$$\text{Acceptable smoke level} = (4F)_{Hex}$$
$$\text{Dangerous smoke level} = (8F)_{Hex}$$

and

Logic 1 on P_{B7} (port B, bit 7) turns on the fan.
Logic 1 on P_{B6} (port B, bit 6) turns on the alarm.

(b) *Software.* The software reads the input A word from the sense electronics on port A and compares it with the acceptable and dangerous levels. It then turns the fan and the alarm on or off, depending on the condition met. Figure 8.6 shows the flow chart, and Table 8.4 shows the listings.

Between 0000 and 000D, initialization is carried out (with the dangerous and acceptable levels loaded into the D and E registers). The fan and the alarm are initially turned off by outputting 00 to port B at I/O location (01).

Between 000E and 001C, the input word on port A is read and compared with the acceptable level (contained in the E register) either to turn on the fan or to branch back.

Similarly, between 001D and 0033, the input A word is read and compared to the dangerous level (contained in the D register) to turn on or off the alarm. The program jumps to appropriate locations to maintain the continuity of the operation.

The above program is simple and straightforward. However, it throws light on handling the I/O and bit instructions, which are perhaps the strongest features of the Z-80 instruction set. As usual, to provide you with more insight

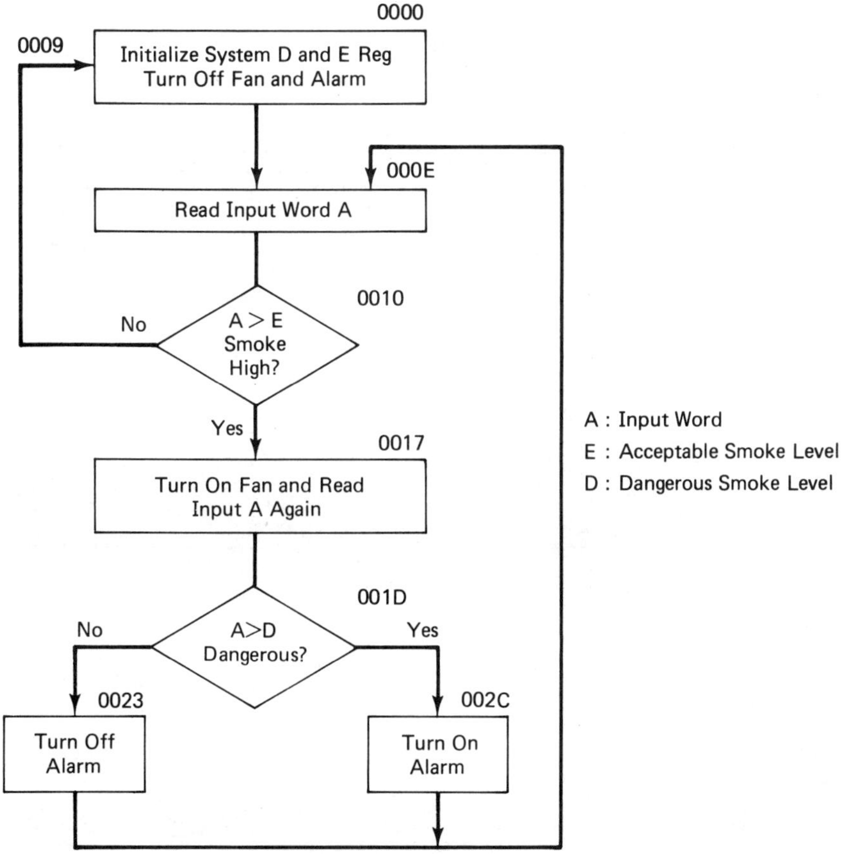

Fig 8.6. Flowchart for the alarm system of Example 4.

Table 8.4. Z-80 Operating Listings for the Alarm Control (Example 8.4).

Location	Label	Mnemonic	Op Code	Add Mode	Comment
0000	Initialize	NOP	00	IMP	Linkage software and initialization done by loading 00 into C register, 8F into D register (danger level), and 4F into E register (acceptable level).
01		NOP	00	IMP	
02		NOP	00	IMP	
03		LD C, n	0E	IMM	
04		00			
05		LD D, n	16	IMM	
06		8F		IMM	
07		LD E, n	1E	IMM	
08		4F			
09	Clear	LD A, n	3E	IMM	Accumulator loaded with 00 and is output to Port B at location 01 to turn off fan and alarm.
0A		00			
0B		OUT (1), A	D301	EXT	
0D		NOP	00	IMP	
0E	Start	IN A, (0)	DB00	EXT	Input A port at location 00 is read into Accumulator and is compared with E register. If A > E, the program jumps to 0017 to turn fan on. If not, it jumps back to 0009 (to clear) to turn off fan and alarm.
0010		CP E	BB	IMP	
11		JP P	F2	EXT	
12		17_L			
13		00_H			
14		JP	C3	EXT	
15		09_L			
16		00_H			
17	Fan On	SET 7, C	CBF9	BIT	Bit 7 of C is set and transferred to A and is output to port B to turn fan on.
19		LD A, C	79	IMP	

Address	Label	Instruction	Code	Mode	Comment
1A		OUT (1), A	D301	EXT	
1C		NOP	00	IMP	
1D	Read A	IN A, (0)	DB00	EXT	Read port A again and compare with D.
1F		CP D	BA	IMP	
0020		JP P	F2	EXT	If A > D, jump to 002C to turn alarm on. If not, proceed to turn off alarm.
21		$2C_L$			
22		00_H			
23	Alarm Off	RES 6, C	CBB1	BIT	Bit 6 of C is reset and transferred to A and is output to port B to turn off alarm. Program jumps to 000E to start new cycle.
25		LD A, C	79	IMP	
26		OUT (1), A	D301	EXT	
28		JP	C3	IMP	
29		$0E_L$			
2A		00_H			
2B		NOP	00	IMP	
2C	→ Alarm On	SET 6, C	CBF1	BIT	Bit 6 of C is set and transferred to A and is output to port B to turn the alarm on. The program jumps to 000E to start new cycle.
2E		LD A, C	D301	EXT	
2F		OUT (1) A	79	EXT	
0031		JP		EXT	
32		$0E_L$			
33		00_H			

(It is assumed that the program resides in the system memory starting at location 0000.)

into I/O instructions, several operating problems have been designed for your use and appear at the end of the chapter.

8.4. SUMMARY

In this chapter, we have introduced the basic architectural features of the Z-80, which is one of the most powerful 8-bit microprocessors.

The instruction set of the Z-80 is presented, and several example problems have been discussed to bring out its features. Of particular importance are the addressing modes, which provide an edge to the Z-80 compared to the other 8-bit processors.

Finally, the instructional timing and I/O features are discussed, to provide the reader with enough background to proceed further.

It is strongly advised that you refer to the Z-80 data books to obtain more information, which cannot be presented here because of space limitations.

Problems

8.1. Figure 8.1 shows the architecture and the bus structure of the Z-80 microprocessor.

(a) What will be the logic values of the control signals (logic 0 or 1) $\overline{\text{MREQ}}$, $\overline{\text{IOREQ}}$ $\overline{\text{RD}}$, $\overline{\text{WR}}$, and $\overline{\text{M1}}$ during a memory read operation?

(b) Repeat (a) during I/O read operation.

8.2. Repeat Problem 8.1 for the

(a) Memory write operation.

(b) I/O write operation.

8.3. The accumulator contains DF, and immediate data of AC is added to the accumulator.

(a) What are the conditions of the flag bits of Figure 8.2?

(b) If the data of 7F is subtracted from the contents of the accumulator of part (a), what are the conditions of the flag bits?

8.4. Can the regular registers A...F and the alternate registers A′...F′ be used simultaneously? Why? Explain the reasons.

8.5. Explain the functional difference between the three modes of interrupts MODE 0, MODE 1, and MODE 2. Provide conceptual examples, using the three modes.

8.6. In a particular application, it is required that all the CPU registers be stored, including the alternates on the stack.

(a) How much stack memory is required?

(b) If the initial value of the stack pointer is set at 01FF, what will be the final value, after storing all the CPU registers?

8.7. Examining the instruction Tables 8.1 and 8.2,

(a) Categorize the instructions as data transfer group, logical group, branching group, etc.

(b) Formulate the additional capabilities of the Z-80, compared to the 8080 and 8085.

8.8. Figure 8.4 shows the instructional format of the Z-80. Identify, using the instruction Tables 8.1 and 8.2, identify at least four instructions, which are

(a) Single-byte

(b) Two-byte

(c) Three-byte

(d) Four-byte.

8.9. Using the instruction set, write simple instructions to

(a) Load $(4000)_{Hex}$ into X register.

(b) Transfer contents of Y register to stack.

(c) Exchange the contents of registers. A...F with A′...F′

(d) Store the contents of A′...F′ on stack.

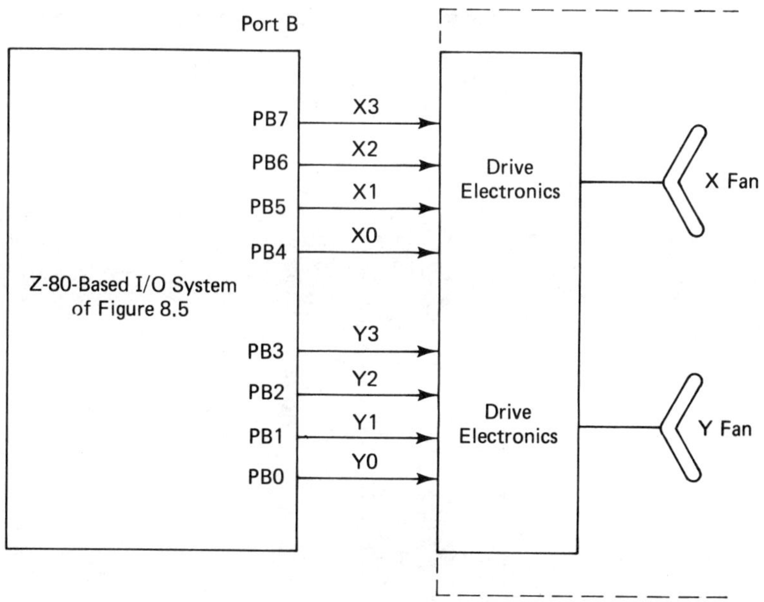

Fig 8.7. Conceptual Z-80-based I/O computer for Problems 8.11 and 8.12.

8.10. Using the software routines of your choice, generate
(a) 100 ms delay.
(b) 500 ms delay.

8.11. Figure 8.7 shows a simple Z-80-based microcomputer, controlling two fans X and Y, which can be operated in two modes:

Control Word (X3 Y3	X2 Y2	X1 Y1	X0 Y0)	*or*	*Mode of Rotation*	*Function*
1	0	1	0		Clockwise	Blower
0	1	0	1		Counterclockwise	Exhaust
0	0	0	0		Stop	

Develop the operating software such that X and Y fans operate in exhaust mode for 30 seconds, stop for 30 seconds, operate for 30 seconds, and so on.

8.12. Repeat Problem 8.11, such that X fan operates in exhaust mode and fan Y operates in blower mode for 30 seconds; both the fans stop for 30 seconds and reverse the condition for 30 seconds; and so on.

8.13. Figure 8.8 shows a simple recreational display system, used in signs, advertising, etc. The optical illusion creates the impression of a continuous movement if the events take place faster than 16 times a second.

Eight lights are driven by port B (PB 7 driving light 7, PB6 driving light 6...). If light 7 is turned on (with other lights off) and after a while light

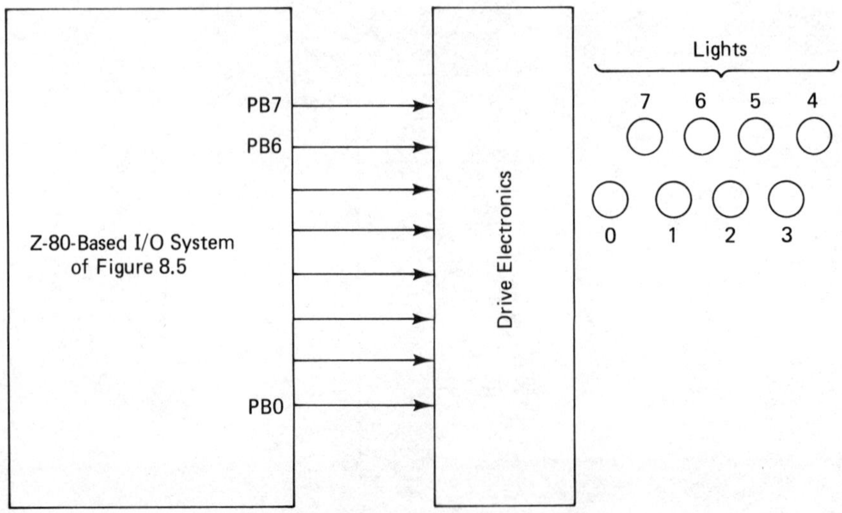

Fig 8.8. A Z-80 computer driving recreation display for Problems 8.13 and 8.14.

6 is turned on (with the rest of them turned off) and so on, it creates the illusion that the optical image is moving in the direction of 7-6-5....

Develop the operating software such that the image moves from 7 to 6 to 5...to 0 in a clockwise circular manner. Consider 100 ms. illumination of each light.

8.14. Repeat Problem 8-13, such that the image

(a) Moves counterclockwise from 0 to 7....

(b) Moves in a zigzag path, as shown.

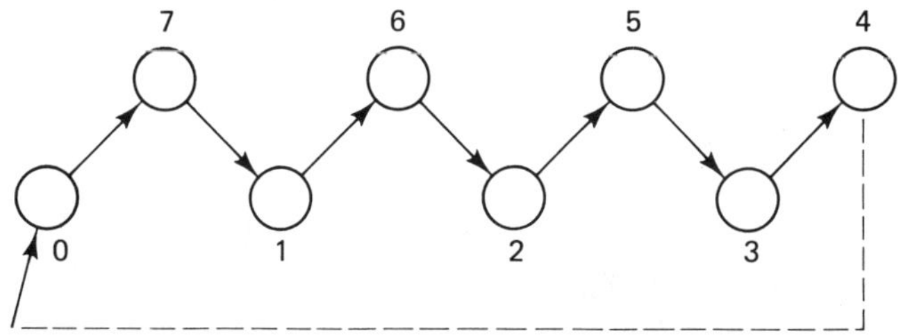

CHAPTER NINE

Z-80-Based Microcomputer System Design

In this chapter, we discuss the actual design of an operating microcomputer system. We will use the Z-80 microprocessor and the associated memory and I/O devices. The flexibility of the Z-80 and its ever-increasing usage in the industry for processing and control applications prompted us to present the actual design of the microcomputer system using the Z-80. The concepts presented here are equally applicable in implementing any other microcomputer system with any other microprocessor.

9.1. MICROCOMPUTER SYSTEM CONFIGURATION

Figure 9.1 shows a typical microcomputer configuration using the Z-80 microprocessor. The minimal operating system, shown above the dotted line, is usually sufficient for most of the control and I/O applications. The expanded operating system has the add-on features of the video display, printer interface, and so on. Popular home computers such as the TRS-80, Sinclair ZX-81™, and Microprofessor belong to this category. We will discuss the actual operating design of the minimal system and show how that can be further extended to become an expanded operating system.

System Components and Structure

As shown in Figure 9.1, the microcomputer system consists of the microprocessor itself for the processing and control of the data; the RAM for the

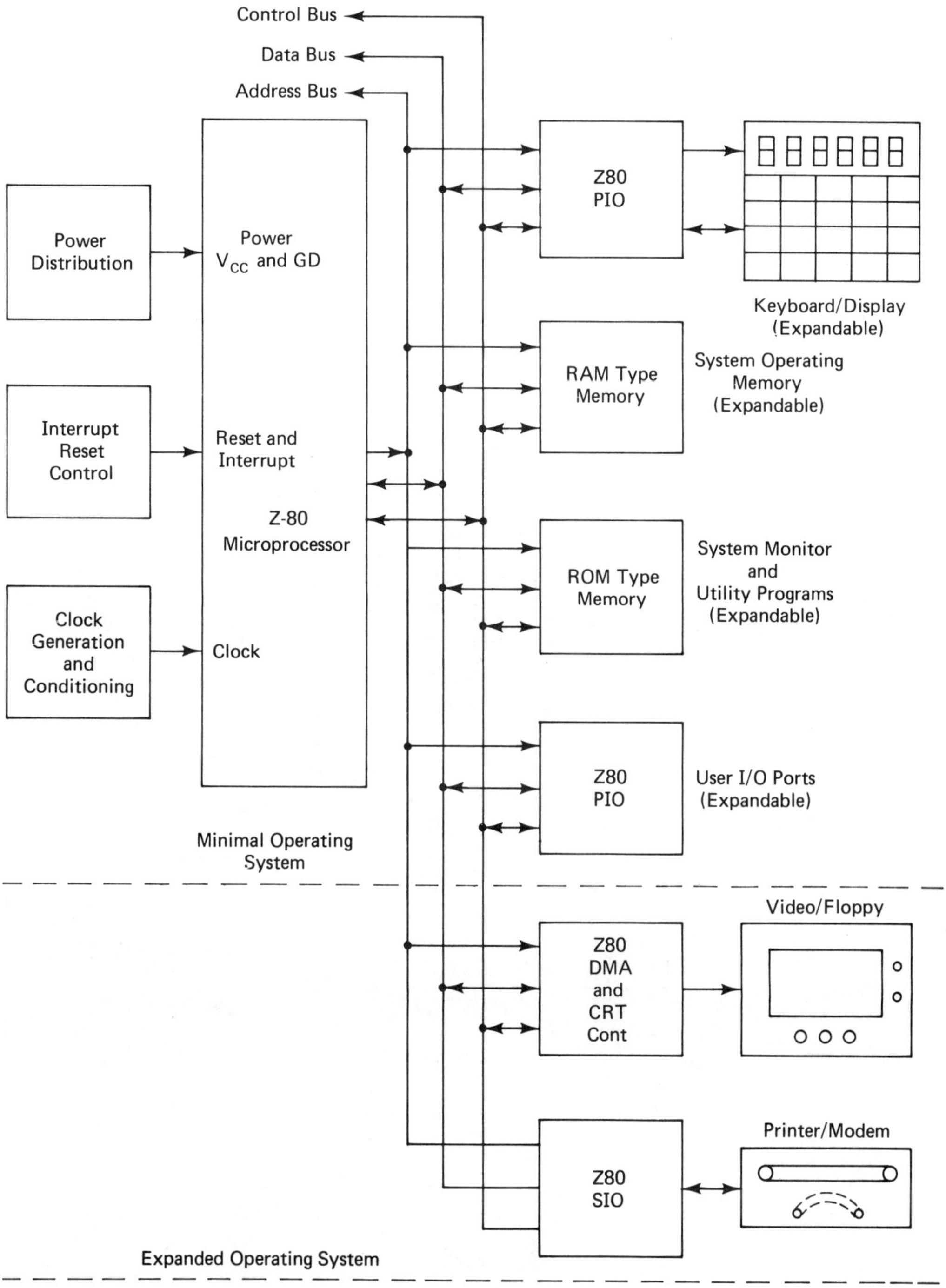

Fig 9.1. A typical Z-80-based microcomputer configuration.

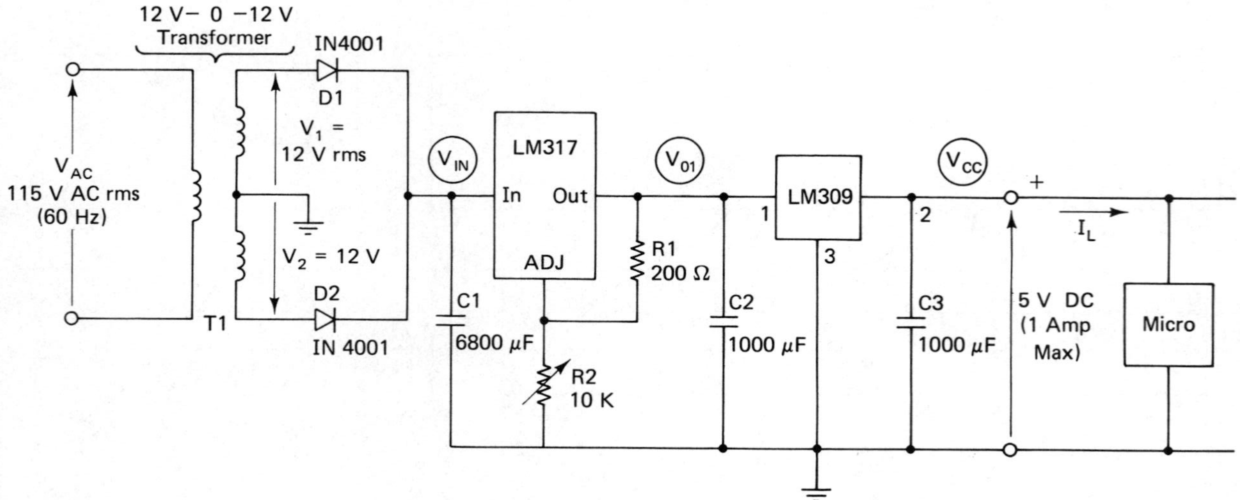

($V_{In} \approx$ 16 V D.C., $V_{01} \approx$ 12 V D.C.
$V_{CC} \approx$ 5V D.C.)

Fig 9.2. A typical 5-volt generation for the microcomputer system.

storage of user programs and variables; and the ROM for the storage of the monitor and utility programs and the fixed constants. In addition, for the input and output parallel interface, there are the PIO (parallel I/O) devices. For the handling of the video floppy disks there are special interface devices such as the DMA CRT and floppy controllers. Proper hardware and software interface of all these devices comprises an operating microcomputer system.

Hardware Concepts

The microcomputer system has to be activated with a clean power supply, with good regulation characteristics. A transient on the power line could send the microprocessor wandering, resulting in the system failure. Z-80 and other similar microprocessor systems operate on a voltage V_{cc} = 5 volts ± 10%. Figure 9.2 shows a typical power supply circuit used in the microcomputer systems. The V_{cc} output can supply up to one amp without loss in the regulation.

Figure 9.3 shows a typical clock generation circuit used with the microcomputer systems. The series resonance of the crystal at 4 MHz completes the oscillating loop of the circuit, consisting of the 7404 inverters ① and ②. Inverter ③ shapes the signal, and the 7474 D flip flop (connected in the ÷ 2 configuration) divides the signal to provide a 2 MHz operating clock to the system.

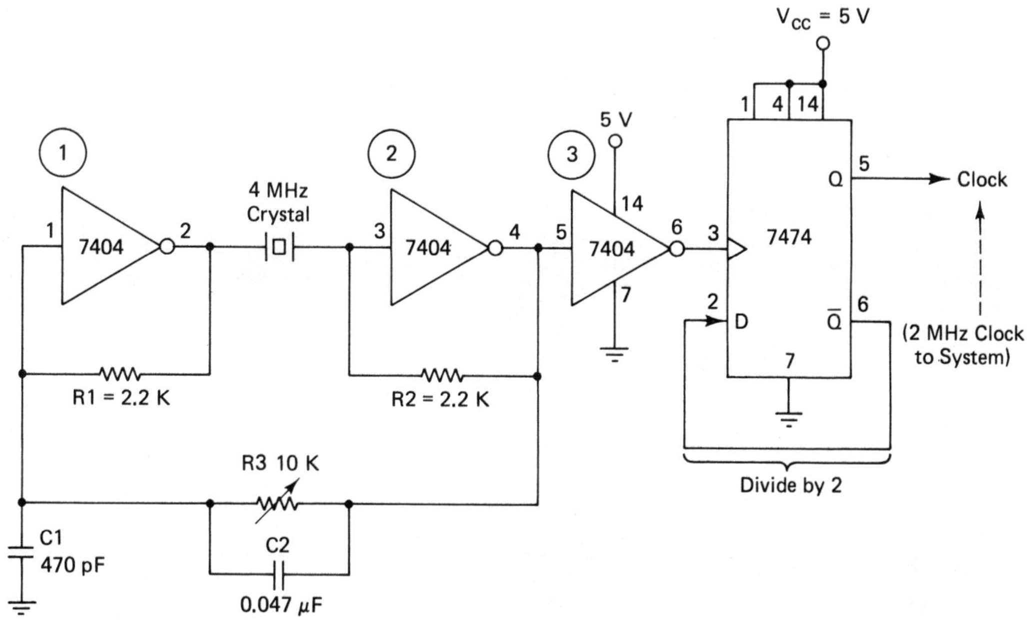

Fig 9.3. A typical clock generation for the microcomputer system.

The rest of the hardware consists of the interface of the memory and the peripheral I/O devices to the Z-80 microprocessor, which we will discuss later.

Software Concepts

With many different hardware devices connected to the microprocessor, it becomes the task of the software to properly address and recognize these devices. Also, the software implements the required data processing and handling operations.

For example, the microprocessor will recognize (under software control), the key being pressed and the type of instruction and the data being entered through the keyboard, as shown in the Figure 9.1. Similarly, under software control, the microprocessor sends the appropriate data to the I/O and memory.

In any microcomputer system, the hardware and software features should be properly integrated to obtain optimum performance.

Example 9.1 Hardware and Software Concepts

In the power supply circuit of Figure 9.2, the input voltage V_{in} dc is 16 volts unregulated.

(a) Find the powers dissipated in the LM 317 and LM 309 regulators, if the load current I_L is 1 amp. Are heat sinks recommended?

(b) In the clocking circuit of Figure 9.3, what is the function accomplished by the resistors R_1 and R_2.

(c) A software instruction such as OUT(c), r takes 12 timing states. With the clocking circuit of Figure 9.3 activating the Z-80, how much time will it take to implement the OUT(c), r instruction.

Solution

(a) *Power Dissipation.*

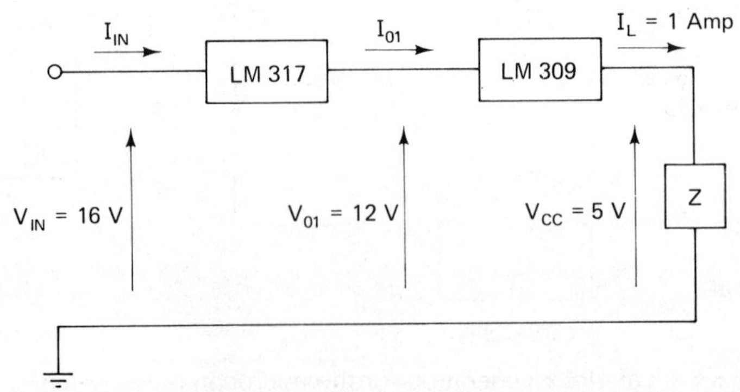

Approximating $I_{in} \cong I_{01} \cong I_L \cong 1$ amp, we can easily observe that the powers dissipated P_{317} and P_{309} respectively in the 317 and 309 devices are

$$P_{317} \cong I_{in} * [V_{in} - V_{01}] \cong 1 * 4 \cong 4 \text{ watts}$$
$$P_{309} \cong I_{01} * [V_{01} - V_{cc}] \cong 1 * 7 \cong 7 \text{ watts}$$

Because of the higher power dissipation, T03 package with appropriate heat sink (such as Wakerfield 680-75) is suggested. Please refer to the National Semiconductor Data Book for details.

(b) *Clock Circuit.* R_1 and R_2 resistors force the 7404 inverters to operate near the threshold and complete the oscillating loop.

(c) *Software Timing.* The effective clock activating the microcomputer system has a frequency of 2 MHz. Thus each timing state takes 1/2 MHz = 0.5 μs.

12 timing states take 6 μs

9.2. MEMORY INTERFACE AND CONFIGURATION

The efficient operation of any microcomputer depends on the way the memory and the I/O are handled by the microprocessor. The address bus should be properly decoded, so that no more than one device (and the corresponding location) is selected and addressed by the microprocessor at any given instant of time. Otherwise, the data will be lost and even the system may get destroyed.

Address Decoding and Interface

Figure 9.4 shows the details of the address decoding and the corresponding memory interface. The Z-80™ pins are respectively connected to the decoder and the memory devices.

When the memory is addressed by the Z-80, the memory request ($\overline{MREQ}$) line goes low, which activates the upper 138 decoder ①. Depending on the condition of the address inputs (A14 and A15) from the Z-80, one of the decoded outputs $Y_0 \ldots Y_3$ goes low.

In our particular case, when A5 and A14 are at logic zero, Y_0 output goes low. This in turn activates the lower 138 decoder ②. Depending on the condition of the A13, A12, and A11 address inputs, one of the outputs goes active low. This decoder tree concept finally results in activating a range of the memory.

Example 9.2 Address Decoding

In the address decoding circuitry of Figure 9.4,

(a) Find the address range activated by each of the outputs of the upper decoder ①.

(b) Repeat (a) for the lower decoder ②.

Solution

(a) *Upper Decoder* ①. Following is the address bus structure.

	A15															A0
	15	14	13	12	11	10	9	8	7	6	5	4	3	2	1	0
$Y_0 = 0$	0	0	x	x	x	x	x	x	x	x	x	x	x	x	x	x
$Y_1 = 0$	0	1														
$Y_2 = 0$	1	0	"		"				"				"			
$Y_3 = 0$	1	1														

Y_0 remains active low over the address range where A15 and A14 remain low, but A13...A0 can change from an all-zero condition to an all-one condition. This corresponds to an address range of 0000 to 3FFF. Thus, extending our argument, we observe that

Y_0 corresponds to 16K range between 0000 → 3FFF
Y_1 corresponds to 16K range between 4000 → 7FFF
Y_2 corresponds to 16K range between 8000 → BFFF
Y_3 corresponds to 16K range between C000 → FFFF

as shown in Figure 9.4

(b) *Lower Decoder* ②. The lower decoder is basically activated by the Y_0 output of the upper decoder (in the address range of 0000 to 3FFF). The condition of the A13, A12, and A11 inputs further define the segments of the address range. Following the same argument, we observe that for decoder ②

Y_0 corresponds to 2K range between 0000 → 07FF
Y_1 corresponds to 2K range between 0800 → 0FFF
Y_7 corresponds to 2K range between 3800 → 3FFF

Notice the chip select redefinition ($\overline{CS0}...\overline{CS7}$) of these decoder outputs.

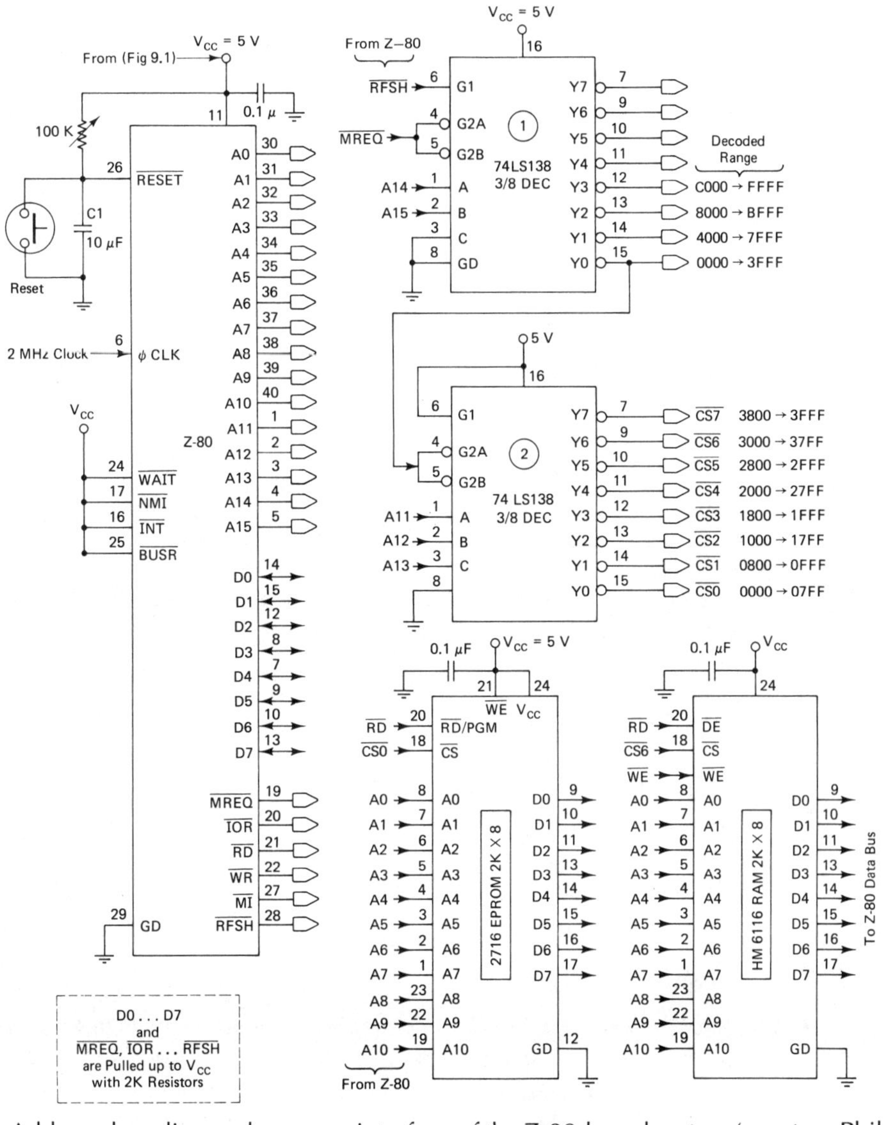

Fig 9.4. Address decoding and memory interface of the Z-80-based system (courtesy Phil Vallejo and Hugo Amezequita, Florida International University).

ROM/RAM Interface

We will now concentrate on the ROM/RAM hardware interface. It should always be emphasized that the operating power supply V_{cc} should be decoupled with adequate capacitance (0.1 μF is acceptable in most cases), to minimize the power supply transients.

In our case, we have chosen the 2716-type EPROM for storing the monitor and utility programs. Similarly, we have the HM6116 CMOS RAM for the user storage. Both these devices are 2K × 8 capacity and are pin compatible. For the microcomputer system we are developing currently, these are adequate, efficient, and cost effective. Proper chip select interface selects the devices one at a time.

For the connections shown in Figure 9.4 ($\overline{CS0}$ connected to the $\overline{chip\ select}$ of 2716 EPROM and $\overline{CS6}$ connected to the chip select of 6116 RAM), we can easily observe that the address range for

EPROM is between 0000 to 07FF
RAM is between 3000 to 37FF

The reader should verify the validity of our statements and the actual operating interface of the memory as shown in Figure 9.4.

Example 9.3 Handling Memory

In many microcomputer systems, one of the main requirements is to be able to clear the operating memory to an all-zero condition.

(a) Develop an operating program for the microcomputer of Figure 9.4, such that the RAM between the locations $(3000)_{Hex}$ to $(3FFF)_{Hex}$ is cleared to the all-zero condition.
(b) Modify the operating program such that FF is loaded in the RAM between 3000 to 3FFF.

Consider that the program can be loaded into the EPROM. You may design the program as a subroutine.

Solution

(a) *Memory All-Zero Condition*. The microcomputer of Figure 9.4 contains all the hardware interface required. The software loads 00 into the accumulator and transfers it sequentially to the memory locations between $(3000)_{Hex}$ to $(3FFF)_{Hex}$. Table 9.1 shows the actual operating listings.

The program is designed as a subroutine, starting at location 01D8. Between 01D8 and 01DB, the contents of HL are stored on the stack. The HL register pair is loaded with $(3000)_{Hex}$, which refers to the beginning of the memory to be cleared.

Between 01DC and 01E5, the memory in the range of 3000 to 3FFF is cleared to all-zero condition. This is accomplished by using the indirect addressing scheme and transferring the contents of the accumulator (00 in this case) to the sequential memory locations.

Table 9.1. Operating Z-80 Listings for Clearing the Memory (Example 9.3).

Location	Label	Mnemonic	Op Code	Mode	Comment
→ 01D8	Clear	Push HL	E5	Indirect	HL push to stack.
Enter 09		LD HL, nn	21	IMM	HL loaded with immediate data of 3000.
DA		00_L			
DB		30_H			
DC	Blank	→ LD A, n	3E	IMM	A loaded with immediate data of 00.
DD		00			
DE		NOP	00	IMM	No operation.
DF		LD (HL), A	77	Indirect	A loaded into memory addressed by HL. HL is incremented and compared with $(40)_{Hex}$.
E0		INC HL	23	IMP	
E1		LD A, n	3E	IMM	
E2		40			If H#$(40)_{Hex}$, branch back to blank at 01DC. This amounts to loading 00 into locations between 3000 to 3FFF sequentially.
E3		CP H	BC	IMP	
E4		JR NZ	20	REL	
E5		F6 (→ Blank)			
E6		POP HL	E1	Indirect	When H = 40, HL are restored from stack and program returns to the calling program.
Return E7		NOP	00	IMP	
← E8		RET	C9	Indirect	

Note: The program is designed as a subroutine, entering at 01D8 and returning at 01E8.

Between 01E6 and 01E8, the HL registers are recovered from the stack and the subroutine returns to the main calling program.

(b) *Loading the Memory with FF.* If the contents of location 01DD in Table 9.1 are changed from 00 to FF (which amounts to loading A with FF), then the memory will be loaded with FF when the subroutine is run.

Several example problems are specially designed and presented at the end of the chapter to help you obtain more experience in handling the memory.

9.3. I/O INTERFACE AND CONFIGURATION

With the proper I/O interface, the usefulness of the microcomputer is greatly enhanced. We will discuss some of these concepts that will enable us to design and implement the I/O interface for any Z-80-based system that uses the I/O mapped I/O concept.

PIO Structure

Z-80 PIO (parallel input/output device) is a 40-pin programmable I/O device that is fabricated with NMOS technology. The structure of the device is as shown in Figure 9.5. The device consists of two 8-bit programmable I/O ports, A and B. Each port consists of two 8-bit registers, the data register and the control register.

The control register contents determine the mode of operation of the corresponding port (whether the port is configured as the input or output or partial input and output, etc.). The data register holds the data for the corresponding I/O transfers.

The Z-80 PIO communicates with the Z-80 CPU through the data, address, and control buses as shown in Figures 9.5 and 9.6. The decoded address bus of the Z-80 CPU drives the select inputs and accordingly selects the PIO internal registers, as shown in Figure 9.6. The control word written into the PIO control register (by the CPU) determines the mode of operation, as shown in Figure 9.7. Mode 3 is perhaps the most flexible mode, with the individual bit programmability.

PIO Interface

Figure 9.8 shows the actual operating interface of the Z-80 PIO to the microcomputer system of Figure 9.4. The PIO is selected when the Z-80 CPU performs an input/output operation and pulls the $\overline{IORQ}$ line low. The address

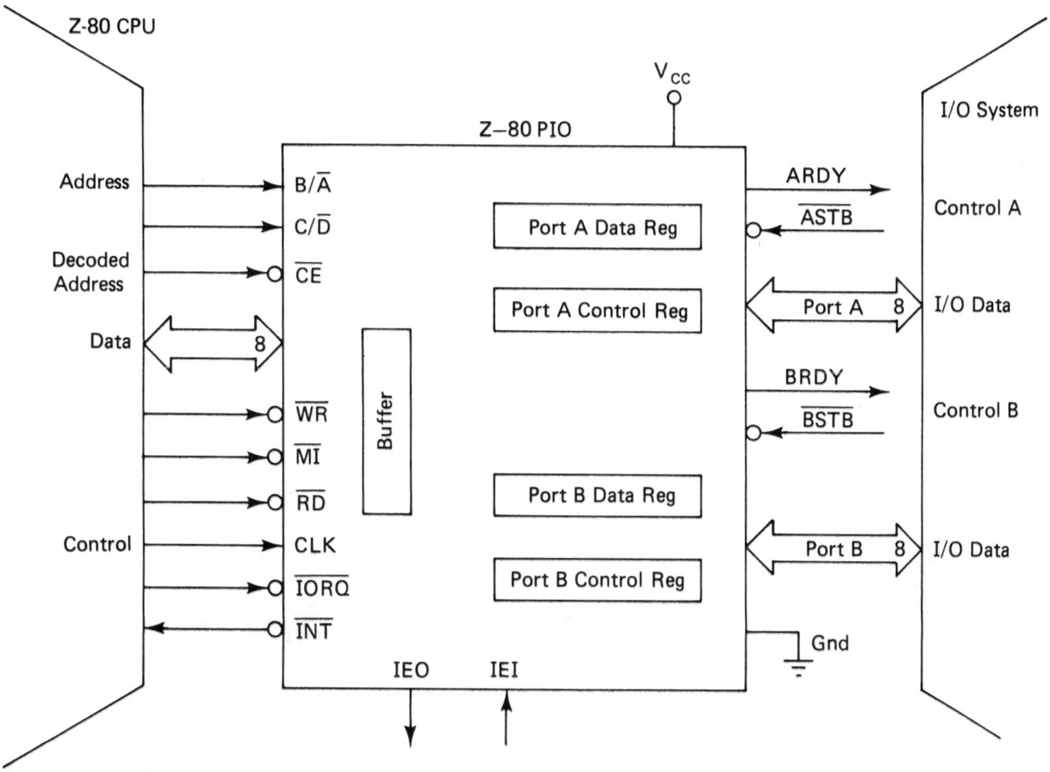

Fig 9.5. The Z-80 PIO structure and configuration.

$\overline{IORQ}$ and $\overline{CE}$ Should be Low to Select the PIO			
C/$\overline{D}$	B/$\overline{A}$	Port Selected	Register Selected
0	0	Port A	Data Register
0	1	Port B	Data Register
1	0	Port A	Control Register
1	1	Port B	Control Register

Fig 9.6. PIO register selection by the Z-80 CPU.

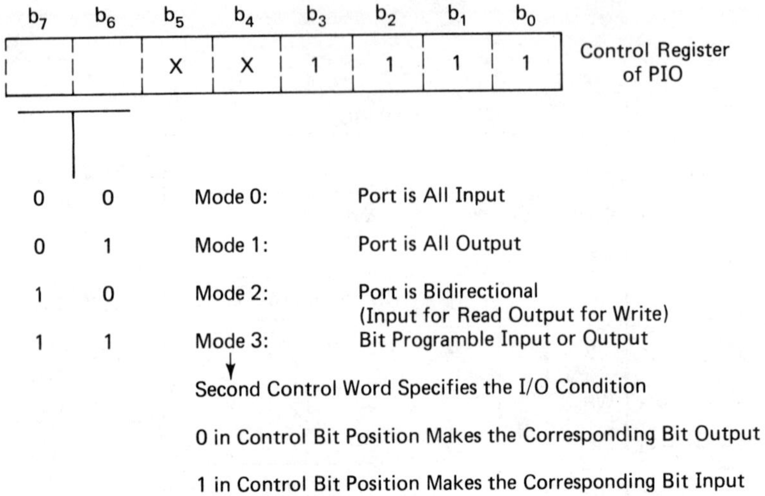

Fig 9.7. Mode selection and I/O configuration.

bits A0 and A1 drive the $B/\overline{A}$ and $C/\overline{D}$ selection inputs of the PIO. Referring to Figure 9.6, this amounts to

I/O Location 00 → Port A data register
" " 01 → Port B data register
" " 02 → Port A control register
" " 03 → Port B control register

For further details of the I/O interface, the data books on the Z-80 and Z-80 PIO should be consulted.

Following is an application involving the actual hardware and software features of the Z-80-based I/O system.

Example 9.4 Z-80 PIO Initialization

Develop the operating software (as a subroutine) such that the PIO of Figure 9.8 operates in mode 3, with port A configured as output and port B configured as input. This subroutine may be called by later system applications.

Solution

The software centers on loading the proper control words into the respective control registers of ports A and B.

Referring to Figure 9.7, we infer that CF should be loaded into the control register to operate the respective port in mode 3. A second control word should be written to make the port bits either output (0 makes it output) or input (1

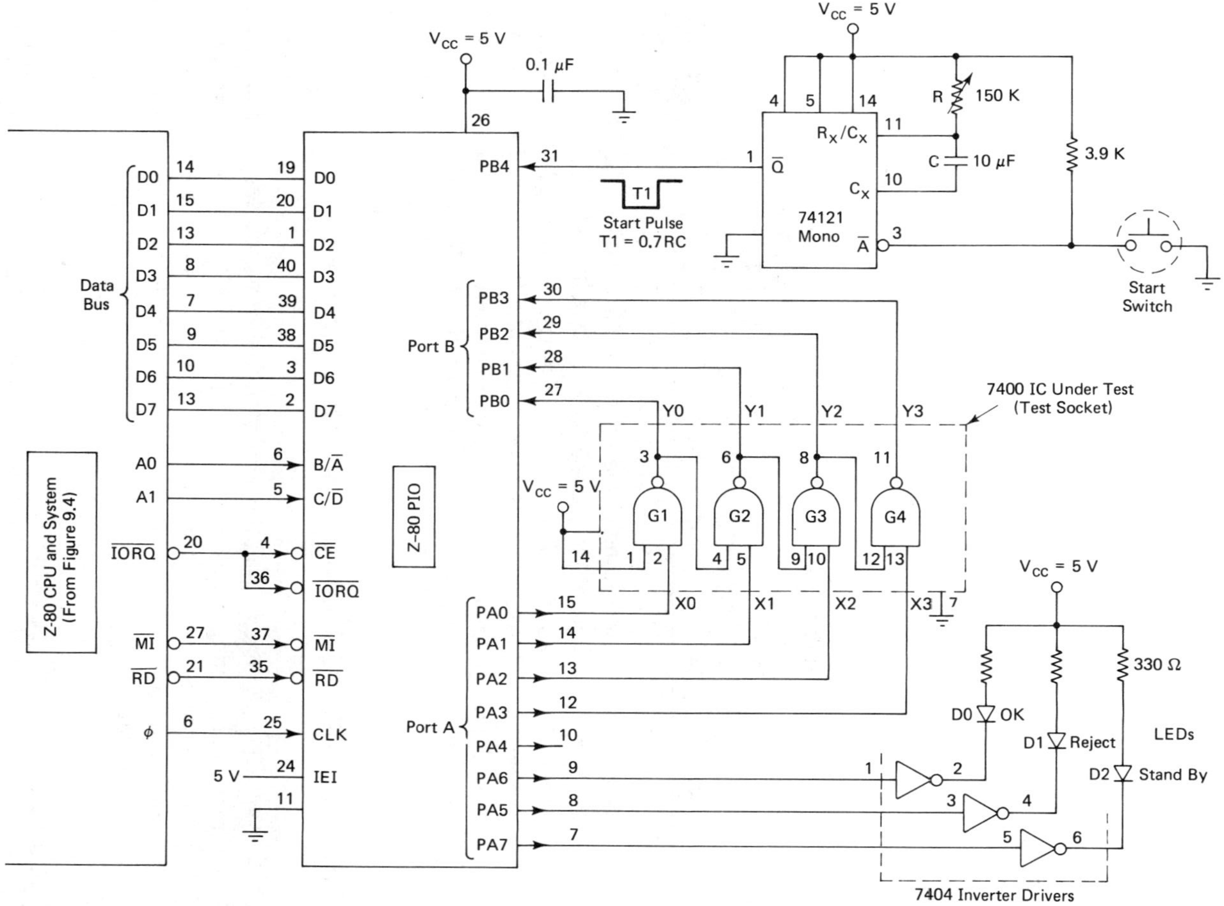

Fig 9.8. The Z-80 PIO interface and structure for the system initialization and IC tester (Examples of 4 and 5).

Table 9.2. Software Listings to Initialize the Z-80 PIO (Example 9.4).

Location	*Label*	*Mnemonic*	*Op Code*	*Comment*
0200	Initialize	NOP	00	Linkage software and delay.
01		NOP	00	
02		NOP	00	
03	Mode 3	LD A, n	3E	Load immediate data of CF into A and transfer it to control registers B and A at I/O locations 03 and 02, to set up mode 3 for both ports.
04		CF		
05		OUT	D3	
06		03		
07		OUT	D3	
08		02		
09		LD A, n	3E	Load immediate data of FF into A and transfer to control register B, to make all bits of port B input.
0A		FF		
0B		OUT	D3	
0C		03		
0D		XOR A	AF	Clear A to all-zero condition and transfer to control register A to make all bits of port A output.
0E		OUT		
0F		02		
10		NOP	00	Return to the calling program.
11	Return	RET	C9	

makes it input). Accordingly, the second control word should be FF to make port B an input port; 00 to make port A an output port.

Table 9.2 shows the actual operating listings. Between 0200 and 0208, both the ports are set to mode 3. Between 0209 and 020F, port B is configured as an input port and port A is configured as an output port. Finally the subroutine returns to the calling program by virtue of the RET instruction at 0211.

9.4. OPERATING MICROCOMPUTER SYSTEMS

We will now integrate all the subsystem concepts developed so far to implement an operating microcomputer system. We will first attempt an I/O bound microcomputer design. Later we will introduce the concepts of the monitor and utility routines. Finally we will present the features of the data entry and the display.

I/O Microcomputer Configuration

Perhaps the easiest microcomputer system that can be designed and implemented is the dedicated I/O bound microcomputer system. Video games, most of the process control and testing type computer systems, and instrumentation-type systems are some of the typical examples of such I/O bound computer systems. The software required to run such a system can be contained in the system ROM or PROM. The data to be manipulated can be obtained through one of the I/O ports. Similarly, the processed data can be output to another I/O port.

We will now integrate the memory subsystem of Figure 9.4 and the I/O subsystem of Figure 9.8 into an I/O bound microcomputer system. We will do that with the help of an example problem.

Example 9.5 I/O Microcomputer System

Implement an automatic IC (integrated circuit) tester (using the Z-80 based memory and I/O subsystems of Figures 9.4 and 9.8) to test the 7400 series of logic devices. For simplicity, choose the 7400-type quad two input NAND gate as the test element. The operator puts the test element and pushes the start button. The micro generates a test pattern and tests the element. If the element is bad, the reject LED should glow. If the system is not actively testing, the standby LED should glow. If the element is good, OK LED should glow.

(a) Develop the necessary hardware and the software to implement the above IC tester system.

(b) Briefly discuss how the concept can be extended to test other 7400 devices; for example, 7408 two input AND gates.

Solution

(a) *IC Tester Hardware*. The hardware of Figure 9.8 is self-contained to test the 7400 two input NAND gates, as shown. If we generate an input pattern such as $X_3X_2X_1X_0 = 1\ 1\ 1\ 1 = F$, for the connections as shown, the output of the good 7400 gate should produce $Y_3Y_2Y_1Y_0 = 1\ 0\ 1\ 0 = A$. Any other output pattern from the IC signifies that the IC is bad.

When the start switch is pressed, the 74121 monostable absorbs the switch bounce and produces a low active test pulse ($\cong$ 1 s duration) at the P_{B4} input of the PIO. The microcomputer senses this pulse and starts the test cycle.

(b) *Software*. The software initializes port A as output and port B as input. It generates the test pattern for the IC under test. It then checks the IC output for the proper pattern. Accordingly it turns on the proper LED lights (1 turns LED on; 0 turns it off). It also restarts the testing sequence properly.

Figure 9.9 shows the flow chart and the corresponding pseudo code. Table 9.3 shows the actual operating listings. We assume that the stack pointer is properly initialized (we will discuss that later).

Between 0300 and 0305, the subroutine at location 0200 (Example 9.4

Table 9.3. Z-80™ Operating Listings for the IC Tester System (Example 9.5).

Location	Label	Mnemonic	Op Code	Comment
0300	Initialize	NOP	00	Linkage software.
01		NOP	00	
02		NOP	00	
03		CALL	CD	Go to initialize subroutine at 0200 to configure port A as output and port B as input (Table 9.2).
04		00_L		
05		02_H		
06	Standby	LD A, n	3E	Turn on the standby light by sending code $(80)_{Hex}$ to port A at I/O location 00.
07		80		
08		OUT	D3	
09		00		
0A	Start	→ IN	DB	Read port B at I/O location 01 and mask other bits except b_4. If $b_4 = 1$ (start pulse is high and inactive), loop back to 030A to read it again. If $b_4 = 0$ (start pulse is active) proceed to test the IC.
0B		01		
0C		AND n	E6	
0D		10		
0E		JP NZ	C2	
0F		$0A_L$		
10		03_H		
11	Pattern	LD A, n	3E	Test pattern to IC 10001111 = 8F is sent to port A to activate the IC. After a brief lapse, port B at location 01 is read to obtain the IC output pattern.
12		8F		
13		OUT	D3	
14		00		
15		NOP	00	
16		NOP	00	
17	Test	IN	DB	
18		01		Upper nibble of the word read is masked out, and the pattern is compared to the expected pattern of 0A.
19		And n	E6	
1A		0F		
031B		CP n	FE	
1C		0A		

Address	Label	Mnemonic	Code	Comments
1D		JR Z	28	If pattern checks out, branch to good IC routine at 0325.
1E		06		
1F	Bad IC	LD A, n	3E	Bad IC. Send $(40)_{Hex}$ word to port A at location 00 to turn on reject light. Branch to check routine at 032A.
20		40		
21		OUT	D3	
22		00		
23		JR	18	
24		05		
25	Good IC	LD A, n	3E	Good IC. Send $(20)_{Hex}$ word to port A to turn on OK light.
26		20		
27		OUT	D3	
28		00		
29		NOP	00	
2A	Check	IN	DB	Read port B at location 01 and check if b_4 is still 0 (implying the same start pulse and same IC). If so, check again at 032A.
2B		01		
2C		AND n	E6	
2D		10		
2E		JP Z	CA	
2F		$2A_L$		
30		03		
31		NOP	00	
32		JP	C3	Jump back to standby at 0306 to start new test cycle.
33		06_L		
34		03_H		
35		NOP	00	
36		NOP	00	

Flow Chart:

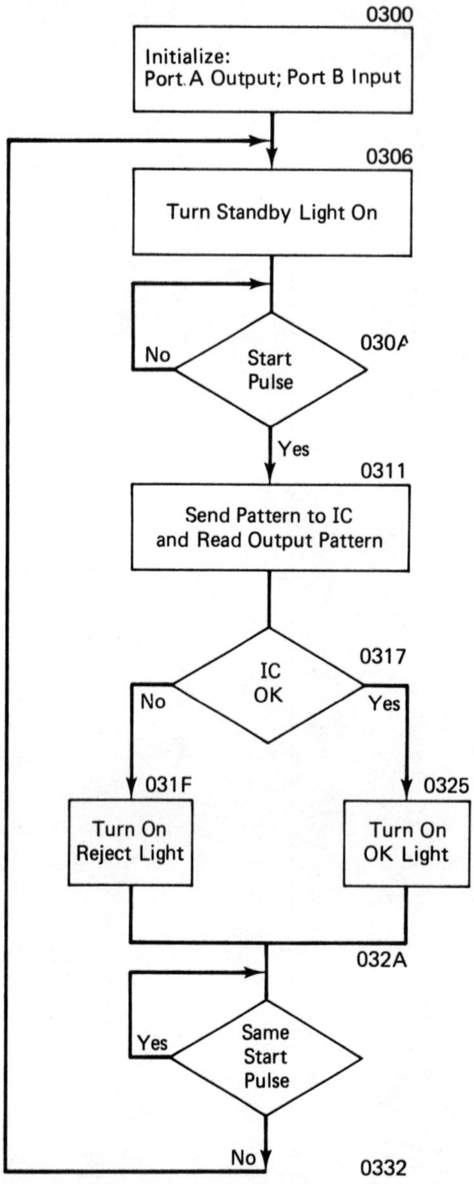

(a) Flow Chart

Pseudo Code:

Initialize:

Configure Port A Output and
Port B Input
Turn Standby Light On

Start Testing:

Read Start Pulse
If Active (Low) Then Start Test Cycle
Otherwise Go Back to Read Start Pulse

Send Pattern and Test:

Send the Pattern to IC Under Test
Read the Output Pattern
If Good IC, Turn On OK Light
If Bad IC, Turn On Reject Light

Check For Next:

If the Same Start Pulse
Loop Around
Otherwise Go Back to Start New Test Cycle

(b) Psuedo Code

Fig 9.9. Flowchart and pseudocode for the IC tester (Example 5).

and Table 9.2) is called to initialize port A as the output and port B as the input.

Between 0306 and 0316, the standby light is turned on, and the test pattern 0F is sent out to port A to activate the IC.

Between 0317 and 0329, the output pattern from the test IC is compared with 0A (the expected output). If the pattern checks, the OK light is turned on. Otherwise the reject light is turned on.

The program loops between 032A and 0330, if it is the same start pulse, implying the same IC in the test socket.

Finally the jump instruction at 0332 starts the new test cycle.

(c) *Extension to Other ICs.* Depending on the IC, the test socket and the test pattern may be changed. Fortunately for the 7408 quad two input AND gate, the pin configuration matches with that of 7400 NAND gate, so the socket connections need not be changed. For the connections shown in Figure 9.8, the output pattern $Y_3Y_2Y_1Y_0$ will be 1 1 1 1 = F for an input pattern of 1 1 1 1 = F. Thus the software may be modified to check for the output pattern of 1 1 1 1 and OK or reject the IC accordingly.

Example 9.5 is simple, but clearly illustrates the concept. The commercial IC testers are more sophisticated and usually check four or five noninteractive input and output patterns before accepting or rejecting an IC device. Also, there will be provisions to use the appropriate test sockets and assemblies (usually called personality modules) to suit the particular IC. Similarly, there will be software provisions to execute the appropriate routines.

Everything looks more sophisticated than it really is. The concept we learned in Example 9.5 can be easily extended to handle all the tasks mentioned above. Special problems are presented at the end of the chapter to help you obtain more insight into the test and instrumentation systems.

Naturally lots of questions should occur to you. How does the micro know that it should start executing the tester program from location 0300? (Refer to Table 9.3: the program starts at 0300). Where is the stack initiated? How to stop the program? How to get started?

Monitor and Initialization Routines

The answers to the questions raised in the previous section are contained in the monitor routines. After the power up (turn on), the microcomputer is structured to go into a definite state to begin the operation. In most cases, this is the reset state, as shown in Figure 9.10. Sometimes this state is also referred to as the "cold start" state.

Each time the reset is activated (remember, reset in any micro has the highest priority), the system reverts to the known reset state. It is a common

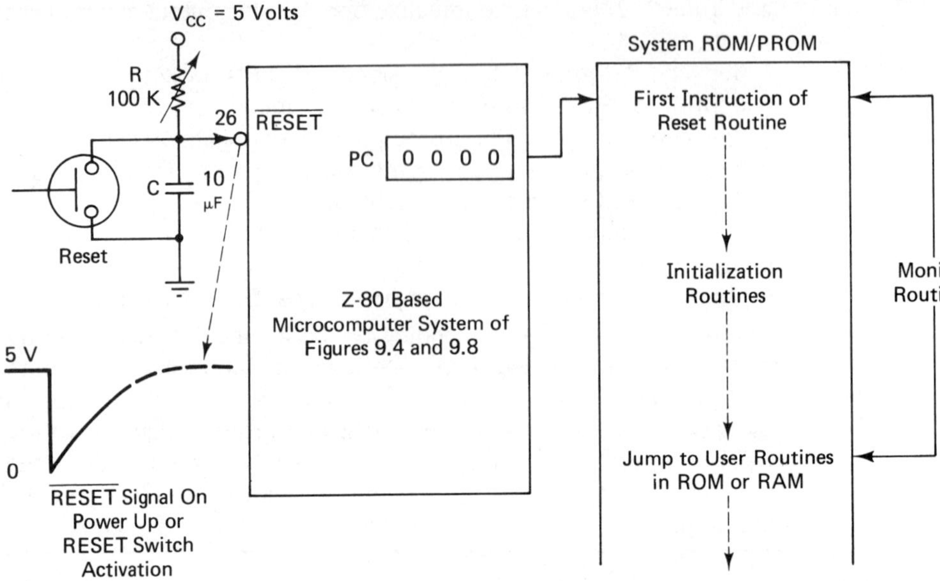

Fig 9.10. System initialization on reset, and the concept of monitor routines.

practice to reset the system when the micro goes wandering or does unusual things.

The reset and other system initialization and control programs are permanently contained in the system control ROM/PROM. These control programs are usually known as the monitor (or utility) routines, since they monitor the system operation.

In our particular case, the Z-80 has the reset address vector at location 0000. On the occurrence of the low active $\overline{\text{RESET}}$ signal, the micro will go to the vectored address location of 0000 and start executing the reset routine (please refer to Chapter 8 on interrupt and reset vectors). Sufficient initialization information can be contained in the reset monitor routine to enable the user to get started and use the microcomputer system.

Example 9.6 Monitor Routines

Develop the required reset and initialization monitor routines for the microcomputer system of Figure 9.10 (for details refer to Figures 9.8 and 9.4) such that

(a) The system is set to interrupt Mode 2.

(b) Stack pointer is initialized to the last RAM location (37FF in our case).

(c) The Y index register is initialized to the beginning of the RAM (3000 in our case).

(d) The RAM between 3000 and 37FF is cleared to all zero condition.

(e) System jumps to the user IC tester program at 0300.

Solution

(a) *Hardware*. The RC network of Figure 9.10 provides the low active $\overline{RESET}$ signal to the Z-80 microprocessor (whenever the power is turned on or the reset button is pushed). The $\overline{RESET}$ signal then recovers to its steady state inactive high level exponentially as shown in Figure 9.10, with a time constant T1 = RC s (variable up to 1 s).

(b) *Software*. When the $\overline{RESET}$ input to the Z-80 micro goes low active, the program counter is loaded with $(0000)_{Hex}$. The system executes the reset and initialization routines starting at location 0000.

The operating listings are shown in Table 9.4. Between 0000 and 000A, the system is set to interrupt mode 2, the stack pointer is loaded with $(37FF)_{Hex}$, and the 1Y index register is loaded with $(3000)_{Hex}$.

The call instruction at 000B uses the subroutine earlier developed (Example 9.3) to clear the memory.

Table 9.4. Z-80 Operating Listings for the Reset and Initialization Monitor Routines (Example 9.6).

Location	*Label*	*Mnemonic*	*Op Code*	*Comment*
0000	Reset	NOP	00	Linkage software.
01		NOP	00	
02		IM2	ED5E	
04		LD SP, nn	31	System set to interrupt mode 2.
05		FF_L		Stack pointer loaded with
06		37_H		$(37FF)_{Hex}$.
07		LD IY, nn	FD21	1Y register loaded with $(3000)_{Hex}$.
09		00_L		
0A		30_H		
0B		CALL	CD	"Clearing Memory" subroutines at
0C		$D8_L$		$(01D8)_{Hex}$ are called to clear
0D		01_H		memory.*
0E		NOP	00	Linkage software.
0F		NOP	00	
10		NOP	00	
11		JP nn	C3	IC tester program at $(0300)_{Hex}$ is
12		00_L		entered via the jump instruction.**
13		03_H		

* Subroutine at 01D8 clears memory (Table 9.1).
** IC tester program at 0300 tests ICs (Table 9.3).

The jump instruction at 0011 finally transfers the control to the user IC tester program (Example 9.5).

It should be emphasized that for our I/O microcomputer system, all the programs and routines are contained in the 2716 PROM. Figure 9.11 shows the memory and I/O map of our I/O computer system.

Example 9.6 clearly demonstrates that a microcomputer system can be integrated and made fully functional with the help of the monitor software contained in the system ROM/PROM. Any amount of sophistication can be built into the monitor routines. The high-resolution graphics, and handling of I/O such as disk drives and printers, are some examples of monitor software.

A microcomputer system with software and user routines contained in ROM/PROM (fixed programs that cannot be easily rewritten) is acceptable as a I/O bound microcomputer for dedicated applications. However, such a system is limited in usefulness for user programs and data that need to be changed frequently.

Interactive Microcomputer System

The limitation of our microcomputer system mentioned above can be easily corrected, and the system capabilities can be further extended to make the I/O microcomputer system a truly interactive microcomputer. Such a sys-

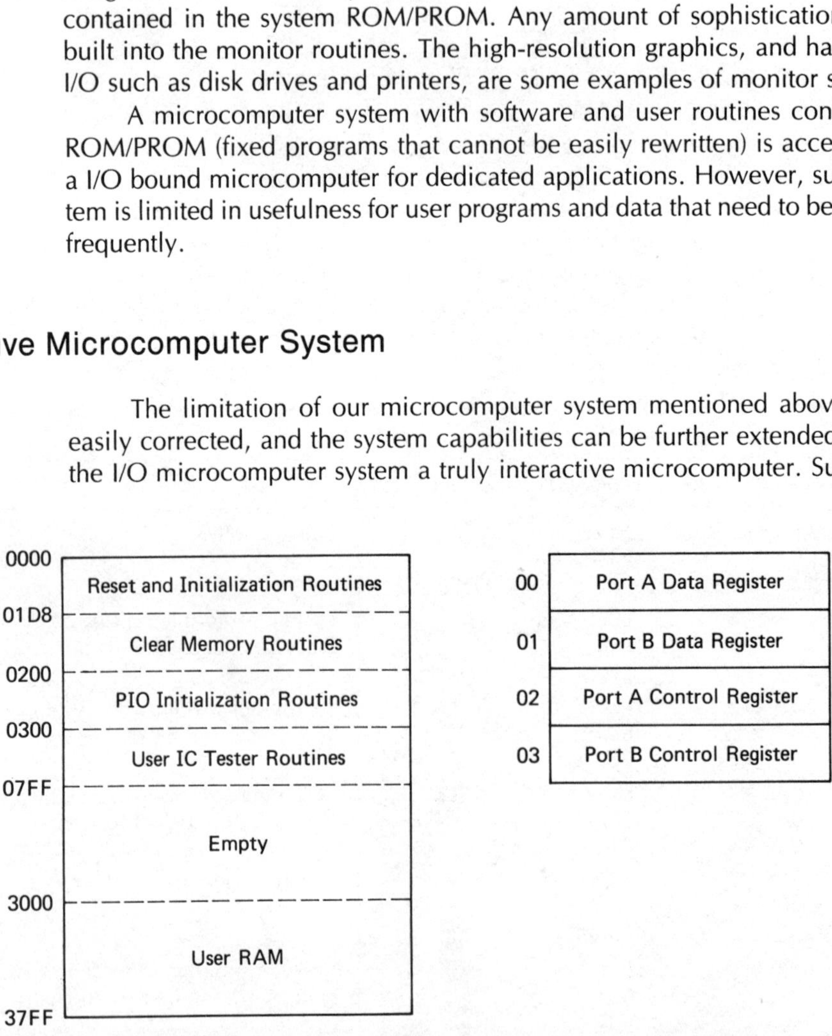

(a) Memory Map (b) I/O Map

Fig 9.11. Memory and I/O map for the microcomputer system.

tem requires the user data entry and display mechanisms as shown in Figure 9.12.

The data and programs can be entered through the keyboard and stored in the RAM, which can be readily modified. The contents of any location or the CPU registers can be examined on the display. Monitor routines can be written to handle the keyboard and display. All commercial microcomputer systems have this feature. Let us see if we can implement it on our system.

Figure 9.12 is a typical example of the interactive microcomputer. We are using additional PIO to interface the display and the keyboard.

When S1 is open, the system is in the program mode. The hex data corresponding to the key pressed is presented to the port B as input. The monitor software (to be written by the user) takes two successive valid hex digits and forms a data or instruction byte. These bytes will be sequentially stored in the RAM. (In our inexpensive system, the instructions have to be entered as the corresponding hex machine codes. Similarly, all data has to be entered as hex numbers.)

While the information is being entered, under software control, this information can be displayed on the 7-segment display. The entire operation seems complicated. However, we have done similar data entry and display operations quite a few times (refer to Sections 3.4, 7.1, and 11.3 for details).

Once the program and data entry is completed, S1 can be switched to the run position. The micro senses this and actually starts executing the program. We have specially designed the end-of-the-chapter problems to help complete the design of the interactive microcomputer system.

9.5. SUMMARY

In this chapter we have designed an operating microcomputer system with the Z-80. Of particular importance are the memory and the I/O handling methods. The memory and I/O decoding should be properly done such that at any given instant of time, only one single location is accessed.

We have extended the concepts of memory and I/O handling to actually design an I/O bound microcomputer system. The example of the IC tester is of considerable significance.

We also introduced the development of the monitor routines and system initialization and integration. Concepts have been discussed to further extend the system into a fully interactive microcomputer.

All the concepts learned in this chapter are very important, especially for individuals who want to specialize in actual microcomputer designs. These concepts can be easily extended to the other micros.

The Z-80 has many more capabilities than what we have been able to discuss here. Further reading is highly recommended, especially the Z-80 Mi-

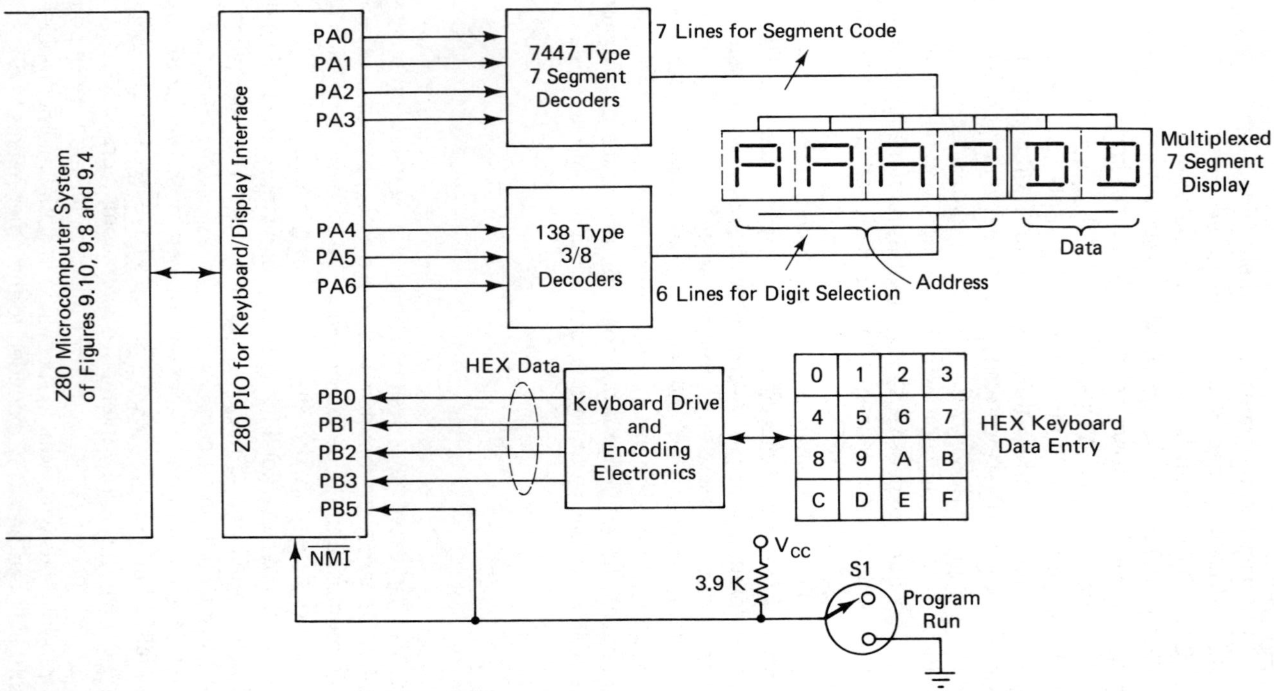

Fig 9.12. A Z-80-based interactive microcomputer system.

croprocessor Applications Reference Book by the Zilog Corporation, and *How to Program the Z-80,* by Rodney Zaks, a Radio Shack publication.

Problems

9.1. Design a conceptual microcomputer system similar to Figure 9.1, which has the Z-80 driving 16K × 8 RAM and 16K × 8 ROM. Show the functional modules with the real devices. Get the information from the corresponding data books.

9.2. In many situations, the microcomputer systems require 24 volts dc (to drive printers, etc.), 12 volts dc (to drive line drivers, etc.), in addition to 5 volts logic supply.

Develop a power distribution system, as shown in Figure 9.13, using the IC regulators of your choice. Show all the details.

9.3. Modify the input section of Figure 9.13 such that it can operate on 220 volts, 50 Hz. Show all the hardware details, with real devices.

9.4. The clock circuit of Figure 9.3 is an industry standard. Modify the circuit so that we can obtain three different clock signals at 6 MHz, 4 MHz and 2 MHz (Hint: You may replace the crystal of Figure 9.3 with a higher frequency crystal, perhaps 12 MHz!).

9.5. Design a clock circuit of your own choice to provide 4 MHz and 2 MHz outputs, with a drive capability of 10-unit TTL loads.

9.6. Design the complete hardware interface such that the memory modules 1, 2, 3 of Figure 9.14 have the following ranges:

Module 1 is 2716 type	2K × 8 PROM between 4000 to 47FF
Module 2 is 2716 type	2K × 8 PROM between 8000 to 87FF
Module 3 is 6116 type	2K × 8 RAM between 1000 to 37FF

9.7. Repeat Problem 9.6 such that the system supports 4K × 8 PROM in the lowest address range and 8K × 8 RAM in the highest address range.

Show all the details of the address decoding, loading, pullup, etc. The designed system should be fully functional.

9.8. Consider the system of Example 9.3, where the EPROM is contained between 0000 to 07FF and the RAM is contained between 3000 to 37FF.

Develop an operating program starting at 0700 (in the EPROM space), which can be called as a subroutine to generate 100 ms delay.

9.9. For the computer system of Problem 9.8, develop an operating software (as subroutines)

(a) At 0600 to store all CPU registers on stack.

(b) At 0650 to restore all CPU registers from the stack.

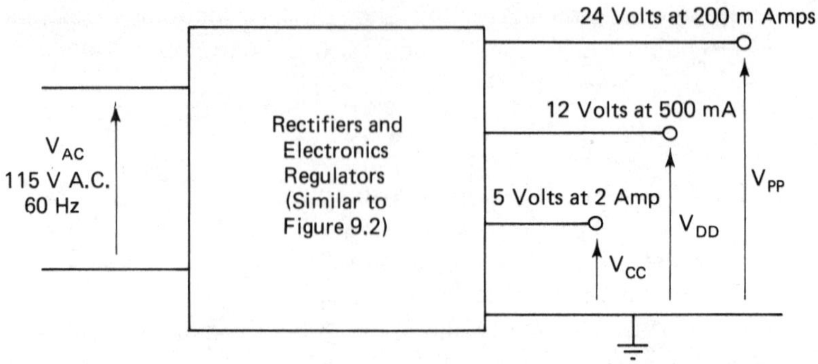

Fig 9.13. General purpose power distribution system for the microcomputer, Problems 9.2. and 9.3.

9.10. Using Figure 9.8 as the guideline for the Z-80 PIO and obtaining the additional information from the data book, design an I/O interface as shown in Figure 9.15 to have the port A and B data and control registers of:

PIO 2 at I/O locations 20, 21, 22, 23
PIO 3 at I/O locations 30, 31, 32, 33

Show the complete details of the hardware and interface. The system should be functional.

9.11. For the I/O computer system of Figure 9.15, develop a software routine to configure all the ports A as inputs and all the ports B as outputs.

9.12. The Z-80 based system can be effectively used as a testing system. Develop the additional software and hardware necessary to use the IC tester

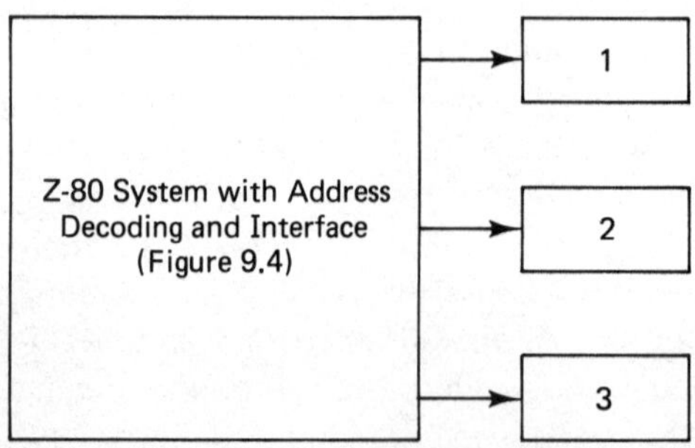

Fig 9.14. A Z-80-based memory interface for Problems 9.6 and 9.7.

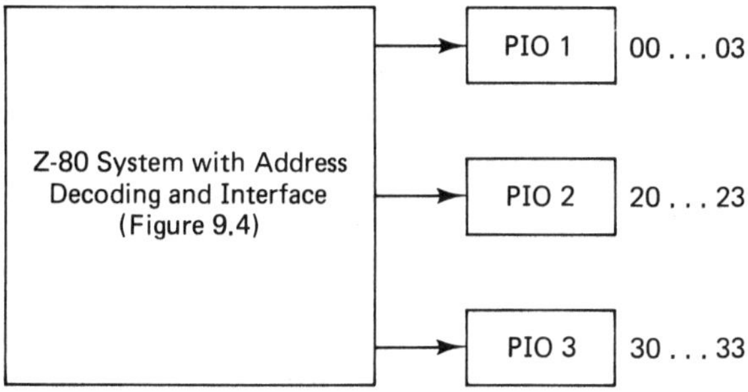

Fig 9.15. A Z-80-based I/O interface for Problems 9.10 and 9.11.

system of Example 9.5 to test

(a) 7474 D flip flops

(b) 7490-type counters

9.13. Repeat the IC tester Problem 9.12, where the Z-80 system alternates between testing the 7400 Nand gates and 7474 D flip flops. Show clearly all the software additions and the hardware (Hint: Multiplexing may be used to route the data between the micro and the test stations!).

9.14. Design a Z-80-based I/O computer system that will act as a function generator to produce

(a) Square wave output

(b) Triangular output

as shown in the Figure 9.16. Consider T1 = T2 and is variable between 100 μs to 100 ms.

9.15. Repeat Problem 9.14, so that the system can be switched between the square wave and the triangular wave generation, on the activation of the $\overline{\text{INT}}$ (interrupt) input.

9.16. As has been mentioned, the monitor routines are vital to the successful

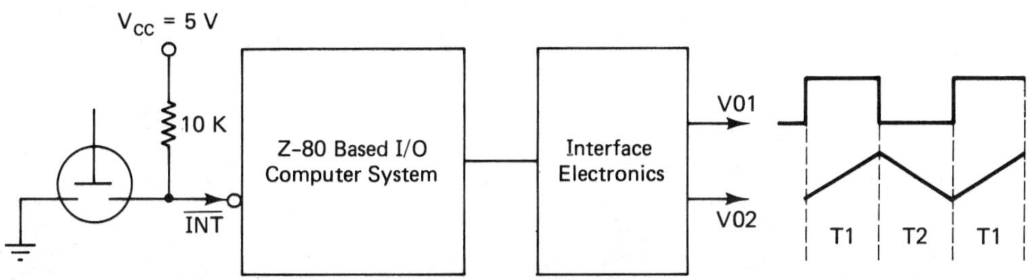

Fig 9.16. A Z-80-based function generator for Problems 9.14 and 9.15.

operation of any system. Develop the monitor routines (as subroutines), for the Z-80-based system being discussed.

(a) Starting at 0500 to generate 100 ms delay.

(b) Starting at 0550 to generate 1 s delay

9.17. Generate the monitor routines for the Z-80-based system

(a) Starting at 05A0 to convert a binary (hex) code to 7-segment code

(b) Starting at 0600 to convert the BCD into 7-segment code

9.18. For the interactive computer system of Figure 9.12, develop the operating hardware and software to

(a) Read the keyboard Hex data, store it in sequential RAM locations starting at $(3000)_{Hex}$.

(b) Display the last stored byte.

9.19. Extend Problem 9.18 so that the system becomes a true interactive computer. Take two successive valid key stores and formulate a hex byte and store it in the program memory space.

(a) Develop the complete operating software to enter the program into the system in the program mode (S1 in program position).

(b) Develop the operating software (as a monitor routine) such that the entered program will be executed in the run mode (S1 in run mode).

CHAPTER TEN

1802 Microprocessor and Microcomputer Systems

The COSMAC 1802 microprocessor developed and marketed by the RCA Corporation is one of the most widely used CMOS 8-bit microprocessors. Because of its low power capability due to the CMOS fabricating technology, the 1802 is well suited for low power applications. It is contained in a standard 40-pin dip package. It is supported by several memory and I/O devices developed with the CMOS technology. In this chapter we will study the important features of the 1802 microprocessor and introduce a typical 1802 microcomputer system.

10.1. GENERAL ARCHITECTURE OF COSMAC 1802

Figure 10.1 shows the basic architectural features and bus structure of the 1802 microprocessor.

Registers, Flags, and Bus Structures

As shown in Figure 10.1, the 1802 consists of:

16 × 16-bit register array	R(N); N = 0...F
8-bit accumulator	D
8-bit temporary register	T

4-bit registers	N
	P
	X
	I
8-bit ALU	ALU

The data manipulation is accomplished with these registers.

Register Structure

Register Array. Consists of sixteen 16-bit scratch pad registers. Each 16-bit register is divided into two 8-bit registers. The higher byte is designated as

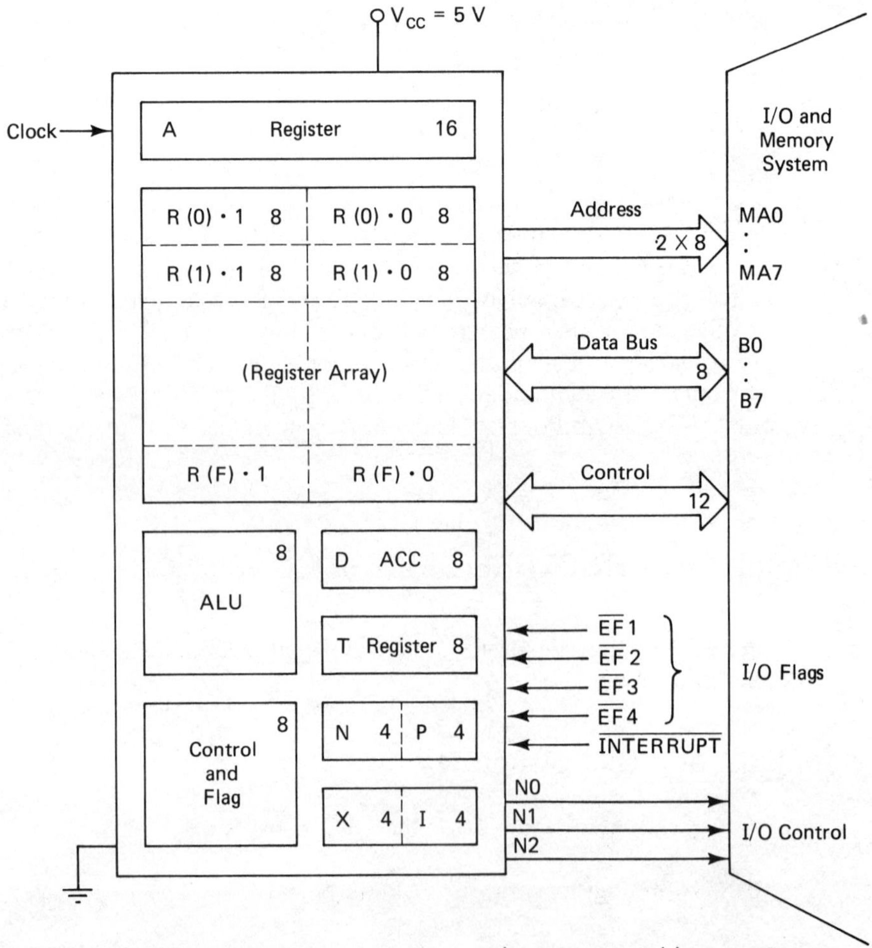

Fig 10.1. COSMAC 1802 programming structure with registers and buses. (Courtesy RCA Corporation.)

R(N) .1 and the lower byte as R(N) .0. The value of N, ranging from 0 to F, designates the particular register pair under consideration.

Under software control any of these registers can be used as a program counter, an index register, and a stack pointer.

Accumulator D. The 8-bit D register is the general purpose accumulator that holds the operand during the program.

Registers N, P, X, and I. These four, 4-bit registers refer to one of the scratch pad registers used for separate functions.

The N register contains the lower nibble of the op code and refers to one of the 16 scratch pad registers for data manipulation.

The P register contains a 4-bit word that sets one of the scratch pad registers as the program counter. This programmable program-counter concept is far reaching and adds an extra dimension to the processing capability of the 1802 microprocessor.

The X register contains a 4-bit word that sets one of the scratch pad registers as the data pointer for data transfer between the CPU and outside memory and I/O.

The I register contains the upper nibble of the op code, which is decoded for the CPU control and operation.

There are software instructions to directly load any number in the P and X registers (SEP and SEX). The I and N registers get loaded by virtue of the op code byte.

Temporary Reg T. This 8-bit T register is used to hold the contents of P and X registers during the interrupt routines.

Buffer Register A. This 16-bit A register is used to help the data transfers between the scratch pad registers and also to handle the address bus multiplexing as we will observe later.

Arithmetic Logic Unit (ALU). This 8-bit unit is similar to ALU in any other 8-bit microprocessor and is used for arithmetic and logical manipulation of the 8-bit data.

It looks as though the architecture of the 1802 microprocessor is overly involved and complicated. However, it can be handled very easily with the proper notation. Fortunately the instruction set of the 1802 is very systematic and logically supports the powerful architecture. The notation we will follow is that of RCA and is shown in Table 10.1.

Flag Structure

The flag structure of the 1802 is different from the other 8-bit microprocessors. Basically it contains three internal flags: DF, 1E, and Q.

Table 10.1. COSMAC 1802 Notation.

R	Register
R(N)	Register N, where N = 0, 1, ... F
R(N).1	High byte of register N
R(N).0	Low byte of register N
R(P)	Register specified by P (program counter)
R(X)	Register specified by X (data pointer)
M(R(X))	Memory pointed by contents of R(X)
M(R(P))	Memory pointed by contents of R(P)

DF Flag. This is similar to the carry and borrow flag and holds the overflow information due to arithmetic and logical operation.

IE Flag. This is the interrupt enable flag, set or cleared under the software control, to enable or disable the interrupts.

Q Flag. This is the I/O flag, whose status is brought outside to control the peripherals. The Q flag can be set or reset under the program control.

In addition, there are four input flags $\overline{EF1}$...$\overline{EF4}$, which can be read for conditional branch operations.

Bus Structure

Address Bus. This is the 8-bit address bus, which provides the high and low address bytes in sequence. The high byte of the address is provided first and is latched in the memory or I/O device connected to the 1802 microprocessor. The lower byte of the address is then placed on the bus. Thus, effectively a 16-bit address vector is provided on the 8-bit address bus, which can be used to address up to 64K locations.

Data Bus. Bidirectional data bus provides 8-bit data transfer between CPU and external devices.

Control Bus. The control bus contains control signals such as memory read and write ($\overline{MRD}$, $\overline{MWR}$); direct memory access ($\overline{DMA}$ In, $\overline{DMA}$ Out); status codes (SCO, SCI); clear and wait ($\overline{CLEAR}$, $\overline{WAIT}$); and timing (Clock In, $\overline{XTAL}$, TPA, and TPB), which will aid the data transfer between CPU and external devices. COSMAC manual and manufacturer's data sheets should be consulted for further information.

Reset and Interrupt Vectors

Reset

The occurrence of the low active $\overline{CLEAR}$ signal resets the 1802 microprocessor. Scratch pad register R(0) is configured as the program counter, with

$(0000)_{Hex}$ loaded into it. Thus, after the reset, the program always starts at location $(0000)_{Hex}$.

Interrupt

On the occurrence of the interrupt, R(1) is configured as the interrupt program counter. P and X nibbles are stored in the T register. After conclusion of the current instruction, the CPU will branch to the interrupt service routine, as specified by R(1) register.

At the end of the interrupt service routine, the occurrence of the RET instruction will restore the main program.

Example 10.1 1802 Architecture

In a particular application, P, X, and N registers are loaded with 3, 5, and 6.

(a) Specify which scratch pad registers are configured as program counter (PC), data pointer (DP), and operand register (OR).

(b) If $\overline{\text{Interrupt}}$ occurs and is accepted, which register is the new PC? What are the contents of T register?

(c) While interrupt is being serviced, if the 1802 microprocessor is reset by $\overline{\text{CLEAR}}$ signal, what will be the contents of the P and N registers?

Solution

(a) *Registers*. The P, X, and N registers specify the PC, DP, and OR. Thus,

Program counter (PC) is	R(3)
Data pointer (DP) is	R(5)
Operand register is	R(6)

(b) *Interrupt*. The new program counter is R(1). This implies that P register is loaded with 1. On the occurrence of the $\overline{\text{Interrupt}}$, P and X registers are stored in T register. Thus,

T register contains $(36)_{Hex}$

(c) *Reset*. When the 1802 microprocessor is reset, the P register is loaded with 0, so that R(0) becomes the program counter. The contents of the N register are unaffected. Thus

P register contains 0
N register unaffected

10.2. INSTRUCTION SET AND ADDRESSING MODES

The 1802 microprocessor is supported by a very powerful instruction set. There are special control instructions to load the P and X registers. Similarly, the short and long branch instructions and the skip instructions provide effective means of handling the conditional branching.

Mnemonics and Op Codes

Table 10.2 provides the instruction summary, mnemonics, and the corresponding op codes. The reader is urged to examine and understand these instructions. Most of them are self-explanatory.

Addressing Modes

There are basically four addressing modes. Fortunately the formatting of the instruction itself identifies the proper addressing mode. There is no necessity to specify the addressing mode separately. However, a clear understanding of these addressing modes will help us use the instruction set very efficiently.

Register Addressing

In this mode, the four lower bits of the instruction byte refer to one of the 16 registers. This allows the manipulation of the data contained in one of the 16 registers.

Example (To decrement register N, with N = 7):

Mnemonic	*General Op Code*	*Specific Op Code*	*Function*
DEC	2N	–	Decrement R(N)
DEC	–	27	Decrement R(7)

Thus N = 0...F, refers to any of the 16 registers (N forms the lower four bits of the instruction).

Table 10.2. 1802 Microprocessor Instruction Set. (Courtesy and copyright RCA.)

INSTRUCTION SET

The COSMAC instruction summary is given in Table I. Hexadecimal notation is used to refer to the 4-bit binary codes.

In all registers bits are numbered from the least significant bit (LSB) to the most significant bit (MSB) starting with 0.

R(W): Register designated by W, where W=N or X, or P

R(W).0: Lower-order byte of R(W)
R(W).1: Higher-order byte of R(W)
NO = Least significant Bit of N Register

Operation Notation
M(R(N)) →D; R(N) + 1

This notation means: The memory byte pointed to by R(N) is loaded into D, and R(N) is incremented by 1.

INSTRUCTION	MNEMONIC	OP CODE	OPERATION
MEMORY REFERENCE			
LOAD VIA N	LDN	0N	M(R(N))→D; FOR N NOT 0
LOAD ADVANCE	LDA	4N	M(R(N))→D; R(N) +1
LOAD VIA X	LDX	F0	M(R(X))→D
LOAD VIA X AND ADVANCE	LDXA	72	M(R(X))→D; R(X) +1
LOAD IMMEDIATE	LDI	F8	M(R(P))→D; R(P) +1
STORE VIA N	STR	5N	D→M(R(N))
STORE VIA X AND DECREMENT	STXD	73	D→M(R(X)); R(X) −1
REGISTER OPERATIONS			
INCREMENT REG N	INC	1N	R(N) +1
DECREMENT REG N	DEC	2N	R(N) −1
INCREMENT REG X	IRX	60	R(X) +1
GET LOW REG N	GLO	8N	R(N).0→D
PUT LOW REG N	PLO	AN	D→R(N).0
GET HIGH REG N	GHI	9N	R(N).1→D
PUT HIGH REG N	PHI	BN	D→R(N).1
LOGIC OPERATIONS♦♦			
OR	OR	F1	M(R(X)) OR D→D
OR IMMEDIATE	ORI	F9	M(R(P)) OR D→D; R(P) +1
EXCLUSIVE OR	XOR	F3	M(R(X)) XOR D→D
EXCLUSIVE OR IMMEDIATE	XRI	FB	M(R(P)) XOR D→D; R(P) +1
AND	AND	F2	M(R(X)) AND D→D
AND IMMEDIATE	ANI	FA	M(R(P)) AND D→D; R(P) +1
SHIFT RIGHT	SHR	F6	SHIFT D RIGHT, LSB(D)→DF, 0→MSB(D)
SHIFT RIGHT WITH CARRY	SHRC }	76♦	SHIFT D RIGHT, LSB(D)→DF, DF→MSB(D)
RING SHIFT RIGHT	RSHR }		
SHIFT LEFT	SHL	FE	SHIFT D LEFT, MSB(D)→DF, 0→LSB(D)
SHIFT LEFT WITH CARRY	SHLC }	7E♦	SHIFT D LEFT, MSB(D)→DF, DF→LSB(D)
RING SHIFT LEFT	RSHL }		

♦NOTE THIS INSTRUCTION IS ASSOCIATED WITH MORE THAN ONE MNEMONIC. EACH MNEMONIC IS INDIVIDUALLY LISTED.

♦♦NOTE THE ARITHMETIC OPERATIONS AND THE SHIFT INSTRUCTIONS ARE THE ONLY INSTRUCTIONS THAT CAN ALTER THE DF.
AFTER AN ADD INSTRUCTION
DF = 1 DENOTES A CARRY HAS OCCURRED
DF = 0 DENOTES A CARRY HAS NOT OCCURRED
AFTER A SUBTRACT INSTRUCTION
DF = 1 DENOTES NO BORROW. D IS A TRUE POSITIVE NUMBER
DF = 0 DENOTES A BORROW. D IS TWO'S COMPLEMENT
THE SYNTAX "−(NOT DF)" DENOTES THE SUBTRACTION OF THE BORROW

Table 10.2 (*Continued*)

INSTRUCTION	MNEMONIC	OP CODE	OPERATION
ARITHMETIC OPERATIONS♦♦			
ADD	ADD	F4	M(R(X)) +D→DF, D
ADD IMMEDIATE	ADI	FC	M(R(P)) +D→DF, D; R(P) +1
ADD WITH CARRY	ADC	74	M(R(X)) +D +DF→DF, D
ADD WITH CARRY, IMMEDIATE	ADCI	7C	M(R(P)) +D +DF→DF, D R(P) +1
SUBTRACT D	SD	F5	M(R(X))–D→DF, D
SUBTRACT D IMMEDIATE	SDI	FD	M(R(P))–D→DF, D; R(P) +1
SUBTRACT D WITH BORROW	SDB	75	M(R(X))–D–(NOT DF)→DF, D
SUBTRACT D WITH BORROW, IMMEDIATE	SDBI	7D	M(R(P))–D–(NOT DF)→DF, D; R(P) +1
SUBTRACT MEMORY	SM	F7	D–M(R(X))→DF, D
SUBTRACT MEMORY IMMEDIATE	SMI	FF	D–M(R(P))→DF, D; R(P) +1
SUBTRACT MEMORY WITH BORROW	SMB	77	D–M(R(X))–(NOT DF)→DF, D
SUBTRACT MEMORY WITH BORROW, IMMEDIATE	SMBI	7F	D–M(R(P))–(NOT DF)→DF, D R(P) +1
BRANCH INSTRUCTIONS–SHORT BRANCH			
SHORT BRANCH	BR	30	M(R(P))→R(P).0
NO SHORT BRANCH (SEE SKP)	NBR	38♦	R(P) +1
SHORT BRANCH IF D=0	BZ	32	IF D=0, M(R(P))→R(P).0 ELSE R(P) +1
SHORT BRANCH IF D NOT 0	BNZ	3A	IF D NOT 0, M(R(P))→R(P).0 ELSE R(P) +1
SHORT BRANCH IF DF=1	BDF	33♦	IF DF=1, M(R(P))→R(P).0 ELSE R(P) +1
SHORT BRANCH IF POS OR ZERO	BPZ		
SHORT BRANCH IF EQUAL OR GREATER	BGE		
SHORT BRANCH IF DF=0	BNF	3B♦	IF DF=0, M(R(P))→R(P).0 ELSE R(P) +1
SHORT BRANCH IF MINUS	BM		
SHORT BRANCH IF LESS	BL		
SHORT BRANCH IF Q=1	BQ	31	IF Q=1, M(R(P))→R(P).0 ELSE R(P) +1
SHORT BRANCH IF Q=0	BNQ	39	IF Q=0, M(R(P))→R(P).0 ELSE R(P) +1
SHORT BRANCH IF EF1=1 (1 = V_{SS})	B1	34	IF EF1=1, M(R(P))→R(P).0 ELSE R(P) +1
SHORT BRANCH IF EF1=0 (0 = V_{CC})	BN1	3C	IF EF1=0, M(R(P))→R(P).0 ELSE R(P) +1
SHORT BRANCH IF EF2=1 (1 = V_{SS})	B2	35	IF EF2=1, M(R(P))→R(P).0 ELSE R(P) +1
SHORT BRANCH IF EF2=0 (0 = V_{CC})	BN2	3D	IF EF2=0, M(R(P))→R(P).0 ELSE R(P) +1
SHORT BRANCH IF EF3=1 (1 = V_{SS})	B3	36	IF EF3=1, M(R(P))→R(P).0 ELSE R(P) +1
SHORT BRANCH IF EF3=0 (0 = V_{CC})	BN3	3E	IF EF3=0, M(R(P))→R(P).0 ELSE R(P) +1
SHORT BRANCH IF EF4=1 (1 = V_{SS})	B4	37	IF EF4=1, M(R(P))→R(P).0 ELSE R(P) +1
SHORT BRANCH IF EF4=0 (0 = V_{CC})	BN4	3F	IF EF4=0, M(R(P))→R(P).0 ELSE R(P) +1

♦NOTE: THIS INSTRUCTION IS ASSOCIATED WITH MORE THAN ONE MNEMONIC. EACH MNEMONIC IS INDIVIDUALLY LISTED.

♦♦NOTE: THE ARITHMETIC OPERATIONS AND THE SHIFT INSTRUCTIONS ARE THE ONLY INSTRUCTIONS THAT CAN ALTER THE DF.
AFTER AN ADD INSTRUCTION:
DF = 1 DENOTES A CARRY HAS OCCURRED
DF = 0 DENOTES A CARRY HAS NOT OCCURRED
AFTER A SUBTRACT INSTRUCTION:
DF = 1 DENOTES NO BORROW. D IS A TRUE POSITIVE NUMBER
DF = 0 DENOTES A BORROW. D IS TWO'S COMPLEMENT
THE SYNTAX "–(NOT DF)" DENOTES THE SUBTRACTION OF THE BORROW

Table 10.2 *(Continued)*

INSTRUCTION	MNEMONIC	OP CODE	OPERATION
BRANCH INSTRUCTIONS—LONG BRANCH			
LONG BRANCH	LBR	C0	M(R(P))→R(P).1 M(R(P) +1)→R(P).0
NO LONG BRANCH (SEE LSKP)	NLBR	C8♦	R(P) +2
LONG BRANCH IF D=0	LBZ	C2	IF D=0, M(R(P))→R(P).1 M(R(P) +1)→R(P).0 ELSE R(P) +2
LONG BRANCH IF D NOT 0	LBNZ	CA	IF D NOT 0, M(R(P))→R(P).1 M(R(P) +1)→R(P).0 ELSE R(P) +2
LONG BRANCH IF DF=1	LBDF	C3	IF DF=1 M(R(P))→R(P).1 M(R(P) +1)→R(P).0 ELSE R(P) +2
LONG BRANCH IF DF=0	LBNF	CB	IF DF=0, M(R(P))→R(P).1 M(R(P) +1)→R(P).0 ELSE R(P) +2
LONG BRANCH IF Q=1	LBQ	C1	IF Q=1, M(R(P))→R(P).1 M(R(P) +1)→R(P).0 ELSE R(P) +2
LONG BRANCH IF Q=0	LBNQ	C9	IF Q=0, M(R(P))→R(P).1 M(R(P) +1)→R(P).0 ELSE R(P) +2
SKIP INSTRUCTIONS			
SHORT SKIP (SEE NBR)	SKP	38♦	R(P) +1
LONG SKIP (SEE NLBR)	LSKP	C8♦	R(P) +2
LONG SKIP IF D=0	LSZ	CE	IF D=0, R(P) +2 ELSE CONTINUE
LONG SKIP IF D NOT 0	LSNZ	C6	IF D NOT 0, R(P) +2 ELSE CONTINUE
LONG SKIP IF DF=1	LSDF	CF	IF DF=1, R(P) +2 ELSE CONTINUE
LONG SKIP IF DF=0	LSNF	C7	IF DF=0, R(P) +2 ELSE CONTINUE
LONG SKIP IF Q=1	LSQ	CD	IF Q=1, R(P) +2 ELSE CONTINUE
LONG SKIP IF Q=0	LSNQ	C5	IF Q=0, R(P) +2 ELSE CONTINUE
LONG SKIP IF IE=1	LSIE	CC	IF IE=1, R(P) +2 ELSE CONTINUE
CONTROL INSTRUCTIONS			
IDLE	IDL	00#	WAIT FOR DMA OR INTERRUPT; M(R(0))→BUS
NO OPERATION	NOP	C4	CONTINUE
SET P	SEP	DN	N→P
SET X	SEX	EN	N→X
SET Q	SEQ	7B	1→Q
RESET Q	REQ	7A	0→Q
SAVE	SAV	78	T→M(R(X))
PUSH X,P TO STACK	MARK	79	(X,P)→T; (X,P)→M(R(2)) THEN P→X; R(2)−1
RETURN	RET	70	M(R(X))→(X,P); R(X) +1 1→IE
DISABLE	DIS	71	M(R(X))→(X,P); R(X) +1 0→IE

#An idle instruction initiates a repeating S1 cycle. The processor will continue to idle until an I/O request ($\overline{\text{INTERRUPT}}$, $\overline{\text{DMA-IN}}$, or $\overline{\text{DMA-OUT}}$) is activated. When the request is acknowledged, the IDLE cycle is terminated and the I/O request is serviced, and then normal operation is resumed.

♦NOTE: THIS INSTRUCTION IS ASSOCIATED WITH MORE THAN ONE MNEMONIC. EACH MNEMONIC IS INDIVIDUALLY LISTED.

Table 10.2 *(Continued)*

INSTRUCTION	MNEMONIC	OP CODE	OPERATION
INPUT–OUTPUT BYTE TRANSFER			
OUTPUT 1	OUT 1	61	M(R(X))→BUS; R(X) +1; N LINES = 1
OUTPUT 2	OUT 2	62	M(R(X))→BUS; R(X) +1; N LINES = 2
OUTPUT 3	OUT 3	63	M(R(X))→BUS; R(X) +1; N LINES = 3
OUTPUT 4	OUT 4	64	M(R(X))→BUS; R(X) +1; N LINES = 4
OUTPUT 5	OUT 5	65	M(R(X))→BUS; R(X) +1; N LINES = 5
OUTPUT 6	OUT 6	66	M(R(X))→BUS; R(X) +1; N LINES = 6
OUTPUT 7	OUT 7	67	M(R(X))→BUS; R(X) +1; N LINES = 7
INPUT 1	INP 1	69	BUS→M(R(X)); BUS→D; N LINES = 1
INPUT 2	INP 2	6A	BUS→M(R(X)); BUS→D; N LINES = 2
INPUT 3	INP 3	6B	BUS→M(R(X)); BUS→D; N LINES = 3
INPUT 4	INP 4	6C	BUS→M(R(X)); BUS→D; N LINES = 4
INPUT 5	INP 5	6D	BUS→M(R(X)); BUS→D; N LINES = 5
INPUT 6	INP 6	6E	BUS→M(R(X)); BUS→D; N LINES = 6
INPUT 7	INP 7	6F	BUS→M(R(X)); BUS→D; N LINES = 7

Register Indirect Addressing

In this addressing mode, one of the 16 CPU registers is used as a memory pointer and holds the address of the operand.

Example [To load from memory specified by R(N)]:

Mnemonic	*General Op Code*	*Specific Op Code*	*Function*
LDN	ON	–	Load via R(N)
	–	07	Load from memory addressed by R(7)

Suppose R(7) contains $(0043)_{Hex}$. The contents of the location 0043 are loaded into the accumulator D, as shown.

Location	Memory	-D- Accumulator
0043 ⟶	[35] ⟶	[35]

Immediate Addressing

In this mode, the operand follows the instruction byte immediately.

Example (Load immediate data into D accumulator):

Mnemonic	*Op Code*	*Function*	
LDI	F8	Load immediate data of A2 into D accumulator	D AC
A2			

[A2]

Stack Addressing

One of the CPU registers is specified as an indexed stack pointer, to allow the sequential data transfers between the CPU and the memory in a stack configuration.

Example [To use R(8) as stack pointer and save R(A).1 and R(A).0 in sequential stack locations]:

Mnemonic	*Op Code*	*Function*
SEX(8) LDI #FF PLO R(8)*	E8 F8 A8	X = 8. So R(8) is data pointer. D loaded with FF and is transferred to R(8) as low byte.
LDI #00 PHI R(8)*	F8 B8	D loaded with 00 and is transferred to R(8) as high byte. R(8) = 00FF
GHI R(A)* STX D GLO R(A)* STX D	9A 73 8A 73	Load R(A) .1 into D and push on to stack. R(X) gets automatically decremented. Load R(A) .0 into D and push on to stack.

* The registers are explicitly specified only to promote the readability and understanding. They are actually specified as the lower 4-bit nibble of the op code.

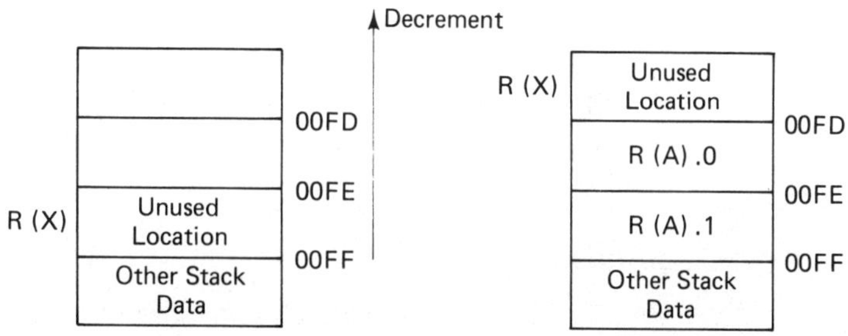

Stack Before Saving   Stack After Saving

The instructions, which effect the stack, are:

IRX	Increment X	LDX	Load via X
STX D	Store via X and decrement	LDXA	Load via X and increment

The long branch, short branch, and skip instructions of the 1802 family of microprocessors are perhaps unique and most versatile in the 8-bit micro-

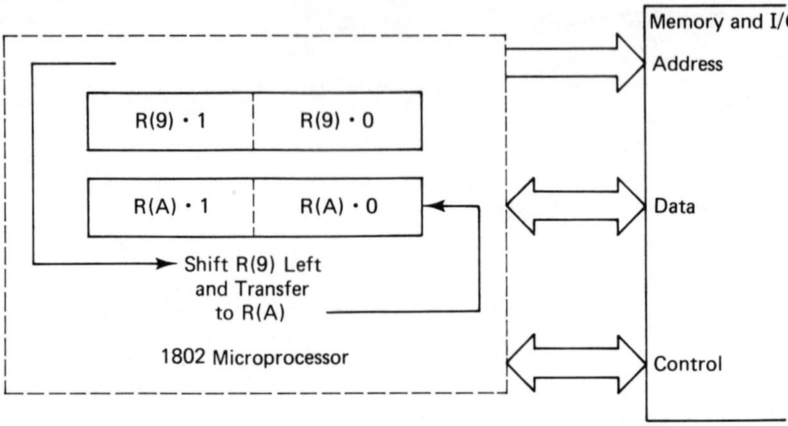

Fig 10.2. Shift and transfer operations (Example 2).

processor family. We will be using them extensively in the example problems discussed later.

Most of the 1802 instructions are 1 or 2 bytes long, with the exception of long branch instructions, which are 3 bytes long.

Example 10.2 1802 Instruction Set

In a particular data base management application, it is required to shift the contents of R(9) two positions left and transfer them to R(A), as shown in Figure 10.2.

(a) Develop the operating software starting at $(0100)_{Hex}$.
(b) If R(9) contains F0C2, what will be the contents of R(9) and R(A) after the operation?

Solution

(a) *Shift and Transfer Software*. The operation involves obtaining the low and high bytes of R(9) in sequence into the D accumulator, shifting them and transferring the resulting bytes into R(A). The SHLC (shift left with carry) ensures that the overflow from the low byte of R(9) is shifted as the LSB of the high byte. Table 10.3 shows the actual operating listings.
(b) *Contents of R(9) and R(A)*. The shift and transfer operations are shown in Figure 10.3. As can be seen, the contents of R(9) and R(A) are

R(9) = F0C2
R(A) = C308

Table 10.3. Operating Listings for Example 10.2.

Location	*Mnemonic*	*Op Code*	*Comment*
0100	GLO R(9)	89	Load low byte of R(9) into D and shift left one bit and store result in R(A).0.
01	SHL	FE	
02	PLO R(A)	AA	
03	GHI R(9)	99	Load high byte of R(9) into D and shift one bit through carry and store result in R(A).1.
04	SHLC	7E	
05	PHI R(A)	BA	
06	GLO R(A)	8A	Shift low byte of R(A) by one bit.
07	SHL	FE	
08	PLO R(A)	AA	
09	GHI R(A)	9A	Shift high byte of R(A) through carry, one bit.
0A	SHLC	7E	
0B	PHI R(A)	BA	
0C	IDL	00	Idle until reset/interrupt

Note: Between 0100 and 0105, the contents of R(9) are shifted one bit left and stored in R(A). The SHLC (shift left with carry) ensures that the overflow from low byte of R(9) is shifted as the LSB of the high byte. Between 0106 and 010B, the contents of R(A) are shifted left (again). Thus, effectively the contents of R(9) are shifted left twice and transferred to R(A).

The above example is fairly simple, but exposes the reader to the powerful instruction set. The register designations such as R(9) are included in the mnemonics to help the reader distinguish among various registers. In reality, the distinction is carried out in the op code (as lower nibble).

The GLO instruction with op code 89 refers to R(9). Similarly the same GLO instruction with op code 8A refers to R(A).

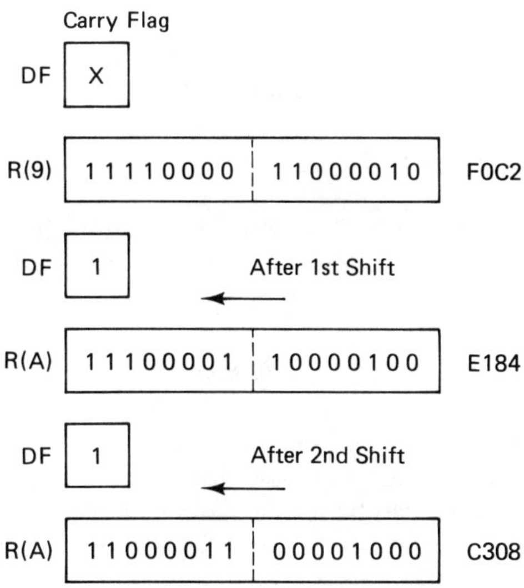

Fig 10.3. Contents of R(9) and R(A) during the shift and transfer operations (Example 2).

Several problems are presented at the end of the chapter to provide insight into the 1802 architectural and instructional features. The reader is encouraged to solve as many as possible.

10.3. 1802-BASED MICROCOMPUTER CONFIGURATION

As mentioned earlier, there are several memory and I/O support devices developed with the low power CMOS technology that can be easily interfaced to the 1802 microprocessor to form an operating microcomputer. One of the self-contained and relatively inexpensive single-board microcomputers is the "COSMAC CDP 185020" by the RCA Corporation. An improved version of the 1802/1804-based microcomputer system is the COSMAC 18S694 microboard computer system, which has an editor, assembler, and cassette and video interface capabilities. Both the systems are shown in Figure 10.4. The discussions presented in this chapter have been related to both systems and are equally applicable to any other 1802-based microcomputer, with few modifications.

System Components and Structure

Figure 10.5 shows a typical 1802-based microcomputer configuration. The 4555 binary decoders and 4028 decimal decoders provide the necessary address decoding and chip selection.

The 1822 RAMs

These RAMS (256 × 4 each) provide the minimum system memory of 256 bytes, which can be further expanded by adding more 1822 devices.

The 1831/1832 ROMs

These ROMS (512 × 8 each) provide the nonvolatile storage for the system utility and monitor programs. The 1824 RAM (32 × 8) is relatively fast and acts as a scratch pad memory for the utility operations.

The 1852 I/O Interface Devices

These function as 8-bit input or output ports and latches under the software control. The keyboard and display can be interfaced through an I/O port.

The system can be further expanded by adding additional devices. RCA has recently introduced more density RAMs and ROMs, and you are advised to consult the RCA data books.

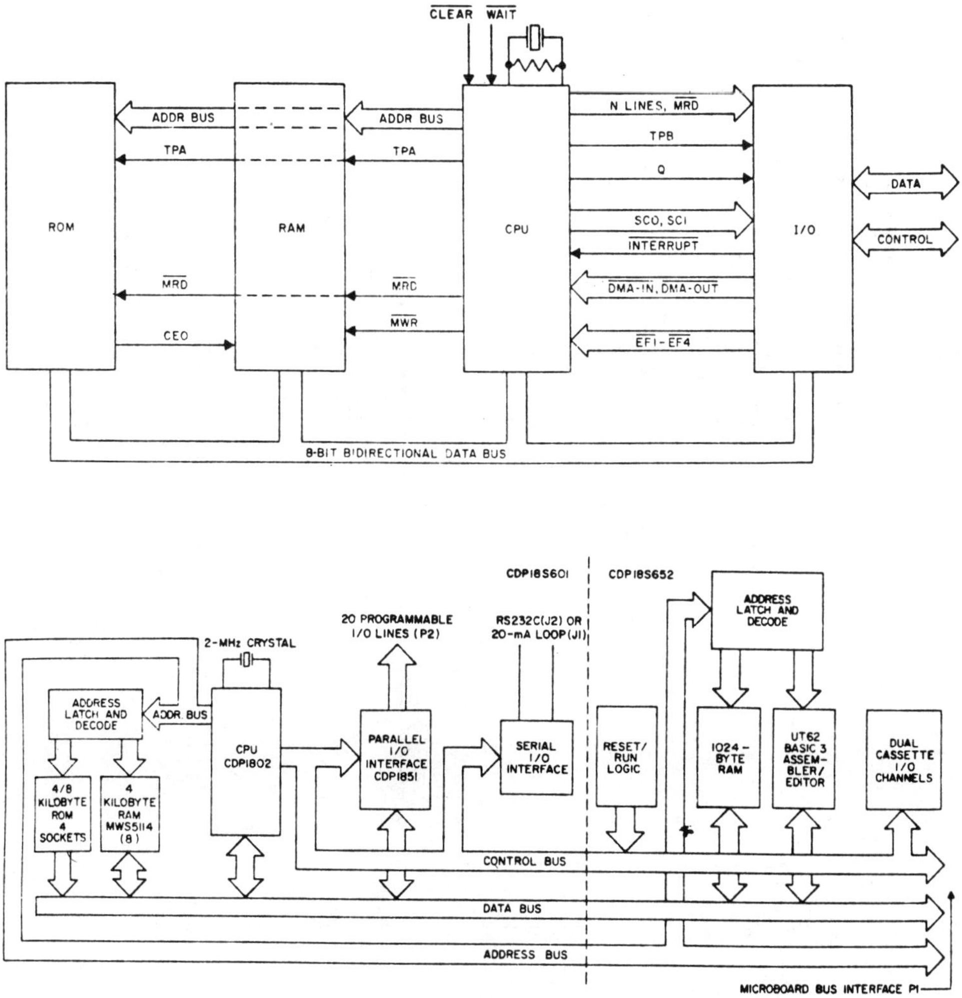

Fig 10.4. The 1802-based microcomputer configuration (courtesy RCA Corporation).

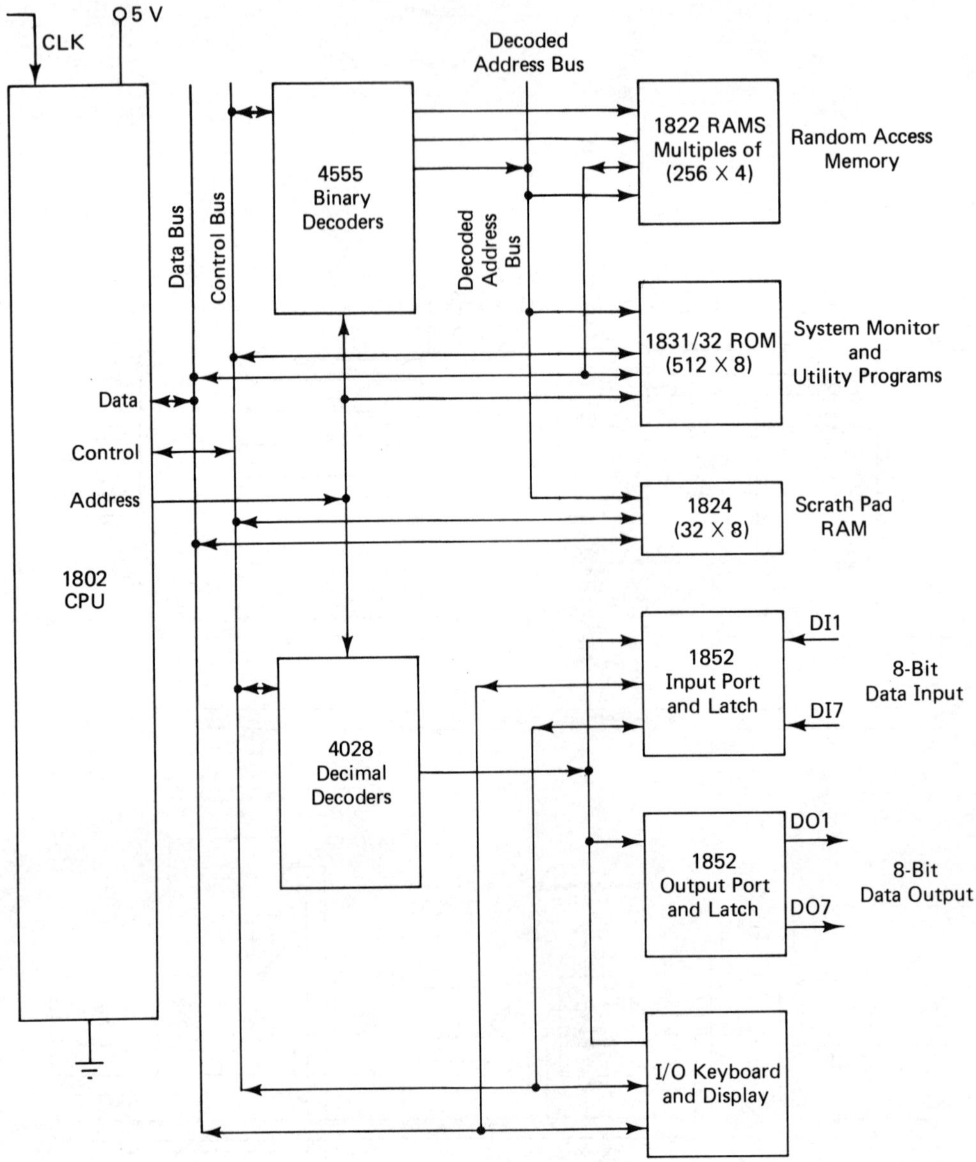

Fig 10.5. The 1802-based microcomputer system. (Courtesy RCA Corporation.)

System Timing and Control

Most of the 1802 instructions take two machine cycles (fetch and execute). Each machine cycle consists of eight clock cycles. The long branch and skip instructions, however, take three machine cycles.

For example, a GLO instruction with two machine cycles takes $2 \times 8 = 16$ clock cycles. If the 1802 is activated by 2 MHz clock, 16 clock cycles would correspond to 16×0.5 μs/cycle $= 8$ μs. This timing information is very important in generating timing and counter loads.

I/O Configuration

The 1802 microprocessor uses the I/O mapped I/O configuration. The specific input/output instructions clearly identify the addressed I/O port without having to go through involved initialization. The instruction "OUT 5" with op code 65 specifies that port 5 is the output port. We will introduce more about these I/O features with the help of an example problem.

Example 10.3 I/O Handling

Shown in Figure 10.6 is a typical I/O configuration, using the 1852 I/O interface devices.

(a) Identify the op codes that will address the output and input ports and explain the operation.
(b) Develop a simple software and hardware interface to read the input port, invert the contents, and drive the LEDs connected to the output port.

Solution

Referring to the manufacturer's data sheets and manual for CDP-1802 Microprocessor, we observe that the device 1852-1 is wired to act as input port (mode 0) and the other 1852-2 is wired as output (mode 1).

(a) *Input and Outport Ports.* From the instruction Table 10.2, we observe that the I/O instruction formatting is as shown.

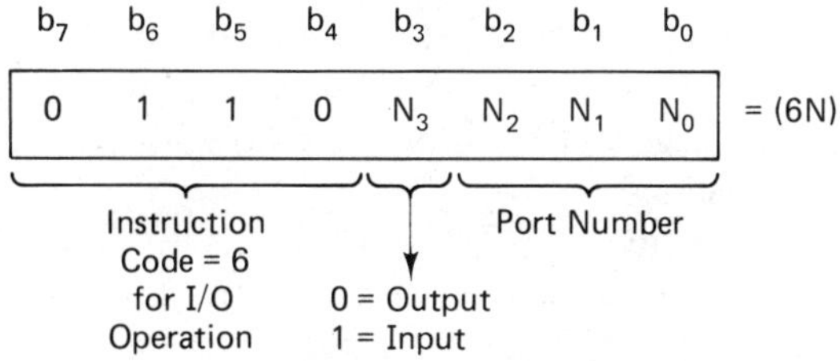

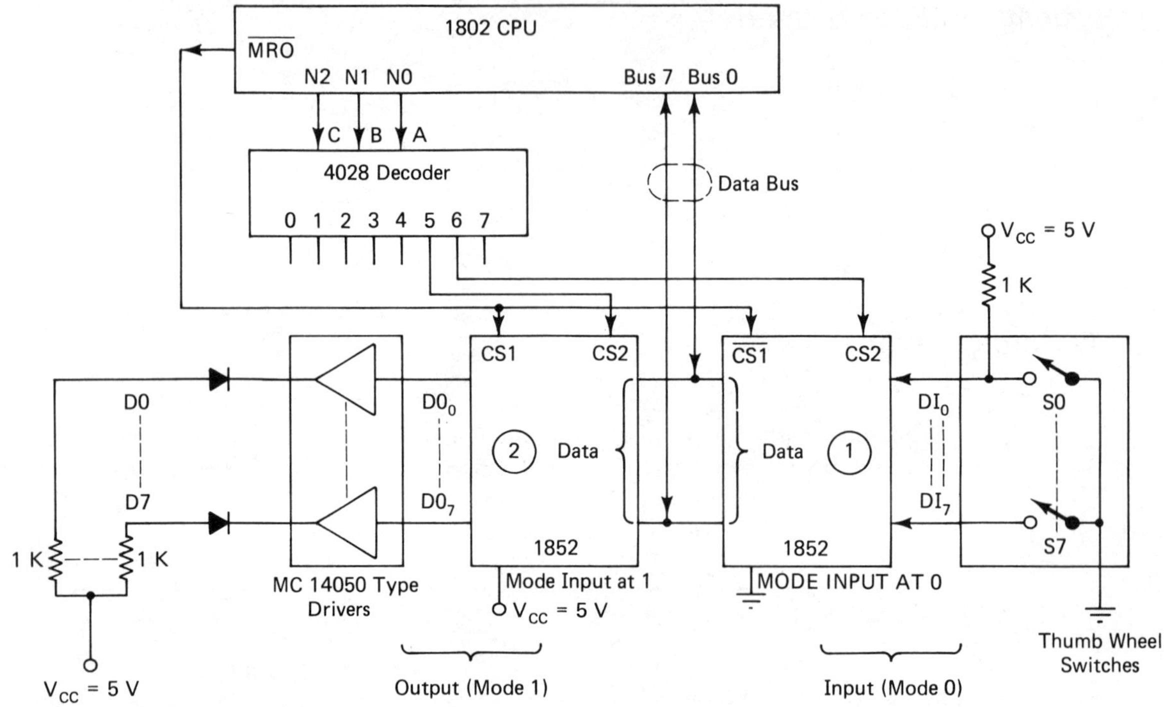

Fig 10.6. I/O configuration and handling for Example 3.

Decoded output 5 from the 4028 decoder ($N_2N_1N_0$ = 101) drives the output 1852 port. Thus the corresponding op code is 65. (make $b_3 = 0$).

Decoded output 6 ($N_2N_1N_0$) = 110 drives the input 1852 port. Thus the corresponding op code is 6E (make $b_3 = 1$).

Output Op Code	65
Input Op Code	6E

(b) *Data Input and Output.* As shown in Figure 10.6, the thumb wheel switch provides the input. The MC 14050 drivers connected to the output port drive the LEDs. Because of the latching action of 1852, D0...D7 information remains unchanged until the next information is written.

Figure 10.7 shows the flow chart and Table 10.4 gives the operating listings.

Between 0000 and 0006, R(6) is configured as the data pointer. The memory location specified by R(6) (in this case 00A0) acts as the entry and exit for all the I/O data operations.

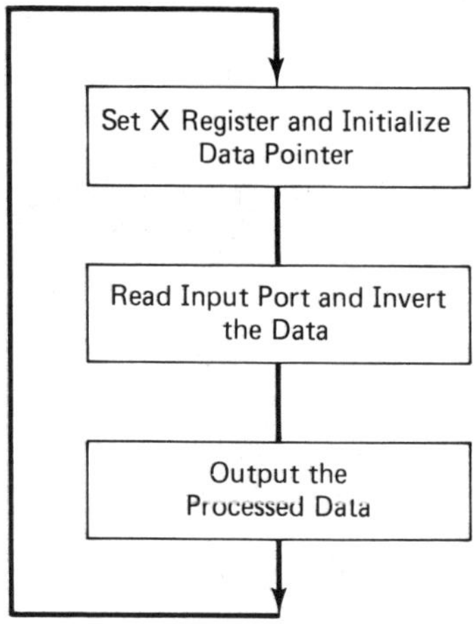

Fig 10.7. Flowchart for the I/O operation of Example 3.

Between 0007 and 000F the input data is read from port 6, inverted and output to port 5. Then the program is branched back to start the next I/O operation.

The reader is urged to solve the several example problems at the end of the chapter specifically designed to provide insight into practical I/O bound applications.

Table 10.4. Listings for I/O (Example 10.3).

Location	*Mnemonic*	*Op Code*	*Comment*
0000	SEX	E6	Load X = 6; R(6) is data pointer.
01	LDI	F8	Load 00A0 into (R6) so that the I/O data is stored at location 00A0, as pointed by R(6).
02	00		
03	PHI R(6)	B6	
04	LDI	F8	
05	A0		
06	PLO R(6)	A6	
07	→INP 6	6E	Input switch data from port 6 and invert it by exclusive Oring with FF and store at data location 00A0.
08	XRI	FB	
09	FF		
0A	STR M(R(6))	56	
0B	OUT 5	65	Output the processed data to port 5. In that process R(6) gets incremented to 00A1. Decrement R(6) to point to 00A0.
0C	DEC R(6)	26	
0D	NOP	C4	
0E	BR	30	Branch to 07 location, to start next I/O operation.
0F	07		

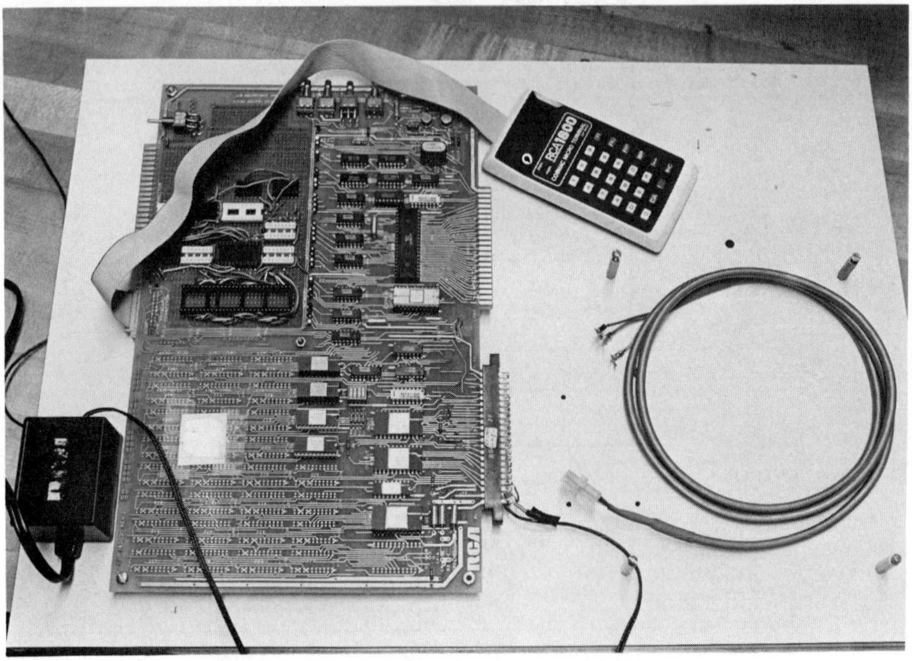

Fig 10.8. Single-board microcomputer systems such as the 18S020/21/25.

10.4. THE CDP=18S020/21 COSMAC MICROCOMPUTER

Developed and marketed by the RCA Corporation, the COSMAC single-board microcomputer system is shown in Figure 10.8. It is relatively inexpensive and contains the required processing and I/O features required for our applications. The data entry into the microcomputer is through the calculator type keyboard/display terminal. To better understand the applications that follow in the next chapter, the reader is requested to read the 18S020/21 operating manual and comprehend it.

While this book was being developed, RCA introduced a more powerful microcomputer system, COSMAC-18S694 (shown in Figure 10.9), which has all the features of the 18S020 and has additional capabilities such as backup storage and assembler. However, the discussions and applications presented in this book are applicable to any 1802-based microcomputer system, with minor modifications.

10.5. SUMMARY

In this chapter, we have introduced the low power CMOS technology 1802 microprocessor, its features and instruction set. Also, we have discussed a

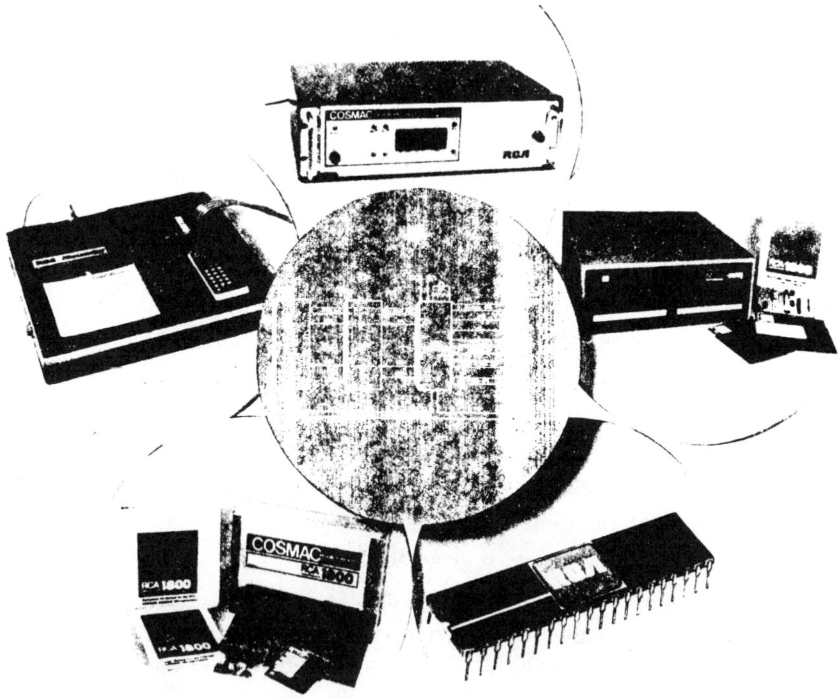

Fig 10.9. Microcomputer subassemblies leading to the 18S694-type microcomputer system.

typica 1802 microcomputer system and other support devices such as 1822 and 1824 RAMS, 1831 and 1832 ROMS, 1852 I/O devices, and so on, fabricated with the CMOS technology.

Because of lower power, the 1802-based microcomputer is well suited for low power applications.

A systematic study of this chapter will provide enough background to understand the system application based upon the 1802 microcomputer discussed in the next chapter. You are encouraged to consult the users' manual for the CDP 1802 Cosmac microprocessor and the RCA microcomputer systems data book for further information.

Problems

10.1. Figure 10.1 shows the architecture of the 1802 microprocessor. N register contains 7, P contains 3, X contains F.

(a) Which registers are configured as the program counter, data register, and the stack pointer?

(b) Which is the program counter on power up reset? Which is the data pointer?

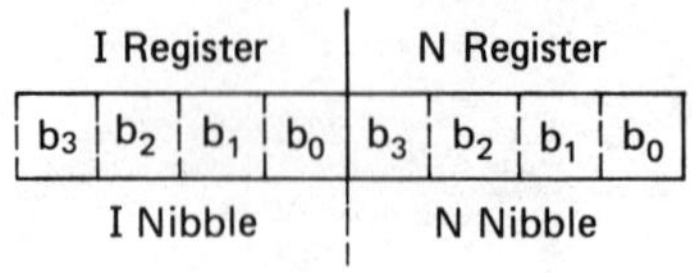

Fig 10.10. Instruction structure of the 1802 for Problems 10.2 and 10.3.

10.2. The op code byte is loaded into the I and N registers, as shown in Figure 10.10.

(a) I nibble refers to the instruction. (T or F)

(b) N nibble refers to the program counter. (T or F)

(c) N nibble refers to one of the 16 registers. (T or F)

(d) I can be directly loaded with data. (T or F)

10.3. Referring to Figure 10.10, if code 1 refers to incrementing, and code 2 refers to decrementing, formulate the op codes that will

(a) decrement register 7,

(b) increment register 9,

(c) double increment register A.

10.4. Using the instruction set of the 1802 micro, write a brief software routine to load 0000 into the scratch pad register bank R(4) to R(A).

10.5. Repeat 10.4, to load FFFF into the register bank R(4) to R(A).

10.6. In a particular application, R(B) has FF79 in it. It is required to set up the stack at 01FF and R(7) to act as the stack pointer, as shown in Figure 10.11.

(a) Initialize R(7) as stack pointer.

(b) Develop the operating listings to transfer R(B) to stack.

10.7. Using the stack organization of Figure 10.11, interchange the lower and upper bytes of R(B). If R(B) contains FF79 initially, after the manipulation R(B) should contain 79FF. Develop all the operating software.

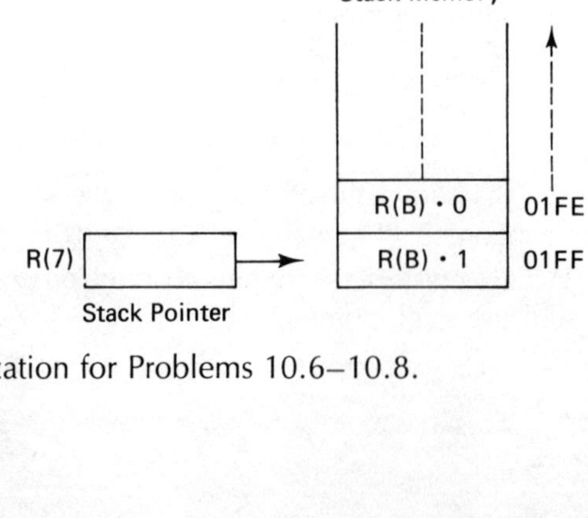

Fig 10.11. Stack organization for Problems 10.6–10.8.

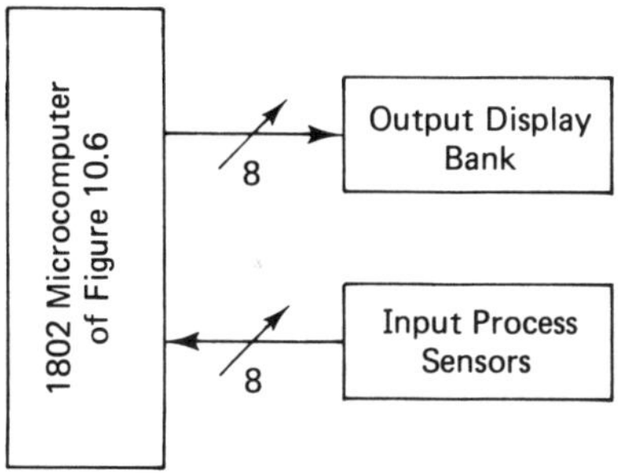

Fig 10.12. I/O applications of the 1802-based system.

10.8. The dynamic stacking can be used to a great advantage. Using the configuration of Figure 10.11, develop the required software to interchange any two registers, such as R(F) and R(E).

10.9. Figure 10.5 shows a typical microcomputer system configuration. Obtaining the information from the RCA data books on 1802 microprocessor products, develop the electronics interface to address the RAM between the locations $(0000)_{Hex}$ and $(03FF)_{Hex}$. Use the 1822 RAM devices.

10.10. Repeat Problem 10.9, such that the system addresses the 2K × 8 RAM, between 0000 and $(07FF)_{Hex}$.

10.11. Figure 10.6 shows the typical I/O configuration of the 1802-based system. Develop the operating software to read the condition of the thumbwheel switches every 1-second interval and store the data in sequential memory locations for a total period of 2 minutes. Use memory starting at $(0100)_{Hex}$.

10.12. In control applications, past (stored) data is usually examined to predict the trend of the process. Considering that the data is stored already between locations 0100 to $(017F)_{Hex}$, (Problem 10.11), develop an operating software to retrieve the stored data and accordingly light up the LEDs of Figure 10.6 at 2-second intervals.

10.13. Figure 10.12 shows a simple I/O control system. Input sensor information should be read in 1-second intervals. The steady state condition of the process is assumed to be reached if the sensor information remains the same for 10 seconds.

Develop an operating software, such that the microcomputer recognizes the steady state condition and then flashes the output LED bank in 1-second intervals.

10.14. Repeat Problem 10.13, if the steady state condition is to be recognized for 20 seconds, before flashing the display LED bank.

CHAPTER ELEVEN

1802-Based Microcomputer Applications

In this chapter we will present some practical applications using the single-board 1802-based microcomputer system, the RCA 18S020/21. With minor modifications, all these operating concepts are applicable to any other 1802-based system such as 185694. As mentioned earlier, using the existing software and hardware features of the system greatly enhances the utility of the microcomputer system.

11.1. USING THE SYSTEM SOFTWARE AND HARDWARE

The 18S020/21 microcomputer is provided with several useful utility software routines contained in the utility-5 ROM. These can be called by the user as subroutines. Also hardwired LED display and serial Q output are provided on the microcomputer board, which will help the user to display any information contained in the microcomputer. These basic features are shown in Figure 11.1. Table 11.1 shows the respective routines contained in the utility ROM-5.

Software Subroutines

The subroutine structure of a 1802-based system is extremely flexible but at the same time very complex. Fortunately the 18S020/21 system contains the utility routines to properly initialize the register bank and help the user

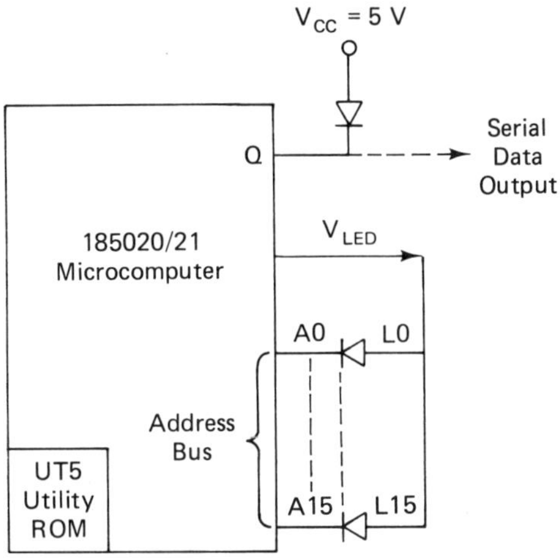

Fig 11.1. The 18S020/21/21 microcomputer with built-in LED display bank.

with the handling of the subroutines. We will clarify these features with an example problem.

Example 11.1 Subroutine Handling

An examination of Table 11.1 shows that R(4) and R(5) are configured as call and return registers for subroutines. The call subroutine listings are as shown in Table 11.2.

Table 11.1. Useful Utility (UT-5) Routines of 18S020/21 Microcomputer System (for details see instruction manual for CDP 18S021).

Name	*Address*	*Function*
Entry	8108	Initializes register bank P = 3; X = 2; R(2): 8C1F (top of stack) R(3): : User PC R(4) = 81E4: call routine R(5) = 81F4: return routine
REG DIS	81A6	Displays R(A) and R(B) on LED bank.
Call	81E4	Saves R(3) as user PC and reconditions R(3) for subroutine PC.
Return	81F4	Restores user PC, at the end of subroutine.

Table 11.2. Call Utility Subroutine Listings (Example 11.1).

Address	*Mnemonic*	*Op Code*	*Comments*
81E3	→SEP 3	D3	Set R3 as program counter.
Entry → 81E4	SEX 2	E2	Set R2 as stack pointer.
E5	GHI 6	96	Contents of R6 are stored on stack.
E6	STXD	73	
E7	GLO 6	86	
E8	STXD	73	
E9	GHI 3	93	Contents of R3* are transferred to R6.R(6) ← R(3).
EA	PHI 6	B6	
EB	GLO 3	83	
EC	PLO 6	A6	
ED	LDA 6	46	Contents of sequential locations pointed by R(6)** are loaded into R3 (this amounts to loading user subroutine address into R3).
EE	PHI 3	B3	
EF	LDA 6	46	
F0	PLO 3	A3	
F1	BR	30	Branch to 81E3 to make R3 the program counter for user subroutine.
F2	E3		

* R3 is the original program counter.
** R6 contains the contents of original program counter of R3.

(a) Explain how to call the "call' subroutine at 81E4.
(b) Explain how this subroutine could be used to call any user subroutine.
(c) Explain briefly how the return from subroutine is accomplished.

Solution

(a) *Call Subroutine*. After asserting that R4 contains the entry address 81E4, one needs to simply specify R4 to be the new program counter by the SEP instruction:

SEP 4 with Op Code D4

The system will start executing the routine at 81E4.

(b) *User Subroutine*. The entry routine at 8108 should be executed to condition the registers for the subroutines. Table 11.1 indicates that R3 is the original user program counter.

Examination of the listings in Table 11.2 indicates that R6 is preserved on the stack. Contents of R3 (current program counter) are transferred to R6. Using R6 as memory pointer, R3 is loaded with the effective address of the user subroutine.

Example (Main Program with R3 as PC):

00A0	SEP	D4	Call to user subroutine at 81A6, via call subroutine
00A1	81		
00A2	A6		

↓
(Program location)

Contents of R3-00A1 are transferred to R6. In turn R3 is loaded with 81A6 (as pointed by R(6), which is the effective address of the user subroutine).

(c) *Return from Subroutine* (Table 11.1). R5 is configured as the return routine pointer. A SEP instruction with op code D5 (making R5 the program counter) will execute the return routine at 81F4, which will restore the user PC and return to the main program. Thus, the last instruction in user subroutine should be SEP with op code D5 (R5 should be preloaded with 81F4)

It looks as though we have gone through a tiring procedure for handling the subroutines. Unfortunately there is no simple way around it, and you really need to study the above example and comprehend it. Any 1802-based system uses similar procedures for the subroutine handling. Several problems are designed to help you with subroutines.

Pulse Width Modulation (PWM)

The Q output of the 18S020/21 microcomputer (Figure 11.1) can be very conveniently used to generate any modulated or coded waveform for industrial control applications. Figure 11.2 shows a simple bio control system that accepts a control input and generates a pulse width modulated wave on Q output to provide electrical shock to the muscular system. These types of systems are extensively used in the biomedical disciplines.

Example 11.2 PWM and Biocontrol

The bio control system of Figure 11.2 generates a PWM signal on its Q output to provide an electrical shock to the muscle. Consider that the duration of the shock is proportional to the input X word.

(a) Develop the necessary hardware and software to make the system fully operational.

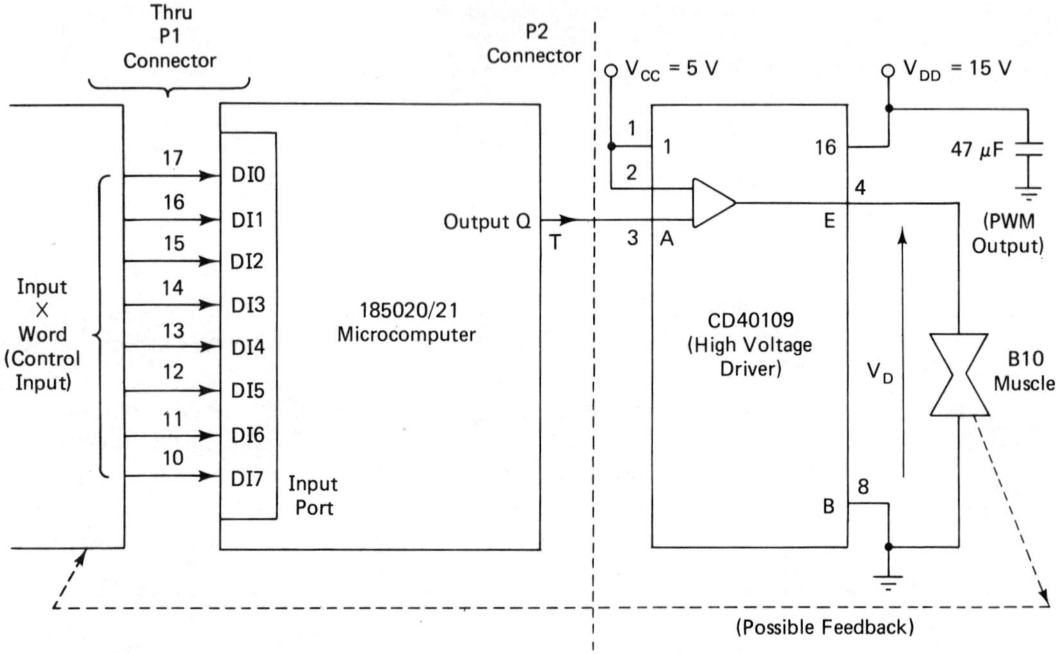

Fig 11.2. PWM generation and biocontrol for Example 2.

(b) Draw the Q output waveform and the shocking voltage waveform if X = $(40)_{Hex}$.

(c) Find the frequency of the shocking waveform. Consider 2 MHz clock frequency.

Solution

(a) *Hardware.* The hardware of Figure 11.2 is self-contained. The CD 40109B driver is used to provide higher shocking voltage up to 15 volts. When the Q output is high, the driver output voltage V_O will be high and provides the necessary electrical shock to the muscle.

(b) *Software.* The input X word is read. The Q output is set high for a duration (delay-1), proportional to the X input word. The Q output is reset low for the rest of the cycle (delay-2). The operation is made repetitive, resulting in the pulse width modulated waveform on the Q output. Figure 11.3 shows the flow chart, and Table 11.3 shows the operating listings.

On power up reset, the system will start executing the program from location 0000. Between 0000 and 0003 the Q output is set high (for shock) and the input X word is loaded into the low bytes of R4 and R5.

Between 0004 and 0007, delay 1 is generated by decrementing R5 to

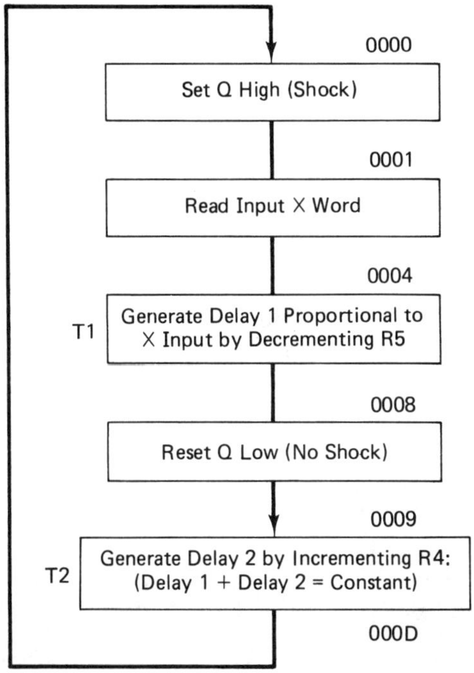

Fig 11.3. Flowchart for biocontrol for Example 2.

Table 11.3. Operating Listings for PWM Biocontrol (Example 11.2).

Location	*Label*	*Mnemonic*	*Op Code*	*Comment*
0000	High	SEQ	7B	Set Q output high (for shock).
01	Input	INP	6E	Read input X word and load it in the low bytes of R4 and R5.
02		PLO 4	A4	
03		PLO 5	A5	
04	Delay 1	→DEC 5	25	R5 decremented and checked for all zero condition to generate delay 1.
05		GLO 5	85	
06		BNZ	3A	
07		04		
08	Low	REQ	7A	Reset Q output low (no shock).
09	Delay 2	→INC 4	14	R4 incremented and checked for all zero condition to generate delay 2.
0A		GLO 4	84	
0B		BNZ	3A	
0C		09		
0D		BR	30	Branch back to 0000 to start new cycle.
0E		00		

all-zero condition. At 0008, the Q output is reset (no shock condition). Between 0009 and 000C, the complementary delay 2 is generated by incrementing R4 to all-zero condition. It should be obvious to the reader that delay 1 + delay 2 = constant (equal to cycle time). More about that later.

The branch instruction at 000D restarts the cycle.

(b) *Waveforms.* X input word is $(40)_{Hex}$. Delay 1 loop is executed $(40)_{Hex}$ times. Similarly, delay 2 loop is executed $(00) - (40)_{Hex} = (C0)_{Hex}$ times. Thus,

$$\frac{\text{Delay 2}}{\text{Delay 1}} = \frac{T2}{T1} = \frac{(C0)_{Hex}}{(40)_{Hex}} = 3$$

The following is the waveform.

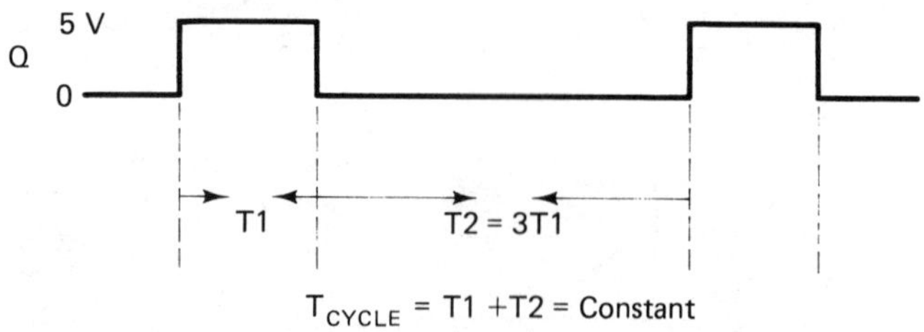

The V_O shocking waveform is similar to the Q waveform, except that it swings between 0 and 15 volts.

(c) *Frequency.* Remember the 1802 timing? (Chapter 10 Section 10.3 on system timing and control). Each instruction used above takes two machine cycles; each machine cycle takes eight clock cycles. Thus 2 MHz clock yields an instruction time of 8 μs.

In our example, each delay loop has three instructions (24 μs). Delay 1 loop is executed $(40)_{Hex}$ times, and delay 2 loop is executed $(C0)_{Hex}$ times.

Thus

$$T1 = (40)_{Hex} * 24\ \mu s$$

$$= 64 * 24 \times 10^{-6} = 1.536\text{ ms}$$

$$T2 = (C0)_{Hex} * 24\ \mu s$$

$$= 192 \times 24 \times 10^{-6} = 4.608\text{ ms}$$

$$T_{cycle} = T1 + T2 = 6.144\text{ ms}$$

$$\boxed{\text{Frequency} = \frac{1}{T_{cycle}} = 163\text{ Hz}}$$

(You should verify that T_{cycle} and frequency remain the same, irrespective of T1 and T2 values.)

This example clearly shows that complex problems can be easily solved with the help of the powerful instruction set and hardware features of the 18S020/21 microcomputer system. In real control application, the X word may be derived from the muscle by biofeedback.

11.2. INPUT/OUTPUT PARALLEL INTERFACE

As mentioned in Chapter 10 (Section 10.3), the parallel interface in a typical 1802-based system is accomplished with the help of 1852 programmable I/O devices. Each 1852 can be structured as an 8-bit input or output port.

1852 Programmable I/O Port

The 1852 is a programmable I/O device contained in a 24-pin dip and is fabricated by the low power CMOS technology. Figure 11.4 shows the basic features.

When the mode input is 0, the device functions as the input port. It accepts the I/O data on the DI0...DI7 input lines and presents the data on DO0...DO7 output lines to the 1802 microprocessor. When the mode input is 1, the device functions as the output port. Each I/O line has unit TTL load drive capability (sink 1.6 mA). Buffering is required for additional drive.

For each input or output port, a separate 1852 device is required, which is hardware configured as either the input or the output (but not both).

Laboratory Controllers

We would like to use the interface and processing capabilities of the 1802-based microcomputer system in developing some real and operating digital control systems. Shown in Figure 11.5 is a typical controller in bio applications for stabilizing the temperature of a thermal chamber. The chamber may contain x-ray films, medicine, surgical equipment, and so on.

The heater H heats the thermal chamber. The semiconductor sensor S provides the thermal feedback. The higher the temperature, the more the leakage current of the sensor diode S, which results in the higher sensor voltage V_{Sense}. V_{Sense} is converted into a digital input X word and is read by the 18S020/21 microcomputer through its 1852 input port. Necessary data processing is done by the microcomputer, which presents the processed digital word on its 1852 output port. This digital word is converted into the necessary

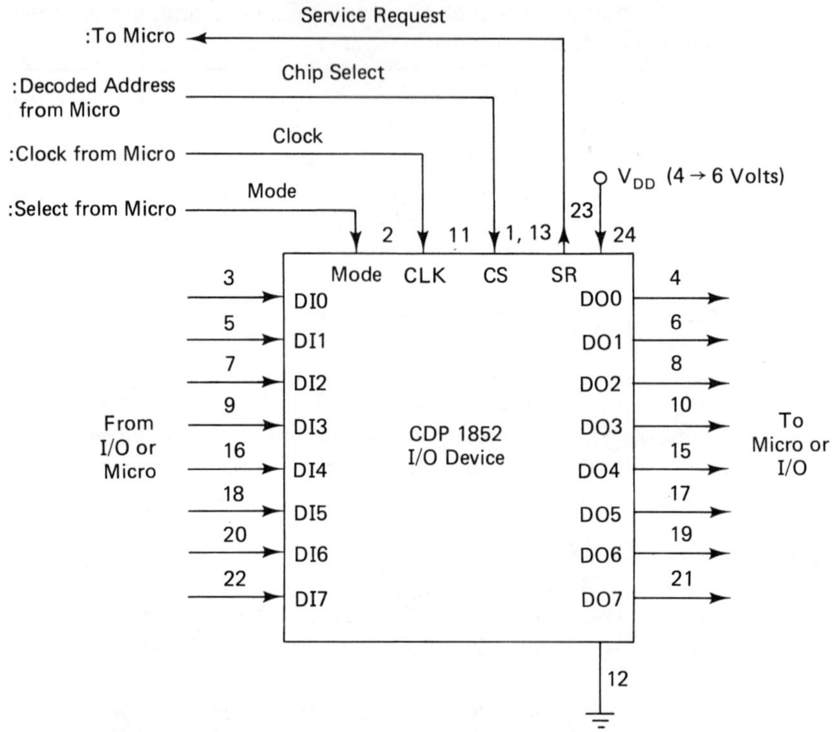

Fig 11.4. The 18S2 I/O device structure.

drive voltage V_{Drive} to drive the heater element. The system operates in the closed loop and regulates the temperature, as determined by the values of components and the digital processing.

Example 11.3 Proportional Controller

Develop the necessary hardware interface and the software to make the system of Figure 11.5 operate as a proportional thermal controller.

Solution

(a) *Hardware*. In the input section, the 14753 comparator amplifiers convert the V_{Sense} voltage into a corresponding digital word. The 14042 quad latch ICs latch this digital word when their CLK input is pulled low by the microcomputer. This latched data appears as the X word at the input of the microcomputer. The micro reads this data, and after processing, presents it as the Y word at its output.

The output 14753 summing amplifier converts the Y word into a linearly scaled output voltage V_{O1}. V_{O1} is then low pass filtered through R_{O1}, R_{O2},

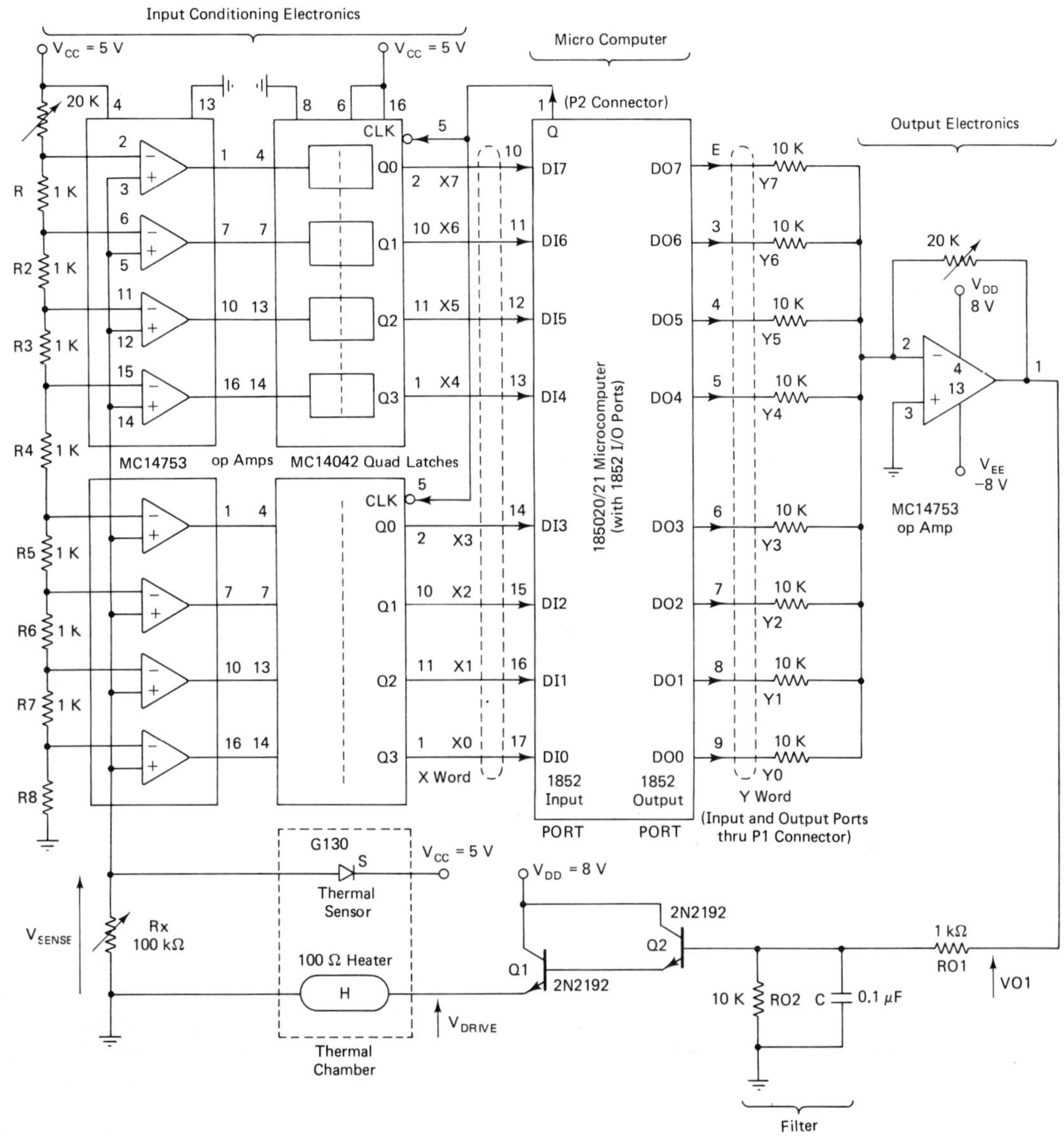

Fig 11.5. Laboratory controller for Example 3.

and C network to remove the switching transients. Q_2 and Q_1 transistors in the darlington configuration provide the necessary drive voltage V_{Drive} across the heating element H.

(b) *Software*. It should be fairly obvious that the X input word has the property of spreading 1, as shown (as temperature and V_{Sense} rise) providing eight-step variation.

	X_7	X_6	X_5	X_4	X_3	X_2	X_1	X_0
Minimum Temp.	0	0	0	0	0	0	0	0
Next Temp.	0	0	0	0	0	0	0	1
Next Temp.	0	0	0	0	0	0	1	1
. .					.			
Maximum Temp.	1	1	1	1	1	1	1	1

If the Y word is made a complement of the X word, it amounts to providing the maximum drive voltage V_{Drive}, when the temperature is minimum and vice versa. This results in the required proportional controller action.

Thus the software centers around latching and reading the X word, complementing it and outputting it as the Y word. Figure 11.6 shows the flow chart and the corresponding pseudo code. Table 11.4 shows the operating listings.

Between 0000 and 0007, R(F) is configured as the data pointer. Value 0030 is loaded into R(F), to refer to the data memory location. Between 0008 and 000A, the input X data is latched and read into the microcomputer. The latching is necessary to prevent the data transition while reading. At 000B, the input latch is released.

Between 000C and 0012, the X data is complemented and is sent to the output port as Y data. The branch instruction at 0013 repeats the operation.

Table 11.4. Operating Listings for the Proportional Controller (Example 11.3).

Location	*Label*	*Mnemonic*	*Op Code*	*Comment*
0000	Initialize	SEX F	EF	R(F) is the data pointer.
01		NOP	C4	
02		LDI	F8	$(30)_{Hex}$ is loaded into D register
03		30		and is transferred to R(F).0.
04		PLO F	AF	
05		LDI	F8	$(00)_{Hex}$ is loaded into D register
06		00		and is transferred to R(F).1 [R(F)
07		PHI F	BF	contains 0030].
08	Latch	REQ	7A	Q is reset to 0 to latch input data
09		NOP	C4	and the input X data is read into
0A	Input X	INP	6E	D register.
0B	Unlatch	SEQ	7B	Q is set to 1 to release input latch.
0C		XRI	FB	Input X data is complemented by
0D		FF		exclusive Oring with FF and is
0E		STR F	5F	stored at 0030, specified by R(F).
0F	Output Y	OUT	65	Stored data is output as Y word
10		NOP	C4	and R(F) gets incremented. R(F) is
11		DEC F	2F	decremented, to offset the
12		NOP	C4	increment.
13	Repeat	BR	30	Branch back to 0008 to repeat the
14		08		operation.

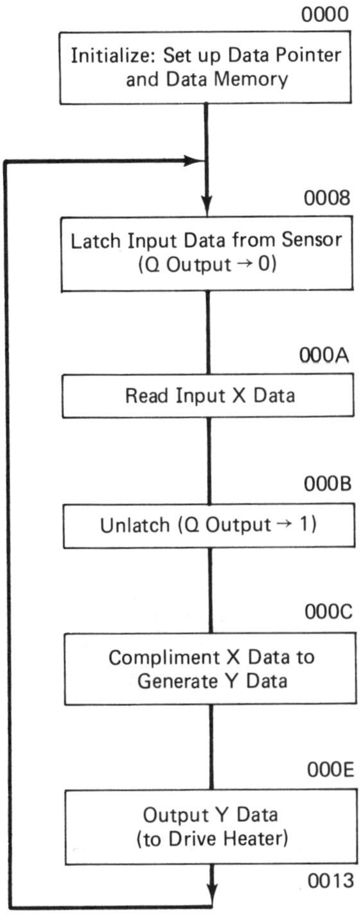

(a) Flow Chart

Initialize:

Set up Data Pointer
Set up Data Memory

Latch Input:

Send Q = 0 to Latch
Read Latched X Data

Release Latch:

Send Q = 1 to Unlatch

Process Data:

Complement X Data
Store Complemented Data as Y Data

Output Data:

Output Y Data from Data Memory

Repeat:

Go Back to Latching Input and Repeat the Operation

(b) Pseudo Code

Fig 11.6. Flowchart and pseudocode for the proportional controller for Example 3.

The above controller is minimal and has only an eight-step control. The input and the output electronic interface is similar to a crude A/D and D/A system. However, for most laboratory applications, eight-step control is more than adequate.

11.3. INDUSTRIAL COUNTING AND DATA ENTRY SYSTEMS

Counting of the events in a given interval of time is one of the most fundamental operations in industrial controls. For example, counting the pulse beat helps to identify the health condition of a patient. Counting the number of persons entering or leaving any commercial organization helps to identify the amount of business turnover.

Industrial Counters

With the flag interrupt inputs ($\overline{EF1}...\overline{EF4}$) readily available, the 18S020/21 microcomputer can be very easily converted into an industrial counting system. Figure 11.7 shows such an application, where the microcomputer is used to count the strokes of a jigsaw in an industrial workshop. Each time the jigsaw makes an excursion, the light beam between the T1L-32 and T1L 78 infra red diode and transistor assembly is interrupted, generating an electrical signal V_{01}. This signal is electronically conditioned and is applied to the $\overline{EF1}$ input of the microcomputer. A timing pulse is applied to the $\overline{EF2}$ input. Necessary software is developed to count and display the EF1 transitions, in a given time interval, which relate to the jigsaw motion.

Example 11.4 Jigsaw Counter

Develop the necessary hardware and software to make the counting system of Figure 11.7: (a) count the jigsaw excursions for 10 seconds and display the count for 5 seconds (b) convert the system into a jigsaw controller.

Solution

(a) *Hardware*. The 555 timer device is used to generate the timing waveform, as shown. For the values used, T1 ≅ 10 s and T2 ≅ 5 s. This timing

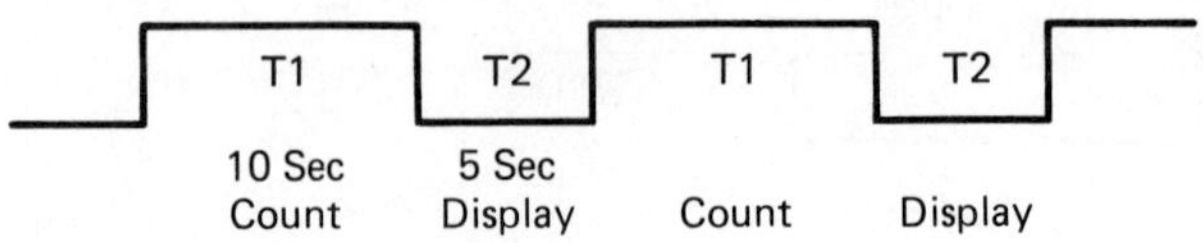

waveform is applied to the $\overline{EF2}$ input. The 3302 fast slew rate comparator device conditions the low amplitude V_{01} signal (generated due to jigsaw excursions) to a TTL compatible signal V_X, as shown.

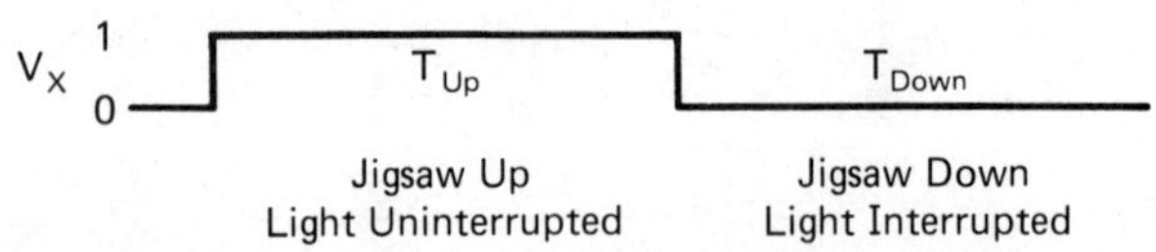

This jigsaw count waveform is applied to the $\overline{EF1}$ input of the microcomputer.

The LED bank of the microcomputer is used to display the count in hexadecimal format.

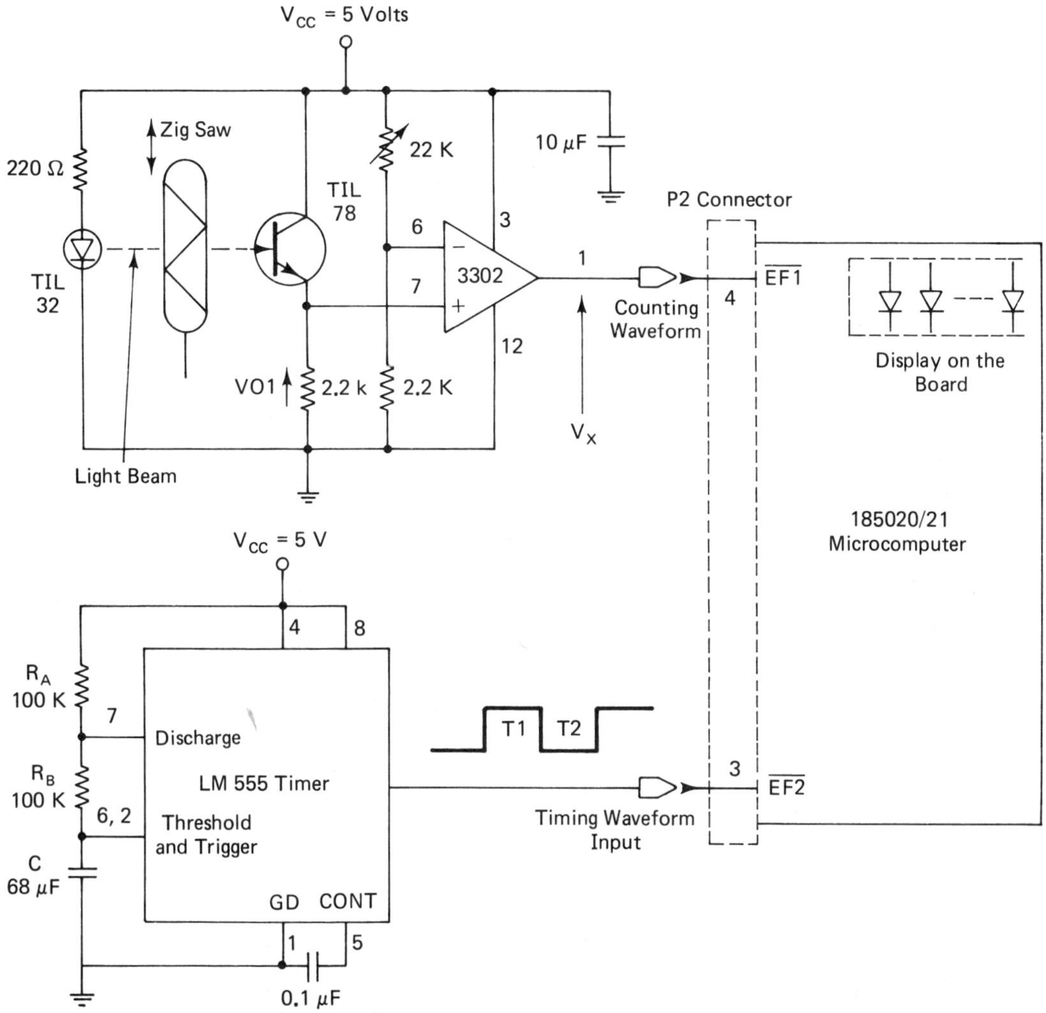

$T1 = 0.69\,(R_A + R_B)\,C = 10$ sec
$T2 = 0.69\,R_B\,C \approx 5$ sec

LM3302 Quad Comparator
LM555 Timer
} From National Semiconductor Co.

Fig 11.7. Industrial counter for counting jigsaw excursions (Example 4).

Software. The software is developed such that the counting and the displaying are done during the T1 and T2 intervals of the timing waveform (on $\overline{EF2}$) respectively. The counting is accomplished by incrementing one of the registers of the CPU [R(A) in our case], each time a positive transition of the counting waveform V_X (on $\overline{EF1}$) is recognized.

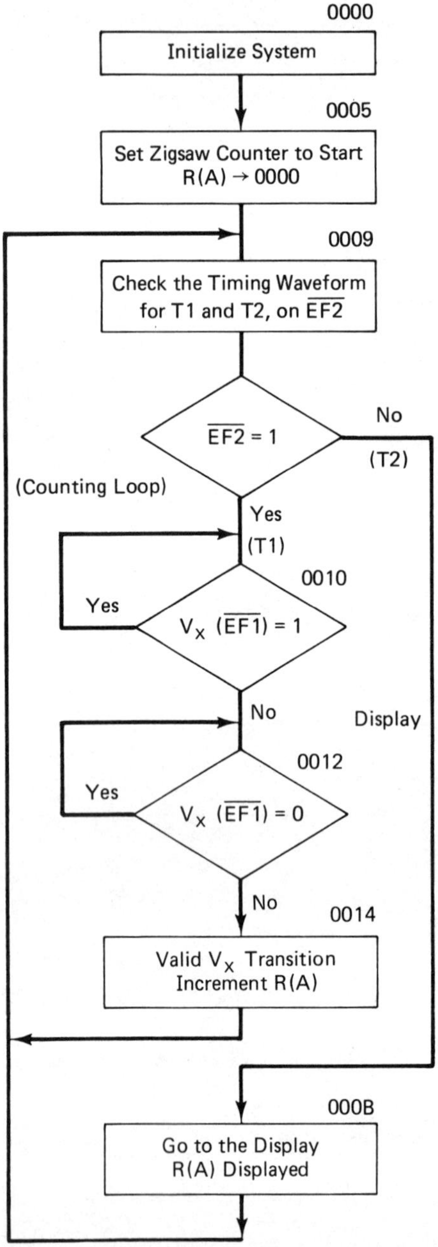

(a) Flow Chart

Initialize:

Set up CPU Registers for Subroutine Handling
Set up Zigsaw Counter R(A) to all-Zero Condition

Check Timing:

If T1 ($\overline{EF2}$ = 1) then Perform Counting Operation
If T2 ($\overline{EF2}$ = 0) then Perform Display Operation

Counting:

Check for Valid V_X ($\overline{EF1}$) Transition
If V_X = 1 Loop Around
If V_X = 0 Loop Around
Increment R(A) on Next V_X Transition
Go Back to Check Timing

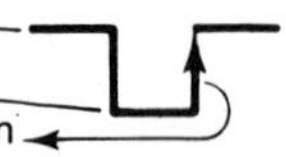

Display:

Use REGDIS Utility Routine to Display R(A) Contents
Go Back to Check Timing

(b) Pseudo Code

Fig 11.8. Flowchart and pseudocode for the jigsaw counter (Example 4).

The display is accomplished by calling an internal subroutine REGDIS, which would display the contents of the register R(A) on the system LED bank.

Figure 11.8 shows the flow chart and the pseudo code, and Table 11.5 shows the operating listings.

Between 0000 and 0004 the microcomputer system 18S020/21 is initialized to handle the subroutines. The system should contain utility ROM-5, to have the entry routine at 8108 to be operational (refer to Table 11.1 for details). The jigsaw counter R(A) is set to all-zero condition, between 0005 and 0008.

Between 0009 and 0017, depending on the condition of $\overline{EF2}$ flag ($\overline{EF2}$ = 1 corresponds to the counting time T1; $\overline{EF2}$ = 0 corresponds to the display time T2), counting or display operations are accomplished. (Refer to Example 11.1 and Table 11.1 to understand the subroutine handling).

(b) *Jig Saw Controller*. The jigsaw count [contents of R(A)] can be interpreted to refer to the speed with which the jigsaw is moving and cutting. A feed-

Table 11.5. Operating Listings for the Jigsaw Counter (Example 11.4).

Location	*Label*	*Mnemonic*	*Op Code*	*Comment*
0000	Initialize	LBR	C0	Longbranch to entry routine at
01		81_H		8108 to initialize the registers
02		08_L		for subroutine handling.
03		NOP	C4	Control is given back to the
04		NOP	C4	user program starting at 0005.
05	Jigsaw Ctr	LDI	F8	Jigsaw counter R(A) is
06		00		initialized to 0000, by loading
07		PLO A	AA	00 in D register and
08		PHI A	BA	transferring to R(A).0 and R(A).1.
09	CHK timing	BN2	3D	If EF2 = 0 ($\overline{EF2}$ = 1), program
0A		10		branches to count at 0010.
0B	Display	SEP	D4	If EF2 = 1 ($\overline{EF2}$ = 0), display
0C		81		subroutine at 81A6 (RegDis) is
0D		A6		called to display R(A).
0E		BR	30	Program branches back to
0F		09		0009 to check $\overline{EF2}$ again.
0010	Count	BN1	3C	Looping if $\overline{EF1}$ = 1 (V_X = 1)
11		10		(T_{up} interval).
12		B1	34	Looping if $\overline{EF1}$ = 0 (V_X = 0)
13		12		(T_{Down} interval).
14	Increment	INC	1A	R(A) incremented, at V_X valid transition (0 → 1).
16		BR	30	Program branches back to
17		09		0009 to check for $\overline{EE2}$ again.

back loop can be easily developed as shown, to generate a drive voltage V_{Drive}, to drive the jigsaw motor depending on the requirement. Perhaps a smaller V_{Drive} voltage can be generated (refer to Example 11.3 on Proportional Controller) to slow down the jigsaw, if a faster movement (higher count) is detected. Examples 11.3 and 11.4 together would yield the required controller.

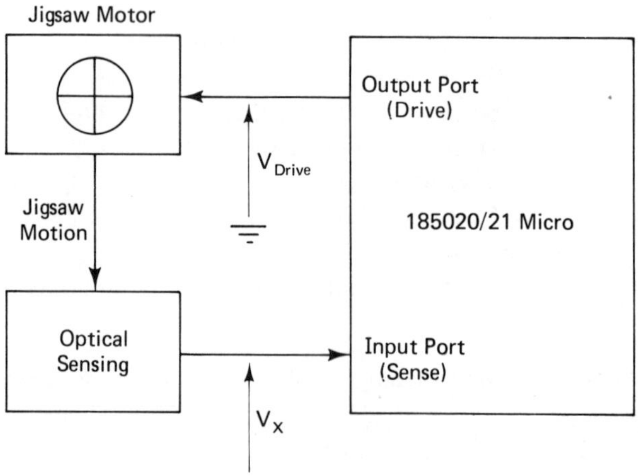

Data Entry and Validation Systems

In any industrial environment, entering the data and validating the entered data is an extremely important operation. Data may be entered through a keyboard or through electronic sensors in an industrial process. Data validation may be accomplished, through the software routines, to identify the nature of the data. The integration of the data entry and validation schemes can result in a very useful operating system.

Sometimes it may be more convenient to get access directly to the address, data, and control buses of the microprocessor and enter the data. This is especially true when the I/O ports of the system are not available.

We will couple the above two concepts and present an example problem.

Example 11.5 Keyboard and Display System

Figure 11.9 shows a typical keyboard and display interface to a microprocessor. Develop the necessary hardware and software so that the micro (1802) reads the keyboard, identifies the key being activated, and displays it.

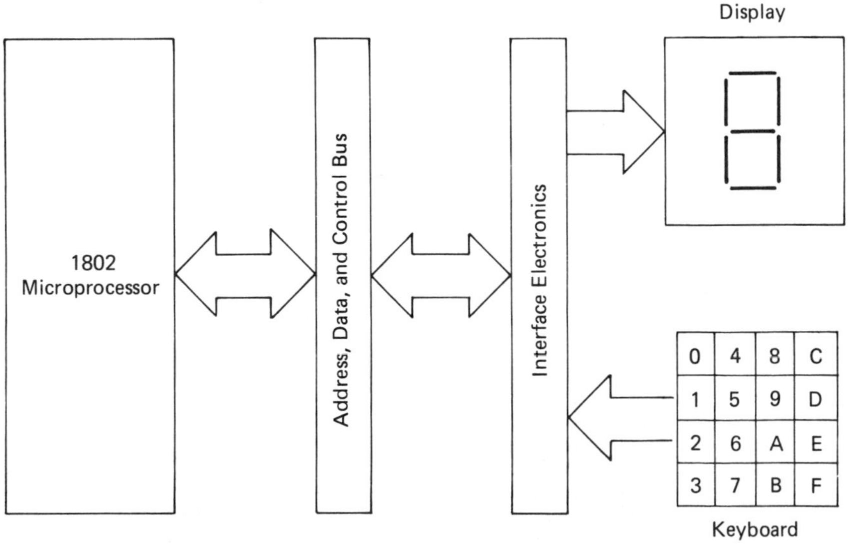

Fig 11.9. Keyboard data entry and display system for Example 5.

Solution

(a) *Hardware*. Figure 11.10 shows the actual operating hardware electronics interface. Access to the 1802 microprocessor is obtained through the P2 connector.

The 74LS 138 decoder ② drives the rows of the keyboard, low, one at a time. When a key is pressed, the corresponding column becomes low. For example, if the Y2 row is driven low and if a logic low is observed on the C1 column, it implies that key number 9 is activated. The 74LS 253 multiplexer presents this column information as the $\overline{\text{EF1}}$ flag input to the microprocessor.

The microprocessor data bus D0...D3 drives the keyboard decoder and the multiplexer through the keyboard latch 14174 ②. The same data bus also drives the 14174 display latch ①. The I/O control bus N2 N1 N0 drives another decoder 74LS 138 1, which in turn activates the key board and the display latches in sequence.

The data bus is latched in the keyboard latch, and the $\overline{\text{EF1}}$ status is observed. If $\overline{\text{EF1}}$ shows logic low (0 level), it implies that a key is pressed whose binary value corresponds to the contents of the data bus. Then the data bus in latched in the display latch, whose output drives the 7447 seven-segment decoder and the display. Thus the pressed key appears in the display.

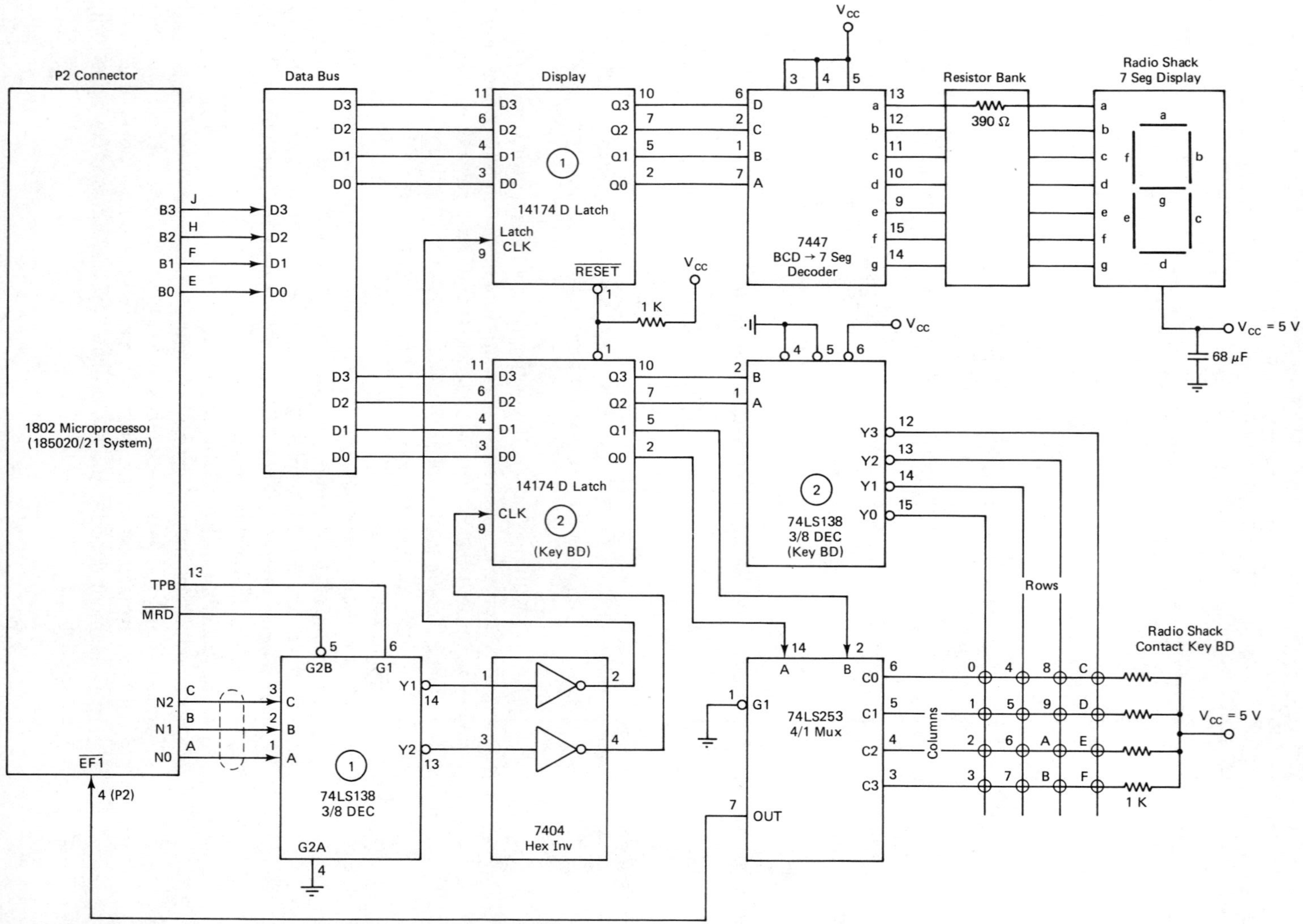

Fig 11.10. Keyboard and display interface electronics for Example 5.

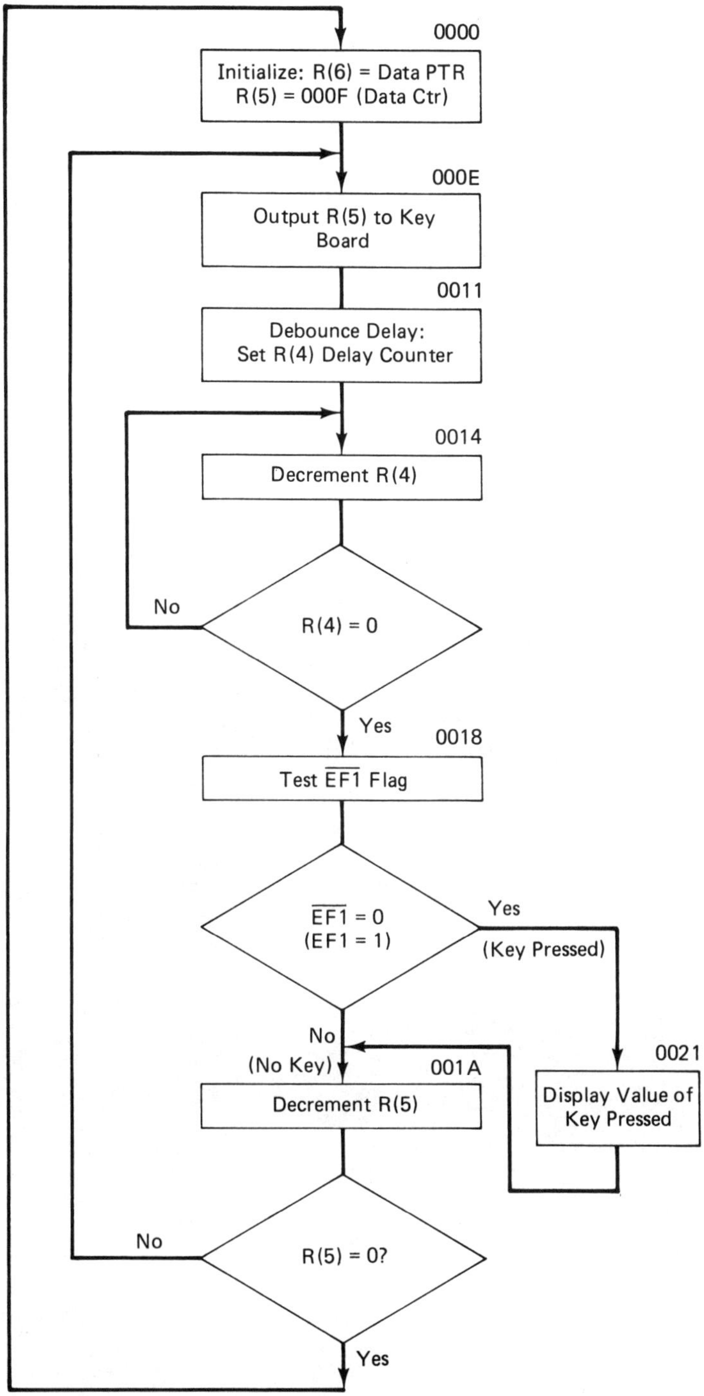

Fig 11.11. Flowchart for the keyboard and display (Example 5).

Table 11.6. Operating Listings for Keyboard and Display (Example 11.5).

Location	*Label*	*Mnemonic*	*Op Code*	*Comment*
0000	Initialize	SEX	E6	R(6) is set as data pointer. D accumulator is loaded with 00 and is transferred to the high bytes of R6, R5, and R4. (High bytes of R6, R5, R4 set to 00).
01		LDI	F8	
02		00		
03		PHI R6	B6	
04		PHI R5	B5	
05		PHI R4	B4	
06		LDI	F8	Low byte of R6 is set at DF, making M R(6) = 00DF as the data memory. R(5) low byte is set at 0F.R(5), which acts as data counter contains 000F.
07		DF		
08	Data PTR	PLO R6	A6	
09	Start Scan	LDI	F8	
0A		0F		
0B	Data Ctr	PLO R5	A5	
0C		NOP	C4	
0D		NOP	C4	
0E	Keybd out	STR MR(6)	56	Low byte of R(5) is output to keyboard latch via data memory. Data pointer reset to 00DF by decrementing R6.
0F		Out 2	62	
10		DEC R6	26	
11	Delay	LDI	F8	Debounce delay generated by loading R(4) with 00FF and decrementing it to 0000.
12		FF		
13		PLO R4	A4	
14		→DEC R4	24	
15		GLO R4	84	
16		BNZ	3A	
17		14		
18	CHK EF1	B1	34	EF1 checked for 1 ($\overline{EF1}$ = 0). If EF1 = 1, program branches to display routine at 0021.
19		21		
001A	Next	DEC R5	25	R(5) decremented for next key position and program branches to keyboard output at 000E, if R(5) #0, and to start scan at 0009, if R(5) = 0.
1B		GLO R5	85	
1C		BNZ	3A	
1D		0E		
1E		BR	30	
1F		09		
20		NOP	C4	
21	Display out	→OUT 1	61	Output contents of data memory to display latch and branch back to 001A, for next scan.
22		DEC R6	26	
23		BR	30	
24		1A		

(b) *Software.* The coordination of all the above events is accomplished under the software control. Initially the data bus is set at 'OF' (D3 D2 D1 D0 = 1 1 1 1), which corresponds to the addressing of the Y3 row and C3 column. The condition of the output of the keyboard multiplexer (which is connected to the $\overline{EF1}$ input of the micro) is checked. If $\overline{EF1}$ = 0, it implies that a key is pressed (in this case it will be key F). Then the contents of the data bus are latched in the display latch, to be displayed at the output. The software decrements the data bus, checks for $\overline{EF1}$ condition, and displays the corresponding digit between F and 0. This method of sequentially activating and observing the keyboard is called "scanning" and is very widely used in the industrial data entry systems.

Figure 11-11 shows the flow chart, and Table 11.6 shows the operating listings.

Between 0000 and 000D, the initialization is carried out, with R(6) as data pointer set at 00DF and R(5) as data counter set at 000F. The location M R(6) = 00DF is used as the data memory for outputting the information.

Between 000E and 0017, the contents of R(5) are ouput to the keyboard latch to activate proper rows. Approximately 6 ms debounce delay is generated, using R(4) as a delay counter. At the end of this delay, condition of the $\overline{EF1}$ flag input is checked.

Between 0018 and 0024, the condition of the $\overline{EF1}$ input is checked, and the key digit pressed is displayed. Also, the scanning of the keyboard is repeated.

The above example is simple, but has unlimited applications in the industrial data entry systems. In case of multiple key closures, the system identifies (without error) the keys closed in the order of the scanning. This feature is known as the "key rollover" and is extensively used in computer, word processing, and typewriter keyboards. Several example problems have been presented at the end of the chapter for your benefit.

11.4. SYSTEM LEVEL INTERFACE

In real world applications, there may be a necessity to interface the microcomputer with a fast I/O system, such as floppy disk, TV display, which require fast data transfers. Similarly the same microcomputer may be used to interface with a slow I/O system, such as a modem, in which data transfers are much slower.

It has been customary in the industry to use the DMA (direct memory access) interface for the fast I/O and SIO (serial input output) interface for the slow I/O. We will now present some of these important concepts.

Direct Memory Access (DMA)

The 1802 microprocessor is provided with the necessary timing and control signals to accomplish the DMA interface. Figure 11.12 shows a typical DMA IN interface. The data from the outside I/O is directly loaded into the system memory, and the 1802 microprocessor generates the necessary timing and control signals.

The 1802 microprocessor operates in four states as shown in the following table:

State Code Lines SC1	SC0	*State and Function*
0	0	S0: Fetch
0	1	S1: Execute
1	0	S2: DMA
1	1	S3: Interrupt

The DMA (IN) operation may be summarized as follows:

A high transition on the external Enter signal will clock an input byte from the external I/O into the input register, consisting of two 14076-type quad latches. Also the DMA in line is pulled low, by clocking the 4013 flip flop into the set state.

Then, the 1802 enters the S2 (DMA) state, after concluding the execution of the current instruction (completion of S0 and S1 states). The 1802 releases the control of the data bus by floating its own data lines (Bus 0...7) into the high impedance state.

The data from the 14076 latch is then written directly into the memory location, referenced by the contents of register R(0). R(0) advances to the next sequential location, for the next data byte transfer. This is a typical DMA IN operation. We will use an example problem to clarify the DMA concepts.

Example 11.6 DMA Operation

Data from the floppy disk interface is flowing into the system of Figure 11.12. The floppy controller generates the enter signal

(a) Draw the DMA timing waveforms.
(b) If R(0) contains $(2000)_{Hex}$, specify where the first data byte is stored.
(c) Modify the above system so that the successive input bytes are stored in the memory, continuously (block transfers).

Solution

(a) *Timing Waveforms.* Figure 11.13 shows the relative timing waveforms (for details, the COSMAC 18S020/21 manual should be consulted).

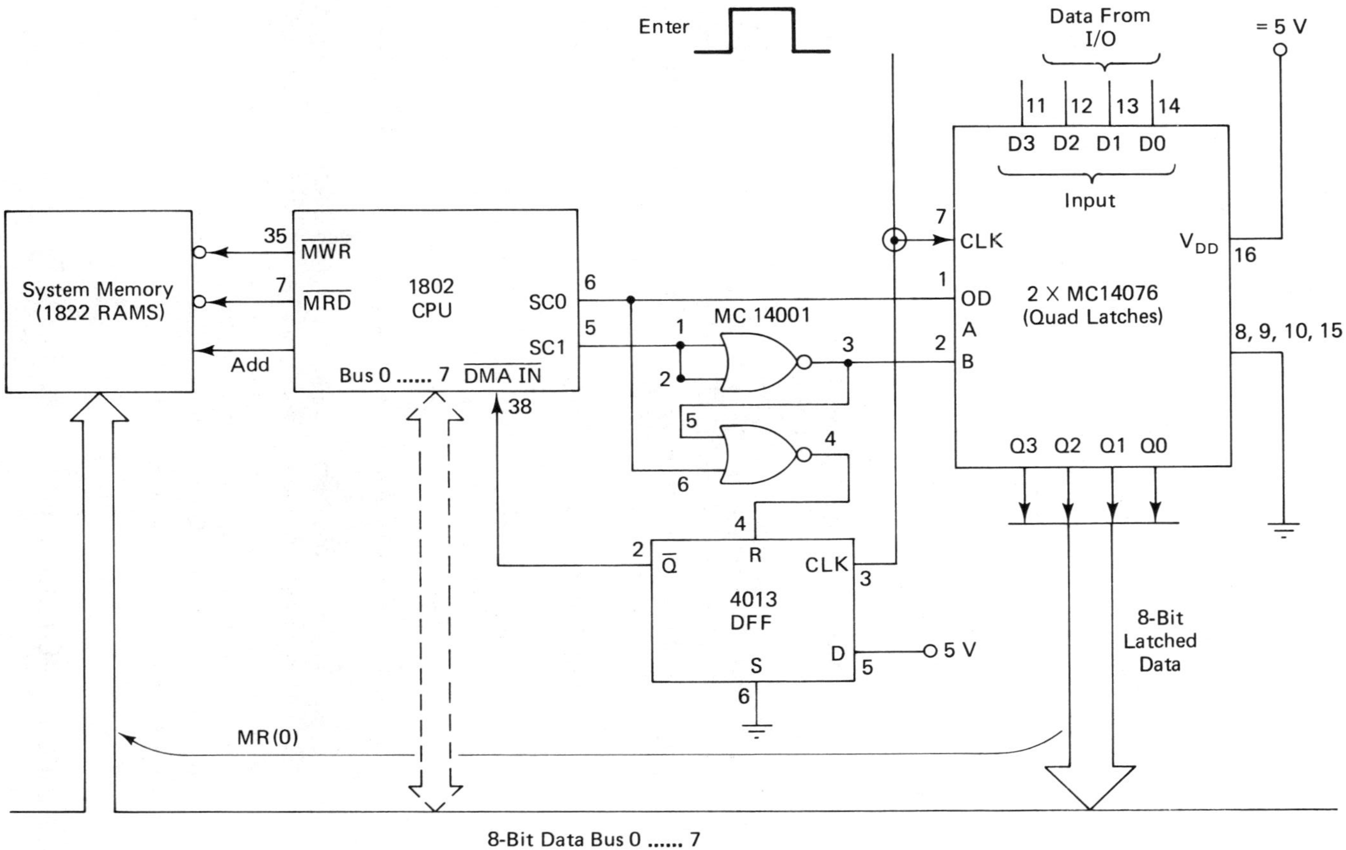

Fig 11.12. DMA interface (for DATA IN) for the 1802 system.

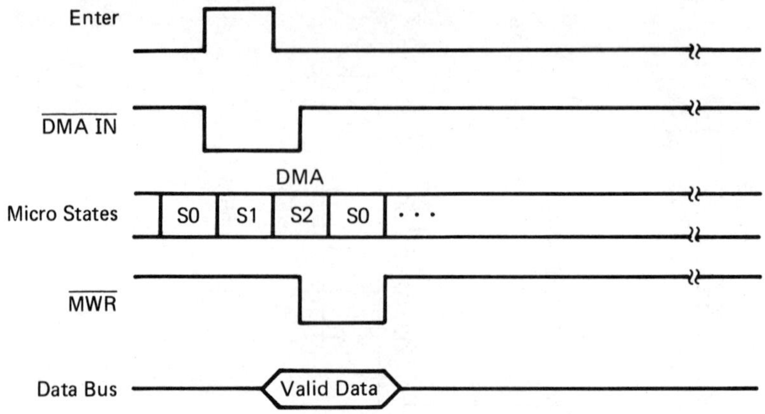

Fig 11.13. DMA IN timing waveforms for Example 6.

The positive transition on the Enter line latches the input data in the 14076 latches and pulls the DMA IN line low.

After the conclusion of the S0 and S1 states, the 1802 enters the S2 (DMA) state. Thereafter the 4013 flip flop gets reset pulling DMA In line high. However, S2 state continues until the data transfer is accomplished.

When the data bus is ready, containing data from the input latches, MWR (memory write control) signal goes low, writing the data bus information into the memory

(b) *First Data Byte.* First data byte is stored at location $(2000)_{Hex}$, as specified by R(0). R(0) increments after each memory write operation.

(c) *Block Transfers.* Block transfer can be accomplished by repeatedly generating the Enter signal and forcing the microprocessor into the S2 state.

Another way of accomplishing the block transfer is to hold the micro in the S2 state, by external logic signals.

The above example is very primitive, but does illustrate the concept. The DMA OUT operation is essentially similar. The external Enter signal may be used to generate the DMA OUT signal to the micro. The data direction gets reversed and flows from the memory to the external I/O. The reader is encouraged to read the COSMAC manual and implement the DMA OUT operation. As usual several end of the chapter problems await you with more applications.

Serial Inout/Output (SIO) Interface

The 1802 microprocessor communicates with the serial I/O systems, using the COP 1854 UART (universal asynchronous receiver and transmitter).

The SIO interface properties are essentially similar to what we have already studied (6850 ACIA in Chapter 5, 8048 and RS-232 Interface in Chapter 3). As such, we prefer not to repeat the same material here, but encourage you to implement the SIO interface with the help of the referenced material. Also the *RCA Microprocessors and Support Systems Data Book* should be consulted to obtain specifics of the 1854 UART.

11.5. SUMMARY

In this chapter, we have concentrated on the applications of the 1802-based microcomputer system. Because of the peculiarity in handling subroutines, we have carefully designed an example to throw light on this important aspect.

We have emphasized the designs of laboratory controllers, through an operating proportional controller example.

The study of the industrial counters and data validation systems will provide insight into the salient features of the 1802-based system such as flag interrupts and conditional branches.

The DMA interface is meant to be an introduction to this important concept. Further reading is definitely recommended on this aspect.

A systematic study of this chapter and implementation of the concepts discussed will provide enough background to understand and design 1802-based operating systems. Also the internal 16-bit architecture will provide a bridge to understand the state of the art 16-bit processors like 8086, 68000, Z-8000, and so on.

For further information, consult the RCA 1800 Microprocessor Evaluation Kit manual for the CDP 1802 COSMAC microprocessor, and the RCA Microsystems manual.

Problems

11.1. Using the 18S020/21 microcomputer configuration of Figure 11.1, develop an operating software such that the system acts as a seconds counter. The seconds count can be displayed on the LED bank.

11.2. Repeat Problem 11.1, such that the system operates as a real time clock, displaying the information as shown in Figure 11.14, using the BCD format.

11.3. In industrial applications, the exact instant of time, when a particular event takes place is of importance. Using Figure 11.14 as the display, develop the operating software such that the display flashes for one minute at 6-second flashing intervals, every 30 minutes. The flashing time should be counted in the real time.

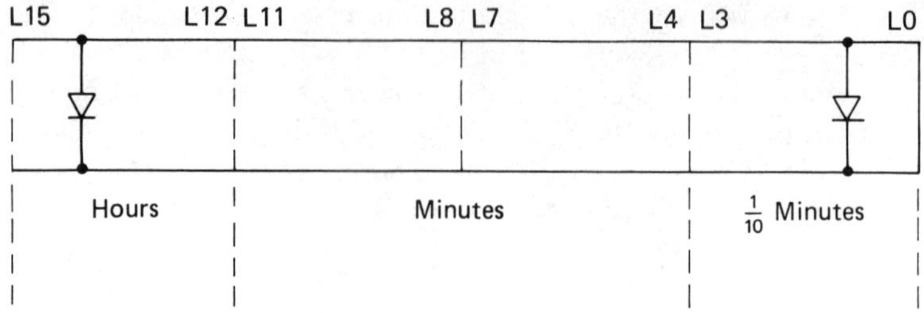

Fig 11.14. Display format for Problems 11.2 and 11.3.

11.4. Develop the operating software, such that the Q output of Figure 11.1 is:

(a) A monostable type output as shown, when the program is run

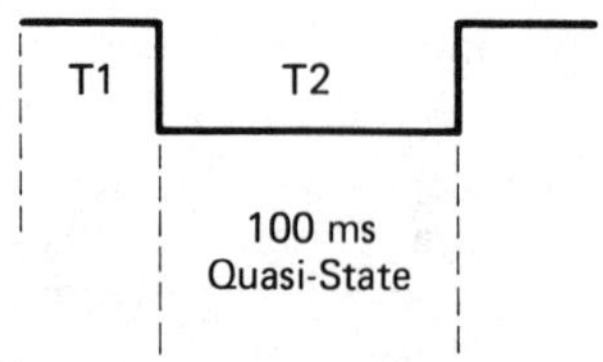

(b) A clock output as shown

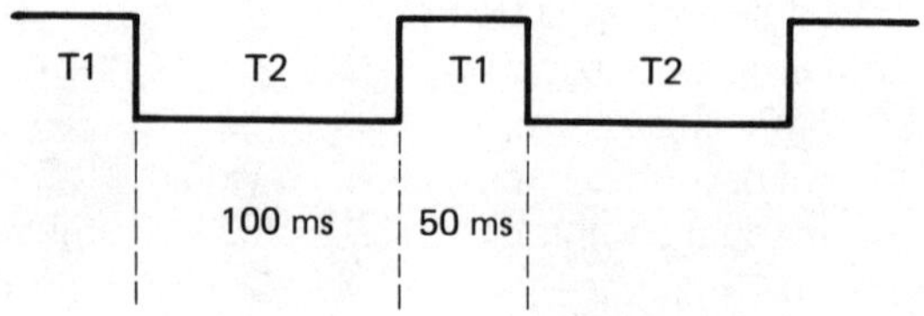

11.5. The PWM system of Figure 11.2 is general purpose and can be used in any control application. Develop the necessary hardware and software such that, in equal intervals of time

(a) The muscle gets shock for 10% of the time and 90% idle; next

(b) Gets shock for 20% of the time and 80% idle; next

|
until
|

The muscle gets shock 90% of the time and 10% idle; and the cycle is repetitive, starting again at (a).

11.6. Repeat Problem 11.5, such that the shocking time progressively increases from 10% to 90% (as in Problem 11.5) and then progressively decreases from 90% to 10%.

11.7. The biofeedback of Figure 11.15 is perhaps very crude, but does provide the concept.

The muscular contraction due to the shock increases the distance d between the optosensor pair, which in turn decreases the sense voltage V_X.

V_X can be conditioned through analog/digital converter (refer to Chapter 5), to provide an 8-bit X word, which is inversely proportional to the amount of contraction and the shock.

Develop the necessary hardware and software such that the system operates as a biofeedback PWM controller, where the X word is read by the micro and a corresponding PWM waveform is generated to shock the muscle. The larger the value of X (implying the contraction and shock were less), shock should be given for a longer time, and so on. Follow the shocking sequence of Example 11.2.

11.8. Repeat Problem 11.7, where the system should operate in burst mode rather than continuous mode. Read X word every second and provide the shock, according to the following format.

(a) X word maximum at FF, provide shock for maximum time of 800 ms.

(b) X word minimum at 00, provide shock for minimum time of 100 ms.

(Note: total cycle time is 900 ms.)

11.9. Design an I/O interface scheme, such that the 1802-based microcom-

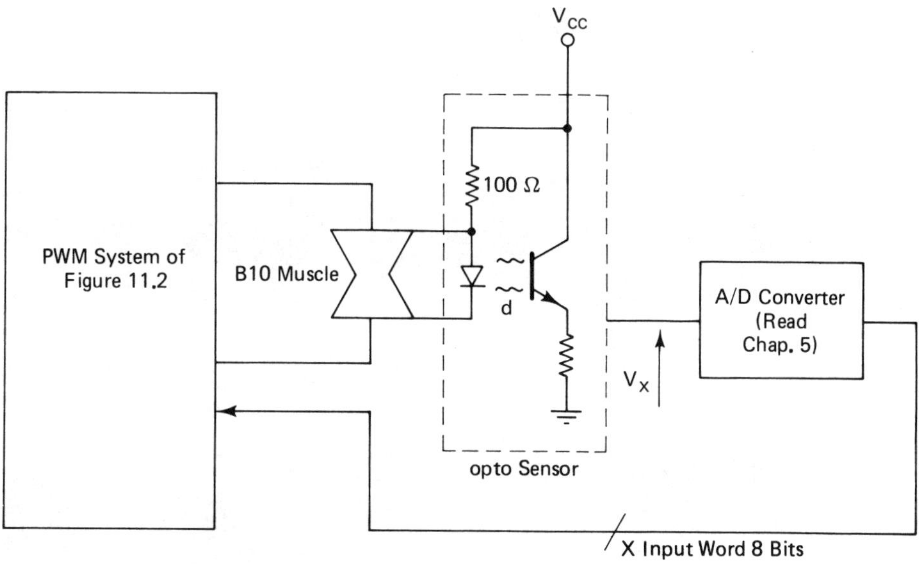

Fig 11.15. Conceptual biosensing for the PWM applications for Problems 11.7 and 11.8.

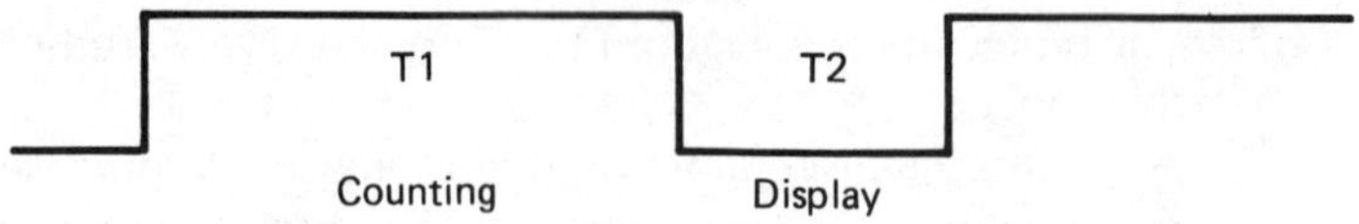

Fig 11.16. Counting and display controller for Problems 11.13 and 11.14.

puter has two input ports and two output ports, consisting of 1852 I/O devices. Show clearly all the hardware features of the system.

11.10. The proportional controllers of Example 11.3 are very widely used in the industry. Following the guidelines of Figure 11.5, design a proportional controller, which will stabilize the temperature of a thermal chamber to within 1°C in a range of 30°C to 90°C. (Hint: requires at least six bits of digital data.)

11.11. Redesign the proportional controller of Figure 11.5 to operate as a linear controller, using the conventional A/D and D/A conversions (refer to Chapter 5).

Show clearly the hardware interface and the software listings.

11.12. Modify the jigsaw counting system of Example 11.4 and Figure 11.7, such that the counting and display intervals as shown in Figure 11.16 are actually generated by the microcomputer, under software control. $T1 = 2\ T2 = 10$ s.

11.13. Develop the necessary hardware and software to make the jigsaw controller of Figure 11.17 fully operational. Assume that the speed range is 25 to 200 excursions per minute, at PWM output of 10% and 80%, for the drive voltage V_{Drive}.

Consider that the input 8-bit X word (0 to 255) specifies the required

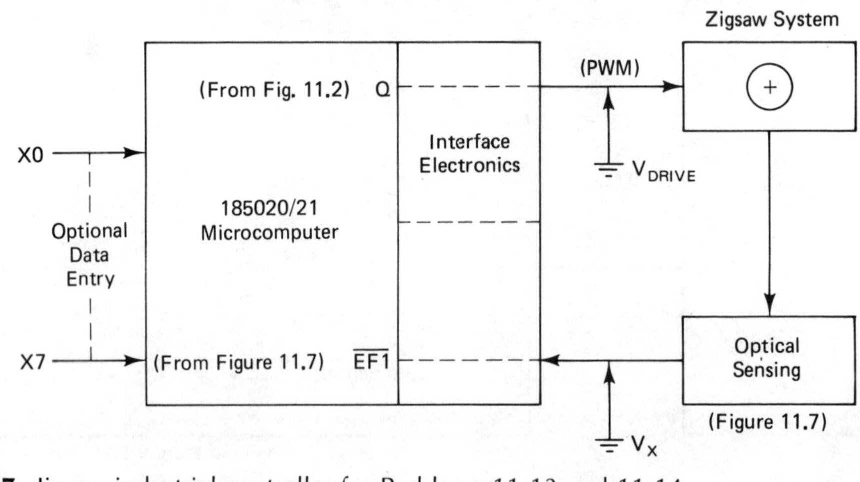

Fig 11.17. Jigsaw industrial controller for Problems 11.13 and 11.14.

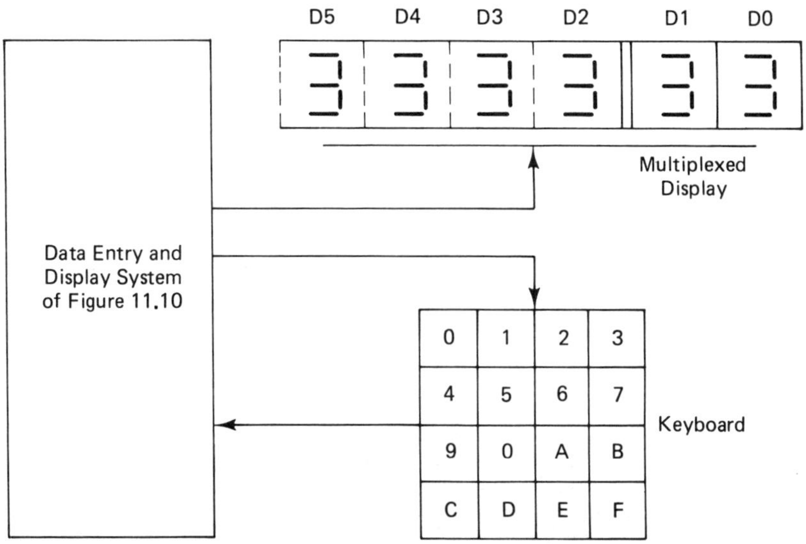

Fig 11.18. Microcomputer data entry and display system.

operating speed initially (For example, if X = $(50)_{Decimal}$, the speed should be initially set at 50 excursions per minute). The micro should then get into the feedback mode, to read V_X and accordingly adjust the PWM output, to maintain the set reference speed.

Clearly show all the required hardware and software.

11.14. Redesign the system of Problem 11.13, with additional safety features built into the controller. Shut off the power to the system, if the speed is counted to be less than 10 per minute (overload condition) and more than 250 per minute (runaway condition).

Develop the complete operating hardware and software to accomplish the safety features in addition to the controller action.

11.15. The data entry and display system of Figure 11.10 can be further simplified. Redesign the system, such that the BCD to seven-segment conversion can be accomplished under the software control.

Show the modified hardware and software listings.

11.16. Repeat Problem 11.15, such that the single seven-segment display can be extended to a multiplexed display. As each digit is entered from the keyboard, the display shifts to the left and the new digit enters the rightmost position. Figure 11.18 shows the concept.

INDEX

B

C

D

E

F

G

H

I

J

K

L

M

N

O

P

U

V

W

X

Z

Number/Name References